ISRAEL

Polity, Society, Economy
1882–1986

About the Author

Michael Wolffsohn, born in 1947, studied history, political science and economics at the Free University of Berlin and in Tel-Aviv. He received his PhD from the Free University of Berlin in 1975 and holds two higher degrees (*Habilitation*) in political science and in contemporary history (both from the University of the Saarland in 1980). He has taught modern history and international relations at the Hochschule der Bundeswehr (University of the West German Armed Forces) in Munich since 1981. His publications include: *Public Works in Germany 1930–1934* (1977), *Die Debatte über den Kalten Krieg* (The Cold War Debate) in 1982, *Politik in Israel* (Politics in Israel) in 1983, *Politik als Investitionsmotor? Deutsche Multis in Lateinamerika* (Politics as an Investment Incentive? German Multinationals in Latin America) in 1984, *West Germany's Foreign Policy in the era of Brandt and Schmidt* (1986), *German–Israeli Relations 1952–1983: What the Polls Say* (1986), and *German–Saudi Arabian Arms Deals, Past and Present: 1936–1939 and 1981–1984. With an Essay on West Germany's Jews* (1986) as well as over forty scholarly articles on topics including Israel, the Middle East, West German and EEC foreign policy, and other issues in international relations.

He has also contributed articles on Middle East and German foreign affairs for the major West German daily and weekly newspapers and has appeared as a foreign affairs commentator for German TV and radio networks. In 1987 he produced a three part TV series on the Arab–Israeli conflict since 1917. He is currently working on a study of German–Israeli relations since 1948/49 and the American–European–Middle Eastern Triangle 1948–1957.

ISRAEL

Polity, Society, Economy
1882–1986
An Introductory Handbook

Michael Wolffsohn

An enlarged and updated
translation of the German edition:
*Israel. Grundwissen Länderkunde.
Politik. Gesellschaft. Wirtschaft*

Translated by
Douglas Bokovoy

Humanities Press International, Inc.
Atlantic Highlands, NJ

First published 1987 in The United States of America by
HUMANITIES PRESS INTERNATIONAL, INC., Atlantic Highlands,
NJ 07716

Library of Congress Cataloging-in-Publication Data

Wolffsohn, Michael.
Israel: polity, society, economy, 1882–1986.

An enlarged and updated translation of: Israel.
Bibliography: p.
Includes index.
1. Israel.   2. Zionism.   I. Bokovoy, Douglas.
II. Title.
DS102.95.W65   1987   956.94   87–3702
ISBN 0–391–03571–1
ISBN 0–391–03540–1 (Pbk)

Manufactured in The United States of America

Contents

Illustrations

Figures

Tables

Preface

Israel: Polity, Society, Economy seeks to present basic information on key aspects of the polity, society and economy of Israel in a condensed format. This volume is thus designed to serve as a reference work offering quick access to basic data for the period from 1882 (the beginning of Zionist-inspired immigration to Palestine) to 1988. The information and analysis are organized according to a kind of building-block principle. Each of the chapters of the text is structured in such a way that it can be referred to independently of the rest of the book, the individual sections devoted to particular aspects of Israel's polity, society and economy each offering a general introduction to and analysis of the topic. For the reader seeking further information, a selected list of suggested reading is supplied for each major section. The scholar wishing to pursue detailed analysis of the sources and topics is referred to the more extensive reference list as well as the references within the text. Numerous maps, diagrams, graphs and statistical tables are included to make the book easier to use for both teachers and students. In many cases, a graph or diagram intended for the general orientation of the reader is followed by a statistical table for the information of the reader requiring greater detail.

The mass of impersonal data must not, of course, be allowed to 'do away with' (Tenbruck) the individual. Instead, the statistics ought to serve as an abbreviated indicator of individual accomplishments and sacrifices, individual hopes fulfilled or abandoned. For example: statistics for the years 1932 to 1938 demonstrate a dramatic rise in Jewish immigration to Palestine. One ought to be conscious of the fact that these numbers reflect the rise of National Socialism. Or: between 1947 and 1948 the status of the Palestinian Arabs shifted from that of a majority to that of a minority. One must also be aware of the pitiful fate of the resulting refugee populations. Because of the limited format of this book, these aspects cannot be discussed extensively here, but there is certainly no lack of appropriate publications from widely differing viewpoints.

Statistics, therefore, do not do away with the individual. Instead, they sketch an outline of his existence.

In view of the increase in annexationist tendencies since 1977 on the part of the Israeli government towards the territories variously designated as 'occupied', 'conquered', 'liberated', or 'administered', a detailed analysis of this problem would seem to suggest itself. The political system involved remains, however, an entity distinct from the both demographically and normatively undeniably Jewish state, and is, therefore, dealt with here only insofar as it is of relevance to Israel within the borders of 4 June 1967. The long-term problems for the Jewish character of the Jewish state entailed by the settlement policies and the politics of (practical) annexation are dealt with in the chapters on demographic developments and the situation of Israel's Arab population.

Readers seeking a confession of faith in or a moral condemnation of Israel may lay this book aside. Those, however, seeking to develop their own insights by examining the facts may find a starting point here.

Introduction

1 ISRAEL AS A PARTY STATE

In the beginning was the organization, and the organization was the party. Political parties had already been formed in the time of the Yishuv, the pre-state Jewish community in Palestine before it was even possible to speak of a Jewish society, much less a Jewish economy. Before the greater part of the immigrant population poured into the country, the handful of settlers who had arrived at the end of the nineteenth century and in the early years of the twentieth had already founded political institutions. They had, in short, created the framework for the party system as well as for the later social and economic structures. The roof had in effect been erected prior to laying the foundations. The parties, especially the socialist parties, were not satisfied with merely creating an organizational structure but went on to build up a network intended to care for their members and supporters 'from the cradle to the grave'. From the very beginning, polity and economy, society and culture – even the question of security – were not only closely connected with, but also determined by, party politics. An analysis of Israel must therefore begin at a point much earlier than that of the founding of the State of Israel in 1948. It must begin in the political sphere, and at the same time be cognizant of the processes of continuity as well as change. The descriptive information offered here on the institutional and organizational aspects of Israel's polity, society and economy is frequently supplemented with data from opinion polls. These materials are, in turn, compared with actual behaviour.

Since politics and the economy, society and culture, as well as military affairs – practically every aspect, therefore, of public and even of private life – continued to be closely linked to party politics in the decades following independence, this book must continually refer to the political parties. For a long time, Israel could be regarded as a model of the party state. Nothing was possible without the consent – not to mention against the will – of the parties. Not even athletics were apolitical. Labour Party supporters met in the Hapoel clubs, middle-class liberals in the Makkabi, 'purist' nationalists – especially Begin sympathizers – in the Beitar, the national-religious in the Elizur. Even today, soccer matches between Hapoel and Beitar teams sometimes take on the character of a surrogate political battle.

2 POLITICAL GEOGRAPHY

Political geography can be normative as well as historical-political. Neither is definitively established and both are predicated on physical geography,

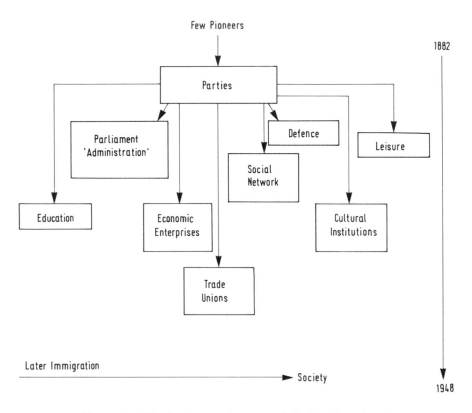

Figure 1   The developmental pattern of the Jewish society in 'Palestine'.

which preconditions the dynamics of both and predetermines the lines of offensive and defensive political and military actions. Examples include the Rhine in French history and the Jordan in the history of Zionism.

The foundation upon which the normative and the political geography of Zionism rests is the Old Testament. But this normative basis is by no means unequivocal, as even the borders of the 'Promised Land' described in the Bible differ greatly. As the laws which were once transmitted only by oral tradition were set down and commented on in the Talmud, numerous and differing descriptions of the borders of Eretz Israel – the Land of Israel – were given (see Isaac, 1976: ch. 2; W. D. Davis, 1982).

In Genesis 15: 18 God promised Abraham the land 'from the Nile to the Euphrates', a claim resurrected in the 1930s by the ultra-nationalist Lehi (or 'Stern Gang') underground organization. Other normative-political references to the Promised Land in the Pentateuch include Deuteronomy 1: 7 and 11: 24 and describe borders resembling those defined in Genesis. In Numbers 34: 3–15, and similarly in Ezekiel 47: 15–20, the area circumscribed is considerably diminished. Although these borders are not clearly reconstructable, they include at least parts of the northern Negev, the West Bank of the

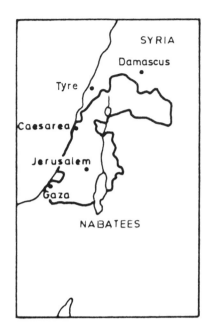

Figure 2 Second temple, sixth century BC to first century AD.

*Figure 3 Roman and Byzantine province, first century to seventh
century AD.*

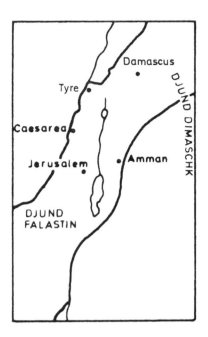

Figure 4   Arab conquest, seventh century to eleventh century.

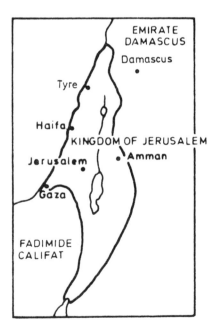

Figure 5   Period of the Crusades, eleventh century to thirteenth century.

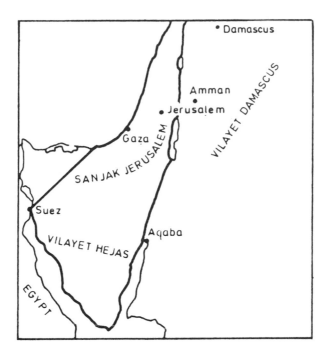

Figure 6   Mamluk and Osmanic period, thirteenth century to twentieth century.

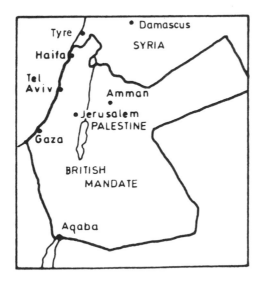

Figure 7   British Mandate, 1921

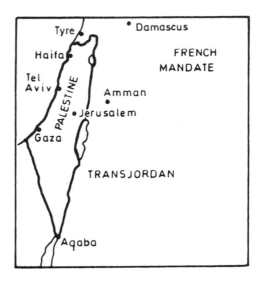

Figure 8   First Partition of Palestine, 1921

Jordan and Galilee. The kingdom promised to the future Messiah in Psalms 72: 8–11 is much more extensive, encompassing the lands bordered by the Nile, the Mediterranean, the Euphrates, the Persian Gulf and the Red Sea. The maps in Figures 2–11 illustrate the dynamics of this historical-political geography. (From: *Tatsachen*, 1975: 28 ff.; Gilbert, 1974: 52, 70.)

(a) THE STATE FRONTIERS

The maps demonstrate the volatility of historical-political geography. Figure 7, for instance, shows that much also depends on the perspective of the political actors and their specific interpretations of geography. Thus both Palestinian and Israeli hawks such as Ariel Sharon are 'right' when they contend that Jordan is, in fact, part of 'Palestine' (on Sharon see *FAZ*, 28 August 1984). For both sides geography serves as a political argument, not as a source of 'truth'.

The currently existing political-historical geography is, as a rule, legally 'secured' – at least unilaterally.

In Israel's Declaration of Independence the borders of the Jewish state are not mentioned, as no agreement could be reached between those demanding a 'maximal' and those favouring a 'minimal' solution (see Wolffsohn, 1983a: 244 ff.). Article 1 of the Law and Administration Ordinance states: 'Every law valid for the entire State of Israel will also be applicable to all of the territory of the State of Israel as well as those parts of Eretz Israel which the defense minister [!] declares as being held by Zahal' (the Israeli Defence Forces; Rubinstein, 1974: 60).

The frontiers resulting from the 1948/9 War of Independence were accepted by force of circumstance, but not established by law. Following the Six Day War, the Knesset (Israel's parliament) amended the Law and

THE FRONTIERS OF THE STATE OF ISRAEL 1949 – 1967

Following the Arab decision to invade Israel in May 1948, the Israelis not only defended the land allocated to them by the United Nations, but extended the area under their control. The frontiers established in 1949 remained the de facto borders until 1967, but during these eighteen years none of Israel's Arab neighbours agreed to make peace with her, or to recognize the permanent existence of her borders

The territory of the State of Israel as proposed by the United Nations in November 1947, but rejected by the Arabs

Territory beyond the United Nations line conquered by Israel, 1948 - 1949

—·— The frontiers of the State of Israel according to the Armistice agreements of 1949, signed between Israel and Egypt (24 January), Israel and the Lebanon (23 March), Israel and Transjordan (3 April) and Israel and Syria (20 July). Transjordan had already occupied all Arab held land west of the Jordan, formally annexing it in 1950, and renaming the whole area 'Jordan'

Transjordan's annexation of the West Bank was opposed by the Arab League States, and only recognized by two members of the U.N., Britain and Pakistan

0   10   20   30
Miles

© Martin Gilbert

Figure 9   The Frontiers Of The State Of Israel 1949–1967

Source: Gilbert, 1974: 52.

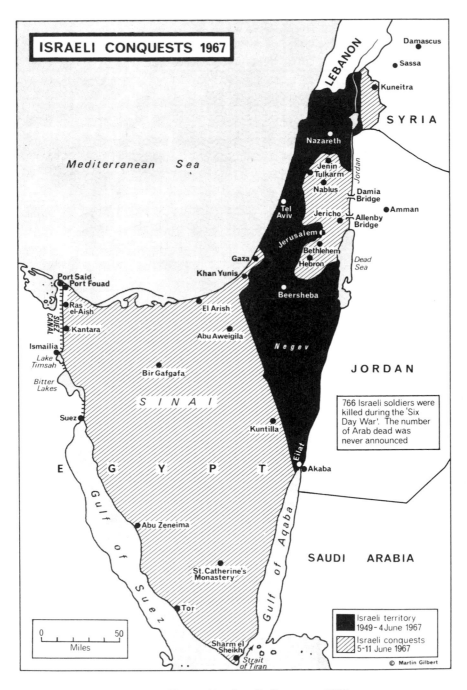

Figure 10   Israeli Conquests, 1967

Source: Gilbert, 1974: 70.

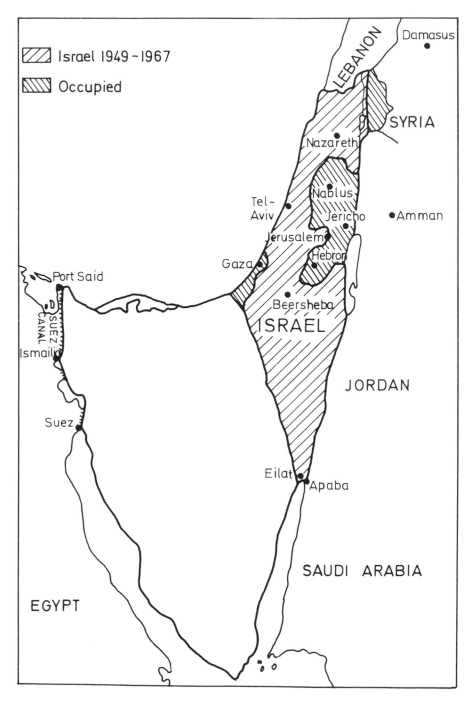

Figure 11   Israeli withdrawals after the peace treaty with Egypt,
1982.

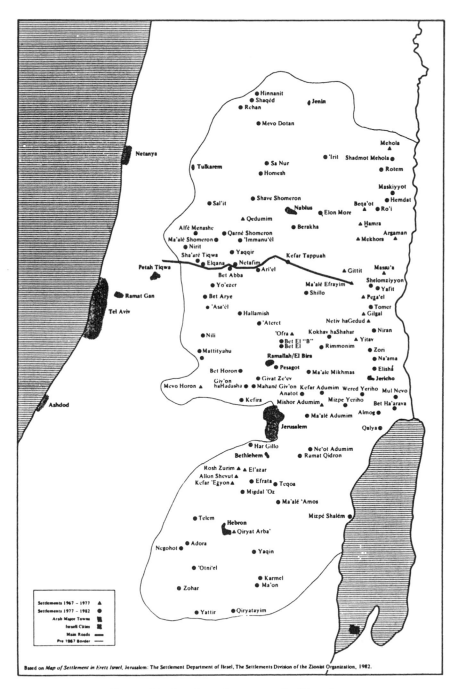

Figure 12   Israeli settlements in the West Bank, 1982.

Source: Sandler and Frisch, 1984: 138.

Administration Ordinance of 19 May 1948, adding Article 11b on 27 June 1967: 'The laws, jurisdiction and administration of the state will be applied in those areas of Eretz Israel which the government [!] mandates by ordinance' (Rubinstein, 1974: 63). On 28 June 1967 Israeli law was extended to East Jerusalem, which was thus annexed. On 30 July 1980 the Knesset passed a basic law declaring Jerusalem to be Israel's 'undivided' capital. On 14 December 1981 Israeli jurisdiction was extended to the Golan Heights by vote of the Knesset.

(b) THE ISSUE OF SETTLEMENTS IN THE OCCUPIED TERRITORIES

The issue of Jewish settlements in the occupied territories, first and foremost in the West Bank, has become the best-known bone of contention between hawks and doves in Israel and entails widespread international repercussions.

First, let us look at some of the relevant facts. There were only 800 Jewish settlers to be found in the West Bank in 1972, but 4,000 in 1977, the last year of the Mapai/ILP era. In late 1981 the number reached 16,200. This rose to 21,000 in December 1982 and to 42,600 by December 1984. (These figures and the following demographic data from various volumes of the annual *Statistical Abstract of Israel*; E. Efrat, *Haaretz*, 24 May 1984; and Benvenisti, data in *Jerusalem Post*, 16 March 1985: 8). Clearly, the Likud-led government lived up to its promise to spur the pace of Jewish settlement in the West Bank, which is usually referred to in Israel as 'Judea and Samaria' – even by many Israeli doves. By the year 2010 the Likud government and the Settlements Department of the World Zionist Organization hope to see about 350,000 Jews living in that area.

Some 700 Jewish settlers were counted in the Gaza Strip in 1972, 3,500 in 1977, and 5,300 in 1981, but only 700 in December 1982, this due to the evacuation of Jewish settlements in that area in accordance with the terms of the Egyptian–Israeli peace treaty of 26 March 1979.

Some 3,000 Jewish settlers were counted in the Golan Heights in December 1977 and 6,700 by December 1982.

Between June 1967 and December 1984, 114 Jewish settlements were created in the West Bank. Most of the settlements in existence before 1981 had been founded by Gush Emunim (Sandler and Frisch, 1984: 140). The total of 42,600 settlers by the end of 1984 gives an average of 2,000 new settlers annually. Most (approx. 46%) live in six urban or semi-urban locations. These are Ariel, Male Adumim, Male Ephrayim, Elkana, Emanuel and Kiryat Arba (the first settlement having been established here in the late 1960s and causing a great deal of trouble for the Labour-led coalition). Ninety-six settlements (or 86% of the total) have 300 or fewer inhabitants. The aim is to make the most of the relatively small numbers of willing settlers in order to accomplish the strategic purpose of surrounding Arab towns and villages, thus separating one from the other (see Benvenisti, 1984; Sandler and Frisch, 1984: chs. 4, 6, 7). In this manner the seemingly minor 'quantity' represented by the Jewish settlements in fact becomes a major political, strategic and social 'quality'.

Before 1977 the Labour-led government had initiated and supported the erection of settlements in the mountains dominating the Jordan Valley and in the Gush Etzion and Jerusalem regions. After 1977 the Likud-led government pursued a stepped-up policy involving a wider geographic pattern.

The geographic pattern of Jewish settlements in 1984 was as follows. Only 3,500 (12·5%) were to be found in the Jordan Valley and 5·3% in the western parts of the West Bank; 9·6% were in the Gush Etzion area; 12·5% near Hebron; 17·1% between the Beit-El and Gilboa ranges; and fully 43% in the environs of Jerusalem. In other words, the bulk of the settlers preferred non-agricultural locations within a short driving distance of either Jerusalem or the coastal plain (i.e. the Tel-Aviv metropolitan area). These facts are not only geographically and politically significant. They also serve as an indicator for the ideology of most of the settlers, who have apparently chosen to break with the traditional Zionist ideal of the *halutz*, that is, the agricultural pioneer who immigrated with the aim of living on the land, of cultivating and living from the soil. The ideal of the *halutz* farmer has given way to the middle-class commuter.

There is a caveat, however. Many of the more motivated (some would say 'fanatical') settlers have indeed been creating small agricultural settlements in which they work very hard. These settlers are continuing the Zionist *halutzic* tradition and are hence admired even by many of their ideological and political opponents. A kind of love–hate relationship exists between hawkish but *halutzic* settlers and their dovish critics. In addition, there is another attraction to moving to the West Bank, especially to the urban settlements. Housing is much cheaper there than in comparably favourable locations in 'old' Israel, so much so that some of the Peace Now and Labour doves who were highly critical of or even hostile to the settlement policy of the Likud-led government proved incapable of resisting this temptation (see Y. Litani, *Haaretz*, 27 July 1984, reporting on Peace Now members who joined a small agricultural settlement because of its *halutzic* approach and its more attractive life-style). Nevertheless, this is rather the exception than the rule. The majority of the non-ideological settlers should be regarded as belonging to the uncommitted public, not to the camp of the doves.

It may be a military solution to surround Arab towns and thus be in a position to cut their lines of communication, but this does not represent a solution to the political, let alone the demographic or ideological problems involved. Those highly motivated settlers who toil in the small *halutzic* communities are by no means capable of altering the demographic imbalance between Jews and non-Jews in the West Bank. True, their Jewishness may be second to none with respect to their sense of identity and their fulfilment of religious duties. Subjectively, it is their intention to assert their Jewishness in the political arena by re-Judaizing 'Judea and Samaria' as part of the Biblical Land of Israel. Objectively, however, they are contributing to the de-Judaizing of the Jewish state, and ultimately to the creation of a bi-national Israel incorporating another 1,224,000 Arabs (1984 figure quoted by Y. Litani, *Haaretz*, 16 August 1984). Would these same Jews then be willing to grant the Arabs the full rights of citizenship, including the 'one man, one vote' principle? If not, this would be tantamount to abandoning the democratic tradition of Zionism. Zionism or democracy?

It could be argued that the super-hawks advocate the expulsion of the Arabs, and, indeed, some do; Rabbi Kahane, for example. But if most of the hawks really favoured expulsion they would not have to surround the Arabs and cut off their lines of communication. They could just as well save the money and the effort. Arab emigration from the West Bank has recently dwindled and the natural increase of the local population remains impressive. Life expectancy has also risen. In other words, neither migration nor natural factors are likely to tip the balance in favour of the Jews (see Zakai, 1984). For the time being, no massive wave of Jewish immigration is on the horizon. The Jewish settlement potential is thus limited and financial constraints make long-term efforts even more difficult.

The Alignment attempted to square the circle by claiming and settling as much territory as deemed militarily 'necessary' while at the same time trying to incorporate as few non-Jews (i.e. Arabs) as possible. The Jewish character of the Jewish state could and should be thus preserved, so the argument ran. This was, in a nutshell, the philosophy of the 'Allon Plan', named after its spiritual father and prominent Labour politician, the late Yigael Allon. (On party politics and the occupied territories, see Kieval, 1983; on the voting behaviour of the settlers and for polls on the settlement issue see A/II/5/a; on the sums spent by the government for the establishment of settlements see C/XV/3.)

FURTHER READING

Kimmerling, Baruch (1983), *Zionism and Territory. The Socio-Territorial Dimensions of Zionist Politics* (Berkeley, Calif.: University of California Press).

Davis, W. D. (1982), *The Territorial Dimension of Judaism* (Berkeley, Calif.: University of California Press).

Gilbert, Martin (1974), *The Arab–Israeli Conflict. Its History in Maps* (London: Weidenfeld & Nicolson).

OCCUPIED TERRITORIES

Benvenisti, Meron (1984), *The West Bank Data Project. A Survey of Israel's Policy* (Washington, DC: American Enterprise Institute).

Sandler, Shmuel, and Frisch, Hillel (1984), *Israel, the Palestinians and the West Bank: A Study in Intercommunal Conflict* (Lexington, Mass.: D. C. Heath).

Davis, Uri (1983), *The Golan Heights under Israeli Occupation 1967–1981* (Durham, NC: Center for Middle Eastern and Islamic Studies).

Kieval, Gershon R. (1983), *Party Politics in Israel and the Occupied Territories* (Westport, Conn.: Greenwood Press).

Elazar, Daniel J. (ed.) (1982), *Governing Peoples and Territories* (Philadelphia, Pa.: Institute for the Study of Human Issues).

Shamgar, Meir (ed.) (1982), *Military Government in the Territories Administered by Israel 1967–1980*, Vol. I (Jerusalem: Hebrew University, Faculty of Law).

Stone, Julius (1981), *Israel and Palestine. Assault on the Law of Nations* (Baltimore, Md., and London: Johns Hopkins University Press).

Harris, William W. (1980), *Taking Root: Israeli Settlement in the West Bank, the Golan and Gaza-Sinai, 1967–1980* (Chichester: Research Studies Press/John Wiley).

Gerson, Allan (1978), *Israel, the West Bank and International Law* (London: Frank Cass).

Nisan, Mordechai (1978), *Israel and the Territories. A Study in Control 1967–1977* (Ramat-Gan: Turtledove).

3 THE PAST AS PRESENT: HISTORICAL FOUNDATIONS

(a) ISRAELI JEWS

The continuing influence of the past on Israeli politics makes itself especially evident in the Holocaust syndrome, in the claim of continuity and in the sense of isolation resulting from the Holocaust syndrome. Moreover, the consciousness of religious Israelis is shaped by the concept of the Jewish people as the chosen people of God, and that of secular Israelis by the conviction that Zionism and Israel embody the 'general will' of the Jewish people (see B/X). The corollary is the same as Rousseau's, namely, that the general will cannot ever be in error.

The Holocaust syndrome refers to the historically anchored self-perception of the Jewish people as a permanently persecuted people. The claim of continuity emphasizes the enduring connection between the people and its land. The absence of the people from the land is attributed to the course of history rather than to the will of the people.

From the statistics on the countries of origin of Jewish immigrants before and after the founding of Israel it can be readily determined where and when persecutions of Jews took place (see B/VI/1/a–d). Very few, if any, immigrants came from countries in which Jews were not being persecuted (see Wolffsohn, 1983c).

The Holocaust syndrome is by no means applicable solely to Germany and German–Jewish or German–Israeli relations. Germany symbolizes the Holocaust in both its concrete and archetypal manifestations, but the Holocaust also serves as a general indicator of the continuing influence of the past on Israel's present. It functions as the filter through which the affected perceive their environment.

The Holocaust syndrome is not only a filter for historical sensibilities. It is also used as a political argument. The PLO, for example, is often equated with the National Socialists, as are those Arab neighbours who continue to refuse to recognize Israel's right to exist.

The continuing impact of the past on the present is frequently reinforced by current events. What is more, the Sabras (the native-born Israelis, i.e. the children of those who experienced 'their' Holocaust in the pogroms of their native lands) were also forced, first in Palestine and later in the State of Israel, to learn what it means to fight for one's very existence. There was the massacre of 1929, the Arab Revolt of 1936/9, the armed struggle against the British Mandate from 1944 to 1947, the 1948/9 War of Independence, the Sinai Campaign of 1956, the Six Day War of 1967, the simultaneous War of Attrition along the Suez Canal in 1969 and 1970 and the military confrontation with Palestinian guerrillas, and the Yom Kippur War of 1973. Although these were not Holocausts, they form part of the syndrome, as they heightened the perception that Jews, that is, Israelis, continue to be persecuted.

The 1982 war in Lebanon was, for the first time, viewed by large segments of the Israeli public as an offensive war and for precisely this reason was perceived as an historical watershed.

A derivative of the Holocaust syndrome is the sense of isolation, which is also conditioned by political geography. At least until the conclusion of the peace treaty with Egypt (26 March 1979), Israel regarded its neighbours without exception as enemies. Its friends were all at a great geographical distance. 'Against the background of the mass destruction of the Nazi period and its direct effects, the impact of isolation was magnified and produced an attitude of pessimism, a feeling of being totally alone in the world' (Elon, 1972: 214).

The reaction of the Israeli public following Nasser's closing of the Straits of Tiran on the eve of the Six Day War was similar. Comparable emotions were also evoked after the Yom Kippur War by the 6 November 1973 declaration on the Middle East by the foreign ministers of the European Community.

The combined syndromes of Holocaust and isolation have given rise to a feeling in Israel that the historical social isolation of Jews, their ghetto existence in the political systems of the various nation states, is comparable to the present-day political isolation of the Jewish state in the international system. Israel is viewed as a modern-day ghetto in the contemporary international community – a tragic irony in the history of Zionism, which arose as an attempt to overcome this very situation.

This sense of isolation is, of course, rendered easier to bear by a pronounced, positive self-image. Among secular Israelis this self-esteem is based on the constructive achievements of the Zionist movement, and it is further strengthened among religious Israelis by the self-confidence of those who count themselves among the chosen of God.

The claim of continuity forges the link between the people and the land. It is not by chance that archaeology has developed into something of a national sport in Israel. It has become 'patriotic archaeology' (Elon, 1972: 307). 'Old stones' are invested with the power of political symbols. The Wailing Wall in Jerusalem and the fortress of Massada on the Dead Sea are particularly poignant examples. Massada symbolizes the physical and psychological link between the people and the land – physical because there were then Jews living in Eretz Israel as there are now, and psychological because the spirit of Massada is diametrically opposed to the passivity seen as characteristic of the Diaspora Jews. It is the spirit of a Jewish resistance which preferred suicide to enslavement.

(b) PALESTINIAN ARABS

Historical perceptions similar to those just described operate among the Palestinian Arabs but lead to opposing value-judgements. For the Arabs living in Israel and the surrounding areas, the events of 1948 and 1949 also constitute a kind of Holocaust trauma with a significant and continuing political impact. The massacre in the Shatilla and Sabra camps near Beirut (16/17 September 1982) may well produce comparable political and psychological effects. For the political psychology of the Palestinian Arabs, the slaughter at Dir Yassin (April 1948) and their massive flight (others would say expulsion) in 1948/9 and again in the wake of the 1967 Six Day War are perceived in a manner not unlike that in which Jewish Israelis regard Auschwitz.

What is important here is not the difference between helpless Jewish concentration camp inmates and Palestinian civilians who were at least in part armed, nor is it a question of 'objective historical truth' (if such exists), but rather the collective, subjective *perception* of history.

The Arabs living in the State of Israel have surely also felt themselves isolated, especially while cut off from contact with the surrounding Arab populations of the West Bank, the Gaza Strip and the neighbouring Arab states in the period from 1949 to 1967. While continuing to live in their historical homeland, they can hardly feel themselves at home in their status as non-Jews living within the Jewish state.

Archaeological evidence was, however, not necessary to an Arab sense of continuity in Palestine, as their ancestors had been living in the land for centuries.

The continuing impact of the past on contemporary Israel therefore affects both Jews and Arabs, although under converse conditions. There is even a parallel to the Jewish concept of the chosen people which manifests itself among the Palestinian Arabs as opposed to other Arabs – positively in the sense of being a step ahead in the processes of modernization, negatively in the sense of being the victims of greater suffering.

PART A
POLITICS

1
System of Government

1 FROM THE OTTOMAN EMPIRE TO INDEPENDENCE

At the time Zionist-motivated immigration commenced in the last decades of the nineteenth century (1882), Palestine was part of the Ottoman Empire. The region was conquered by British forces between October 1917 and September 1918. On 19 April 1920 the League of Nations granted Great Britain the Mandate for Palestine and on 24 July 1922 the League confirmed the statutes of the Mandate, which came into effect in September 1923.

On 23 August 1903 the Knessiyat Hayishuv, the first assembly of the Yishuv, met in Sihron Yaakov, but only held seven sessions.

Although there had been political parties within the framework of the World Zionist Organization since 1902 and in Palestine since 1905, renewed attempts to establish a representative Jewish institution in 1908, 1910 and 1911 all failed, due in no small part to the obstacles the Ottoman authorities placed in the way of any systematic and continuous political organization of the Yishuv from 1908 onwards.

The British conquest of Palestine rekindled hopes for 'the establishment in Palestine of a national home for the Jewish people', which, as stated in the Balfour Declaration of 2 November 1917, 'His Majesty's Government view with favour . . . and will use their best endeavours to facilitate the achievement of this object . . .'.

The first preparatory conference for a representative assembly met on 2 January 1918 in Jaffa, the conferees consisting of party and community leaders who were invited rather than elected. This conference chose a thirty-six-member 'Provisional Council of the Jews of Eretz Israel in the Conquered Territories'. A second preparatory conference in July 1918 established the rules for the election of a 'Constituent Assembly'. These elections took place on 19 April 1920 (see Table 1) and this quasi-legislative body was given the name Aseffat Hanivharim (Assembly of Delegates).

The effective political leadership of the Yishuv lay in the hands of the National Council (Vaad Leumi) from 1920 to 1948, which varied in size from twenty-three to forty-two members chosen by the Assembly of Delegates (Aseffat Hanivharim). The National Council met several times each year and progressively assumed the legislative functions intended for the Assembly.

The executive organ of the National Council was the National Council Executive (Hanhalat Havaad Haleumi), consisting of from six to fourteen members chosen by the National Council from among its ranks. The members of the Executive headed the following 'departments': politics, local affairs, rabbinical affairs, education, culture, health services, social services, sports and information. The work of the National Council was financed by the World Zionist Organization (WZO) as well as by taxes on the Yishuv. Greater political influence rested, however, with the Executive of the Jewish Agency in Eretz Israel, made up of representatives of the WZO and other Jewish organizations of the Diaspora.

With its 'Regulations for the Organization of the Jewish Community in Palestine' of 1 January 1928, the Mandate government granted the Jewish institutions of self-government legal status and recognition. These regulations empowered the officially registered members of the Jewish community in Palestine (= Knesset Israel) over the age of 18 to elect a seventy-one-member Constituent Assembly for a period of three years (later changed to four, but also not adhered to). The Assembly was to determine the taxes and the budgets for the religious and secular institutions of Knesset Israel. The Orthodox party Agudat Israel boycotted Knesset Israel, which it regarded as lacking a scriptural basis and therefore blasphemous. Large numbers of Jews of strict religious persuasion were opposed to Zionism on the principle that the movement represented an interference in 'God's handiwork' in that it was attempting to end the exile of the 'Children of Israel' through the establishment of a new Jewish state by the hand of man rather than by God.

The United Nations Resolution of 29 November 1947 provided for the partitioning of Palestine into a Jewish and an Arab state, called for the internationalization of Jerusalem and also stipulated that elections to constituent assemblies be held in both states prior to 1 October 1948. These assemblies were to install provisional governments and to prepare constitutions securing a parliamentary form of government with a legislature 'elected on the basis of proportional representation', universal suffrage and a secret ballot. During the transitional phase from November 1947 to October 1948 a Provisional Governing Council to be appointed by a special commission by 1 April 1948, at the latest was to gradually assume responsibility for governmental administration and the police. Moreover, the Provisional Governing Council was to prepare elections to be held within two months of the withdrawal of the Mandate troops (to take place by 1 August 1948).

In view of the fact that the British government prevented the implementation of the partition resolution by refusing to allow the UN commission to enter Palestine until just before the expiration of the Mandate and by withdrawing its troops without providing for an orderly transfer of power to the institutions of self-government called for in the UN resolution, the National Council, together with the Executive of the Jewish Agency in Eretz Israel, decided in March 1948 to take the initiative in creating the Provisional Council provided for in the partition resolution. This took the form of the People's Council (Moetzet Haam), consisting of the fourteen members of the National Council Executive, the eleven-member Executive of the Jewish Agency in Eretz Israel and twelve delegates from groups not represented in the aforementioned bodies: Sephardic Jews (longtime residents of Spanish and Oriental descent), rightist-nationalistic Revisionists (who had previously been excluded), Orthodox representatives from Agudat Israel (who had not participated before in the Jewish self-governing organizations) and Communists. This body then elected an executive committee of thirteen members, the People's Directorate (Minhelet Haam).

On 29 April 1948 the British Parliament passed the Palestine Act setting 15 May of that year as the date for the termination of the Mandate. The People's Council met in Tel-Aviv on 14 May 1948 to proclaim the *independence* of the Jewish state 'Israel' effective the following day. The People's Council was then renamed the Provisional State Council (Moetzet Hamedina Hazmait) and the People's Directorate became the Provisional Government (Hamemshala Hazmanit). Due to the outbreak of hostilities immediately following the declaration of independence, the elections set for 10 October 1948, could not be carried out until 25 January 1949.

Table 1   The Precursors of Israel's Government and Parliament

Government:	*Parliament:*
	1903 Yishuv Assembly
1918 Provisional Council	1918 preparatory conference
1920 National Council Executive (+ Executive of the Jewish Agency in Eretz Israel)	1920 Assembly of Delegates chooses National Council
March 1948 People's Directorate	March 1948 People's Council (National Council Executive + Executive of the JA in Eretz Israel)
14 May 1948 Provisional Government	14 May 1948 Provisional State Council
	2 February 1949 Constitutional Assembly becomes First Knesset
8 March 1949 Government	

The Constitutional Assembly (Haassefa Hamehonenet) convened on 14 February 1949, and two days later passed the Transition Law (Hok Hamavar) adopting the name 'Knesset' (assembly) for the legislature and declaring the Constitutional Assembly as the First Knesset. At the same time, provisions were made concerning the presidency, the government, and the relations between the government and the Knesset.

2   'CONSTITUTION', LEGAL SYSTEM, CITIZENSHIP

(a) 'CONSTITUTION'

Israel has no written constitution. The Declaration of Independence and a set of 'basic laws' serve in its stead. The basic laws include the following:

Knesset (1958); Land (1960); Presidency (1964); Government (1968); State Economy (1975); Military (1976); Jerusalem, the Capital of Israel (1980) and Judiciary (1984). Three additional basic laws are in preparation: (1) Basic Law: The State Comptroller; (2) Basic Law: Citizens' Rights; and (3) Basic Law: Legislative Process. It is then expected that these eleven basic laws will collectively make up Israel's constitution.

The basic laws are the product of a compromise agreed on by the members of the First Knesset on 13 June 1950, following deep differences among the parties over the extent and application of religious regulations. In accordance with this Knesset decision, the constitution was to be created as a collection of individual chapters, each consisting of a basic law to be passed separately by the Knesset (see Likhovski, 1971: 18; Rubinstein, 1974: 21 ff. and 271 ff.; Wolffsohn, 1983a: 499 ff.).

While all other legislation can be passed or amended by a simple majority of the members present and voting, an absolute majority of the Knesset (at least sixty-one members) is required to modify or annul a 'protected article' of a basic law. However, this provision does not apply to a basic law as a whole. Basic laws thus do not take precedence over other legislation.

The Knesset alone is supreme, so that in Israel, unlike in the United States, there is no constitutional principle of judicial review. In Israel the Supreme Court is merely the organ responsible for the binding interpretation of existing legislation. Laws which have passed the Knesset with the proper majorities – as determined by the Knesset itself – cannot be declared unconstitutional by the Supreme Court. What passes the Knesset is law. If, however, the Knesset makes a formal technical error in passing a piece of new legislation, the Supreme Court is, if called upon, empowered to declare such legislation invalid.

(b) LEGAL SYSTEM

A commission of nine members recommends to the president the candidates for appointment to the Supreme Court, which consists of ten justices. The commission is chaired by the justice minister and includes the president and two other justices of the Supreme Court, a minister delegated from the cabinet, two members of the Knesset chosen by secret ballot and two delegates from the Israeli Bar Association (Rubinstein, 1974: 222; Freudenheim, 1973: 279 ff.).

Previous to 1984 the tenure·of a justice was terminated by his resignation or death, by mandatory retirement (at 70), or if the president and five additional members of the Supreme Court reached the finding that he had committed a 'disciplinary offence'. The same terms of tenure apply to the judges of the lower courts. The Basic Law: Judiciary (1984) introduced an important change. Now, seven of the nine members of the commission for the selection of judges may determine that a judge is no longer fit to serve. The motion may be put forward by the minister of justice or by the president of the Supreme Court.

The Supreme Court also serves as Israel's only court of administrative law, from which there is therefore no appeal. In this function the court is called the Beit Ha-Mishpat Hagavoa Lezedek and it is in this role that the court's responsibilities as an instance of control on the executive are particularly important. It has been made both relatively easy and inexpensive for citizens to turn to this court in the case of an abuse of administrative authority. As the Supreme Court's powers of judicial review in this area also encompass the actions of the military government in the occupied territories, it has become highly popular among the residents of the West Bank as an instance of relief.

Only in recent years have charges of political partisanship on the part of the Israeli courts been heard in increasing numbers, the main accusation being that the Likud government had pressed for the nomination of judges close to its own political views. On the other hand, it must be conceded that residents of the occupied territories have often, and successfully, fought appeals against expropriations before the Supreme Court in its function as the High Court of Justice. This is, despite the criticism of alleged political favouritism, an indication of the independence of this institution (for further details see Shamgar, 1982; Lustick, 1981). The Israeli Bedouins have also been able to mount successful appeals to the Supreme Court to prevent expropriations of their lands.

The independence of the judiciary was again demonstrated by the three-man commission which investigated the events leading up to the massacre of Palestinians near Beirut in September 1982. A sitting as well as a retired Supreme Court justice served on the commission, which reached conclusions hardly construable as favourable to the government.

The Supreme Court showed its mettle as an institution for the 'active defence' of democracy based on Zionist principles in its prohibitions of the Arab-nationalist al-Ard Group in 1964 and 1965. Slightly overstating the point, one could speak of the Supreme Court as an institution of 'Zionist democracy'. (On the al-Ard Group see B/VI/3/f; Landau, 1971: ch. 4; Likhovski, 1971: ch. 3; Lustick, 1980: 128 and Wolffsohn, 1983a: esp. 209 f., 425 ff.).

Article 9 of the Law and Administration Ordinance of 19 May 1948 authorized the Provisional State Council to declare a state of emergency whenever necessary. This was then done the very same day (see Bracha, 1978). The state of emergency was at first supposed to last for only three months but has been successively extended by vote of the Knesset up to the present. Accordingly, military courts and military administrations can be instituted, a fact which affected the status of the Israeli Arabs until December 1966 and continues to apply to the residents of the occupied territories insofar as these have not been annexed (for details see Shamgar, 1982; Wolffsohn, 1983a: 502 f.).

In addition to the emergency powers legislation, military courts are also authorized by the Ordinance for the Prevention of Terrorism of 1948. Suspected terrorists are therefore tried before military courts in Israel. The competencies of the military courts are subject to the supervision of the Supreme Court (Gutmann and Levy, 1976: 536 ff.).

The attorney general (also referred to as the legal adviser) not only offers his advice to the government on legal matters but also serves as the state procurator general. The attorney general is appointed and dismissed by the government, but due to the authority of this office as well as the office holders this has happened only once, in 1962. The government is not empowered to give the attorney general any written or verbal instructions, and it is his decision whether to open or close legal cases.

In 1976 Aharon Barak, then attorney general, later a Supreme Court judge, ordered the prosecution of the wife of Prime Minister Rabin. It was discovered that she held an illegal bank account in the United States, and in the end Rabin was forced to give up his candidacy for a further term as prime minister.

The attorney general is not formally a member of the cabinet, but it has become customary that he participate in the weekly cabinet sessions usually held on Sundays (see Klein, 1983).

(c) CITIZENSHIP

As a result of the Law of Return, passed by an overwhelming majority of the Knesset on 5 July 1950, any Jew arriving from abroad is automatically granted Israeli citizenship upon application (for the text of the Law of Return see Laqueur, 1970: 162 f.). Otherwise, the *de natu* principle (parentage) applies. Under special conditions, citizenship was also granted on the basis of residency in the case of the non-Jewish residents of Palestine living within the borders of Israel. In addition, citizenship can also be achieved through naturalization or by special grant (Rubinstein, 1974: 397 ff., and 1980: 401 ff.).

While for Jewish Israelis the word 'Jew' is entered as their 'nationality' in their identity papers, the entry for Arab Israelis is 'Arab'. Thus no distinction is made between nationality and religion with regard to Jews (whether religious or not) and Arab religious diversity (Christian, Sunni, or Druse) is disregarded.

Table 2   The Means of Obtaining Israeli Citizenship

Israeli citizenship can be obtained on the basis of:

1   The Law of Return
2   Birth (*de natu* principle)
3   Residence
4   Naturalization
5   Special grant

Non-Jewish residents of the territories conquered in 1967 and since then formally annexed to Israel (East Jerusalem and the Golan Heights) are nevertheless *not* citizens of Israel. If they desire to obtain Israeli citizenship, they must apply for naturalization (Rubinstein, 1980: 420 f.). In this way it is possible to annex territories without adding the residents to the voter rolls. More precisely, these residents are not allowed to vote in elections for the Knesset, but may participate in local elections, where not only Israeli citizens but all residents have the right to vote. Thus Israel remains a Jewish democracy with Arab territories and a politically stratified bi-national society in which one nation holds a dominant position (see A/I/3/f on Israel's identity crisis).

3 THE KNESSET

(a) LEGAL FRAMEWORK

Article 7a of the Law and Administration Ordinance (LAO) of 19 May 1948 designated the Provisional State Council as the legislative organ of the state. Article 3 of the Transition Law of 16 February 1949 transferred all powers of the Provisional State Council to the Constitutional Assembly, which simultaneously declared itself as the First Knesset. On 29 March 1949 the Knesset approved procedures for the passage of legislation, defining the fact of official publication as 'proof of the legitimacy of a law' (Article 10, LAO).

The seat of the Knesset is Jerusalem. The Knesset has 120 members elected for a legislative period of four years. The Knesset can be dissolved before the expiration of its term only when a majority of the members voting passes a 'special law' to this purpose. This was done to advance elections in 1951, 1961, 1977, 1981 and 1984.

Knesset rules call for twelve standing committees. Both the government and individual members may introduce bills, although about 95% of all bills now originate with the government. Three readings of a bill are required before passage.

As the successor of the Constitutional Assembly, the Knesset functions both in this capacity and as Israel's legislative body. In addition, it must pass the budget as well as follow-up legislation, is permitted to create subcommittees, and serves as a check on the executive. The office of the State Comptroller acts as a further check on the government (for details see section A/I/4).

(b) POLITICAL STATUS AND FUNCTIONS

The counterpart to the constitutional supremacy of the Knesset is the continuing reality of the omnipotence of party structures. The Knesset is only as strong, or as weak, as the structures of the parties represented in it permit. It is not possible to speak in terms of the independence of the Knesset member from his party, even though neither the Basic Law: Knesset nor parliamentary rules oblige the member to party loyalty. The rigid system of candidate lists, however, constitutes such an effective method of party discipline that formal legal sanctions remain unnecessary as long as the party leadership retains control over the candidate lists and the distribution of political spoils (see Elections, section A/I/3/e).

One result of the dominance of the party machine was that the 'sovereignty' of the Knesset came to depend less on its legally defined powers (Basic Law: Knesset) than on the power structures within the parties, the balance of power within and among the Knesset factions, and most of all on the assertiveness of the government, especially of the prime minister. The political parties and blocs have only been able to gain in strength when the authority of the government grew weaker.

The Knesset serves the politicians as a public platform. Its debates supply arguments for public discussion and thus the Knesset also acts as the nation's central exchange for information and experience, as it offers the shortest lines of communication. The Knesset is also the place where both those who make and those who carry out decisions come together. At the same time, it can serve as a stepping-stone for those who aspire to higher positions in the government, although only as an addendum to other qualifications.

Up until the beginning of the 1970s, belonging to the generation of the 'founding fathers' was practically a prerequisite for a seat in the cabinet. From 1948 to 1971, 43·5% of Israel's cabinet ministers came from this group. By way of contrast, only 8% of the ministers were selected on the basis of their non-political achievements. Nevertheless, the 'founding fathers' were also members of the Knesset, and their names headed their parties' candidate lists. Also, the prime minister must be a member of the Knesset. Knesset membership has, in the last decades, become almost indispensable for achieving cabinet rank. Whereas in Rabin's cabinet (1974/7) only six of the nineteen ministers were members of the Knesset, in cabinet 18b under Begin (1977/81) there was only one non-parliamentarian and in Begin's cabinets 19a and 19b (1981/3) all of the ministers were legislators. When Arens replaced Sharon as defence minister (in early 1983) another non-parliamentarian joined the government. In the Shamir cabinet, Arens remained the only non-parliamentarian. In the government formed in September 1984 all of the ministers, were also members of the Knesset.

Knesset approval is not required after the government has negotiated a treaty with a foreign power (cf. A/I/5/a). In 1984, however, Israel's attorney general proposed that treaties be subject to a Knesset vote (G. Alon, *Haaretz*, 7 August 1984).

(c) THE SELF-IMAGE OF KNESSET MEMBERS

Polls conducted during the Eighth Knesset (1973/7) showed that 76% of the Knesset members of the governing coalition wished to act in the role of a 'trustee' and 79% of the opposition parliamentarians considered this role 'desirable' (Caspi, 1976: 169). In other words, they did not conceive of themselves as 'delegates' in the strict sense of functioning as automatic executors of a mandate given by the electorate, but rather as politicians to whom the voters had given their trust for a certain period, that is, as trustees. At the same time, an acute awareness of the gap between this idealized self-image and political reality was demonstrated, especially among the members of the opposition.

(d) ELECTORATE AND ELECTED: LEADERSHIP VS RESPONSIVITY

What we are concerned with here is the ability of legislators to adapt and supply leadership to changing conditions within the society, especially to respond to ideological shifts among the voting public and the resulting discrepancies between the electorate and the elected (for further discussion see Wolffsohn, 1983a: ch. 33). While Arian (1971) found a significant ideological gap between the electorate and the elected in the 1960s, Caspi (1976) concluded that the differences had diminished by the early 1970s. According to Caspi, Israel's parliamentarians perceived a considerably smaller area of common ground shared by themselves and their voters than the much broader consensus actually measured by empirical means. Caspi explained this as a 'possible internalization' of the criticisms directed against the parliamentarians. The gap was found to be much narrower concerning foreign policy and territorial questions than on domestic and social issues.

(e) ELECTIONS

The basic principles of the election system for the future State of Israel were agreed upon in the third 'Preparatory Conference', which called itself the 'Council of Eretz Israel' and met in Jaffa on 18 December 1918. Suffrage was to be universal and equal, voting direct, secret and nationwide (the entire state as a single constituency), and representation proportional. The system of candidate lists determined by the party leadership was also agreed upon in 1918. The voting age was set at 20, the minimum age for office-holding at 25. The question of female suffrage was hotly contested between secular and religious Zionists. The Orthodox AI boycotted both the elections and participation in the Assembly of Delegates because women were allowed to vote.

The decision in favour of the rigid party candidate lists was probably of the greatest consequence for the election system in terms of discouraging party members from mobilization and active participation. Since the founding of the state, the nomination of candidates has been increasingly centred within the innermost circles of party leadership. Significant changes were made in most parties in 1977 (see A/II/3). Since then the process of nomination has become somewhat more open and democratic, the rank-and-file participating more actively.

Discussion of electoral reform has never ceased. The most frequent suggestions have been to elect Knesset members by simple majority in constituencies (as in the British parliamentary system). Another proposal calls for requiring a party to achieve a higher minimal percentage of the total vote before receiving any seats in the Knesset. Although the larger parties have shown interest in initiating reforms, they have always been forced to look out for the interests of their respective smaller coalition partners, who felt their very existence threatened by such measures.

Just once, in 1931, an exception was made to the principle of proportional representation, when eighteen of the seventy-one mandates were reserved for 'ethnic' groups: fifteen for the Sephardim and three for the Yemenites. (For details on the elections of the Yishuv period see Horowitz and Lissak, 1978: chs. 4 and 5; Wolffsohn, 1983a: 437 ff.)

The legal framework for the election system in the State of Israel is provided by the Basic Law: Knesset as well as by the election laws passed by the Knesset in 1959 and 1969, including recent modifications. Campaign financing and the day-to-day expenditures of the parties are regulated by the Party Financing Law of 24 January 1973 (see section A/II/4). Elections are held at the end of a legislative period on the third Tuesday of the Jewish month of Heshvan (October/November) or, if preceded by a leap year, on the first Tuesday of that month. If the Knesset is dissolved before the end of its term, the special law to this effect simultaneously sets the date for the advanced elections.

All men and women who are 18 years of age or older and citizens of Israel have the right to vote in Knesset elections and can be elected to office at the age of 21. Voting is not compulsory. There is no provision for absentee balloting.

The voting procedure is as follows. Individual ballot papers for each of the candidate lists are to be found in the polling booth. A ballot paper is printed for each party list with the letter or letters which constitute the official party abbreviation. The voter selects the ballot paper for the list of his choice and places this paper into an envelope which he then drops into the ballot box.

A party must receive at least 1% of the total vote in order to be represented in the Knesset. The number of seats assigned to each list is calculated by dividing the total number of valid votes in the election by 120 (the number of Knesset seats). This number is then divided into the number of votes cast for the individual list. Up to 1969 the remaining seats were distributed according to the lists with the largest remainders – a practice which favoured the smaller parties. Since 1973 this distribution has been carried out according to the modified d'Hondt method, which benefits the larger parties.

If a member of the Knesset resigns his seat or assumes an office excluding him from the Knesset (such as the presidency or a Supreme Court judgeship) the vacancy is automatically filled by the next candidate down his party's list.

(f) CAMPAIGN HISTORY, ELECTION RESULTS, VOTING PATTERNS

Table 3 shows, in simplified form, the three major political groupings in Israel together with the political parties belonging to each. Chapter A/II/1 (on party history) will sketch out further details concerning the individual parties and their 'genealogy', but first a general overview.

From the first elections to the Constituent Assembly onwards, the labour-oriented parties, led by Ahdut Haavoda (AH), the predecessor of Mapai, outdistanced all other groupings. The era of Mapai, later the Israeli Labour Party (ILP), thus began in 1920. It ended in 1977. Despite its dominant position, however, Mapai was always in need of a coalition partner, which it sought among the moderate religious and middle-class parties (HPM and Liberals).

The elections for the Constitutional Assembly, which constituted itself as the First Knesset on 16 February 1949, were held on 21 January 1949, in the wake of the War of Independence. With 35·7% Mapai was the clear victor, but without an absolute majority. It was followed by Mapam with 14·7%, Herut with 11·5%, the General Zionists (GZ) with 5·2%, the Progressives (PP) with 4·1% and the Communists with 3·5%.

David Ben-Gurion became prime minister, leading a coalition of Mapai, the religious parties, Sephardim and the PP. Difficulties soon arose with the religious parties over the issue of education policy in the camps for the newly arrived immigrants and with the middle-class religious Mishrahi over economic questions (rationing). The First Knesset was dissolved two years before the end of its regular term when an additional controversy arose with the religious parties over the issue of military service for women. In the elections of 30 July 1951 Mapai remained the strongest party with 37·5%, but the General Zionists made the largest gains. In 1953 Ben-Gurion resigned as prime minister.

In the election campaign of 1955 Mapai was led by Prime Minister Sharett, but it was an ill-kept secret that the name of the new prime minister would be Ben-Gurion.

The shift to the right noticeable in the elections of 1951 (gains by the GZ) took a different course in the elections of 26 July 1955. Within each of the

Table 3   The Political Camps and Their Chief Parties*

	Labor and Leftist Parties	Bourgeois and Rightist Parties	Religious Parties
Largest Party	MAPAI (1930) social democratic ISRAELI LABOUR PARTY (1968; merger of Mapai, Ahdut Haavoda, Rafi)	HERUT (1948) nationalistic	NATIONAL RELIGIOUS PARTY (as NRP since 1965, before then; Hapoel Hamisrahi + Misrahi), moderate religious
Other Parties	Mapam (1948), leftist socialist Ahdut Haavoda (1944), socialist Rafi (1965), rightist social democratic Communist Party (1919) New Communist List (1965), Moscow-oriented	General Zionists (1948) GZ/Liberals (1965), rightist liberal Progressive Party (1948) Independent Liberals (1965), leftist liberal (AZ and PP united as Liberal Party 1961–65) Tehiya (1979)	Agudat Israel (1912), Orthodox Poale Agudat Israel (1925), Orthodox socialist (merged in 1984 with R. Druckmann's Morasha) Tami (1981), Oriental religious Shass (1983/84), Oriental Orthodox
Bloc**	SMALL MAARAH (1965): Mapai, Ahdut Haavoda BIG MAARAH (1969): ILP, Mapam (joined in 1981, left in 1984), Independent Liberals, Yahad (E. Weizman, joined in 1984)	GAHAL (1965): Herut, Liberals LIKUD (1973): Gahal + 3 smaller parties, since 1982 practically only Herut and Liberals	

* Date of founding in parenthesis.
** Within a "bloc" the individual parties retain their organizational independence while presenting a single list of candidates at elections and maintaining a common faction in the Knesset or in local representative bodies.

major political constellations (Labour, religious, bourgeois/'right'), the greatest gains were made by the parties of the right wing of each camp. Whereas Herut almost doubled its proportion of the vote (to 12·6%), the GZ fell back to 10·2%, while Mapai shrank to 32·2%. The moderate socialist New Ahdut Haavoda (founded in 1944) did better (with 8·2%) than the more leftist Mapam (with 7·3%).

In the elections of 3 December 1959 Mapai profited from the prestige gained in the successful Sinai Campaign of 1956. It received 38·2% of the vote and thus increased the gap between itself and the second-strongest party, Herut (with 13·5%).

The early elections of 15 August 1961 took place in the glare of the Lavon affair, which was largely an internal Mapai controversy. The party thus suffered a setback and received only 34·7% of the vote. The biggest loser, however, was the new Liberal Party (uniting the GZ and PP in 1961), which had hoped to come in at least in second place but was beaten by Herut. In 1963 Ben-Gurion stepped down as prime minister and was succeeded by Levi Eshkol (Mapai).

The elections of 2 November 1965 were dominated by the upheavals that had previously occurred within the largest parties. Mapai was led by Prime Minister Levi Eshkol, who had prevailed in an internal party struggle. Ben-Gurion had led a challenge against his own hand-picked successor but failed to regain control of Mapai and thus led his followers out to form the Rafi Party. Forced to fight an election campaign on two fronts (against traditional rivals as well as the former prime minister and Rafi), Eshkol prevailed again. His task was made somewhat easier by the creation of the 'Small Maarah' (- Alignment) with AH.

Due to the forging of the Gahal bloc between Herut and the General Zionist wing of the Liberals that same year, Begin's party was able to break out of its ghetto and attain political legitimacy as well as increased acceptance. Of the two communist parties that had just resulted from a split, the Moscow-oriented Rakah (New Communist List) received the most votes.

With the 'Government of National Unity'composed from a broad coalition on the eve of the Six Day War (1967) still in office, the parties were less polarized in the elections of 28 October 1969. In 1968 Mapai, AH and Rafi had merged to form the Israeli Labour Party (ILP) which, under the leadership of Golda Meir, joined with Mapam in forming the 'Big Maarah' (Labour Alignment). With 46·2% of the vote, the new Alignment fell just short of an absolute majority.

The elections of 31 December 1973 were overshadowed by the Yom Kippur War (October 1973). The government of Golda Meir was accused of having failed to recognize the approaching danger and thus of responsibility for the high number of casualties. The public was particularly angered by the refusal of the Maarah leadership to make changes in the candidate list which had been drawn up for the elections originally scheduled for 31 October and then postponed. There were no changes made, even though, in the opinion of many Israelis, the failure of a number of highly placed politicians had been manifest. As expected, the Labour bloc suffered losses, but (with 39·6%) still remained clearly the largest faction, ahead of the Likud bloc, which had been formed in the summer of 1973.

Among the short- to middle-term causes of the Maarah's disastrous showing in the elections of 17 May 1977 was the delayed reaction to the protest movements which followed the 1973 war. Demands had been raised for 'more democracy' both inside and among the political parties, as well as for an end to the political, economic and social dominance of the elite.

A new party, the Democratic Movement for Change (DMC), made this 'the' issue of the 1977 campaign, promising both renewal and Zionist continuity. Moreover, the ILP had been damaged by diverse scandals and corruption affairs. The high rate of inflation also contributed little to the party's prestige. The ILP had neglected the Oriental Israelis both before and during the campaign, while the Likud paid them particular attention. Last but not least, the divisiveness within the ILP resulting from a leadership crisis intensified by the biological factor of age contributed to the end of the Mapai/ILP-dominated era. With Golda Meir's resignation in April 1974, the last of the charismatic personalities of the generation of the 'founding fathers' passed from the political stage of the Labour parties. The transition from a charismatic, 'natural' elite to an 'elected' leadership (Fein, 1967: 196 f.) did not prove successful.

On the opposite side of the political spectrum, the Likud bloc had in Menachem Begin a candidate capable of projecting both the charisma of the founding generation and a strong personal image. Viewed in this light, the election results appear to evince a certain nostalgia on the part of Israeli voters for the 'good old days' of the 'founding fathers' when there had, of course, been security problems to face, but when a basic consensus on the goals and the borders of the Jewish state had prevailed and Israel's society had not been plagued by an identity crisis.

The Six Day War was the prime cause of this identity crisis, as it posed new and fundamental questions about the character and the borders of the state (see Political Geography, section 2 of the Introduction). Was the goal to be a return to an historic 'Eretz Israel'? If so, which one? How were the Arabs living there to be treated? Should they not be granted Israeli citizenship? But would not this spell the end of the Jewish character of Israel? If the Arabs were not to be treated as equals, this would entail the loss of democracy in Israel. Zionism or democracy? If all the territories were to be returned, would not this endanger Israel's security? To these questions so vital to the future of the state, the ILP not only had no clear answers to offer in 1977, but was not even able to agree on a common line.

The crisis of identity in Israeli society, the crisis of legitimacy within the dominant party and its leadership, the crisis of participation (the challenge mounted against the traditional elite cartels), the crisis of integration (the polarization of Israeli society into Afro-Asian and Euro-American Jews), as well as the closely related crisis of distribution (the gap between rich and poor) – all of these led to the change of government in 1977. The elections of 17 May 1977, were 'critical elections' (Key, 1955) in that they resulted in far-reaching changes in the power structure.

The elections of 30 June 1981 confirmed the end of the ILP's dominance of the party system, which since then has been characterized by competition between two almost equally strong groupings, either one capable of displacing the other (see Arian, 1981). The elections to the Tenth Knesset were moved up as a result of the gradual dissolution of the governing coalition formed in 1977. The DMC was particularly affected, disintegrating into politically diverse fragments. It is worthy of note that the crisis in the government and the divisions within the coalition parties coincided both in chronology and in political content with the problems of the peace-making process (beginning with the Sadat initiative in 1977). The dialogue for peace repeatedly brought the government to the verge of breaking apart. The crises were further intensified by controversies over economic policy. In 1981 Israel held the world record for inflation. None other than the minister for religious affairs (from the NRP) was indicted for fraud and corruption. The settlements policy, the issue of peace with Egypt (vs 'peace on the back burner'), continuous labour strife, the 'Maarahization' of the Likud, and Israel's increasing international isolation led to a steep drop in the polls for the Likud coalition.

The turnabout came in January 1981, when the new finance minister, Aridor, introduced his populistic measures (i.e. election-time gifts to the voters). The Lebanese missile crisis in April, Begin's attacks on West German Chancellor Helmut Schmidt and French President Giscard d'Estaing, and certainly not least of all the destruction of the Iraqi nuclear reactor outside Baghdad increased the popularity of the Likud (Diskin, 1982b: 103). Last, and important, the Likud built on the support of Oriental Jews, a tactic which led to an up until then unprecedented 'ethnic' polarization in Israeli politics and society.

Seen in retrospect, the 1984 campaign actually began with the resignation of Prime Minister Begin, announced in late August 1983. Begin's successor, Yitzhak Shamir, had to first surmount the challenge of internal rivalries in the Herut party. In September 1983 he managed to defeat David Levy (a politician of Moroccan origin) in order to become Herut's candidate for the prime ministership, but later on he was unable to push through the economic austerity package proposed by his new finance minister, Yigael Cohen-Orgad. Aridor (the ousted predecessor) did his best to torpedo Cohen-Orgad's programme, even though both belonged to Herut. Moreover, the small Tami Party led by Ahron Abuhatzira (the former minister of religious affairs who in the meantime had been convicted of corruption and sentenced to three months in prison, Israel's first minister ever to have been convicted of such a crime while in office) also rejected Orgad's austerity programme, lest Tami lose the support of its lower-class Oriental constituency. Ariel Sharon, minister without portfolio since early 1983, repeatedly tried to undermine the authority and policy of his successor as minister of defence, Moshe Arens, who was, like Sharon, a member of Herut. Sharon demanded a 'tougher' line in Lebanon and in the occupied territories. Whereas the Orthodox Agudat Israel Party insisted on additional religious legislation (first and foremost measures that would hit hard at Reform and Conservative Judaism), the Liberal Party, also part of the Likud, firmly opposed any such action. The coalition disintegrated and the Knesset was prematurely dissolved. The campaign for the 23 July 1984 elections saw an additionally weakened Shamir, who defeated Sharon in the internal Herut contest over the candidacy for the prime ministership by the relatively narrow margin of 6:4.

The Labour Alignment, on the other hand, succeeded in closing ranks. The Peres–Rabin rivalry was buried (at least for the time being) and popular former president Yitzhak Navon ran in place two of Labour's 'leadership quartet' (Peres, Navon, Rabin and Bar-Lev).

The campaign proper was dominated by three issues: the economy, the continued presence of Israeli troops in Lebanon, and the issue of the West Bank settlements. Among other cuts in public expenditures, the Labour opposition demanded reductions in spending for new settlements and called for the IDF to be withdrawn from Lebanon as soon as possible in order to end this drain on the budget. Both the Likud and Labour were unanimous in declaring their intention to leave Lebanon, but differed in their approaches to accomplishing this aim. On the settlements issue, the Alignment proposed to tolerate existing settlements but to freeze further construction in areas heavily populated by Arabs. Instead, Labour preferred to stimulate settlements which it considered vital for security – not just for territory and ideology. The Alignment and its allies argued that the inclusion of almost 2 million Arabs living in the territories would jeopardize the Jewish character of Israel. The Likud and its partners countered with the question of why Jews should be allowed to settle in New York or Los Angeles but not in the Land of Israel, the land of Abraham, Isaac and Jacob.

During the campaign most observers predicted a clear-cut Alignment victory. This seemed all the more probable as, for the first time in its history, the Likud had to run without the charismatic personality of Menachem Begin. The former prime minister had totally withdrawn from public life and in no way participated in the campaign, not even to issue statements of endorsement.

The result of the 23 July 1984 elections was a stalemate. The left (Alignment, Citizens' Rights Movement, Shinui, Communists, Progressive List for Peace, Lova Eliav) won a total of 45·8% of the votes cast, as compared to 44·5% in 1981 (Alignment, Shinui, Communists, Citizens' Rights Movement, Shelli, Independent Liberals). Thus the left gained only 1·3% in 1984. The right (Likud, Tehiya, Rabbi Kahane) won 37·1% in 1984, whereas Likud and Tehiya had obtained 40·7% in 1981. The right thus lost 3·6% (see S. Weiss, *Haaretz*, 1 August 1984).

According to Shevach Weiss, the political centre was represented by Telem in 1981 and by Ometz (Yigal Hurvitz, formerly of Rafi, State List, Laam and Telem) as well as by Ezer Weizman in 1984. This 'centre' increased its share of the vote from 1·6% in 1981 to 3·4% in 1984. The religious parties (where Tami was included in 1981 and 1984, together with Shass in 1984) remained stable. They received 11·8% of the vote in 1981 and 11·4% three years later (ibid.; it may make sense also to include Kahane in the religious camp). 'Other' lists mustered 1·4% in 1981 and 2·3% in 1984.

The turnabout in the 1984 elections came late, within four weeks of the voting. According to Diskin, dramatic changes in favour of the Likud took place among the voters on election day proper. The governing coalition's economic campaign presents to the voters apparently accomplished their purpose (*Haaretz*, 5 August 1984; see sections B/VI/2/d–e and C/XII/6/a).

A total of six religious parties entered the Eleventh Knesset: the National Religious Party (which lost two seats), Shass (which had only just broken away from Agudat Israel in 1983 but promptly obtained four mandates from Orthodox-Oriental voters), Agudat Israel (which lost two seats), Morasha (a combination of hawkish former NRP dissidents and members of PAI), Poale Agudat Israel (with two parliamentarians), Abuhatzira's Tami Party (which lost two of its former three seats, probably to Shass) and Rabbi Kahane's superhawkish Kach.

Early in the campaign the Central Elections Committee had banned Kach as well as the Arab-Jewish Progressive List for Peace (PLP), but both parties were later allowed to run by the Supreme Court. In the end the PLP obtained two Knesset seats and became the most important competitor for the new Communist List among Israel's Arabs.

Figures 13 and 14 and Tables 4–6 give the detailed results of the elections from 1920 to 1984. (For more information concerning elections during the Yishuv period, see Horowitz and Lissak, 1978: chs. 4 and 5; Wolffsohn, 1983a: 437 ff.)

Ecological analyses (i.e. the analysis of precinct voting patterns) have demonstrated that before 1969 voters shifted not only within the larger political camps (the Labour, religious and bourgeois groupings) but also moved from one to the other (Diskin, 1980a: ch. 5). The net fluctuations among the blocs remained, however, almost perfectly balanced through 1969, so that the overall size of the larger groupings varied minimally (Diskin, 1982a: 57; Levy and Gutmann, 1979: 9; Wolffsohn, 1984: 50).

Since sociological data on voter fluctuation are easily obtainable from other sources (Arian, 1972a, 1975, 1979, 1980; Diskin, 1982a; Caspi, 1972; Wolffsohn, 1983a: 452 ff.), the following summary can suffice here. Sabras, the native-born Israelis, proved to be especially independent voters, although evincing a general preference for Herut/Gahal/Likud. Traditionally, the ILP was able to rely more on voters of Euro-American origin than on Oriental Jews. The younger generation identified itself with the Mapai/ILP era to a lesser degree than its parents. For the new generation, the state and the parties represented accomplished facts rather than institutions of its own creation, so that it could more easily go over to the opposition without bothering its political conscience. Quantitatively, the most significant change in voting patterns was the shift in 1977 from the Labour bloc to the Likud and DMC, although the Likud also lost some voters to the latter.

In 1981 both the Likud and the Maarah were especially successful in winning back former supporters. The Labour Alignment picked up its additional votes among former DMC supporters. The Likud won back voters who had gone over to the religious parties, most probably former National Religious supporters responding to the secularization of the NRP (following its turn to more general economic issues and settlements policy). The Likud was able to lure these voters with its emphasis on religious values as well as its promise of an active settlements policy. While profiting from crossovers, the Likud and the Maarah lost few of their 1977 voters. The Maarah also gained numerous additional voters among the Arabs.

The analysis of voter fluctuations nevertheless presents a deceptive picture. Among those who had voted for the Likud in 1977, only 22·5% were prepared to do so again in January 1981; 31·2% declared for the Maarah (Diskin, 1982a: 58). It was apparently only in the course of the campaign

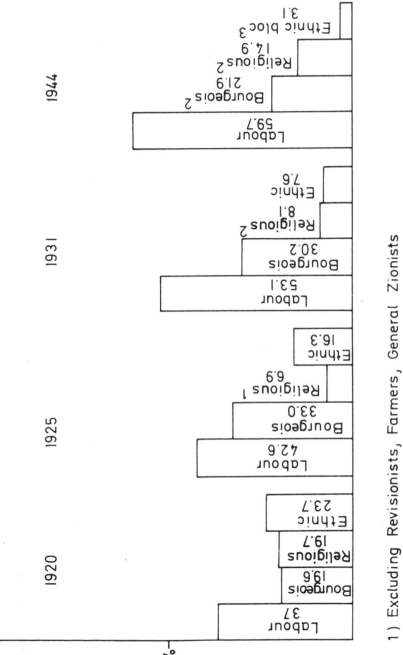

Figure 13   Elections to the Assembly of Delegates in the Yishuv, 1920–44.

1) Excluding Revisionists, Farmers, General Zionists
2) Excluding Al
3) Excluding Sepharadim

Table 4 Knesset Elections 1948–84: Votes per Party

	1st Knesset 25 Jan. 49	2nd Knesset 30 July 51	3rd Knesset 26 July 55	4th Knesset 3 Dec. 59	5th Knesset 15 Aug. 61	6th Knesset 2 Nov. 65	7th Knesset 28 Oct. 69	8th Knesset 31 Dec. 73	9th Knesset 17 May 77	10th Knesset 30 June 81	11th Knesset 23 July 84
Total Population	872,700	1,370,100	1,789,100	2,088,700	2,179,500	2,598,400	2,929,500	3,338,200	3,575,400	3,921,700	4,120,000
Eligible voters	506,567	924,885	1,057,795	1,218,483	1,271,285	1,499,709	1,748,710	2,037,478	2,236,293	2,490,014	2,654,610
Voters	440,095	695,007	876,085	994,306	1,037,030	1,244,706	1,427,981	1,601,098	1,711,726	1,954,609	2,091,402
Valid votes	434,685	687,492	853,219	969,337	1,006,964	1,206,728	1,367,743	1,566,855	1,747,820	1,937,366	2,073,321
Big Maarah	—	—	—	—	—	—	632,035	621,183	430,023	708,536	724,074
Small Maarah/ Yahad	—	—	—	—	—	443,379	—	—	—	—	46,302
Rafi	—	—	—	—	—	95,323	—	—	—	—	—
Mapam	64,018(a)	86,095(a)	62,401	69,469	75,654	79,985	—	—	—	—	—
Mapai	155,274	256,456	274,375	370,585	349,330	—	—	—	—	—	—
AH	(a)	(a)	69,475	58,043	66,170	—	—	—	—	—	—
Minority Lists (allied w. Maarah)	(b)	32,288	37,777	37,782	35,376	39,894	47,989	48,961(a)	24,185(c)	11,590	73,560
NRP	13,413	56,730(d)	77,936	95,581	98,786	107,966	133,328	130,349	160,787	95,232	31,103
Tami	—	—	—	—	—	—	—	—	—	44,466	—
Shass	—	—	—	—	—	—	—	—	—	—	63,605
AI	52,982(e)	13,799	39,836	45,569	37,178	39,795	44,002	60,012	58,652	72,312	36,079
PAI/Morasha	—	11,194	—	—	19,428	22,066	24,968	—	23,571	17,090	33,287
Kach	—	—	—	—	—	—	—	—	—	—	25,907
Likud	(f)	—	—	—	—	—	—	473,309	583,968	718,941	661,302
Shlomzion	—	—	—	—	—	—	—	—	33,947	—	—
Gahal	—	—	—	—	—	256,957	296,294	—	—	—	—
State List	—	—	—	—	—	—	42,654	—	—	—	—
Telem/Ometz	—	—	—	—	—	—	—	—	—	30,600	23,845
Herut	49,782	45,651	107,190	130,515	138,599	—	—	—	—	—	—

Tehiya	—	—	—	—	—	—	—	—	—	44,700	83,037
Liberal Party	22,661(g)	111,394	87,099	59,100	137,255(i)	—	—	—	—	—	—
Indep. Liberals	17,786(h)	22,171	37,661	44,889	(i)	45,299	43,933	56,560	20,384	11,764	49,698
CRM	—	—	—	—	—	—	—	35,023	20,621	27,921	54,747
DMC/Shinui	—	—	—	—	—	—	—	—	202,265	29,837	—
Free Centre	—	—	—	—	—	—	16,393	—	—	—	38,012
Shelli/PLP	(j)	—	—	—	—	—	—	—	27,281	8,691	—
OZ	—	—	—	—	—	14,124	16,853	10,469	—	—	—
Moked	—	—	—	—	—	—	—	22,127	—	—	—
CP	15,148	27,334	38,492	27,374	42,111	13,617	15,712	53,353	80,118	64,918	69,815
DFP	(k)	—	—	—	—	27,413	38,827	3,269	6,780	10,900	—
Others	—	—	4,484	8,469	3,896	5,536	—	—	—	—	—
Minority lists	—	—	—	—	—	—	—	—	35,049	10,823	—
Other lists	43,620	24,380	16,133	21,422	3,181	15,369	14,845	52,220	40,189	29,040	—

(a) AH in Mapam.
(b) Already allied with the Labour parties before the creation of the Maarah.
(c) United Arab List (at first only a single list).
(d) Including Misrahi and Hapoel Hamizrahi.
(e) United Religious Front.
(f) Including Gahal, State List, Great-Israel Movement.
(g) Until the 4th Knesset: General Zionists.
(h) Including the Progressive Party.
(i) Until the 4th Knesset: Progressive Party.
(j) Shelli, including Moked and Haolam Haze.
(k) Until the 8th Knesset: 'Rakah' – New Communist List, including the Democratic Front for Peace and Equality (NCL), the Black Panthers (Oriental and Sephardic Jews) as well as 'independent' Jews and Arabs in the elections for the 9th Knesset.
For explanation of abbreviations see List of Abbreviations (pp. 000–0).

Sources: Elections, 1977, and 1981: table 1; Central Bureau of Statistics; Central Election Committee; *Statistical Abstract of Israel*, 1984: 568 f.

Table 5   The Knesset Elections, 1949–84: Relative Strength of the Parties (%)

Knesset	I	II	III	IV	V	VI	VII	VIII	IX	X	XI
Valid Votes	*100·0*	*100·0*	*100·0*	*100·0*	*100·0*	*100·0*	*100·0*	*100·0*	*100·0*	*100·0*	*100·0*
Participation	86·9	75·1	82·8	81·6	81·6	83·0	81·7	78·6	79·2	78·5	78·8
Big Maarah	—	—	—	—	—	—	46·2	39·6	24·6	36·6	34·9
Small Maarah/Yahad	—	—	—	—	—	36·7	—	—	—	—	2·2
Rafi	—	—	—	—	—	7·9	—	—	—	—	—
Mapam	(a)14·7	(a)12·5	7·3	7·2	7·5	6·6	—	—	—	—	—
Mapai	35·7	35·7	32·2	38·2	34·7	—	—	—	—	—	—
AH	(a)—	(a)—	8·2	6·0	6·6	—	—	—	—	—	—
Minority lists (allied with Maarah)	3·0	4·7	3·3	3·9	3·5	3·3	3·5	3·1	(c)1·4	0·6	—
NRP	( )[1]	(d)8·3	9·1	9·9	9·8	8·9	9·8	8·3	9·2	4·9	3·5
Tami	—	—	—	—	—	—	—	—	—	2·3	1·5
Shass	—	—	—	—	—	—	—	—	—	—	3·1
AI	(e)12·2[1]	2·0	4·7[2]	4·7[2]	3·7	3·3	3·2	3·8[2]	3·4	3·7	1·7
PAI/Morasha	( )[1]	1·6	( )[2]	( )[2]	1·9	1·8	1·8	( )[2]	1·3	0·9	1·6
Kach	—	—	—	—	—	—	—	—	—	—	1·2
Likud	(f)—	—	—	—	—	—	—	30·2	33·4	37·1	31·9
Shlomzion	—	—	—	—	—	—	—	—	1·9	—	—
Gahal	—	—	—	—	—	21·3	21·7	—	—	—	—

State list/Telem/Ometz	—	—	—	—	—	—	3·1	—	—	1·6	1·2
Herut/Tehiya	11·5	6·6	12·6	13·5	13·8	—	—	—	—	2·3	4·0
Liberal Party	(g)5·2	16·2	10·2	6·2	13·6	—	—	—	—	—	—
Independent Liberals	(h)4·1	3·2	4·4	4·6	—	3·8	3·2	3·6	1·2	0·6	2·4
CRM	—	—	—	—	—	—	—	2·2	1·2	1·4	2·6
DMC/Shinui	—	—	—	—	—	—	1·2	—	11·6	1·5	—
Free Centre	(j)—	—	—	—	—	—	—	—	—	—	—
Shelli/PLP	—	—	—	—	—	1·1	1·2	—	1·6	0·4	1·8
OZ	—	—	—	—	—	—	1·2	0·7	—	—	—
Moked	3·5	—	—	—	—	1·2	1·2	1·4	—	—	—
CP	(k)—	4·0	4·5	2·8	4·2	2·3	2·8	3·4	4·6	3·4	3·5
DFP/NCL	—	—	—	—	—	0·5	0·0	0·2	0·4	0·5	—
Other minority lists	—	1·6	0·8	0·4	—	—	—	—	2·0	1·6	—
PS	—	—	—	—	—	—	—	—	—	—	—
Other lists	10·1	3·6	1·9	2·2	0·3	1·3	1·1	3·3	2·2	1·6	2

[1] NRP, AI and PAI formed a bloc with a single list in 1949.

[2] AI and PAI formed a bloc with a single list in 1955, 1959 and 1973.

See Table 4 for explanation of lettered notes.

For abbreviations see Glossary of Abbreviations (pp. 00–0).

Source: *Elections*, 1981: table 1.

Table 6   The Knesset Elections, 1949–84: Mandates per Party

Knesset	I	II	III	IV	V	VI	VII	VIII	IX	X	XI
Total Mandates	120	120	120	120	120	120	120	120	120	120	120
Big Maarah	—	—	—	—	—	—	56	51	32	47	44*
Small Maarah/Yahad	—	—	—	—	—	45	—	—	—	—	3*
Rafi	—	—	—	—	—	10	—	—	—	—	(6)*
Mapam	19	15	9	9	9	8	—	—	—	—	—
Mapai	46	45	40	47	42	—	—	—	—	—	—
AH	—	—	10	7	8	—	—	—	—	—	—
Minority lists (allied with Maarah)	2	5	5	5	4	4	4	3	1	—	—
NRP	( )[1]	10	11	12	12	11	12	10	12	6	4
Tami	—	—	—	—	—	—	—	—	—	3	1
Shass	—	—	—	—	—	—	—	—	—	—	4
AI	16[1]	3	6[2]	6[2]	4	4	4	5[2]	4	4	2
PAI/Morasha	( )[1]	2	( )[2]	( )[2]	2	2	2	( )[2]	1	—	2
Kach	—	—	—	—	—	—	—	—	—	—	1
Likud	—	—	—	—	—	—	—	39	43	48	41
Shlomzion	—	—	—	—	—	—	—	—	2	—	—
Gahal	—	—	—	—	—	26	26	—	—	—	—

State List/Telem/Ometz	—	—	—	—	—	—	4	4	—	2	1
Herut/Tehiya	14	8	15	17	17	—	—	—	—	3	5
Liberal Party	7	20	13	8	17	—	—	—	—	—	—
Independent Liberals	5	4	5	6	—	5	4	4	1	1	—
CRM	—	—	—	—	—	—	—	3	1	1	3*
DMC/Shinui	—	—	—	—	—	—	—	—	15	2	3
Free Centre	—	—	—	—	—	—	2	—	2	—	—
Shelli/PLP	—	—	—	—	—	—	2	—	2	—	2
OZ	—	—	—	—	—	—	2	1	—	—	—
Moked	—	—	—	—	1	1	1	—	—	—	—
CP	4	5	6	3	5	3	3	4	5	4	—
DFP	—	—	—	—	—	3	—	—	—	4	4
Other minority lists	—	—	—	—	—	—	—	1	1	—	—
PS	—	—	—	—	—	—	—	—	—	1	—
Other lists	7	3	3	—	—	—	—	—	—	—	3

Notes:

* In September 1984 Mapam (6 MKs) broke with the Maarah, which Yahad (3 MKs) had joined in August. In September 1984 one ILP MK joined the CRM.

1 NRP, AI and PAI formed a bloc with a single list in 1949.

2 AI and PAI formed a bloc with a single list in 1955, 1959 and 1973.

See Table 4 for explanation of further notes.

For abbreviations see List of Abbreviations (pp. 00–0).

Source: Elections, various vols.

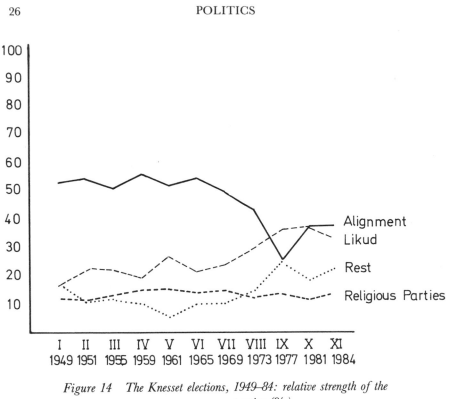

*Figure 14   The Knesset elections, 1949–84: relative strength of the
parties (%).*

that the Likud succeeded in winning back its former supporters. The
bombing of the nuclear reactor near Baghdad appears to have been decisive
(Diskin, 1982a: 58; Peretz and Smooha, 1981: 508). By way of contrast, of
those who had voted Maarah in 1977, 83% were prepared to do so again in
January 1981 (ibid.). Among former DMC supporters, only 2·3% preferred
the Likud in January 1981, but 14% actually voted Likud in June. (For
further details see section A/II/5/e.)

To sum up: the number of uncommitted voters has grown significantly in
recent years and the preferences of these Israeli voters can shift with
extraordinary rapidity, as demonstrated by the swing in public opinion
between January and late June of 1981.

A number of currents can be identified in the floating vote in 1984. The
Likud's greatest losses were to Tehiya. Here, the 'purists' were obviously
dissatisfied with what they perceived as the 'catch-all' (O. Kirchheimer)
character of the Likud, which also lost voters to Kahane, Weizman, Hurvitz
and, of course, to the Alignment.

The Alignment lost its more 'purist' 1981 voters to the Citizens' Rights
Movement, Shinui and Lova Eliav (who did not win a Knesset seat).
Weizman and the Progressive List for Peace also attracted former Maarah
voters.

The National Religious Party lost 1981 voters mainly to Rabbi Druckman's Morasha (which was joined by the PAI), but also to the hawkish

Tehiya and the Orthodox-ethnic Shass, which, in turn, absorbed about 46% of Agudat Israel's 1981 supporters. Tami, too, lost many voters to Shass and a somewhat lesser number to the Likud, Weizman and the Alignment.

Tehiya, the Citizens' Rights Movement, Shinui, Kahane (who may also have won over a few former Tehiya voters), Agudat Israel, PAI, Morasha and Ometz (Hurvitz) gained significant numbers of young and, more important, 'new' voters, who went to the polls for the first time. This conclusion is derived from an analysis of the election results from the Israel Defence Forces, where the voters are younger than the general electorate (see Y. Galnnor, *Haaretz*, 2 September 1984). Among IDF voters Tehiya won 9·7% (as compared with the 3·7% it received from the civilian electorate); Shinui 4·2% (vs 2·6%); the Citizens' Rights Movement 3·3% (vs 2·3%); Agudat Israel 4·5% (vs 1·6%); Morasha/PAI (Druckman) 2% (vs 1·6%); Ometz 3·4% (vs 1%); and Kahane 3% (vs 1·1%).

Much of the floating vote in 1984 was Oriental (H. and R. Smith, *Jerusalem Post*, 3 August 1984) and went to Tehiya, the Likud and Kahane, and away from the Alignment (see Figure 42).

Ashkenasi Israelis voted mostly for the Alignment and its allies (Shinui, Citizens' Rights Movement, Weizman), and also for Tehiya, but not for the Likud (ibid.). The bulk of the voters who had supported the Democratic Movement for Change in 1977 could be counted among the floating voters of 1984. Some of these may have broken away from their former allegiances as early as 1965, when some of them switched from Mapai to Ben-Gurion's Rafi, then to the State List in 1969 and the Citizens' Rights Movement in 1973 (when, as in 1984, it also gained three mandates).

It must not be forgotten, however, that much of the flow took place during the final four weeks before the balloting (H. and R. Smith, *Jerusalem Post*, 17 July 1984), and even on election day itself (A. Diskin, *Haaretz*, 5 August 1984).

As for the Arab floating vote in 1984, the main movement away from the Communists (NCL) was to the Progressive List for Peace (PLP). A small proportion went to the Alignment, which, together with its affiliated 1981 minority list, lost most heavily to the PLP and less to the NCL. Shinui and Yahad (Ezer Weizman) also profited from Alignment losses among the Arabs of Israel.

(g) THE SOCIOLOGY OF ISRAEL'S LEGISLATORS

1 Immigrants and 'natives'

Figures 15 and 16 show the longstanding dominance of the second *aliya* (the second wave of immigration, which arrived in Palestine between 1904 and 1914). This *aliya* constituted the political elite of the Yishuv from 1918 to 1948 and continued to lead Israel in the first decades following independence. (The various *aliyot* are discussed in section B/VI/d.)

The numbers given for the period since 1948 refer only to the members of the Knesset from the largest Knesset faction – Mapai/Maarah from the First to the Eighth Knessets and the Likud bloc since 1977. After Mapam's defection from the Maarah in September 1984 the Likud again became the largest single faction.

The dominance of the second *aliya* was particularly striking in the parties of the Labour bloc, both in the Yishuv period and in the years after independence. (On the Yishuv see Horowitz and Lissak, 1977: 159, and 1978: 114; Lissak, 1981: ch. 14; Wolffsohn, 1983a: 222 ff., esp. table 22.)

The quantitatively diminishing importance of the second *aliya* within Mapai is traceable to biological rather than political factors. In 1974 there were still relatively few *Sabras* – only 33% – in the Maarah faction, whereas Sabras made up over 50% of the Likud faction. Only in 1977 did they top 50% in the Maarah, but by then already represented 71% of the Likud. In 1981 as well, the Likud outdistanced the Maarah in this respect, but less strikingly than in 1977.

Within the Mapam, the founder generation, which arrived with the third *aliya*, was also able to maintain its quantitative and political dominance. The data for AH reflects the continuing importance of the fourth *aliya* for this party on the one hand and the significance of the Sabras on the other, particularly in comparison with Mapam.

The leftist-socialists and the Communists profited especially from the third and the fifth *aliyot*. It must be noted, however, that from the Seventh Knesset onwards the non-Jewish legislators among the ranks of the Communists were, as Arabs, also native-born.

The extent to which Rafi/State List constituted the party of the 'youth' (led by the 'old man' Ben-Gurion) is indicated by the relatively high proportion of Sabras in the party. In this respect, however, the DMC may be considered 'the' party of the Sabras. The fourth and fifth *aliyot* were of decisive importance for the Orthodox parties AI and PAI, as well as for the middle-class parties. The Oriental immigrants who have arrived since 1948 form the backbone of Tami.

In the Eleventh Knesset, elected in 1984, the Sabras reached their second highest level of representation in the largest parliamentary faction, making up 68% of the Likud deputies (as opposed to 71% in 1977 and 63% in 1981 but only 33% in 1973). Sabra representation in the previous Knessets was, of course, much lower. With 10% of the members, the fifth *aliya* (which arrived between 1932 and 1939/47) was the most veteran *aliya* of the Eleventh Knesset; 22% of the members had immigrated since 1948 (see Figure 16). The fifth *aliya* was also the most veteran among the other Knesset factions; there were no longer any members from the previous *aliyot*. The generation of the 'founding fathers' has passed from the political stage; their children and grandchildren have taken over.

2 Age

The Eighth and Tenth Knessets show the first signs of a slow turnabout in the ageing trend observable in almost all of the parties. Figure 17 documents this general, gradual change, but also shows the continued ageing of the Communist faction as well as of the Herut/Gahal/Likud camp. In the Eleventh Knesset the average age rose once again (to 53·8 years). The Orthodox-Oriental Shass faction sent by far the youngest group of deputies into the Knesset. Their average age was 42. A comparison with the average age of its Ashkenasi counterpart, Agudat Israel, shows that the competition between these parties has something to do with generational change as well.

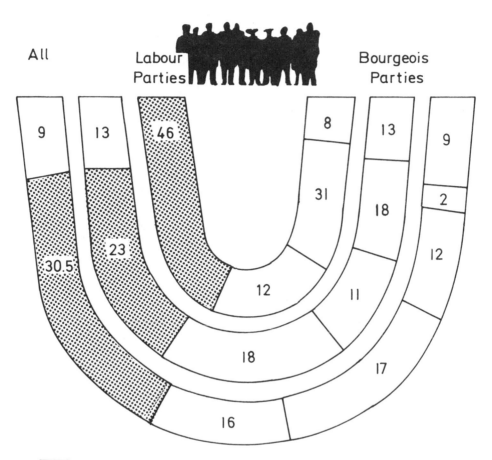

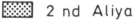 2 nd Aliya

* Not 100% because data unavailable for all aliyot

Figure 15   The political elite in the Yishuv, 1918–48 by immigration
*wave (*aliya) (in %).

Source: Horowitz and Lissak, 1978: 114.
Key:

	All	Bourgeois Parties	Labour Parties
1st *aliya*	9	13	—
2nd *aliya*	30·5	23	46
3rd *aliya*	16	18	12
4th *aliya*	17	11	31
5th *aliya*	12	18	8
1940 ff.	2	—	—
Zabarim	9	13	—

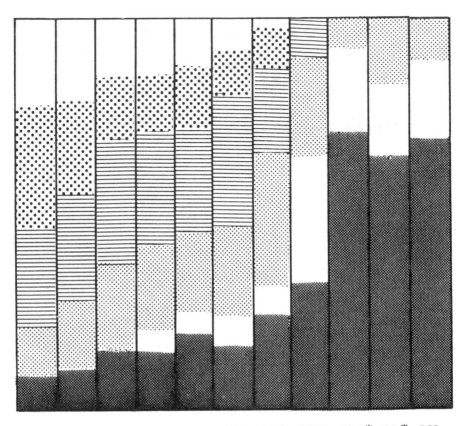

*Figure 16   Knesset members of the largest parliamentary group,
1949–84, by* aliya *(in %)*.

* IX and X Likud; earlier Mapia/Maarah.

Legislature	I	II	III	IV	V	VI	VII	VIII	IX	X	XI
2nd *aliya*	26	21	17	12	13	8	2	2	—	—	—
3rd *aliya*	30	23	12	10	10	8	7	—	—	—	—
4th *aliya*	24	28	38	33	31	42	27	9	—	—	—
5th *aliya*	11	17	21	20	21	18	33	25	7	17	10
1948 ff.	—	—	—	6	6	8	7	31	22	20	22
Zabarim	9	11	12	15	19	16	24	33	71	63	68

Tami's one-man faction (Abuhatzira, aged 46) was placed a poor second (see Wolffsohn, 1984: 55).

It is also worth noting that the Likud faction (average age 50·2) was younger than the Maarah (53·3) and that Ometz's one-man faction (Yigael Hurvitz, 66) represented the oldest faction.

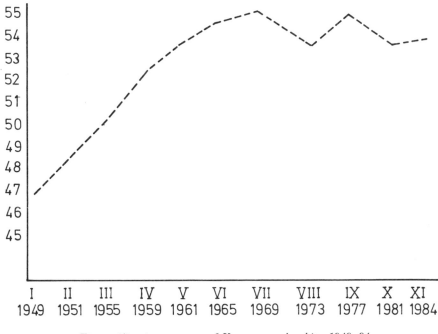

Figure 17   Average age of Knesset membership, 1949–84.

In summary, one can hardly speak of a changing of the political guard in 1984, and not even of a rejuvenation, except for the Orthodox camp (Shass vs Agudat Israel). This phenomenon by no means contradicts the statement made above that the children and grandchildren have taken over from the founding fathers. Instead, it shows that the latter clung to power over an unusually long period, so that their children had long grown up by the time their turn finally came. Furthermore, the successor generation does not seem to be eager to carry out the next changing of the guard in a fundamentally different manner.

3   Origin

Figure 18 documents the long-term dominance of Eastern European Jews in the political leadership elites (see Wolffsohn, 1984: 57 ff.).

Undoubtedly, the wind was blowing from the East in the first years of the young nation, while the influence of politicians from Western and Central Europe remained negligible. The numbers of politicians of Afro-Asian descent were extraordinarily low, but slowly increased with time. Although far more Israelis of Oriental heritage voted for the Likud than the Maarah in 1981, the latter actually seated more Oriental Jews in its parliamentary faction.

For biological reasons, the trend has been towards an ever greater proportion of native-born Sabras in the Knesset. Of Israel's seven prime ministers, however, six have been from Eastern Europe and only one, Yitzhak Rabin (1974/7), was a Sabra. Of the two leading contenders in 1984, Shamir was born in Poland, as was Peres, although the latter arrived in Palestine at the age of 11.

In the Eleventh Knesset (1984) the Citizens' Rights Movement and the Likud proved to be the most 'Sabra' of the parties with 75% and 68% respectively of their parliamentarians having been born in Israel. Shinui, Yahad (Weizman) and Mapam followed with about two-thirds of their Knesset members being Sabras. In the ILP Sabras made up 54% of the delegates. The overall dominance of Sabras is, of course, the result of biological rather than political processes. It thus makes more sense to make distinctions between Sabras of an Oriental or Ashkenasi background, but these data are more difficult to obtain, as they are not usually discussed by the Knesset members or mentioned in their biographies.

Eastern Europeans were well represented in the New Communist List (25%), Mapam and Likud (17% of the respective factions), but also in the Labour Party (with 11%). In terms of absolute numbers – which are more telling here – the most Eastern Europeans were to be found in the Likud, followed by the Labour Party. Party traditions were effective even as late as 1984 in these cases. Shinui, NRP and Tehiya were the only parties in 1984 which nominated Central and Western Europeans for top positions on their lists. As a result, this ethnic group was represented in the Knesset exclusively by these parties.

Immigrants from the Balkan countries were to be found only in the Labour Party (3 out of 37 MKs), Mapam (1 out of 6) and Agudat Israel (1 of 2). In absolute numbers, the most immigrants from North African and Asian countries in the Knesset were to be found in the ILP faction (9 out of 37 MKs). The Likud sent six Afro-Asian deputies in its total of forty-one MKs (despite the overrepresentation of this group among its voters). In terms of percentages, Tami was the most Oriental party in 1984 (100%), but then it had only a single Knesset seat. Shass returned two immigrants from Morocco, one from Afghanistan and a Sabra of Moroccan origin.

There were only three members of the Knesset from Anglo-Saxon countries in the Eleventh Knesset: one in the Labour Party (Abba Eban), one in Tehiya (Rabbi Waldman, who was born in Israel, moved to the USA as a child and returned to Israel in the 1950s) and the third was Rabbi Kahane! If we interpret these latter data from a different perspective, we can say that one Anglo-Saxon MK is a dove (Eban) and two are hawks (Waldman and Kahane). Figure 18 summarizes the data for the two major parliamentary factions from the First to the Eleventh Knessets.

4 Occupation

Figure 19 offers information on the occupational backgrounds of Knesset members (Wolffsohn, 1984: 62 f).

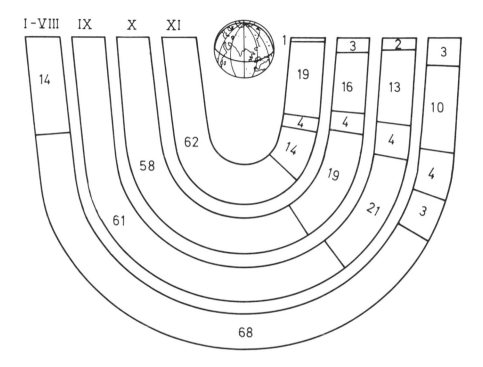

Figure 18   Origin of the Knesset membership of the two largest factions (in %).

Key:

Legislature	I–VIII	IX	X	XI
Israel	14	61	58	62
East Europe	68	21	19	14
Central and West Europe	3	—	—	—
Balkans	4	4	4	4
Africa/Asia	10	13	16	19
Anglo-Saxon countries	3	2	3	1

Professional politicians made up 54% of the Mapai faction between 1949 and 1955 (Brichta, 1972: 287). In the Ninth Knesset, the percentage increased to 65% in the ILP (Weiss, 1977: 35). Among the legislators of the Likud from 1949 to 1965, 45% were professional politicians (Brichta, 1972: 290), but this was true of only 13% in 1977. In the NRP the proportion dropped from 65% in the First Knesset to 25% by 1977. Professional politicians made up an overwhelming 100% of the AI faction in the Ninth Knesset, although its average for 1949–65 was only 29% (Brichta, 1972: 289; Weiss, loc. cit.).

The long dominance of the professional politicians finally led to a situation in which only those who had 'made it', who had survived the long march through the ranks of the party apparatus, were able to enter the Knesset.

5   Bourgeois Image

The political elite of the Yishuv was predominantly Labour and naturally tried to present a 'proletarian' image, although many of its members were professional politicians. In the intervening decades this image has changed. Now, the bourgeois image prevails – despite the fact that most voters are working class.

This trend can be clearly seen in the numbers of legislators who had previously been educators, other professionals, or self-employed. The smallest changes are to be observed among the parties of the Maarah. During the first six legislative periods (1949–65) 21% of the Maarah faction came from these occupational groups and the proportion grew only slightly to 29% in 1977.

For the Herut faction the comparable figures were 48% for the period from the First to the Sixth Knessets, and 60% for the General Zionists/Liberals. This increased to 75% in 1977. The increase is also very large for the NRP: from 35% to 58% (Brichta, 1972: 287 ff.; Weiss: 1977: 35 ff.).

Despite the 'proletarian', that is, working class quantitative dominance, the 'bourgeois' professions enjoyed great prestige. Again, Labour reacted belatedly to value changes. The trend to a bourgeois image was accentuated earlier and more strongly by the Likud.

Figure 19 illustrates the continuing trend towards middle-class, 'bourgeois' occupations in the Eleventh Knesset (1984). It also demonstrates that the Likud has best managed to keep up with this development, at least as far as the two largest parties are concerned.

In 1984 there were only eight farmers and two blue-collar workers among the 120 Knesset members. Gone were the days when parliamentarians boasted of their pioneer, *halutzic* backgrounds. The Labour Party did not send a single delegate with a blue-collar profession to the Eleventh Knesset. Instead, it was the Likud which accounted for 50% of the parliamentarians presenting a 'left-wing' occupational image. There were, however, only two blue-collar workers elected to the Eleventh Knesset and both of them, David Levy (Herut/Likud) and Charly Biton (Black Panthers/NCL), had long turned professional politicians. The Likud was also more *halutzic* than Labour in its image in 1984.

Except for the professional politicians, who were most strongly represented in the Labour faction (11 out of a total of 24 were Labour MKs), lawyers constituted the most numerous occupational group in the Eleventh Knesset (20 of the 120 MKs), of which 65% (13) belonged to the Likud faction. Teachers represented the third largest group.

In public opinion polls the prestige of middle-class occupations has risen steadily (Eisenstadt, 1973: 180; V. Krauss, 1976: 87; Wolffsohn, 1983a: 334 ff.). Krauss (1976) found that the highest status was accorded to biologists, dentists, lawyers and judges. Mayors ranked fifth, members of the Knesset ninth. Doctors, economists and university professors held places ten, eleven and twelve, whereas cabinet ministers came in twenty-ninth and *kibbutz* officials ranked only seventieth (*kibbutz* finance secretaries, that is; *kibbutz* general secretaries were still further down in place eighty). Parties such as the ILP and Mapam, which attempted to attract votes with the image of the

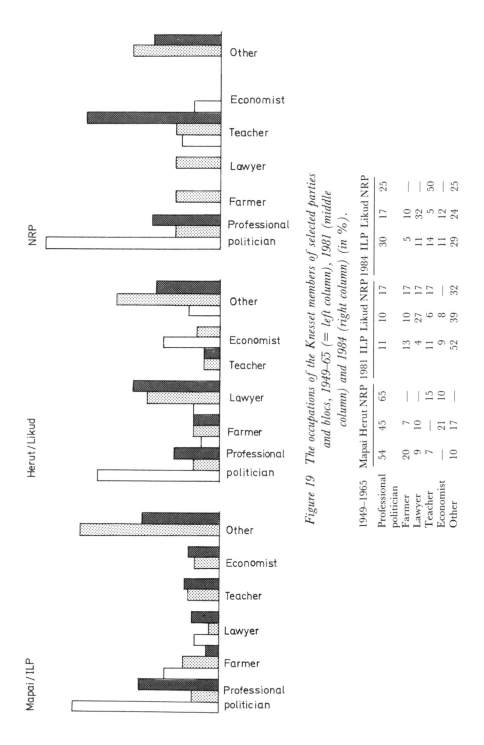

Figure 19 The occupations of the Knesset members of selected parties and blocs, 1949–65 (= left column), 1981 (middle column) and 1984 (right column) (in %).

1949–1965	Mapai	Herut	NRP	1981	ILP	Likud	NRP	1984	ILP	Likud	NRP
Professional politician	54	45	65		11	10	17		30	17	25
Farmer	20	7	—		13	10	17		5	10	—
Lawyer	9	10	—		4	27	17		11	32	50
Teacher	7	—	15		11	6	17		14	5	—
Economist	—	21	10		9	8	—		11	12	—
Other	10	17	—		52	39	32		29	24	25

agricultural pioneer, were thus forced to labour at a distinct disadvantage. The prestige of 'bourgeois' professions is also a clear indication of the abandonment of pioneer (i.e. *kibbutz*) values in the society as a whole. Where pioneers and creators (as well as propagators) of ideology were once in demand, Israeli society and politics in the 1970s and 1980s seemed to prefer the technocrat.

6   Military Background

In 1977 eleven parliamentarians (9%) could look back on a career in the military. This had been true for 90 of the 374 Knesset members (24%) during the eight preceding legislative periods (Gutmann and Landau, 1975: 178, 181).

The proportional decline in the number of Knesset members with a military background (i.e. officers of the rank of colonel and higher) could also be observed in the Tenth Knesset (1981), where only seven parliamentarians (or 6%) had been career officers. The Labour Party alone returned three former chiefs of staff (rank of lieutenant general): Rabin, Bar-Lev and Gur. Chaim Herzog, elected president in 1983, had left the IDF as a major general. Telem had another former lieutenant general: Moshe Dayan, who passed away in October 1981, shortly after the opening session of the Knesset.

The highest ranking retired officers in the Likud faction were Major General (Res.) Ariel Sharon and Brigadier General (Res.) Mordechai Zippory. Tehiya could present a former colonel (Professor Neeman).

The proportion of former career officers (again, colonel and higher) rose slightly in the Eleventh Knesset to a total of eleven (or 9%). Labour returned Rabin, Bar-Lev and Gur, and the Likud faction once more included Sharon. Tehiya also returned Professor Neeman, but he was now 'outranked' by Lieutenant General (Res.) Raphael Eitan ('Raful'). Two of Yahad's three Knesset seats were occupied by high-ranking former officers: Major General (Res.) Ezer Weizman himself and Brigadier General (Res.) Benyamin Eliezer ('Fuad'). Like Yahad, the Citizens' Rights Movement, led by Mrs Shulamit Aloni, also presented two officers among its three-member faction. Mordechai Bar-On and Ran Cohen had attained the rank of colonel (Res.). The Arab-Jewish Progressive List for Peace sent Major General (Res.) Mattityahu Peled into the Knesset.

7   The General Occupational Structure

The occupational data clearly show that the Likud and DMC could be labelled as 'the' bourgeois parties of the professional classes, the NRP as the party of the teachers (at least of former teachers) and the Maarah as the party of civil servants and professional politicians.

8   Formal Education

Of the members of the Mapai faction from the First to the Sixth Knessets, 58% held university degrees (Brichta, 1972: 305), and in the Ninth Knesset it was still 53% (Weiss, 1977: 33). In the Herut the percentages were 69% (First to Sixth Knessets) and 55% (1977) (ibid.; Brichta, 1972: 307). Here the decline in the number of university graduates was relatively large and can, to a degree, be interpreted as an adaptation to the 'proletarization' of the Likud voters. The proportion of university graduates declined insignificantly from 67% to 65% in the three religious parties (Weiss, loc. cit.; Brichta, 1972: 308).

The following two legislative periods evinced a virtual explosion of university graduates (including representatives with equivalent degrees such as rabbinical ordination).

The Alignment faction in the Tenth Knesset (1981) included thirty-five university graduates (or 74%); and of the Labour Party faction in the Eleventh Knesset (1984), thirty-two members (or 86%) held degrees. The other large bloc, the Likud, seated thirty-five graduates (or 73%) in the Tenth and thirty-two (or 78%) in the Eleventh Knessets. One out of the four New Communist List MKs was a university graduate in 1981 and 1984. Two out of the three Tami delegates in 1981 held degrees.

The following parties were represented only by university graduates (100%) in 1981 and 1984: Citizens' Rights Movement, the National Religious Party, Agudat Israel, Shinui, Tehiya and Telem (Moshe Dayan's party, 1981 only). The Eleventh Knesset included the following additional groups represented exclusively by graduates: Shass, Morasha, Progressive List for Peace and Kach (Kahane).

To sum up, the recent trend indicates that the chances of getting into the Knesset for would-be politicians without a degree are disappearing. Nevertheless, we have to be careful not to draw a precipitate conclusion based merely on numbers. The man who became prime minister in 1984, Shimon Peres, possessed only a secondary education. (Although he did study at Harvard, no mention of an academic degree is to be found in any of his biographies.) His predecessor, Foreign Minister Yitzhak Shamir, is also only a high school graduate. The same was true of Israel's fifth prime minister (and minister of defence in 1984), Yitzhak Rabin, and of Herut's leader David Levy.

9 Women

As in many other countries, women also remained 'underrepresented' in Israel, even though equality for women has been of high ideological priority in Israel's political culture, particularly during the Yishuv period. With the increasing trend towards bourgeois culture observable in both Israeli society and politics (see the section on occupational prestige), the clock of history has been turned back. The increasing 'Orientalization' of Israeli society, that is, the growing importance of Jews of Afro-Asian backgrounds with their traditional, patriarchal family structures, has certainly also been a significant contributing factor.

That the place of the woman in the eyes of the Orthodox AI and PAI is in the home is documented by the number of women in their factions, namely, none; nor has there ever been more than a handful of women in the ranks of the NRP. The proportion of women has been low in all of the middle-class parties, but also in the leftist-socialist Mapam and AH, and the prospects for women have been even worse among the Communists. The chances for women were better, however, in Mapai (data in Wolffsohn, 1983a: 341 f.).

Table 7   Votes Cast by Women as a Proportion of the Total Vote for
          Various Parties, 1973 and 1977 (%)

Party	1973	1977
Maarah	56	53
Likud	50	56
DMC	—	58
NRP	58	58
AI/PAI	57	59
Others	51	52

Table 7 shows the proportions of the vote totals for the various parties cast
by women in the 1973 and 1977 elections.

Largely 'male-dominated' parties (as indicated by the percent of total
votes for the party cast by male voters in 1981) included Tehiya (66%) and
Shinui (58%). As shown in Figure 21, 71% of the CRM voters in 1981 were
women, who also formed the majority in the totals for the NRP (56%), Shelli
(53%), Maarah (52%) and Likud (51%) (Levy and Gutmann, 1981: table 4).

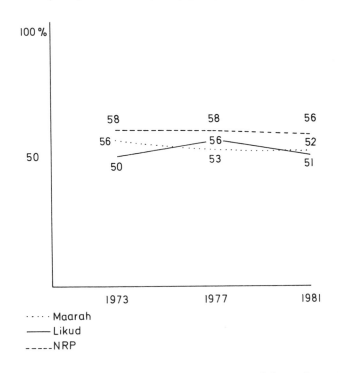

*Figure 20   Votes cast by women as proportion of the total vote for
the major parties, 1973, 1977 and 1981.*

Sources: Levy and Gutmann, 1979b: 33, and 1981: table 4.

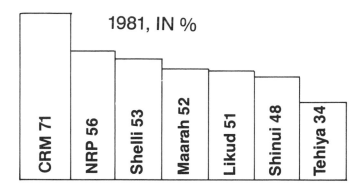

Figure 21   Votes cast by women as a proportion of the total vote for the major parties, 1981 (%).

4   THE STATE COMPTROLLER

The state comptroller functions as the chief auditory agency within the government and as the official ombudsman for public complaints in Israel.

The agency was established by the State Comptroller Law passed by the Knesset on 18 May 1949, subsequently amended fourteen times and revised in 1958 (for the text see State Comptroller, 1983). In accordance with Article 9, the state comptroller is responsible for auditing all government ministries, the Bank of Israel, the social security administration, the state-owned radio and television networks, local government agencies, state corporations as well as enterprises under partial public ownership, local religious councils, and even the university administrations (ibid.: 678; Gutmann and Levy, 1976: 457 ff.).

The state comptroller himself is responsible solely to the Knesset and is appointed for a term of five years by the president on recommendation of the Knesset Rules Committee. He is not allowed to hold a seat in the Knesset or in any local government body.

In March 1971 the duties of the state comptroller were expanded, making him the chief ombudsman for pursuing complaints from the public (Article 31 ff.; State Comptroller, 1983: 683 ff.). In this function he holds the title of Commissioner for Public Complaints. This extension of the duties of the office was carried out partly in response to the rising numbers of written complaints being brought to this agency by the public. The data in Table 8 show the dramatic development.

In 1960, 900 Israelis turned to the state comptroller with written complaints and the number of complaints rose steadily until 1967. Probably as a result of the Six Day War, this number dropped to 2,625 in that year but increased once again steeply thereafter. Like the Six Day War, the Yom Kippur War apparently had a 'soothing' effect on the minds of the public and fewer complaints were filed. The decrease may also have to do with the fact that many people were called up for duty in the army, where red tape and other annoyances were, at that time, more likely to be tolerated. The decline

Table 8   Complaints Filed with the Commissioner for Public Complaints,
          1960–82

1960	900
1964	1,980
1966	3,120
1967	2,625 (Six Day War)
1968	3,562
1969	4,143
1970	5,120
1971/72	7,490
1972/73	6,762
1973/74	4,937 (Yom Kippur War)
1974/75	5,561
1975/76	6,063
1976/77	5,542
1977/78	5,917
1978/79	6,832
1979/80	7,857
1980/81	7,326
1981/82	6,172 (War in Lebanon)

Sources: *Annual Report of the Commissioner for Public Complaints*, no. 10, 1981:
             16, and no. 11, 1982: 16; Blustein, 1975: 56.

in 1981/2 may also be explained by the War in Lebanon, which was called
'Operation Peace for Galilee'. (The cut-off date for the data for 1981/2 was
September 1982.) Taken together, the numbers for the period 1960–82
document rising frustration, or at least an increase in the articulation of
frustrations which may have been quietly 'swallowed' in the past. The data
are thus significant for social and political change in Israel.

5   THE EXECUTIVE

(a) THE LEGAL FRAMEWORK

The Yishuv had a double executive structure with the National Council on
the one hand and the Executive of the Jewish Agency on the other. In March
and April 1948, on the eve of the founding of the state, the executive bodies
were given a unified structure with the creation of the People's Directorate.
Following independence, the Provisional Government held office until the
first government was confirmed by the First Knesset on 3 March 1949. The
legal basis for the Provisional Government was provided by the LAO passed
by the Provisional State Council on 19 May 1948, making the former
responsible to the latter body. Article 4 of the Transition Law of 16 February
1949 prescribed that the Provisional Government would remain in office
until a new one could be designated by the Constitutional Assembly. The

LAO and the Transition Law remained the 'constitutional' basis of the government until passage of the Basic Law: Government on 13 August 1968 (Gutmann and Levy, 1976: 4 ff.; Rubinstein, 1974: 31 ff., and 1980: 26 ff.; Wolffsohn, 1983a: 691 ff.).

An outline of the evolution of the organs of government in Israel is to be found in the introduction to this book. Figure 24 presents a schematic diagram of the system of government as a whole.

Article 6 of the Basic Law: Government (BLG) grants the president the power to assign a member of the Knesset the task of forming a government, for which Article 7 allows a period of 21 days with a possible extension of an additional 21 days. Other articles of the BLG considerably restrict the president's options and place greater emphasis on the role of the Knesset in the formation of the government.

Article 5 of the BLG requires the prime minister to be a member of the Knesset, but non-parliamentarians are allowed to become cabinet ministers. With permission of the cabinet, ministers may name one or two deputy ministers, who must be members of the Knesset.

Treaties with foreign governments are negotiated, signed and ratified by the prime minister and the cabinet. The diplomatic recognition of foreign states and governments, the granting of diplomatic privileges to foreign governments and the power to declare war are also the privilege of the executive (Rubinstein, 1974: 362 ff., and 1980: 343 ff.).

The executive is not required to seek the assent of the Knesset in such matters, but has often done so for political reasons (i.e. justification by reason of parliamentary approval) in the case of highly controversial issues such as the negotiations leading to the reparations payments by the Federal Republic of Germany and the 1978 Camp David Agreement. Legitimacy was thus added to legality, and the legitimizing function of the Knesset became significant.

For a long time the legal status of the prime minister was only that of first among equals. In 1981 an amendment to the BLG gave him the power to dismiss cabinet ministers. Prior to 1962 the PM had first to resign himself, a step equivalent to the resignation of the entire government. In that year, the principle of 'collective responsibility' was formally adopted, permitting the cabinet as a whole (but not the prime minister acting alone) to dismiss ministers who, either on their own or with their party faction, voted against the coalition.

(b) COALITIONS AND GOVERNMENT CRISES

Table 10 presents an overview of the parties composing the coalitions led by Mapai/ILP up to May 1977, and later by the Likud. The table does not include the Provisional Government, which held office from 14 May 1948 to 9 March 1949, and consisted of Mapai, Mapam, General Zionists, New Immigration, Mishrahi, Hapoel Hamizrahi and Agudat Israel (Yaacobi, 1980: 337).

It is highly important to note that the Mapai/ILP era was characterized by coalitions with slim majorities in the Knesset (Diskin, 1976 and 1980a; Sirkin, 1971: 363 f.; Nachmias, 1975: 146).

The tendency to broaden the parliamentary base of the government by coalition continued after the change of government in 1977, but the generally increasing polarization led to sharper confrontations, a decline in the willingness to compromise, and even slimmer majorities in the Knesset. The formation of the government in September and October 1983 demonstrated the lack of common ground necessary for a broad coalition. The 'National Unity Coalition' agreed upon in September 1984 was a direct result of the election deadlock, a marriage of necessity rather than a love affair, and one in which the marginal parties of the left (Mapam) and right (Tehiya) refused to join.

Until May 1977 no government was formed without Mapai/ILP because this would only have been numerically possible on the basis of an alliance ranging from the Communists to the Orthodox. This most unlikely situation occurred in fact just once, on the occasion of the election of the president of the Knesset in 1959, when the Mapai candidate was defeated. The office involved, however, was relatively unimportant.

Table 9   Main Coalition Partners

Until 1977:	Mapai/ILP + National Religious + Independent Liberals
1977–84:	Likud + National Religious + Orthodox Agudat Israel
(1984–	National Unity Cabinet)

The formation of a Likud/NRP coalition on the national level was the culmination of developments which had already been in progress on the local level since 1965. In addition, Diskin's studies of precinct voting patterns show a continuous, gradual drift on the part of national-religious voters towards the nationalist right since the 1950s, so that the shift in the national coalition appears as merely the final adjustment to changes which had already taken place in society. Diskin found that in the 1950s religious voters had already begun to prefer Herut/Gahal/Likud to the labour parties as a possible second choice. But this fact had long remained invisible. Only in 1977 did it become a matter of visible and effective politics (Diskin, 1976, 1980a, 1980b).

In addition to the office of the prime minister, Mapai/ILP also retained the chief cabinet posts during its period of dominance: the Foreign Ministry and the Ministries of Defence, Finance and Agriculture, as well as Education and Culture. Beginning in the mid-1960s, these Mapai bastions began to crumble. Key ministries had to be given to Labour 'dissidents' (the Defence Ministry to Moshe Dayan in 1967, for instance) or to other parties. From 1977 to 1981 the Likud was considerably more cautious, but from 1981 on an increasing predominance of Likud partisans in key cabinet posts was to be observed. The Likud had learned its lesson from the Maarah well.

Religious issues were the most common source of crises within coalitions (resignations or cabinet shuffles). Of the 111 controversies within the cabinet in the years 1949 to 1984, 35 were over questions of religious policy. Foreign policy issues were the cause of fourteen such crises, internal party struggles were responsible for twelve and territorial issues for nine.

(c) PUBLIC SATISFACTION WITH THE GOVERNMENT

Since 1967 the Israel Institute for Applied Social Research (IIASR) in Jerusalem has conducted regular and systematic public opinion research. Figure 22 gives an overview of trends in the confidence of the Israeli public in its government from 1967 to 1983. (Data from Levy and Gutmann, 1978: 18 and 1979a: 48; Stone, 1982: 221; Diskin, 1982a: 103; Peretz and Smooha, 1981: 108; and from the regular reports in *Haaretz* and the *Jerusalem Post*. See also the yearly volumes of the *Index to International Public Opinion* and the monthly *World Opinion Update*.) It must be noted, however, that the earlier polls are somewhat limited in their comparability with data from 1982 onwards, which were gathered by other institutions (mostly by PORI).

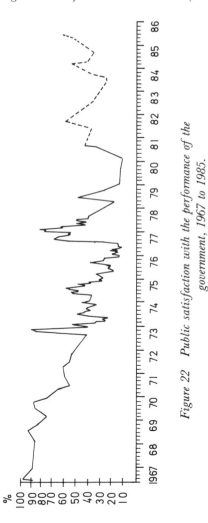

Figure 22 Public satisfaction with the performance of the government, 1967 to 1985.

Table 10   Israel's Governments, 1949–86

I Knesset		1949–51
	1	2
Assumed Office[1]	8 Mar. 1949	1 Nov. 1950
Resigned	15 Oct. 1950	14 Feb. 1951
Prime minister	Ben-Gurion	Ben-Gurion
Coalition parties	Mapai, RF, Sephardim, Progr.	(same)
Knesset mandates	73[2]	73[2]

II Knesset			1951–55		
	3 A	3 B	4	5	6
Assumed Office[1]	8 Oct. 1951	23 Sep. 1952	23 Dec. 1952	26 Jan. 1954	29 Jun. 1955
Resigned	23 Sep. 1952	19 Dec. 1952	6 Dec. 1953	29 Jun. 1955	
Prime minister	Ben-Gurion	Ben-Gurion	Ben-Gurion	Sharett	Sharett
Coalition parties	Mapai/Mis., HPM, AI, PAI	Mapai, HPM	Mapai, AZ, Progr., HPM, Mis.	(same)	Mapai, Progr., HPM, Mis.
Knesset mandates	67[2]	60[2]	87[2]	87[2]	66[2]

III Knesset		1955–59	
	7	8	9
Assumed office[1]	3 Nov. 1955	7 Jan. 1958	1 July 1958
Resigned	31 Dec. 1957	1 July 1958	5 July 1959
Prime minister	Ben-Gurion	Ben-Gurion	Ben-Gurion
Coalition parties	Mapai, Mapam, AH, Progr., HPM, Mis. (=NRP)	(same)	Mapai, Mapam, AH, Progr., HPM
Knesset mandates	80[2]	80[2]	69[2]

IV Knesset		1959–61
	9 A	9 B
Assumed Office[1]	17 Dec. 1959	—
Resigned	—	31 Jan. 1961
Prime minister	Ben-Gurion	Ben-Gurion

Coalition parties	Mapai, Mapam, AH, Progr., NRP	same + PAI from 18 July 1960
Knesset mandates	86[2]	88[2]

V Knesset		1961–65	
	10	11	12
Assumed Office[1] Resigned	2 Nov. 1961 16 June 1963	26 June 1963 15 Dec. 1964	— 23 Dec. 1964
Prime minister	Ben-Gurion	Eshkol	Eshkol
Coalition parties	Mapai, AH, NRP, (PAI)	(same)	(same)
Knesset mandates	68[2]	68[2]	68[2, 3]

VI Knesset		1965–69	
	13 A	13 B	14
Assumed Office[1] Resigned	12 Jan. 1966 —	5 June 1967 26 Feb. 1969	17 Mar. 1969 —
Prime minister	Eshkol	Eshkol	Golda Meir
Coalition parties	Mapai, Mapam, AH, IL, NRP (PAI)	Mapai, Mapam, AH, Rafi, Gahal, NRP (PAI)	(same)
Knesset mandates	75[2]	111[2]	111[2]

VII Knesset	1969–73	
	15 A	15 B
Assumed Office[1] Resigned	15 Dec. 1969ˉ 6 Aug. 1970	1 Sep. 1970 —
Prime minister	Golda Meir	Golda Meir
Coalition parties	Maarah, Gahal, IL, NRP	Maarah, IL, NRP
Knesset mandates	102[2]	76[2]

VIII Knesset		1973–77	
	16	17 A	17 B
Assumed Office[1] Resigned	10 Mar. 1974 11 Apr. 1974	3 June 1974 —	30 Oct. 1974 22 Dec. 1976

Table 10   Israel's Governments, 1949–86 (*continued*)

Prime minister	Golda Meir	Rabin	Rabin
Coalition parties	Maarah, IL, NRP	Maarah, IL, CRM	Maarah, IL, NRP
Knesset mandates	68^2	61^2	68^2

IX Knesset		1977–81	
	18 A	18 B	18 C
Assumed Office[1] Resigned	29 June 1977 23 Sep. 1977	24 Oct. 1977 —	6 Sep. 1978 —
Prime minister	Begin	Begin	Begin
Coalition parties	Likud, NRP, (PAI), (AI) Dayan, (Flatto-Sharon)	same + DMC	Likud, NRP, Rump of DMC after split
Knesset mandates	64	79	71^4

X Knesset		1981–84	
	19 A	19 B	20
Assumed office[1] Resigned	5 Aug. 1981 —	28 July 1982 15 Sep. 1983	10 Oct. 1983 23 Mar. 1984
Prime minister	Begin	Begin	Shamir
Coalition parties	Likud, NRP, (AI), Tami	Likud, NRP, Telem, Tehiya	(same)
Knesset mandates	61	64^5	64

XI Knesset	1984–
	21
Assumed Office[1] Resigned	13 Sep. 1984
Prime minister	Peres 1984–6, Shamir 1986–? (agreed 1984)
Coalition parties	Likud, Labour, NRP, Shass, Shinui, Yahad (Weizman), AI, Morasha/PAI,[6] Ometz
Knesset mandates	97

Notes:

[1] Dated from vote of confidence in the Knesset. Only dates of resignation are given, as all governments remain in office as caretakers until replaced by successor.
[2] Minority lists allied with ILP included.
[3] Seven Mapai members (but no cabinet minister) join Rafi.
[4] 1978–80: Moshe Shamir, Geula Cohen leave the Likud; Josef Tamir leaves Liberals, joins Shai.
[5] Telem disbands in 1982, its MKs remain in coalition; two Likud MKs cross over to Maarah.
[6] PAI left the coalition in 1985 but remained in bloc with Morasha.

Between 1967 and 1970 satisfaction with the government remained relatively high. This is a most interesting result, for it indicates that a broad governing coalition does not necessarily lead to dissatisfaction. In the stated period Israel was governed by a 'National Unity' cabinet including the Labour parties, Gahal, the NRP and other minor partners.

From that period up to the 1973 Yom Kippur War public satisfaction declined steadily. During the war the popularity of the government rose dramatically, only to take a steep plunge in early 1974 and then to recover by mid-year. Until the end of the Mapai-led era the trend was downwards, but there were two significant exceptions. One was the result of the disengagement agreement with Egypt in September 1975 and the other was due to the liberation of the hostages in Entebbe (Uganda) in July 1976.

Following its formation in 1977 the Likud-led government first enjoyed a brief honeymoon with the public and then lost popularity, but recouped its losses after the signing of the peace treaty with Egypt (March 1979). Satisfaction with the government hit another low in 1980 but then rose again up to the June 1981 elections.

In April 1982, on the eve of the War in Lebanon against the PLO, 39% of those polled responded that they were 'satisfied' or 'very satisfied' with the government, but 53·7% replied they were 'not very satisfied' (*Haaretz*, 7 May 1982). In mid-July, after the outbreak of hostilities but before the massacre in Beirut, 60% were 'satisfied'. This dropped to 37·8% by June of 1983 and to only 34% in July (*Jerusalem Post*, 18 July 1982, and 2 August 1983, also with data on the popularity of the prime minister and other cabinet members).

According to PORI, 56% rated the performance of the government as 'very good' or 'good' in July 1982 (before the Beirut massacre) whereas these evaluations were given by only 43% in April 1983 (*Index to International Public Opinion*, 1982/3: 141).

According to Hanoch and Rafi Smith (*Jerusalem Post*, 17 July 1984), 31% of the Jewish public evaluated the 'general' performance of the government as 'successful' or 'fairly successful' in December 1983, whereas only 24% did so in April 1984. The public's esteem rose only slightly by June (to 25%) but reached 34% by the time the Knesset elections took place in July. Although we are dealing here with a similar (but not identical) question posed by a different polling institute, the data nonetheless can give an overall impression of the shifts in public opinion.

In summary, two basic phenomena can be observed in the polls. First, wars (1973, 1982) or other dramatic events (the disengagement agreement of 1975, the Sadat initiative in November 1977, the Camp David peace treaty with Egypt in March 1979) lead to short-term shifts in public opinion. Second, the Jewish Israelis polled have always shown greater confidence in the government's security policies than in its economic policies. (See Figure 56 as well as Wolffsohn, 1983a: 705 f.; Stone, 1982: 229, 235.)

The desire for a national unity *cabinet* was very strong in Israel in the early 1980s. A PORI poll taken in 1982/3 showed that about two-thirds of the public favoured such a government (*Index to International Public Opinion*, 1982/3: 146, 425; *Haaretz*, 25 July 1984, also quoting PORI poll results). By April 1984 the percentage of those in favour of a broad governing coalition rose to 73% and to 81% by late July (PORI polls, *Haaretz*, 25 and 27 July 1984). After the actual formation of such a coalition in September 1984, however, its popularity rating following the initial 'period of grace', that is, after its first hundred days in office, proved low indeed. Some 45% responded that its handling of economic problems was 'very bad' or 'bad' and 44% chose to label both the coalition's overall policy and its security policy in particular as 'mediocre' (PORI poll, *Haaretz*, 20 December 1984).

(d) DECISION-MAKING

During the era of Mapai/ILP governments as well as since 1977 the responsible policy-makers have only rarely called in experts to advise them in the decision-making process (see Wolffsohn, 1983a: 706 ff. for numerous examples and Wolffsohn, 1979a on economic policy; Globerson, 1970; Dror, 1971, 1978; Brownstein, 1977 and Shlaim and Tanter, 1978 on the Mapai/ILP era).

That improvisation proved to be the order of the day is astounding insofar as a government frequently facing decisions not only on the distribution of extraordinarily limited financial resources but often the choice between war and peace as well might be expected to consult intensively with competent experts. Instead, it has usually been the responsible cabinet minister – especially if he was a strong political personality – who managed to have his way in the Cabinet without calling in expert opinion, even when serving under a 'strong' prime minister. (On the problems of planning see Bilski, 1980.)

Table 11 Types of Prime Minister

'Strong' prime ministers:
Ben Gurion, Golda Meir, Begin

'First-among-equals':
Sharett, Eshkol, Rabin, Shamir, Peres

The authority of the prime minister has always been particularly critical with regard to the extent of participation by others in the decision-making process. At the high tide of their political authority Ben-Gurion, Golda Meir and Begin commonly arrived at decisions alone. Sharett, Eshkol, Rabin and Shamir, on the other hand, never achieved such a dominant position in the cabinet. Finally, the coalition agreement of September 1984 contained a built-in structural weakness in the role of Prime Minister Peres.

(e) THE BUREAUCRACY

1 Creation and Professional Background

Following the achievement of independence, it was neither possible nor considered desirable for the newly created administrative bodies to retain more than a few of the 4,800 Jews who had served the British Mandate authorities. On the one hand, the public attitude towards them was ambiguous. On the other hand, it was hardly practical to try to get along entirely without the experience of seasoned bureaucrats. As a result, 1,724 of the 5,041 civil servants employed by the state in March 1949 had previously worked for the Mandate government (Reuveni, 1974: 16 ff.; for further details see Wolffsohn, 1983a: 523 ff.).

In surveys conducted in 1965/6 and 1970, Globerson (1970: 53) found that 20% of the bureaucrats in the top levels of the Israeli civil service had been employed by the Mandate authorities and 44% by institutions of the Yishuv or the Histadrut; 12% had come from private firms, 8% had been self-employed and 16% had had no previous employment.

Among the bureaucratic elite in 1978, the great majority consisted of those who had entered public service after independence – this due in no small degree to the age factor. Only 2·8% had been part of the government bureaucracy in 1947 or before; 17·5% had entered government service in 1948 or 1949, 35% between 1950 and 1959, 30·4% between 1960 and 1969, and 14·3% between 1970 and 1976 (Haberfeld and Nadler, 1979: 117).

2 'Ethnic' Origin of the Bureaucratic Elite

As in other top political positions, more Israelis of Euro-American backgrounds and Sabras were to be found in government service than Oriental Israelis. In 1953, 14·3% of the civil servants were immigrants from Islamic nations, 35·1% from Eastern Europe, 15% from the Balkan nations, 17% from other European states, 0·5% from North or South America and 18·1% were Sabras (Reuveni, 1974: 26).

The rule of thumb that the higher the level, the fewer Oriental Israelis also applies to the government bureaucracy. In Globerson's (1970: 38) samples for 1965/6 only 3% of Israel's top bureaucrats were of Afro-Asian heritage, 54% had come from Eastern Europe, 23% from Western Europe and Anglo-American nations, and 20% were Sabras. The distribution in 1970 was 52% Eastern Europeans, 23% Western Europeans or Anglo-Americans, 21% Sabras and still only 3% Oriental Jews.

In 1978 Haberfeld and Nadler found that among the 217 top positions in government service (Globerson had taken the top 294) the Sabras had in the meantime, for mainly biological reasons, overtaken the Eastern and Western European immigrants: 34·6% were Sabras, 29·4% were from Eastern or Western Europe, 20·4% from the USA, 11·4% from Central Europe and 4·3% from Asia or Africa (op. cit.: 116). The increase among Oriental Jews in comparison with Globerson's studies is extraordinarily small.

3   Party Politics and the Bureaucracy

Beginning in the 1950s a gradual trend towards de-politicizing government service in Israel has made such criteria as training, ability and special skills more important than party membership. Nevertheless, the dominant party, Mapai/ILP, continued to maintain and even expand its dominant influence in the government bureaucracy until into the late 1970s. (For details see Robinson, 1970; Wolffsohn, 1983a: 525 ff.) After the change in government in 1977, a slow trend set in in favour of the Likud, the National Religious Party and later Tami. The Likud's takeover of the bureaucracy accelerated in 1981 and Tami dealt most rigorously with its ministry: Labour, Social Affairs and Immigrants Absorption.

4   Bureaucratic Culture

Protekzia (a network of personal connections) is a special characteristic of the bureaucratic culture of Israel. A wealth of information on this phenomenon can be found in the works by Dent (1972) and Caiden (1970) and in the thorough study conducted by Nachmias and Rosenbloom (1978). Dent shows that the longtime residents of Israel had grown more accustomed to *protekzia* than more recent immigrants, but that the latter adapted themselves relatively quickly. The systematic manner in which the ministers Levy (Herut) and Abuhatzira (NRP, since 1981 Tami), both of Moroccan background, 'took care of' their political friends demonstrates the process of adaptation. Both politicians secured positions for their clients and cronies in their ministries and thus consolidated their *protekzia* network.

In the case of immigrants from the USA, however, certain difficulties in adaptation have been observed (Avruch, 1981). With their belief in the principles of the meritocracy, many American immigrants had a difficult time accommodating themselves to the Eastern European customs of clientelism.

5   Public Opinion

The attitude of the Israeli public towards its bureaucracy is anything but benevolent. Despite the low public esteem for bureaucrats, however, the latter maintain a much more flattering self-image. In fact, the reciprocal images Israeli society and its bureaucrats entertain of each other are anything but identical. (For extensive data on both see Nachmias and Rosenbloom, 1978: 170 ff.)

6 THE PRESIDENT

(a) THE LEGAL FRAMEWORK

Article 3 of the Basic Law: Presidency of 1964 states that the Knesset is to elect the head of state for a term of five years. The powers of the president include the following. (1) The president signs into law all measures not directly relating to his own prerogatives as well as 'treaties with foreign states approved by the Knesset'. (2) He participates in the formation of the government, accepts the resignation of the cabinet or of members of the cabinet and is kept informed about its meetings. (3) He appoints Israel's diplomatic representatives, accepts the credentials of foreign diplomats and confirms the appointments of consular officials of foreign nations. (4) He appoints the judges of the Supreme Court and of other courts, as well as the state comptroller and the president of the Bank of Israel. It is important to note that the president does not personally select officeholders whom he appoints. The Knesset, for instance, actually selects the state comptroller, who is then appointed by the president. (5) He can grant pardons, reduce or alter sentences. The president, however, has little political weight.

(b) THE PRESIDENTS AND THEIR ELECTIONS

On 16 February 1949 Chaim Weizmann was elected president on the first ballot with 83 votes. His only opponent, Professor Josef Klausner, received 15 votes. Since Weizmann, a General Zionist, had served as president of the WZO for many years, his candidacy aroused little controversy. A new election became necessary on 19 November 1951 as the rules then in force coupled the term of the president to the legislative period of the Knesset. Unopposed, Weizmann was re-elected with 85 votes (against 11 negative votes) on the first ballot. Chaim Weizmann died on 9 November 1952 (Zidon, 1971: 289; Weiss, 1973: 103; Wolffsohn, 1983a: 723 ff.).

After prevailing by a narrow margin in an internal party vote, Yitzak Ben-Zwi (Mapai) was elected head of state on the third ballot on 8 December 1952, over Yitzak Grünbaum of the General Zionists and Rabbi Nurok, the candidate of the National Religious Party. Ben Zwi was re-elected without opposition on 28 October 1957, and again without controversy for a third term of office on 30 October 1962. He died on 23 April 1963, and on 21 May Zalman Shazar (Mapai) was elected as his successor with 67 votes against 33 for Peretz Bernstein of the GZ. Shazar was re-elected without opposition on 26 March 1968.

In 1973 Golda Meir worked her will in the ILP, cultivating favour with the party hierarchy and thus with the party as a whole for her candidate, Professor Ephraim Katzir. On 10 April 1974 Katzir, who was not a member of the ILP, defeated A. M. Urbach, the candidate of the NRP.

Although the ILP had been out of power since the previous year, differences of opinion among the parties of the government coalition paved the way for the unopposed election of the ILP candidate, Yitzhak Navon, to the presidency on 19 April 1978. Navon proved to be an unusually popular president and numerous rumours about his running for a still higher office circulated. He did not stand for re-election in 1983 in order once again to become politically active in his party, and he ran as the second-ranking candidate on the Alignment ticket in the 1984 elections. During the campaign, however, Navon's political star failed to shine as brightly as expected.

Although the governing coalition was able to count on 64 votes on a day-to-day basis, Chaim Herzog of the ILP was elected president on the first ballot (with 61 votes) on 22 March 1983. His opponent, Menachem Elon, a justice of the Supreme Court, received only 57 votes (*Haaretz*, 23 March 1983).

Figure 23 compares the political party of the various presidents at the time of their election to the then largest political party in the governing coalition.

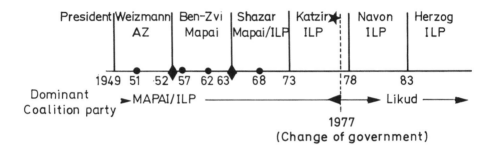

Figure 23   Israel's presidents and the dominant party in the government.

Key:
    = re-election
    = death in office
    = independent but nominated by ILP

7 LOCAL GOVERNMENT

(a) HISTORICAL BACKGROUND

In contrast to their lack of influence in the larger institutions of the Yishuv, the bourgeois parties found opportunities to gain and maintain real strongholds on the level of local politics. This was especially true of Tel-Aviv (Horowitz and Lissak, 1978: 340).

Among other factors, the existence of tax-paying qualifications for voting favoured this development. In order to be eligible to vote in Tel-Aviv, for example, the citizen was required to have paid yearly taxes of at least 50 piastres. Although not a large sum, it was sufficient to limit voter participation (see Gutmann, 1958; Giladi, 1973: 243 f.; Wolffsohn, 1983a: 162 ff., 639 f.).

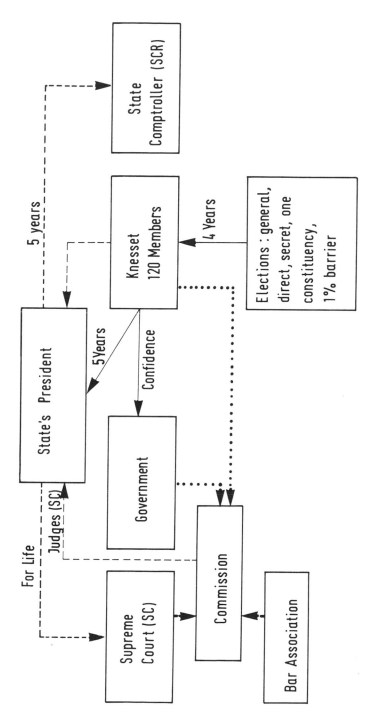

Figure 24 Israel's system of government.

Key:
appoints
nominates
sends members to Commission
elects

(b) POWERS

Neither during the Mandate nor since have local governments in Israel achieved any wide radius of action. Under the Mandate, the British high commissioner held sweeping powers, which were in large part transferred to the interior ministry following independence.

To a certain extent the Histadrut may also be regarded as a rival of local governments, as the union undertakes its own local initiatives to secure jobs, maintains its own centres for recreation, adult education, and so on, and supplies social services such as health insurance.

(c) FINANCES

The interior ministry may authorize city and village governments to levy taxes, but even these taxes, together with the fees collected for the services of the local institutions, are by no means sufficient to cover the expenses of the local administrations (Weiss, 1972: 69 ff.; Wolffsohn, 1983a: 638 f.; Kalcheim, 1979: 103). Since 1979 numerous local governments, including the city of Tel-Aviv, have teetered on the edge of bankruptcy. In recent years it has not even been possible to pay the salaries of municipal employees without subsidies from the national government. In fiscal 1979/80, 46·1% of all income available to local authorities came from the national government. In 1980/1 the proportion decreased slightly to 43·5% (*Statistical Abstract of Israel*, 1982: 578 f., and 1983: 606).

(d) POPULARITY

Despite their limited powers and financial difficulties, local governments seem to have gained in popularity, especially in comparison to the growing dissatisfaction with the central government, at least if the frequency of political protest can be taken as an indicator. In the 1950s, 50·8% of all protest demonstrations were directed against local political institutions, 40% against the central government and 9·3% against other institutions. In the 1960s only 30·8% were directed against local authorities, 52·9% against the central government, and 16·2% against other institutions. The percentages for the 1970s were, in the same order, 31·2%, 58·3% and 10·4% (Lehman-Wilzig, 1982: 104).

This may, among other things, have to do with the fact that the group with the largest potential for protest, namely, Oriental Israelis, has long been better represented at the local level, and that since 1978 mayors have been chosen directly by the voters in elections simultaneous with those for city and local councils.

(e) 'ETHNICITY' IN LOCAL POLITICS

As late as 1955, only 23·6% of the members of local governmental bodies were of Afro-Asian extraction, but by 1965 this had risen to 44·2%. Moreover, the percentage tends to be significantly higher in the development towns founded since 1948, where many Oriental immigrants were settled. Increased representation has led to rising satisfaction (Smooha, 1978: 315; further data in: Wolffsohn, 1983a: 413 f.).

(f) INTEREST IN LOCAL POLITICS

It nevertheless cannot be overlooked that Israelis tend to be less interested in

Table 12   Voter Participation in Local Elections, 1950–83 (%)

	Local Elections Only	Local Elections Concurrent with Knesset Elections
1950	79·6	—
1955	78·6	82·7
1959	80·2	81·4
1965	82·7	83·1
1969	79·0	81·5
1973	73·2	78·6
1978	57·3	—
1983	58·0	—

Sources: Weiss, 1970: 7, and 1972: 107; Elections, 1973: XXIII; Local Authorities, 1979: VII; *Haaretz*, 26 October 1983.

local political issues than in national issues. The levels of voter participation, as shown in Table 12, can be taken as a useful indicator. (As the voting in local elections takes place in two stages, the figures for 1978 and 1983 refer to the first of the two ballots.)

In 1950, 1978 and 1983 local elections were held separately from Knesset elections. Of the eligible voters who failed to participate in the 1978 elections, 56% openly admitted that they were 'not interested' (IIASR, 1980: 1).

(g) LOCAL ELECTIONS

The results of Knesset and local elections through 1973 can be easily compared, as the election laws were largely similar for both. Local elections in Israel are direct, proportional and based on the one-man, one-vote principle. Here, too, the voter casts his ballot for a party rather than individual candidates.

The minimum age for voters is 18, for candidates 20. Those persons who are not Israeli citizens but who have been residents for at least six months preceding the election may vote in local elections.

District councils differ from city and village councils in that the former are composed of delegates from the settlements in the district. Thus, local elections do not take place in rural settlements such as *kibbutzim* and *moshavim*.

Up to and including the local elections of 1973, each city or local authority council elected the mayor as well as the deputy mayor and other magistrates from among its members. Since 1978 the mayor has been elected directly by the citizens. As a result of the law passed on 7 August 1975, a candidate is elected mayor if he receives at least 40% of the total valid votes cast (according to the law as amended on 9 April 1976; 50% had been required before, see Baker, 1976: 79, and 1977: 126.). If no candidate receives 40% on the first ballot, a run-off election is held fourteen days later between the two candidates receiving the highest vote totals on the first ballot. Members of the local authority councils are still elected by party list.

A comparison between the results of local and Knesset elections clearly

demonstrates that even before 1977 Mapai/ILP had been forced to share –
and sometimes even turn over – power on the local level to the Likud or its
predecessors, Herut and Gahal (for specifics see Wolffsohn, 1983a: table
108).

The coalitions which began to be formed in local governments in 1965
proved a sign of things to come. In contrast to their behaviour in the Knesset,
the NRP, Rafi and Gahal began to join in coalitions against the Labour bloc
on the local level.

A selection of comparative data on Knesset and local elections is to be
found in Figure 25.

(h) ARAB LOCAL GOVERNMENT

The Arab communities have increasingly evolved into 'states within the
state', but the possibility cannot be dismissed that the Communists (who
have become more and more active in this sphere since 1965 but had to
absorb a setback in 1978) may succeed in building a bridge between Arabs
and Jews on the basis of the fact that they are not Zionists, but do explicitly
recognize Israel's right to exist within the borders of 4 June 1967.

In 1978, however, the 'Sons of the Village' and the 'Progressive National
Movement' were able to achieve significant gains. In contrast to Rakah
(NCL), both of these groups question in principle Israel's right to exist. In
1983, both Labour and Rakah claimed victory, but localism proved to be
much more decisive for the Arab local authorities than party politics (see
A. Mantzur, *Haaretz*, 13 November 1983). The religiously fundamentalist
'Muslim Youth' also made a good showing at the polls in 1983.

The stronger identification with local issues among the Arab population is
reflected in higher levels of voter participation, which regularly exceeded
90%. In 1978, when participation among Jewish voters was particularly low,
88·6% of the eligible Arab voters went to the polls (Local Authorities, 1979:
VII). In 1983 Arab participation reached 74%, whereas only 51% of the
Jewish electorate turned out (*Haaretz*, 26 October 1983). This may, among
other factors, be attributable to the fact that the Communists, as well as the
more radical, and particularly the local groups, present real alternatives to
the Zionist parties. Moreover, immediate concerns of the Arab population
are aggregated and articulated by local Arab lists. This, in turn, indicates
that there is a vast political potential for a non-communist Arab list at the
national level.

FURTHER READING

HISTORICAL BACKGROUND

David Vital, *Zionism: The Formative Years* (Oxford: Oxford University Press, 1982) and
   The Origins of Zionism (London: Oxford University Press, 1975).
Shlomo Averini, *The Making of Modern Zionism: The Intellectual Origins of the Jewish State*
   (New York: Basic Books, 1981).
Howard M. Sachar, *A History of Israel. From the Rise of Zionism to Our Time* (Oxford:
   Blackwell, 1976).
Walter Laqueur, *A History of Zionism* (London: Weidenfeld & Nicolson, 1972).

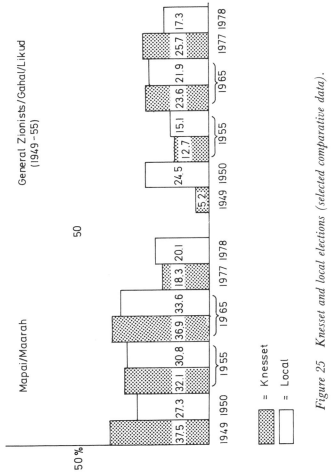

Figure 25 Knesset and local elections (selected comparative data).

POLITY OF THE *YISHUV*

Dan Horowitz and Moshe Lissak, *Origins of the Israeli Polity. Palestine Under the Mandate* (Chicago: University of Chicago Press, 1978).

LEGAL SYSTEM

For recent developments consult the *Israel Year Book* under 'Legal System', where H. E. Baker deals with the latest data.

Ariel Bin-Nun, *Einführung in das Recht des Staates Israel* (Darmstadt: Wissenschaftliche Buchgesellschaft, 1983).

Hedva Porat-Martin, 'Rabbinical and civil courts in Israel: A dual legal system in action', PhD dissertation, University of California, 1979.

Robert H. Eisenmann, *Islamic Law in Palestine and Israel* (Leiden: Brill, 1978).

David M. Sassoon, 'The Israel legal system', *American Journal of Contemporary Law* (Baltimore, Md.), vol. 16, pp. 405 ff.

THE KNESSET

Gregory S. Mahler, *The Knesset. Parliament in the Israeli Political System* (Rutherford, NJ: Fairleigh Dickinson University Press, and London/Toronto: Associated University Press, 1981); legal framework, attitudes, behaviour.

Eliahu S. Likhovski, *Israel's Parliament. The Law of the Knesset* (Oxford: Clarendon Press, 1971).

Asher Zidon, *Knesset. The Parliament of Israel* (New York: Herzl Press, 1967); older but highly informative, and written by a man who knew – he was secretary general of the Knesset.

ELECTIONS

Indispensable, and more than analyses of elections, are the books edited by Asher Arian, *Elections in Israel*, available for the campaigns from 1969 to 1981. See also his *The Choosing People* (Cleveland, Ohio: Press of Case Western University, 1973).

Dan Caspi, Abraham Diskin and Emanuel Gutmann (eds), *The Roots of Begin's Success. The 1981 Israeli Elections* (New York: St Martin's Press, and London: Croom Helm, 1983).

Howard R. Penniman (ed.), *Israel at the Polls* (Washington, DC: American Enterprise Institute, 1979 and 1984); one volume on the 1977 elections, the other on the 1981 campaign.

STATE COMPTROLLER

Gerald E. Caiden, *To Right Wrong: The Initial Ombudsman Experience in Israel* (Tel-Aviv: Ashdown Press, 1980).

Nathalie Kerbe, *L'Ombudsman israelien* (Paris: A. Pedone, 1975).

GOVERNMENT AND ADMINISTRATION

For general data see *The Government Yearbook* which contains a list of ministries and ministers as well as policy guidelines.

Gad Yaacobi, *The Government* (New York: Praeger Publishers, 1982).

David Nachmias and David H. Rosenbloom, *Bureaucratic Culture. Citizens and Administrators in Israel* (New York: St Martin's Press, 1978).

Gerald E. Caiden, *Israel's Administrative Culture* (Berkeley, Calif.: University of California Press, 1970).

LOCAL POLITICS

See the articles by S. Weiss and D. Elazar in the volumes edited by Arian on the
    elections of 1969 and 1973.
Emanuel Gutmann, 'The development of local government in Palestine. Background
    to the study of local administration in Israel', PhD dissertation, Columbia Univer-
    sity, New York, 1958.
There are no other comprehensive analyses on this subject in English, but this one is
    very in-depth. In Hebrew, see the various publications by S. Weiss.

II

The Parties

1 HISTORY

The 'genealogy' of Israel's political parties is shown in Figure 26 (see also
Table 3). What follows is a sketch of the development of the most important
parties and groupings.

Only a few years after the creation of the League of Nations-sanctioned
British Mandate for Palestine (1922), three large political groupings, or
'blocs', were formed within the Yishuv. These consisted of the previously
mentioned groupings of religious, bourgeois and labour parties. A fourth,
'ethnic' bloc consisting mainly of Sephardim (i.e. Jews whose original
ancestors came from Spain) was steadily losing influence. Because the vast
majority of Jewish immigrants to Palestine at the end of the nineteenth
century were from Eastern Europe, the Sephardim, together with the remaining 'ethnic' groups such as the Yemenites, who had been living in
Palestine since 1882, soon became a small minority in the Yishuv. This bloc
still held several seats in the First and Second Knessets, but slowly disap-
peared from the political landscape in the course of the 1950s, their leadership largely going over to Mapai or the General Zionists.

(a) RELIGIOUS PARTIES

The religious parties were the first to organize politically, joining in the
Misrahi ('Spiritual Centre') Movement in 1902. The development of Religious Zionism was hardly a matter of historical inevitability. The Orthodox
approach to history was, after all, passive, whereas Zionism was activist in its
view of the world. Traditional Orthodoxy held to the belief that the exile of

the Jewish people (the Diaspora) was God's punishment for the sins of the Jews. It was up to God to end the Diaspora and any human interference in this process would be blasphemous or, at best, secular. Overstating the point, one could say that religious Zionism tried to prevent the de-Judaization of Judaism by Zionism. In contrast to traditional Orthodoxy, it undertook to work within the World Zionist Organization (WZO) rather than outside or against it.

Following a split among the religious groups in 1911/12, Agudat Israel (AI, 'Union of Israel') was founded. The division was triggered by the decision of the WZO to initiate activities in the cultural and educational spheres. Orthodox Jews viewed this as a direct challenge on the part of the non-religious majority of Zionists. Since many of the Orthodox were already convinced that Zionism was blasphemy, the Zionist challenge in cultural and educational affairs prompted them to leave the WZO to found their own Orthodox movement (see Marmorstein, 1969; Schiff, 1977; Isaac, 1981: chs. 2 and 3).

In 1922 the left wing of Misrahi split off to create Hapoel Hamisrahi (HPM, 'Worker's Misrahi'). HPM tried to realize a synthesis of religion and non-Marxian, mainly agrarian, socialism. A group on the left of AI founded Poale Agudat Israel (PAI, 'Worker's AI') in 1925, bringing together Orthodox industrial and agrarian workers. From the very beginning, their anti-Zionism was much more moderate. Those Orthodox Jews for whom AI's resistance to the Zionist parties was not energetic enough joined together in 1935 to form the predecessor organization of the present-day Neture Kartha ('Guardians of the City'), rejecting any form of contact with 'blasphemous' Zionists. Today, they are to be found living mainly in the Meah Shearim quarter of Jerusalem.

Under the impact of the Holocaust, AI was ready to work together with the Zionist parties without accepting Zionism in principle. AI utilized its coalition with the Likud (1977/84) to maximize religious inroads into secular fields and to solidify its financial structure.

Before the elections to the First Knesset, the religious parties formed a political bloc on the basis of a common election list and a joint faction in the Knesset. In 1956 HPM and Misrahi merged to create the National Religious Party (NRP).

Gush Emunim, a group of settlements activists, loosened their affiliation with the NRP after the 1973 war. Many joined the hawkish Tehiya ('Resurrection') Party, founded in 1979 by Likud dissidents opposed to the peace treaty with Egypt. Others joined with Rabbi Druckmann in founding Mazad ('Zionist-Religious Bloc') in 1983. Mazad and Poale Agudat Israel presented a joint list ('bloc') in the 1984 Knesset elections. The new amalgamation was called 'Morasha'.

In 1981 a group of NRP members, mainly of Moroccan origin, who felt themselves disadvantaged within the NRP, and who were led by Minister for Religious Affairs Abuhatzira, joined with some break-away members of the Labour Party in founding Tami ('Movement for the Tradition of Israel'). Their image is Moroccan, national religious and lower class. Welfare politics is their domain.

In 1984 Torah and Labour, one of the numerous factions of the NRP, left the religious camp under the leadership of David Glass to join the Labour Party, where it has begun to form the nucleus of a Labour religious faction in hopes of attracting former religious voters to the ILP.

Two other religiously based parties deserve attention because of the results of the July 1984 Knesset election: Shass (Hitachdut Haspharadim Shomre Torah = 'Torah Observing Union of the Sepharadim') and Rabbi Kahane's Kach ('Just So').

Shass is basically the Oriental break-away faction of the Jerusalem branch of Agudat Israel. Its spiritual (and politically highly skilled) leader is former Sephardic Chief Rabbi Ovadia Joseph. The rupture in the Jerusalem AI took place just before the local elections held in late October and early November 1983. Its resounding success encouraged Shass to seek national representation as well. This bid also proved successful, as Shass gained four Knesset seats.

Rabbi Kahane created his militant Jewish Defence League in the United States in 1968. He later immigrated to Israel and presented his 'Kach' list in the 1973, 1977 and 1981 Knesset elections, but to no avail, as it failed each time to garner the required minimum 1% of the total valid vote. In 1984 Kach received one mandate and Kahane announced that he would use his parliamentary immunity to encourage Israel's Arabs to leave the Jewish state. It appeared he intended to use the Knesset as an additional forum to propagate his radical extra-parliamentary anti-Arab activities.

(b) LABOUR PARTIES

Until 1977 the Labour parties were the most significant parties, both politically and in terms of organization. Two groups had crystallized early on: a small, radical and permanently anti-Zionist minority, and a majority which attempted to fuse Zionism with socialism. The leadership of the anti-Zionist left was assumed by the Communist Party. In 1919 its predecessor, the Socialist Worker's Party (SWP) split from the leftist-socialist Poale Zion (PZ, 'Workers of Zion', founded in 1905) after PZ decided to join with socialists previously uncommitted to any party to form Ahdut Haavoda (AH, 'Unity of Labour'; see Shapiro, 1976).

For the Communists the class struggle took priority over the 'national' (i.e. Jewish-Arab) conflict, so that they were thus able to create the first and only genuinely Jewish-Arab party. Zionism was rejected because its nationalism conflicted with communist internationalism and 'class politics' (Greilsammer, 1978). On the other hand, it was precisely this goal which led to frequent internal party struggles and splits. A break with far-reaching consequences occurred in 1965 when the bi-national group founded Rakah, the New Communist List (NCL), which emerged from the elections in a considerably stronger position than the increasingly leftist-Zionist CP. In 1983 the Progressive Movement Nazareth broke with Rakah. The PMN appealed to moderate, educated, Arab middle-class voters. In 1984 the PMN merged with a group of Jewish doves led by Matty Peled and Uri Avnery to form the Progressive List for Peace (PLP). The PLP favours a bi-national state in Israel alongside a Palestinian state in the Gaza Strip and the West Bank.

The Jewish remnants of the Communist Party carried on under the old name. They made their peace with other leftist-Zionist groups such as

Moked and Shelli, which favoured moderation in territorial issues and conciliation with the Palestinians, including the PLO (Schnall, 1979: 104 f.). The NCL attracted some, albeit not a great deal, of additional support in 1977 by joining in an election alignment known as the DFF, Democratic Front for Freedom and Equality, consisting of the NCL and a number of independent and Oriental Jewish candidates, each group preserving its own organizational independence but maintaining a common faction in the Knesset.

Hapoel Hazair (HP, 'Young Workers', founded in 1905) did not join Ahdut Haavoda in 1919, as it considered AH too Marxist-oriented. By 1930, however, AH had largely rid itself of radical elements and a merger between AH, HPZ and Mapai ('Party of the Workers of Eretz Israel') was effected. David Ben-Gurion and Berl Katznelson were the most prominent Mapai politicians of that time.

The more radical Zionist socialists who had resisted the founding of AH in 1919 joined in creating PZL (Poale Zion Left) in 1920. Following diverse splits and reconciliations, PZL merged in 1946 with the left wing of Mapai (which had split off in 1944 and again called itself AH) to form AH-PZL. This party amalgamated with Hashomer Hazair ('Young Guardians', founded in 1915), thus creating Mapam ('United Workers' Party') in 1948.

Hashomer Hazair had originated as a youth movement inspired by the *halutzic* ideal of the agricultural pioneer and began to found *kibbutzim* in the 1920s.

On the eve of the elections to the Third Knesset in 1959, a split occurred within Mapam. The less pro-Soviet AH, which also favoured a more active military policy, broke with Mapam and was joined by the majority of the former PZL.

Following the protracted controversies of the early 1960s surrounding the Lavon affair (which arose over the question of political responsibility for the disastrous failure of an intelligence mission which had taken place in 1954), Ben-Gurion and his supporters broke with Mapai to found Rafi ('List of the Workers of Israel'). A further reason for the split was that Ben-Gurion's faction, which included Shimon Peres and Moshe Dayan as well as the later presidents Navon and Herzog, was opposed to the formation of the 'Small Maarah' alignment (common election list and Knesset faction) with Ahdut Haavoda.

In 1968, under the influence of the euphoric feelings of unity following the Six Day War, Mapai, AH and Rafi merged to form the Israeli Labour Party (ILP). Roughly 40% of the members of Rafi, including Ben-Gurion, refused to go along with the merger and banded together as the State List (SL). Since 1969 the ILP and Mapam have cooperated in the 'Big Maarah' alignment, which was joined by the Independent Liberals, who were no longer represented in the Knesset, and by the Citizens' Rights Movement in 1981. The latter was founded in 1973 by Shulamit Aloni, a former ILP member of the Knesset. She stood for more religious liberalism and for women's rights.

Following the creation of the 'National Unity Government' in September 1984, Mapam left the Maarah. Like Mapam, some ILP members left their party in protest against the coalition with the hawkish Likud. Yossi Sarid, the ILP's 'super-dove', joined the Citizens' Rights Movement. Before Mapam's defection, Ezer Weizman's Yahad had joined a thus newly reconstituted Maarah in August 1984.

(c) THE BOURGEOIS PARTIES

Beginning in 1907, the 'civic' parties began coalescing into loose confederations, but the extent of their organization, which suffered continuous reversals due to their tendency to spin off splinter groups, remained limited until well into the 1930s. A total of thirty-three middle-class groups, as opposed to 'only' twelve religious and eleven leftist parties, offered lists of candidates in the four elections to the Constituent Assembly during the Yishuv period. At first, the middle-class groups simply called themselves 'Zionists' or 'General Zionists'.

The acknowledged leader of the nationalist right was Zeev (Vladimir) Jabotinsky, who founded the Revisionist Zionists in 1925 (see Isaac, 1981: chs. 2 and 5). With regard to the future borders of the Jewish state, the Revisionists were 'maximalists', already favouring what amounted to a militant line with regard to the Mandate authorities, whom they accused of having abandoned the Balfour Declaration of 1917 in favour of a pro-Arab policy. As the Revisionists were convinced that the other Jewish parties would simply accept the policies of the Mandate authorities and did not expect any change in policy on the part of the WZO, they created their own New Zionist Organization as a rival to the WZO in 1935.

Following early signs of activity in 1931, Ezel ('National Defence Organization') was built up in earnest, beginning in 1937. At first merely the party militia of the Revisionists, Ezel gradually grew more independent, particularly after Jabotinsky's death in 1940. In 1942 Menachem Begin took over as commander, after which the Revisionists lost all influence.

After the outbreak of the Second World War Ezel's majority was prepared to fight alongside the British against Hitler's Germany, but a minority within the organization was not prepared to do so. The latter founded Lehi ('Fighters for the Freedom of Israel'). Their leader was Abraham Stern.

One of Lehi's three leaders after Stern's assassination by the British was the future foreign minister and then prime minister Yitzhak Shamir. While Lehi was dissolved after independence, Ezel reconstituted itself as a political party in 1948, as the Herut Movement. At first Herut did not include the Revisionists, who subsequently joined in 1951, as did the remnants of Lehi.

The General Zionists were divided into a left and a right wing. The former, the GZ(A), favoured cooperation with the moderate parties of the left, whereas the latter, the GZ(B), preferred an alliance with the Revisionists. The best-known politician of the GZ(A) was the later president Chaim Weizmann. Both parties reunited in 1945 only to part ways again in 1948. Liberals on the left formed the Progressive Party (PP), which was joined by the Zionist Workers as well as a group from Germany known as the New Immigration.

In 1961 the PP and the GZ merged to form the Liberal Party, but this re-reunification was short-lived, the parties falling apart once more in 1965. Those General Zionists who continued to call themselves the Liberal Party joined with Herut to form the Gahal bloc. This event proved a decisive turning point for Herut, which until then had been shunned by the Zionist parties as a 'terrorist' organization. The legitimization of Herut had taken a giant step forward.

The majority of the former PP was not prepared to form a bloc with Herut in 1965 and therefore decided to re-found its old party, calling itself the Independent Liberals.

The tendency towards concentration among the middle-class parties reached its zenith in the summer of 1973 with the founding of the Likud, amalgamating the Gahal bloc, the Free Centre (which had bolted from Herut in 1966/7), the Eretz Israel Workers' Movement (founded after the 1967 Six Day War, its membership consisting mainly of former Mapai supporters) and, finally, the State List (see Isaac, 1976: ch. 3).

The apparent chaos presented by the numerous shifts of allegiance, splits, mergers and jumps from one political camp to the other since the mid-1960s graphically illustrates the dissolution of the boundaries between the traditional political blocs.

In 1976 the smaller parties within the Likud (State List, Eretz Israel Movement, Independent Centre) broke off to form the Laam Party. Personal rivalries between former members of the State List (led by Yigael Hurvitz) and former members of the Independent Centre led to a split. The IC was composed of former Herut members who had broken with their party in protest over its participation in the Histadrut beginning in 1965. The IC was close to the National Workers' Organization of the Revisionist unions. While the IC remained within the Likud as part of Laam and finally rejoined Herut in 1982, Hurvitz (re)founded the new/old Rafi, which allied itself with Dayan's newly formed Telem Party in April of 1981 in the hope of repeating the events of 1965. The new party experienced a debacle at the polls, receiving only two Knesset seats. This disastrous showing, followed by Dayan's death in October 1981, pushed Telem into its terminal crisis. In 1982 Hurvitz returned to the Likud (which he left again in 1984). The remainder of his Rafi Party went over to the ILP.

The founding of the Tehiya ('Resurrection') Party can be interpreted as a protest against the signing of the peace treaty with Egypt. Tehiya unites 'hawks' from Herut, Laam, the Eretz Israel Movement and Gush Emunim. The name of the party deliberately reinvokes the political programme of Abraham Stern. In 1984 Tehiya presented a common list in the Knesset elections together with another newly formed super-hawkish party, Zomet, which had been founded by Rafael Eitan, Israel's chief of staff from 1978 to 1983. Their common list received five mandates and the two parties merged in 1985.

Since 1965 a number of new parties have entered into Israel's body politic, forcing their way like wedges between the traditional camps. The phenomenon began with Uri Avnery's non-Zionist, highly dovish Haolam Haze ('This World' – also the title of Avnery's weekly magazine; see Schnall, 1979: ch. 4).

The new party with the greatest impact proved to be the previously mentioned Democratic Movement for Change which, following its founding in 1977, attracted followers from all camps, won fifteen Knesset seats in its first appearance at the polls and joined the governing coalition in October of the same year, but then proved unable to bridge the widening gaps within its own ranks. The DMC subsequently broke up into its constituent parts and failed to present an election list in 1981. Its founder, Yigael Yadin, former chief of staff and an archaeologist, resigned.

2   ORGANIZATION

The formal organization of the parties is generally patterned after that of Mapai/ILP (Yanai, 1981: chs. 3, 4 and 5; Wolffsohn, 1983a: 661 ff.). The organs of the party on the local and district levels consist of the party council, secretariat and offices. The *moshavim*, the *kibbutzim* and local party units with more than 15,000 members (Tel-Aviv, Jerusalem and Haifa) constitute districts. As in the ILP, the organs on the national level are the party congress, the central committee (CC) with its secretariat and the party offices with their secretariat. In principle, the party congress is the chief decision-making body, the CC assuming its functions between conventions. The actual decisions are made either in the party offices (that is, by party officials) or, more frequently, in informal groups.

The ultra-Orthodox Agudat Israel Party has a somewhat different organizational structure. Here the Council of the Torah Greats, the party's supreme rabbinical body, has the final say. Interestingly, this authority was challenged in the 1984 campaign by those AI politicians who had been ordered by this council to renounce their Knesset candidacy. The highest decision-making body of the Oriental-Orthodox Shass is their Council of the Torah Scholars.

Apart from the formal party bodies, the informal but sometimes more influential 'factions' (i.e. former parties operating as factions; for example, Ahdut Haavoda and Rafi within the ILP) and 'circles' (i.e. issue-, organization- or personality-oriented groups within a party) are deserving of analytical attention. Unfortunately, however, it is not possible here to even begin to describe the complex internal structures of the parties with their plethora of sometimes cooperating, sometimes competing groups. (For case studies see Schiff, 1977: ch. 4; Yishai, 1980; Yanai, 1981: chs. 6–8; Wolffsohn, 1983a: 688 ff.; Goldberg and Hoffman, 1983.)

3   DECISION-MAKING

The party apparatus had already achieved dominance during the Yishuv, and attained virtual omnipotence following independence (see Wolffsohn, 1983a: 658 f. for documentation and literature). Unprecedented mass protest against the various decision-making cartels in the government and parties arose immediately after the Yom Kippur War (1973). The DMC rode the crest of this wave in 1977, campaigning under the banner of more democracy within the parties.

A systematic examination of the procedures employed in nominating candidates for the Knesset between 1949 and 1984 demonstrates that one result of the protest movement and the rise of the DMC was an increased

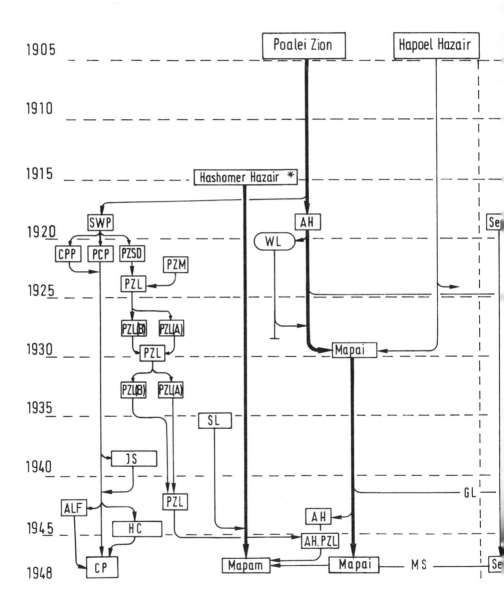

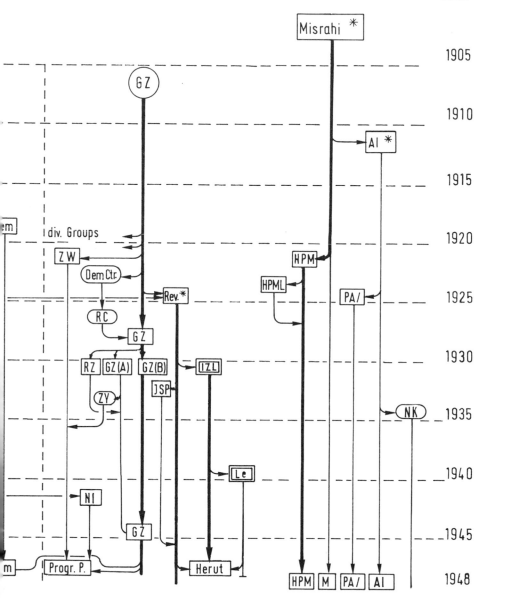

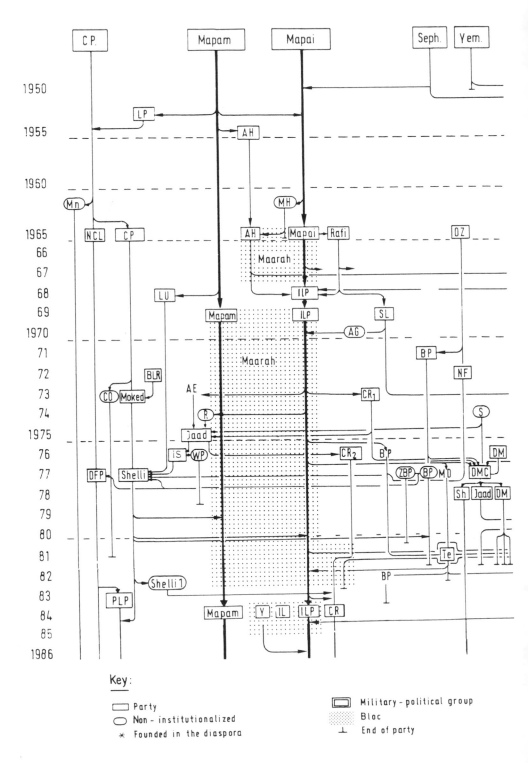

Key:

☐ Party
⬭ Non - institutionalized
✳ Founded in the diaspora

▭ Military - political group
▦ Bloc
⊥ End of party

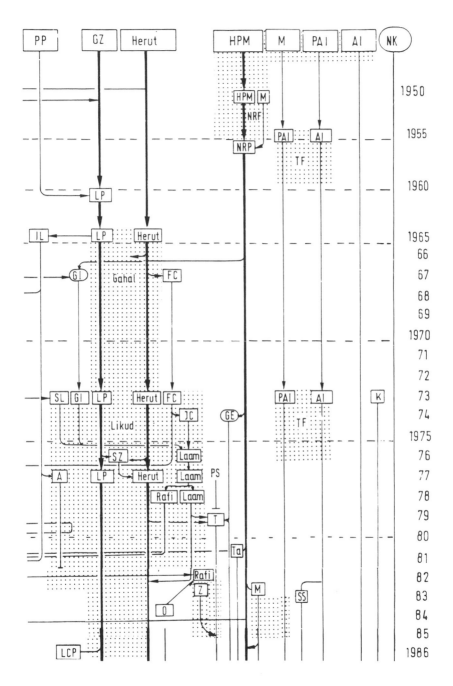

Figure 26   The genealogy of Israel's parties.

measure of internal party democracy in 1977. The clock was turned back in this respect in 1981, although not completely. Irrespective of political orientation, most observers agreed in 1984 that the nomination of Herut's Knesset candidates was the most 'democratic' in terms of grass-roots participation. The Alignment tried to combine grass-roots participation with considerations of party factions and societal sectors. In 1984 even Agudat Israel witnessed a challenge to traditional authority mounted by party bosses against its supreme governing body, the Council of the Torah Greats. (For further information see Goldberg, 1980; Hoffman, 1980; Yanai, 1981: ch. 2; Brichta, 1977; Wolffsohn, 1983a: 664 f.; Goldberg and Hoffman, 1983.)

All attempts to legislate a greater degree of internal party democracy in Israel have thus far failed. Every party is allowed to make its own rules concerning its internal decision-making processes.

4   PARTY FINANCES

Until 1968 most parties depended on membership dues, donations, support from the Jewish Agency, and profits from party enterprises. Following an act of the Knesset, the parties participating in the Histadrut as well as those parties with union organizations of their own (HPM, PAI), were permitted to collect party membership dues by payroll deduction. If the individual party member consents, his membership dues are deducted from his paycheck by the government and the resulting funds are centrally distributed to the parties. Party finances were put on a permanent legal footing by the Knesset on 24 January 1973, in a law regulating both the financing of election campaigns and the day-to-day expenses of the parties by means of a programme of state support. (For further details see Boim, 1972 and 1979; Wolffsohn, 1983a: 469 ff., 240 ff., 562 ff.)

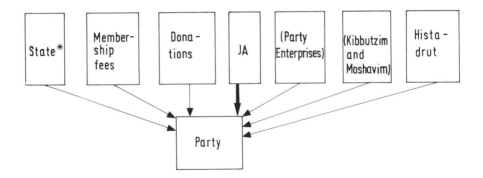

Figure 27   Party finances.

Key:
 *   = most important source
 ( ) = where these exist and generate a profit

Table 13   Public Financing of Israel's Parties as a Proportion of the
National Budget (%)

Fiscal Year	% of National Budget
1974/75	·05%
1976/77	·04%
1977/78	·08%
1978/79	·09%
1980/81	·02%
1981/82	·04%
1982/83	·03%
1983/84	·02% (est.)
1984/85	·02% (est.)

Source: Statistical Abstract of Israel, various vols.

When taken as a proportion of total government expenditures, the public
financing of Israel's parties has proved unusually modest, as shown in
Table 13.

5   STRUCTURAL AND IDEOLOGICAL CHARACTERISTICS

(a) HAWKS AND DOVES

This polarization is almost as old as political Zionism itself. It was only
during the period between independence and the Six Day War, a time in
which the parties all more or less accepted the new circumstances, that the
discussion ebbed somewhat.

Furthermore, as already discussed in the preface to this volume, the
problem is closely related to normative political geography. The first plan for
the division of Palestine worked out by the World Zionist Organization and
presented at the Paris Peace Conference in February of 1919 is not without
relevance to the present discussion. Not only the territory of Israel within the
borders of 4 June 1967, but also parts of what is now southern Lebanon (up
to the Litani River), the Golan Heights, the West Bank of the Jordan and
the eastern bank of the river up to the Hedjaz railway line (not currently
claimed by anyone) were included in this plan (Gilbert, 1974: 11).

It is important to note that the dividing line between hawks and doves
does not run between but rather within the political parties. Nonetheless, it is
possible to speak, albeit somewhat simplistically, of an increasing tendency
since the mid-1970s on the part of politicians of the Labour bloc as well as the
parties cooperating with it to lean towards the side of the doves, whereas the
leadership of the Likud and the parties which joined its coalition can be
counted among the hawks. It is, of course, necessary to take note of differences within the parties and groupings.

The main bone of contention between hawks and doves is the issue of
settlements on the West Bank. The settlements on the Golan Heights, in the
Jordan Valley, near Jerusalem and in the Gaza Strip have proven less

controversial, as have the question of negotiations with the PLO (largely rejected), the near total opposition to a Palestinian state (not even in the occupied territories – much less as a replacement for the state of Israel) and the refusal to expel the Arab residents from these territories or from Israel proper. Only Rabbi Kahane, who garnered 1·2% of the vote in the 1984 Knesset elections, advocates the last extreme proposal. Table 14 offers a synopsis of the positions of the parties on various issues. (For a similar table for the 1977 elections, see Wolffsohn, 1983: 264 f.)

Since 1977 the polls have also shown that moderate attitudes on territorial issues are more likely to be found among voters supporting the Maarah. But this refers to the West Bank only, not to the Jordan Valley, the Golan Heights or Jerusalem (see Levy and Gutmann, 1978: 5 ff.; Levinsohn, 1979: 8 ff.; Wolffsohn, 1983a: 257 ff.).

Table 15 documents attitudes in Israeli society towards the return of occupied territories for the period from 1968 to 1983.

Although the problem of comparability inevitably arises when the results of various surveys conducted by different institutes are presented together, as they are here, the basic tendency should become sufficiently clear. With regard to specific territories, the poll results show a simultaneous decline in 'maximalist' positions and a polarization into two almost equally strong camps: one for, the other opposed to, territorial compromise. These findings undoubtedly represent a cache of political dynamite.

The division is, of course, mainly over the question of the return of the West Bank rather than of the Golan Heights, concerning which there is a widespread consensus of opinion against the surrender of any of the remaining territory. Consequently, the formal annexation of the Golan Heights in December 1981 not only won the overwhelming approval of the Knesset but of the Israeli public as well. Annexation 'now' (i.e. in January of 1982) was welcomed by 57% and 'at some later date' by another 11%. Negotiations on the final status were supported by 18% and a return to Syria by only 5% (with 9% replying 'don't know' or 'no answer'; PORI poll in *World Opinion Update*, vol. IV, no. 1982: 54).

The 'Jerusalem Law' (i.e. the formal annexation of the eastern part of the city) was approved without reservation by 60% of the public, conditionally by another 3% and opposed by 15% (with 22% replying 'don't know' or 'no answer'; PORI poll of July 1980 in *Index to International Public Opinion*, vol. III: 202). There is further widespread agreement – a steady 70% and more in the polls since 1967 – that there ought to be no negotiations with the PLO (Wolffsohn, 1981 and 1983a: 275 ff.; Z. Peled, 1979 and 1980. Highly revealing polls on the PLO and the Palestinians since the mid-1970s are also to be found in the *Index to International Public Opinion*, vol. I: 7, 61, 63, 66–8, 129; vol. II: 101, 104–6, 172; vol. III: 66, 200, 205; vol. IV: 223, 227 f., 250; and a more recent survey in *World Opinion Update*, vol. VIII, no. 4, 1983: 57 f.)

Responses in the polls have been largely unchanging when the question is framed in general terms of willingness to 'return the occupied territories' (Table 16). Here the proportion of those totally rejecting compromise rose from 38% in 1969 to 50% in 1981. If one adds the totals of those willing to give up only 'some' territory or 'none at all', the results are 90% for 1969,

Table 14 Hawkish and Dovish Parties in Israel

	Matzpen Arab 'Rejection'	NCL	PLP	Mapam CRM Shinui	Labour Weizman	Ometz	Likud	Tehiya	Kahana	NRP	Tami	PAI Morasha	AI	Shass
Expulsion of Arabs from Israel or territories	–	–	–	–	–	–	–	–	+	–	–	–	–	–
Golan concessions	+	+	+	–	–	–	–	–	–	–	–	–	–	–
Formal annexation of West Bank	–	–	–	–	–	–	(–)	+	+	–	–		–	–
Citizenship for West Bankers												+		
Concessions populated areas of West Bank	+	+	+	+	+	(+)	–	–	–	(+)	+	–	+	–
Settlements everywhere in West Bank	–	–	–	–	–	(–)	+	+	+	(+)	–	+	–	+
Settlements in West Bank where militarily necessary	–	–	–	+	+	+	+	+	+	+	+	+	+	+
Settlement freeze to open negotiations with Jordan	+	+	+	+	+	(+)	–	–	–	(–)	(+)	–	+	–
Development freeze for all settlements except for:	+	+	+	+	+	+	–	–	–	(+)	–	–	–	–
Development freeze for settlements in Jordan														

Table 14 Hawkish and Dovish Parties in Israel

	Matzpen / Arab 'Rejection'	NCL PLP	Mapam / CRM / Shinui	Labour / Weizman	Ometz	Likud	Tehiya	Kahana	NRP / Tami	PAI / Morasha	AI	Shass
Valley, Gush Etzion, West Bank mountain tops, Jerusalem area	–	–	–	–	–	+	+	+	+	+	–	–
Jerusalem annexation (East)	–	–	+	+	+	+	+	+	+	+	+	+
Negotiations with PLO if it renounces terror and recognizes Israel	+	+	+	+	(+)	–	–	–	(+)	(+)	(+)	+
Negotiations with PLO (no preconditions)	+	+	–	–	–	–	–	–	(+)	–	–	–
Palestinian State in West Bank and Gaza	+	+	–	–	–	–	–	–	–	–	–	–
'Democratic, secular state' there and Israel	+	–	–	–	–	–	–	–	–	–	–	–

Key:
+   affirmative
–   negative

Table 15 Attitudes towards the Return of Occupied Territories, 1968–85

Question (in Guttman, 1978): What (territorial) concessions would you be willing to make in order to achieve peace with the Arab states?

Date	Event	% willing to return 'some' territory or 'none'				
		West Bank	Gaza Strip	Sinai	Golan Heights	Sharm el-Sheik
1968 Feb.	Actions of/against PLO	91	85	57	99	93
1969 Feb./Mar.	Poll during War of Attrition	75	75	52	95	87
1971 Mar./Apr.	Poll	56	70	31	92	91
1972 Sep.	Olympic Massacre in Munich					
Oct.	Soviet airlift to Syria					
Oct./Nov.	Israeli air raid on PLO bases in Syria					
	Poll	69	78	54	97	96
1973 5 Oct.	Poll	82	80	69	94	92
6 Oct.	Yom Kippur War					
Nov.	Poll	58	62	36	86	87
Dec.	Poll	60	66	38	93	91
1974 Jan.	Sinai Disengagement I					
May	Disengagement with Syria					
July	Poll	65	—	—	86	83
1975 Mar.	Maale Adumim settlers removed by IDF					
	Poll	36	—	—	83	80
Sep.	Terrorists occupy Hotel Savoy in Tel-Aviv					
Oct.	Sinai Disengagement II					
	Poll	56	57	38	85	88
Nov.	UN Resolution: Zionism = racism					
1976 Sep.	Poll	68	69	39	80	88

Table 15 Attitudes towards the Return of Occupied Territories, 1968–85

Question (in Gutmann, 1978): What (territorial) concessions would you be willing to make in order to achieve peace with the Arab states?

		% willing to return 'some' territory or 'none'				
Date	*Event*	*West Bank*	*Gaza Strip*	*Sinai*	*Golan Heights*	*Sharm el-Sheik*
Dec.	Rabin's resignation					
1977 Jan.	Poll	59	60	—	83	84
May	Elections					
Nov.	Sadat in Israel					
19 Nov.	Poll	61	51	17	19	77
30 Nov.–4 Dec.	Poll	60	50	16	84	84
Dec.	Sadat's break with the 'Rejectionist Front', Cairo conference, Begin in USA					
Dec.	Poll	60	46	19	74	74
1978 Jan.	Breakdown of Jerusalem conference					
Mar.	PLO massacre on coastal road					
	IDF in Lebanon					
Apr.	Poll	63	49	28	83	73
Sep.	Camp David negotiations					
Nov.	Poll[1]	52	—	—	—	—
1979 Mar.	Israeli-Egyptian treaty, poll	—	33[2]	—	—	—
June	Poll[1]	66	—	—	—	—
July	Poll	35[2]	—	—	74[2]	—
1982 May	Poll[3]	58	—	—	—	—

		West Bank + Gaza	Golan
June	War in Lebanon, poll	53	
Aug.	Poll before Beirut massacre	47	
1983 Mar.	Lebanon, poll	82[4]	
May	Lebanon, poll	86[5]	
Sep.	Begin resigns, poll	52[6]	
Dec.	Poll	62[6]	
1984 Mar.	Poll	58[6]	
Jul.	Elections, poll	50[6]	
1985 Dec.	Poll		88

Notes:

— Question not posed.

[1] PORI poll conducted for *Haaretz*; question: return of territory but retention of military bases

[2] 'Return nothing, even in the event of peace with Arab states.'

[3] With regard to peace with Jordan: 'nothing'; *Modi'in Ezrahi* poll.

[4] Including 32% willing to return 'some' territory.

[5] Including 36% willing to return 'some' territory.

[6] West Bank and Gaza Strip in the event of peace with Jordan; *Modi'in Ezrahi* poll.

Sources: Gutmann, 1978: table 1; Levy and Gutmann, 1978; *Haaretz*, 3 July 1979; Z. Peled, *Yediot Aharonot*, 22 July 1979; *Jerusalem Post*, 3 September 1982 and 10 June 1983.

Table 16   General Willingness to Return Occupied Territories (%)

Return	1969	1973	1977	1981	1984
None	38	31	41	50	42
A small part	52	52	43	42	44
Most	5	10	7	4	6
All	1	2	7	3	8
No answer	4	5	2	1	—

Sources: IIASR data and 'Dahaf' data in Arian, 1981: 14; Stone, 1982: 41; Arian, 1985: 269.

83% in 1973, 84% four years later and 92% in the election year 1981. The range of manoeuvrability for politicians seeking compromise is apparently limited. It must, however, also be noted that, despite the extraordinarily important role Sharm el-Sheik once played in public opinion in Israel, this strategic point was returned to Egypt within the framework of a peace treaty. The citizens of Israel, too, can be manipulated.

(b) VOTING BEHAVIOUR OF THE SETTLERS

Aspects of political geography involving the occupied territories, the settlements, the settlers and the settlement policies of the major parties were dealt with in the introduction to this volume. The following section examines the voting behaviour of the settlers as an important manifestation of their political culture. In fact, the existence of a distinct political subculture can be traced along geographical lines, first and foremost along the 'Green Line', that is, Israel's pre-1967 border (see Goldberg and Ben-Zadok, 1983).

Table 17 shows that a political upheaval took place among the settlers in 1981 and that the resulting trend became even more pronounced in 1984 due to the continuing expansion and restructuring of this population, which, simply put, was packed with rightists. Up to 1981 both Labour and Likud achieved better results in the country as a whole than among the Jewish settlements in the occupied territories. In 1984, however, Maarah losses were dramatic (down from 24·9% to a mere 6·5%), whereas the Likud obtained slightly better results in the territories (33%) than in the rest of the country (31·9%).

Until 1977 the Jewish electorate in the territories was more religious (NRP) in its voting behaviour, but still basically middle-of-the-road. The votes cast for the Democratic Movement for Change (DMC) in 1977 can also be added to the moderate Maarah tendency. The gap in favour of the NRP in the territories as opposed to the rest of the country remained, but was considerably reduced in 1981 and even more so in 1984.

Tehiya did extremely well in the territories, but to some settlers it was obviously no longer 'purist' enough in 1984. This may explain the disproportionate success of Kach (Rabbi Kahane), which received 5·1% of the vote in the territories, compared to 1·2% overall. Rabbi Druckman's Morasha may have also won over some Tehiya potential, but the majority of his support came from the NRP reservoir. Druckman had been a member of the Knesset

Table 17   Selected Data on the Voting Behaviour of Jewish Settlers in
            the Occupied Territories, 1973–84 (%)

		1973	1977	1981	1984
Likud	Territory	29·5	30·5[1]	30·4	33·0
	Country	30·2	35·3	37·2	31·9
Maarah	Territory	34·5	22·5[2]	24·9	6·5
(Labour)	Country	39·6	24·6[3]	36·6	34·9
NRP	Territory	21·1	26·8	11·9	5·9[4]
	Country	8·3	9·2	4·9	3·5
Tehiya	Territory	—	—	23·1	20·6
	Country	—	—	2·2	4·0
Kach	Territory	n.a.	n.a.	n.a.	5·1
(Kahana)	Country	n.a.	n.a.	n.a.	1·2

Notes:
[1] Including 'Shlomzion' (= Ariel Sharon).
[2] Democratic Movement for Change 12·1.
[3] Democratic Movement for Change 11·6.
[4] Morasha (Rabbi Druckman, the former NRP Knesset member, with Poale
Agudat Israel) 16·8%.

Sources: Elections, 1977: 42; Elections, 1981: 38; Y. Litani, *Haaretz*,
            8 August 1984.

from the NRP, and a reunification was on the agenda of the 1984 pre-election
negotiations but failed to materialize.

   With these data in mind, it is difficult to imagine how a Maarah-
dominated government (much less just a Maarah-led coalition like the one
agreed upon in September 1984) could press through far-reaching territorial
concessions. The authority of such a government would be shaky among the
settlers.

(c) PUBLIC ATTITUDES ON SETTLEMENTS

The last section focused on the political culture within the Jewish settlements. This section focuses on the political culture surrounding these settlements,
that is, the attitudes of the general public towards their activities.

   The results of polls conducted by the Israel Institute of Applied Social
Research (IIASR) between May 1972 and July 1979 underline the necessity
of making basic distinctions between the different occupied territories. We
have already observed this phenomenon while examining the willingness to
make territorial concessions. The following data are from Levinsohn (1979:
3, where the reader can also find the data according to socio-demographic
variables). For the settlements on the Golan Heights and in the Jordan
Valley there was practically unanimous support.

   The figures for the Golan Heights settlements varied from 99% in the
period from May to July 1972 to 88% in July of 1979. The weakest level of
support was 79% in March of 1978 (responses: 'support' or 'support definitely'). Opposition ('against' or 'definitely against') was lowest from May to

July 1972 with 5%, and highest in January of 1978 with 24%. In July 1979, 11% were opposed. For the settlements in the Jordan Valley support was at its highest from May to July 1972 with 90%, at its lowest in January of 1978 with 67% and was at 79% in July of 1979.

Polarization was more noticeable in the support for the settlements in 'Judea and Samaria', but hardly extreme. Settlements in 'Judea' enjoyed the most support in May–July 1972 with 65%, the least in February of 1978 with 56% and attained 62% in July 1979. Support for the Jewish settlements in 'Samaria' was similar, but a few percentage points lower (62% in May–July 1972 as well as in July 1979, with a record low of 56% in February and March of 1978).

If we are to believe the polls conducted by Public Opinion Research Israel (PORI), polarization subsequently sharpened. In June 1980, 44% favoured 'additional settlements' in the West Bank whereas 44% were opposed, with 7% lending conditional support and 9% giving no response (*Index to International Public Opinion*, vol. III: 205). In March 1981, however, such settlements were 'strongly approved' or 'approved' of by 51% and 'somewhat' or 'strongly' disapproved of by 42% (ibid.: 206). 'Hawkishness' increased again between July and October 1981 (in the wake of the Likud election victory) with 58% 'for' new settlements on the West Bank in October, as opposed to 49% in July. Opposition decreased by only 1%, from 30% to 29%, but the number of undecided interviewees fell from 17% to 9% (with 'conditional support' remaining at a stable 4%; ibid., vol. IV: 229).

When the question was posed somewhat differently in July 1983, 51% agreed with the proposal to 'establish settlements in strategic areas only' (the Maarah approach), 26% wanted to build them 'anywhere . . . , even in heavily populated Arab areas' (the position of the settlement activists and of the government), only 16% wanted no more settlements, and 7% expressed no opinion (*World Opinion Update*, vol. no. 7, 1983: 99). Nearly a year before, in August 1982, the Maarah approach had obtained the support of 45% and the 'anywhere' position of the activists 24%. Most significantly, the plea for no more settlements was supported by 26% in 1982, 10% more than in 1983 (ibid., vol. no. 8, 1982: 8).

With economic problems becoming evident and the personal financial situation of the average citizen worsening in December 1983, 72% of Jewish Israelis agreed that 'in the framework of a national austerity programme the first budget to be cut should be the one for settlements in Judea and Samaria' (Modi'in Ezrahi poll, *Jerusalem Post*, 3 January 1984).

In summary: an increasing polarization is observable among Jewish Israelis concerning settlement activities in the West Bank. It is possible to speak of two camps of about equal strength. As soon as their personal situation is affected by expenditures for settlements, however, most Israelis seem to have second and third thoughts concerning their support. In other words, there are 'intervening variables' which somehow dilute ideological positions. In terms of political engineering, the consequences are self-evident: the Israeli public can be manipulated on this issue, first and foremost when it begins to affect bread-and-butter issues (see Levinsohn, 1979: 10 on the higher approval rates for settlements in principle than for their budget priority).

(d) RELIGIOUS POLICY

Since the early 1960s polls have continually shown that between 25% and 30% of Jewish Israelis regard themselves as 'religious' or as 'traditionalists', this all the more so among 'Orientals' as opposed to 'Westerners' (Zelniker and Kahan, 1976: 33; Antonovski and Arian, 1972: appendices A and E; Arian, 1972a: 187 ff.; Wolffsohn, 1983a: 278 f.; Goldscheider and Friedlander, 1981: 10 ff.). If these results are compared with the election returns for the religious parties, it can be seen that the latter have succeeded in mobilizing only about half of their potential voters. (On religious voters see Tables 18 and 19.)

Among the parties of the Yishuv, the Communists, PZL and HHZ were the most secularly oriented, followed by the religious centre, consisting of both parts of the GZ, Mapai and the Revisionists. The degree of religiosity then increased over the range Misrahi, HPM, PAI and AI to Neture Kartha, insofar as this group can be considered a political party at all. The spectrum of parties since Israel's independence presents the following scale (from most secular to most religious): Communists, Mapam, Shelli, Citizens' Rights Movement, Independent Liberals, DMC (while it existed), Liberals, Mapai/ILP, Herut, Laam, Tehiya, Kahane, NRP, Mazad/PAI, AI, Shass, NK.

Here, too, the overall picture may be misleading with regard to particular political constellations. The Labour Party, for example, has an institutionalized religious faction (The Religious Worker) and the Tehiya Party consists of a secular as well as of a religious group with close links to Gush Emunim. Within the religious parties themselves there are numerous groups or factions which reflect traditional religious cleavages in Judaism. A good example is the centuries-old rivalry between mythological-populist Chassidism and its sharpest adversaries, the Mitnagdim from Vilna. Incredible as it may sound, this rivalry, long institutionalized in Agudat Israel, formed part of the background of bitter clashes in the 1984 campaign, the two groups fighting over the leadership of the AI Knesset list.

With regard to the religiosity of the voters of the various parties, it is important to note that the religious parties were almost exclusively supported by Jews of strict religious observance, whereas Moked, Shelli, the Citizens' Rights Movement and, to a lesser degree, the Independent Liberals and the DMC drew their support from secular Israelis. The Likud, Tehiya and Labour electorates were religiously varied, the first two parties more so than Labour. Again, of Israel's two 'catch-all' parties, the Likud is the 'catch-more' party.

The Jewish religion has frequently had a greater polarizing than harmonizing effect on the politics of the Jewish state, but Israel is nonetheless far from being on the verge of a 'Kulturkampf'. An increasing militancy can be observed among the Orthodox, especially since 1977, from which point on they have been able to rely on AI as a coalition partner in the government. (For revealing data on religious protest see Lehman-Wilzig and Goldberg, 1983: esp. table 1. On the political function of religion in Israel see Abramov, 1976 and Wolffsohn, 1978. On the connections between territorial and social issues see Wolffsohn, 1983a: 260.)

The general truce declared between the parties on religious issues resulted

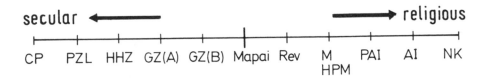

Figure 28   Israel's secular-religious party spectrum during the
Yishuv.

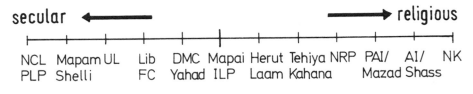

Figure 29   Israel's secular-religious party spectrum since
independence.

in an agreement to maintain the status quo in this area. The basis for this
unofficial pact is the letter of 19 June 1947 from Ben-Gurion (in the name of
Mapai), Yitzhak Gruenbaum (of the GZ) and Rabbi Fischman-Maimon
(Misrahi) promising the AI leadership significant concessions on religious
questions in the future state. As a result, AI not only agreed to participate in
the institutions of Israel, but also actually became part of the first three
governments and did so again between 1977 and 1984. In the course of the
years, the status quo has proved extraordinarily dynamic, at first favourable
to both religious and non-religious groups, but since 1977 shifting to the clear
advantage of the religious, whose activities subsequently intensified greatly
(Lehman-Wilzig and Goldberg, 1983: table 1).

(e) PARTIES OF THE RIGHT AND LEFT

In Israel, those parties which (1) support the strong position of the Histadrut,
(2) advocate a progressive, levelling tax system and (3) are rooted in the
tradition of the Israeli labour movement, the political culture of which is
strongly influenced by agrarian elements (*kibbutzim, moshavim*), can be considered parties of the 'left'. (On the problematic nature of these categories see
Arian and Shamir, 1983; Wolffsohn, 1983a: ch. 22.) If, with certain reservations, the political parties of present-day Israel and their predecessor groups
can be aligned in a continuum from left to right, the order would be the
following. On the extreme left one would find the extra-parliamentary leftist
groups such as Matzpen (Schnall, 1979: 89 ff.), followed by Rakah (NCL),
the National Communists, the diverse Zionist-socialist groups and parties,
especially Mapam, then AH. The transition to the centre and to the right
becomes fluid in the case of Mapai/ILP, as some of this party's members and
voters can be counted as part of the left, centre or right. For a time, the
DMC constituted 'the' party of the centre, followed by the Independent

Liberals. The religious parties would be placed to the right of centre, Herut, Tehiya and Mazad still further to the right.

With regard to the overall development of the parties from the Yishuv to the present, a general trend to the right can be observed in the party system as a whole, as well as within the individual political camps, as a result of which the party on the right in each camp has increased in strength. In the course of time, the moderate and therefore more 'rightist' Mapai has come to represent the dominant force in the Labour camp. In the bourgeois camp, Herut prevailed. The ideological development of formerly leftist parties has tended ever more to the 'right'. Even Mapam is a case in point.

The shift to the right in public opinion is documented by Figure 54 and Table 50.

(f) FOREIGN POLICY

The most important foreign policy issue during the Yishuv period concerned relations with Great Britain as the Mandate power. The attitudes of both Weizmann's GZ(A) and the New Immigration party were decidedly pro-British, whereas the feelings of the Revisionists and the GZ(B) were much more ambivalent. Lehi, and later Ezel, were militantly anti-British.

Despite all criticism, Mapai believed that there was no alternative to cooperation with the Mandate power, but after the British White Book of May 1939 announcing the imposition of severe restrictions on Jewish immigration and land purchases the sympathies and activities of Mapai in foreign affairs shifted to the United States in the hope that it would apply pressure to Great Britain.

Although the religious parties avoided taking positions on foreign policy, they could hardly help having reservations with regard to the atheistic Soviet Union. For the Communists, however, Moscow was and remained the lodestar of their political course. The left-wing socialists, particularly the PZL, carried on a balancing act between international solidarity with the Soviet Union and Zionist interests which not infrequently collided with those of the Soviets.

Following independence, differences of opinion arose over the issue of East–West tensions. Ben-Gurion and Mapai at first preferred to steer a neutral course, but finally opted in favour of the USA after the outbreak of the Korean War and in view of the massive help given Israel by American Jews. Moreover, beginning in 1949, the Soviet Union had begun to attack Zionism both at home and in Soviet bloc countries as well (Greilsammer, 1978: 191 ff.: Ro'i, 1980: pts. III and IV).

Mapam held its pro-Soviet course until the middle of the 1950s and has attempted since then to maintain an equal critical distance with regard to both of the superpowers, but has not succeeded in improving its relations with the Soviet Union.

AH was more leftist nationalist and therefore more reserved, despite all its sympathies for the USSR.

The left-leaning liberal Progressive Party at first argued for neutrality in the Cold War, but abandoned this stance in the mid-1950s in favour of a clearly pro-Western attitude, which it has continued to maintain, despite transient neutralist phases. The same applies for the right-leaning liberal GZ/Liberal Party.

Herut views itself as a 'part of the free world', but is guided, according to its own definition, by 'national interests' for the sake of which it was and remains prepared to risk a deterioration in Israeli–American relations.

On the issue of relations with the Federal Republic of Germany, Mapai followed the lead of Prime Minister Ben-Gurion, who resolutely proceeded to establish contacts, beginning in 1951/2 with negotiations on reparation payments and since the mid-1950s on military affairs. Ben-Gurion's long-term goal was the establishment of diplomatic relations, a feat accomplished under Eshkol in 1965. The nationalists of Herut were vehemently opposed to any relations with Germany, as were the two leftist socialist parties, Mapam and AH, as well as the Communists, for whom the West Germans were merely tools of 'US imperialism'. In June 1973 Willi Brandt became the first West German chancellor to visit Israel and in July 1975 Yitzhak Rabin became the first Israeli prime minister to visit the Federal Republic. Relations took a turn for the worse under Begin as a result of his attacks on Chancellor Schmidt and the 'German people' for their behaviour during the Nazi period. Due to Begin's resignation, Chancellor Helmut Kohl's visit to Israel (planned for the summer of 1983) had to be postponed until January 1984.

(g) VOTERS

Some data concerning the voters of the various parties are treated in this book in the specific context of the respective population group or political issue (see sections A/I/3/f; A/II/5/a–c, f; B/VI/1/d; B/VI/2/d–e; B/VI/3/i; B/VIII/4, 5). What follows in this section is a general description of the chief characteristics of the Israeli voting public.

Until 1977 the voters of the NRP and Mapai/ILP exhibited the greatest diversity in their sociological make-up, whereas those of AI were the least diverse, coming mainly from the ranks of the well-to-do Orthodox of central European heritage with very little representation of groups from lower educational and economic levels. This picture changed to a degree in the mid-1970s as AI began to make inroads among Orthodox industrial workers with Oriental backgrounds.

Voters attracted to the ILP are mainly of Euro-American backgrounds, whereas voters with higher levels of income and education have gravitated towards the Independent Liberals, the Citizens' Rights Movement and, in 1977, to the DMC, which in that year also drew middle-class voters away from the ILP. In 1981, however, the ILP succeeded in winning back these voters. The proportion of voters from the lowest income and educational levels is particularly small for Mapam, which draws its support mainly from its reservoir of voters in the *kibbutzim*, who are commonly regarded as a sort of 'planter aristocracy'. AH also depends mainly on voters from the *kibbutzim*. Among ILP voters up to 1977, women, senior citizens and the middle classes were most strongly represented. In addition, there was the support of the party-sponsored *kibbutzim* and *moshavim*, although voters from the *moshavim* had already begun to desert Mapai/ILP in the 1960s.

The proportion of working-class and thus also Oriental voters is especially high among the supporters of Herut/Gahal/Likud. Here, too, the sociological polarization between the Euro-American leadership and the voters is the greatest, although it must be noted that in the meantime about half the membership of the Herut Central Committee comes from Oriental backgrounds.

The majority of Sabras vote Likud, the proportion reaching 75% among Sabras of Oriental heritage in 1981. PAI largely represents Orthodox *kibbutzim* and *moshavim* as well as strictly religious industrial workers. Increasing numbers of the latter have, however, recently begun to prefer AI. (For further data and sources see Wolffsohn, 1983a: ch. 27.)

Tables 18 and 19 show socio-economic characteristics of the voters of the various parties for the years 1973, 1977 and 1981.

In 1981 Shelli, the Citizens' Rights Movement, Shinui and Tehiya were especially popular among Israelis under the age of 30, these parties receiving roughly half of their votes from this age group. The ages of the Likud voters were more widely distributed but the tendency was on the whole also towards the younger age groups. The oldest voters overall were those of the Maarah, whereas the NRP showed the greatest age spectrum. Upper income groups preferred Shinui, Tehiya, CRM, Shelli and the Maarah in 1981. 'The' party of the hawks, Tehiya, was most strongly supported by Sabras of Euro-American backgrounds, as were Shelli, CRM and Shinui (data from Levy and Guttman, 1981: table 4). In 1981 Tami did best in the new development towns as well as in those urban areas populated largely by Oriental Jews (Elections, 1981: tables 4, 5 and 18). The majority of the non-religious were to be found among Shelli, CRM and Shinui voters in 1981 (Levy and Gutmann, loc. cit.).

As in 1973 and 1977, the Likud attracted more religiously oriented voters than the Labour Alignment. In view of the traditional affinity of religious voters for Herut/Gahal/Likud (Diskin, 1980a), this result comes as no surprise. The both secular and religious composition of the hawkish Tehiya is reflected by its electorate as well. As in many other ways, the Democratic Movement for Change proved to be middle-of-the-road in 1977.

The data in Table 19 must be interpreted with care, as the voter fluctuation between January and late June 1981 was extraordinarily high and this particular poll was conducted in February and March 1981. On the other hand, only people who knew (or pretended to know) how they were going to vote were interviewed.

The results of the 1984 elections can be summed up as follows: the Alignment and such allies as Shinui and the Citizens' Rights Movement, as well as Ezer Weizman's Yahad, were preferred mostly by Israelis of Euro-American backgrounds (first and later generations), the more well-to-do and better educated, by older voters (exception: Shinui and CRM, whose voters were younger) and less religious citizens (cf. A/I/3/f).

According to the Israel Institute for Public Opinion Research poll conducted by Dr Abraham Diskin (professor of political science at Hebrew University, Jerusalem), 55% of all Maarah voters had fathers who were immigrants from Euro-American countries, 29% had fathers who came from Africa or Asia and 16% had fathers born in Israel (poll taken from 6 to 8 July 1984, and kindly supplied to the author by Dr Diskin). A comparison of the loyalists among the various age cohorts of the 1984 Alignment voters yields a

Table 18   Socio-Economic Data on 1973 and 1977 Voters (voters of the party = 100%)

	Maarah		Likud		NRP		AI/PAI		CRM		Moked/IL /Shelli		DMC	
	73	77	73	77	73	77	73	77	73	77	73	77	73	77
Education														
Up to 4 years	3	3	6	6	9	7	4	3	1	—	1	—		1
5–10 years	36	35	35	39	30	27	27	27	12	10	12	13	14	14
11–12 years	33	35	32	34	28	28	25	24	29	30	29	29	38	32
13 years or more	38	27	27	21	33	38	44	46	58	60	58	58	50	53
Income														
Up to 3,999 IL	17	19	18	20	20	17	30	32	7	14	12	8	9	10
4,000–7,999	41	42	45	45	47	42	46	44	34	34	33	32	38	30
More than 8,000	42	39	37	35	33	39	24	24	59	52	55	60	53	60
Age														
20–29	18	18	28	37	30	28	24	31	38	47	52	47	10	29
30–39	19	13	27	21	20	19	23	21	28	20	15	26	13	22
40–49	18	17	19	16	17	13	17	17	15	17		10	29	19
Over 50	45	52	26	26	43	40	36	31	19	16	21	17	57	40
Occupation														
White-collar worker	51	46	51	48	52	50	44	46	68	53	61	55	45	61
Self-employed	8	7	14	12	7	8	11	8	9	9	14	13	20	11
Housewife	24	21	24	26	25	20	30	30	10	25	6	9	12	11
Other	17	27	11	14	16	22	15	16	13	13	19	23	22	27

Origin of Interviewee and Father													
Israel, Israel	5	5	8	8	6	6	13	12	12	8	13	9	3	7
Israel, Oriental	8	6	16	19	6	8	6	8	8	8	5	11	2	5
Israel, Euro-American	17	17	19	15	17	23	24	25	37	43	45	39	14	36
Oriental, Oriental	19	15	28	29	26	18	14	15	5	6	2	11	5	6
Euro-Am., Euro-Am.,	51	57	29	29	45	45	43	40	38	35	35	30	76	46
In Israel since														
Zabarim	31	27	44	43	28	38	42	45	57	57	63	57	20	47
Before 1948	23	28	17	15	25	23	18	17	15	11	15	9	36	19
1948 and after	46	45	39	42	47	39	40	38	28	32	22	34	33	34
Religious Observance														
Very traditional	5	4	11	10	60	62	91	89	3		3	2	3	2
Traditional	12	10	18	19	32	29	9	9	7	1	6	7	6	7
Somewhat traditional	48	47	48	48	7	8	2		33	39	39	31	37	42
Not traditional	35	39	23	23	1	1	—	—	60	57	68	67	54	49

Source: Levy and Gutmann, 1979a: 33 ff.

Table 19   Socio-Economic Data on 1981 Voters (voters of the party = 100%)

	Tehiya	Likud	Labour	NRP	Shinui	CRM	Shelli
Sex							
Men	66	49	48	44	58	29	47
Women	34	51	52	56	42	71	53
Total (%)	100	100	100	100	100	100	100
Education							
No education	—	3	1	4	—	—	1
4 years	—	3	2	2	2	—	—
5–8 years	8	18	18	22	4	—	7
9–10 years	6	17	14	12	9	11	4
11 years	6	9	7	5	7	2	9
12 years	34	28	28	19	21	25	28
13+ (no academic degree)	21	12	16	19	32	32	20
University degree	25	9	13	17	26	30	30
Total (%)	100	100	100	100	100	100	100
Age							
20–24	29	20	13	12	12	16	30
25–29	13	17	13	13	26	30	27
30–34	15	13	12	12	19	18	11
35–39	3	7	8	7	9	16	11
40–44	8	8	9	10	9	4	4
45–49	10	7	8	10	9	2	4
50–54	8	8	8	11	2	4	4
55–64	9	9	15	13	5	9	3
65+	5	11	15	12	9	2	4
Total (%)	100	100	100	100	100	100	100
Monthly Income							
Under 7,000 IL*	6	5	6	6	2	6	11
7,001–15,000	1	7	6	8	2	6	6
15,001–20,000	3	8	8	10	2	2	13
20,001–25,000	9	14	10	11	13	12	8
25,001–30,000	14	13	13	11	4	8	5
30,001–35,000	10	13	10	13	12	10	8
35,001–40,000	10	10	10	8	13	14	13
40,001–50,000	11	10	12	12	12	14	11
50,001+	36	20	26	21	40	28	24
Total (%)	100	100	100	100	100	100	100
Religious Observance							
Very strict	24	14	5	66	—	—	7

Strict	15	23	13	27	5	2	9
Somewhat strict	40	41	45	7	44	34	26
Not strict	21	22	37	—	51	64	59
Total (%)	100	100	100	100	100	100	100

*About $90.

Source: Levy and Gutmann, 1981: table 4; poll taken in Feb./Mar. 1981.

revealing view of their age structure. Some 14% of those aged 18 to 29 who had cast their vote for this list in 1981 intended to do so again on 23 July 1984. The number of loyalists in the age bracket from 30 to 49 was 54%, and 32% among voters over 50. Some 54% of the Maarah loyalists in 1984 had received post-secondary education, 26% had completed a course of secondary education and 30% had not done so (Diskin poll, Israel Institute for Public Opinion Research, 20 June 1984).

Likud was the choice of Oriental Jews, many of them belonging to the lower economic strata with less formal education and a stronger religious orientation than Alignment voters. As to the age factor, the Likud seems to have performed almost equally well in most of the age cohorts (see Y. Galnoor, *Haaretz*, 2 September 1984).

Diskin's poll (loc. cit.) found that Likud loyalists were once again much younger than Maarah loyalists. Of the Likud loyalists, 34% belonged to the 18 to 29 age cohort, 47% to the group between 30 and 49 and only 19% were over the age of 50. The education of the Likud loyalists was clearly inferior in comparison with that of the Alignment supporters of 1981 and 1984. Only 13% had received post-secondary education, 36% had completed secondary school and 51% had 'less than complete secondary education'. In view of these facts it cannot come as a surprise that 61% of all those who claimed in early July 1984, that they would vote Likud had an Afro-Asian father, only 22% an Euro-American and 17% a Sabra father.

Tehiya could count upon Oriental Jews to about the same extent as on Ashkenasi Israelis. Actually, the support for Tehiya was slightly less strong among Oriental Israelis. It also attracted younger citizens, and both religious and secular voters.

The religious parties were predominantly Oriental, with the notable exception of the National Religious Party, which received more or less balanced support. Whereas the NRP and Shass got most of their votes from older Jews, Agudat Israel, Marasha and Rabbi Kahane's Kach were supported disproportionately by younger voters (see H. and R. Smith, *Jerusalem Post*, 3 August 1984; Y. Galnoor, *Haaretz*, 2 September 1984; S. Weiss, *Haaretz*, 1, 2 and 5 August 1984).

Arab voters were more pluralistic in 1984 than ever before. The Progressive List for Peace presented a serious challenge to the Communists.

(h) RURAL AND URBAN STRUCTURES

Among the socialist and Zionist parties of the left, including HPM, PAI and the IL, the *halutzic* ideal, the spirit of the agricultural pioneer, continues to be revered. With regard to HHZ/Mapam and AH, it can even be said that the *kibbutz* existed before the party. Because of their ideological and political importance, the *kibbutzim*, and to a lesser extent the *moshavim*, have been overrepresented in the leadership circles of the Labour parties when their influence is compared with their strength as a percentage of the total vote. Sections B/VIII/4 and 5 attempt to convey an impression of the *halutzic* activities of the parties within the framework of their *kibbutzim* or *moshavim* organizations. Not even Herut was willing to do without *moshavim* of its own.

The *moshavim*, and especially the *kibbutzim*, still enjoy considerable public prestige, although this is to be seen more among Israelis of Euro-American heritage than others. The strong political appeal of the settlement activists in the West Bank areas may, among other things, be based on their ability to tie in their methods with the Zionist ideal of the *halutziut*.

The membership and the voters of the General Zionists, Gahal/Likud and the left-leaning and middle-class protest parties (Avnery, for example) as well as of the larger part of the religious parties have remained predominantly 'urban'. The NRP, however, once enjoyed the support of Hapoel Hamisrahi agricultural settlements (for data see sections B/VIII/4 and 5).

(i) THE SIZE OF THE PARTIES

Figure 48 illustrates the tendency towards concentration in Israel's party system, a trend which became particularly pronounced in the 1981 elections to the Tenth Knesset.

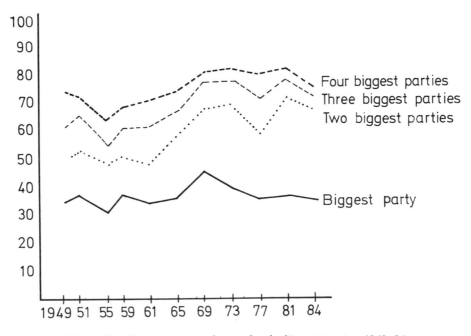

Figure 30   Concentrations of votes for the biggest parties, 1949–84.

In 1984 the trend was reversed. The marginal or more 'purist' voters of the great 'catch-all' parties (Otto Kirchheimer) were obviously dissatisfied with what they perceived as all too vague positions on clear-cut problems such as the occupied territories, settlements, the economy, relations with the Arabs, religious issues or Lebanon. They therefore turned either to the parties to the right of the Likud (especially to Tehiya) or to the parties left of (i.e. more 'purist' than) the Alignment, especially to Shinui and the CRM.

(j) THE LEGITIMACY OF THE PARTIES

The legitimacy of the parties, that is their fundamental, subjective acceptance on the part of the citizenry, is hardly a measurable quantity. But if the increasing numbers of protest groups and grass-roots citizen's initiatives can be taken as an indicator of legitimacy problems among the traditional parties, it can be concluded that dissent began to develop on a larger scale after the Six Day War, almost certainly in connection with the necessity which then arose to rethink certain fundamental concepts concerning the character of the Jewish state (Isaac, 1976).

Truly serious problems of legitimacy arose following the Yom Kippur War of 1973 with the increasing activities of an extra-parliamentary opposition. Most important among these extra-parliamentary groups are the Gush Emunim settlement activists (who maintain personal and organizational connections with parties in the Knesset, particularly the NRP, Tehiya and Mazad) and their opponents grouped in the Peace Now movement. (For further details and literature see Weisbrod, 1981; Yishai, 1981; Wolffsohn, 1983a: ch. 32; Sprinzak, 1981; Schall, 1979.)

The recovery of the marginal parties in 1984 may also signal a certain disillusionment with the traditional big parties. Nevertheless, neither Tehiya on the right, nor Shinui, nor the Citizens' Rights Movement on the 'left', are anti-system parties challenging the legitimacy of Zionism. The democratic legitimacy of Zionism has recently been challenged, however, by extra-parliamentary Jewish terrorists (a number of whom were convicted in 1984) and by Rabbi Kahane's Kach (see also A/II/5/a and the Conclusion of this volume). Zionist legitimacy is also called into question by the Communists as well as by the Arab-Jewish Progressive List for Peace. (For an indication of the legitimacy of the political system as a whole see section B/VI/1/f.)

FURTHER READING

GENERAL

See the titles for 'comprehensive works' on page 277 and also the most informative survey of parties and politics: Rael J. Isaac, *Party and Politics in Israel. Three Visions of a Jewish State* (London and New York: Longman, 1981), analysing the three main political camps.

See also the historical books listed on page 56 as well as Horowitz and Lissak, 1978 for the Yishuv period.

SPECIFIC PARTIES

On Mapai, Peter Y. Medding, *Mapai in Israel* (Cambridge: Cambridge University Press, 1972).

On Mapai's forerunner, Yonathan Shapiro, *The Formative Years of the Israeli Labour Party. The Organization of Power 1919–1930* (London: Sage, 1976).

On the Israel Labour Party, Myron J. Aronoff, *Power and Ritual in the Israel Labour Party* (Assen and Amsterdam: Van Gorcum, 1977).

On the Communist parties, Alain Greilsammer, *Les Communistes israeliens* (Paris: Presses de la Fondation Nationale des Sciences Politiques, 1978).

On the parties of the left in general, Peretz Merhav, *The Israeli Left: History, Problems, Documents* (Cranbury, NJ: A. S. Barnes, 1980).

On the Revisionist Movement and Herut, Nachum Orland, *Die Cherut* (Munich: Tuduv, 1983); Joseph Schechtman and Y. Benari, *History of the Revisionist Movement* (Tel-Aviv: Hadar, 1970).

On the religious parties, Gary S. Schiff, *Tradition and Politics: The Religious Parties in Israel* (Detroit, Mich.: Wayne State University Press, 1977); Sam N. Lehman-Wilzig and Bernard Susser (eds.), *Public Life in Israel and the Diaspora* (Ramak-Gan: Bar Ilan University Press, 1981), with several articles on these parties.

See also the books mentioned in 'Elections' on page 58.

On the marginal parties and extra-parliamentary groups, David J. Schnall, *Radical Dissent in Contemporary Israeli Politics. Cracks in the Wall* (New York: Praeger, 1979); Rael Jean Isaac, *Israel Divided. Ideological Politics in the Jewish State* (Baltimore, Md.: Johns Hopkins University Press, 1976); on the 'Land of Israel' and 'Peace Movement' since the Six Day War.

III

The Military

(a) HISTORICAL AND POLITICAL ASPECTS

From the very beginning of the Yishuv, military affairs were subject to the primacy of party politics. In 1909 Poale Zion founded Hashomer ('The Watchman', dissolved on 20 July 1920). Following the bloody clashes between Jews and Arabs in April 1920 and May 1921, all the major Labour parties, under the leadership of the Histadrut, participated in the founding of a successor organization of 15 June 1921. It was given the name Hagana ('Defence').

In 1931, two years after the massacres of Jewish residents in Hebron, the first 'hawks' began to break away from Hagana because they had not been able to press through their demands for a more activist policy of retaliation. The final break took place in 1937 over the issue of how to deal with events arising in connection with the Arab Revolt, which had erupted in 1936. At this time the General Zionists and Misrahi began to cooperate with Hagana, the leadership of which was expanded to include non-socialists.

On 31 May 1948 Hagana was declared Israel's official army and was given a new name: Zahal, which is translated as Israel Defence Forces (IDF). In order to make Zahal truly the army of the entire nation, two larger party-controlled military forces had to be dissolved: the leftist Palmach of Mapam and the rightist Ezel.

In the autumn of 1947 Hagana included some 42,000 members, Palmach 3,000, Ezel 2,000 and Lehi 400 (Brecher, 1972: 74).

Under extreme pressure from Ben-Gurion and Palmach, intensified in the wake of the *Altalena* incident, Ezel acquiesced to its integration into Zahal in June of 1948. The crew of the *Altalena*, a ship laden with weapons and ammunition intended for Ezel, refused orders to turn its cargo over to Zahal; the ship was subsequently fired upon and sunk with loss of life just off Tel-Aviv. In order to avoid further bloodshed, Ezel – more precisely: its commander, Menachem Begin – yielded. Lehi was outlawed as a military organization following the 17 September 1948 assassination of the UN emissary Count Bernadotte. Lehi was generally considered to have been responsible for this act. On Ben-Gurion's orders Palmach was formally absorbed into Zahal on 7 November 1948.

Long after the integration of the four previous Jewish military organizations into a single army, in fact until well into the 1960s, former Hagana members continued to dominate the upper ranks of the IDF officer's corps, whereas former Palmach and Ezel fighters experienced extraordinary difficulties (see Peri, 1973: 56, and 1983: chs. 3 and 4; Wolffsohn, 1983a: 509 f.). Although the originally independent Palmach brigades later constituted the elite units of Hagana, the top positions in the IDF remained closed to 'Palmachnikim' for a long time. Yitzhak Rabin, Israel's chief of staff from 1964 to 1967, was the first former Palmach officer to achieve this rank. Chaim Bar-Lev (1968/72) was the second, David Elazar (1972/3) the third and Rafael Eitan (1978/83) the fourth (for further details see Wolffsohn, 1983a: 509 f.). On the other hand, it must also be noted that former Ezel members constituted one of the main manpower reserves of Herut. Until the Seventh Knesset around three-quarters of Herut's Knesset deputies were Ezel veterans (Lichtenstein, 1974: 20).

(b) POLITICAL INVOLVEMENT

For a considerable period of time, the chiefs of staff practised a policy of political non-involvement. There were, however, some exceptions to this rule. In 1977/8 Chief of Staff Mordechai Gur protested repeatedly that Egypt's president was not to be trusted and became one of the sharpest critics of the Camp David Agreement. His successor, Raphael Eitan, was even less restrained in his political pronouncements, issuing frequent calls for harsh measures against the Palestinians, whom he claimed understood only the language of force. Under Eitan's command the army became, according to Peri (1983: 268 ff.), at least in part an 'ally of Gush Emunim', i.e. of the leading group of settlement activists. In a way, the network of Jewish terrorists uncovered and convicted in 1984 demonstrated the partial truth of Peri's argument.

This development was a sign of the dramatic changes that had taken place among Israel's highest ranking officers, who until into the 1970s had tended to articulate moderate views on territorial and political questions (polls in

Peri, 1973: 93 ff. and 1974: 145 f.). By 1983, however, it no longer came as a surprise when Eitan, following the completion of his tour of duty as chief of staff, proceeded to found the hawkish Zomet movement, which then joined forces with Tehiya in 1984 and received five seats in that year's Knesset elections. It is noteworthy that Tehiya–Zomet, as well as Rabbi Kahane's Kach, were disproportionately successful among soldiers in the 1984 elections (Y. Galnov, *Haaretz*, 2 September 1984; for 1977 see Diskin and Wolffsohn, 1977: 814). This, of course, has to do with the previously described trend towards the political right, a trend stronger among younger Israelis than among their elders. This shift first favoured Gahal/Likud, then, more recently, Tehiya–Zomet and Kach.

Since the appointment of Moshe Dayan to the post of defence minister in 1967, the phenomenon of 'officers in grey suits' (in ministerial positions) has become increasingly prevalent. Ezer Weizman, minister of defence from 1977 to 1980, and Ariel Sharon, who held that post from 1981 to 1983, are but two outstanding recent examples. Peri (1983: 283 ff.) does not rule out the danger of a 'military democracy' with the IDF furnishing the nation's political leaders. It must, however, be taken into consideration that for a long time Zahal was, especially for Sabras, the only alternative channel of upward political mobility outside the party machines dominated by the party bosses (see Wolffsohn, 1983a: ch. 13, for data).

Criticism aside, it must be noted that the political rise of the officers since 1967 has taken place within rather than outside, or in avoidance of, the democratically elected institutions of the country.

That these democratically elected institutions were capable of maintaining civilian control over the military was evidenced in 1982/3 when the Kahan Commission investigated the role of the military and the politicians in the Beirut massacre and subsequently called both to a public accounting. Defence Minister Sharon as well as high-ranking officers were forced to resign. Chief of Staff Eitan was censured and was not reappointed following the expiration of his tour of duty.

Details concerning Israel's military expenditures may be found in section C/XV/3.

(c) ZAHAL'S NON-MILITARY DUTIES

Among the most significant of the IDF's non-military assignments is to serve as an agent promoting equal opportunity for disadvantaged groups, especially for Oriental immigrants, but also for new immigrants in general, all of whom receive a basic education as well as occupational training during their term of service, if these are lacking.

(d) COMPULSORY MILITARY SERVICE

Men between the ages of 18 and 29, as well as unmarried women between 18 and 26, are liable for military service.

The changes which have been made in the length of compulsory service are shown in Table 20.

Since the time of Israel's most striking military victory, the 1967 Six Day War, the length of compulsory service has continuously increased.

Those exempt from military service include Orthodox religious Jews such

Table 20 Changes in the Length of Compulsory Military Service, 1949–75

| Year | Length of compulsory service in months | |
	Men	Women
1949	24	12
1950	24	24
1952	30	24
1963	26	20
1966	30	20
1968	36	20
1975	36	24

as *yeshivot* students and Orthodox women. Paradoxically, it became easier for the latter groups to secure exemptions from military service under the more hawkish Likud-led coalition (1977/84), when the government was dependent upon the parliamentary support of the Orthodox parties.

As a rule, women are assigned to non-combat units and often fill clerical positions.

The Druze population opted for compulsory military service in the late 1950s. There are also some Bedouin volunteers, and in late 1984 it was decided to open Zahal's ranks for about two hundred volunteers from 'Arab villages' (A. Maatzur, *Haaretz*, 18 December 1984).

(e) RESERVES

The IDF relies heavily on its reserve system. Following compulsory service, men remain in the reserves until the age of 54, women until the age of 38. Reservists are called up for an average of thirty days every year, and not uncommonly for longer periods. This generates an enormous burden, not only for the individual, but also for the economy as a whole.

Of the 174,000 members of Zahal in 1981/2, 120,300 were conscripts. Within 24 hours the IDF can mobilize a manpower potential totalling 500,000 (*Middle East Contemporary Survey*, vol. VI: 662; further information there or in *Military Balance*, published by the Institute for Strategic and International Studies, London).

(f) CONSCIENTIOUS OBJECTION

Statistics on the numbers of conscientious objectors are kept secret, but due to the high prestige of the military, which can in fact be described as a 'people's army', the few cases which have become public knowledge may be assumed to be virtually equivalent to the total. Zeev Schiff and Eitan Haber, two of the most reliable military commentators in Israel, speak of several dozen such cases (Schiff and Haber, 1976: 511).

However, the number of soldiers who have refused to serve in the occupied territories or in Lebanon has risen dramatically in the last several years.

From the beginning of the War in Lebanon (6 June 1982) until April 1985 a total of 140 Israeli soldiers (mainly reservists) received prison sentences of up to 35 days for refusing to serve in the West Bank region or in the 'North Bank' (i.e. Lebanon; *SZ*, 12 April 1985). That Zahal is truly a 'people's army' is once again demonstrated by this spillover of the political polarization of Israeli society into the military.

FURTHER READING

Yoram Peri, *Between Battles and Ballots. Israeli Military in Politics* (Cambridge: Cambridge University Press, 1983).

Amos Perlmutter, *Politics and the Military in Israel, 1967–1977* (London: Frank Cass, 1978); and his first volume, *The Military and Politics in Israel. Nation-Building and Role Expansion*, 2nd ed. (London: Frank Cass, 1977); narrative.

Edward Luttwak and Dan Horowitz, *The Israeli Army* (New York: Harper & Row, 1975).

See also Nathan Yanai, *Party Leadership in Israel. Maintenance and Change* (Ramat-Gan: Turtledove, 1981), ch. 12.

IV

The Media

(a) NEWSPAPERS

The 'People of the Book' was, during the Yishuv period, a people of the newspaper as well, and the readership of party-affiliated newspapers was wide. Since independence, the party newspaper has gone into decline as a result of the decreasing role of ideology in Israeli society. (For further details see Wolffsohn, 1983a: ch. 48; Galnoor, 1982: 226 ff.)

Yediot Aharonot (with a weekend circulation of approx. 360,000) and *Maariv* (approx. 135,000), both independent but politically right of centre, are the two largest daily newspapers in Israel, followed by the liberal, somewhat left of centre *Haaretz* with a weekend circulation of approx. 65,000, the Histadrut-owned *Davar* with approx. 30,000 and the *Jerusalem Post* with approx. 20,000. The weekday circulation of *Yediot Aharonot* averages 180,000, that of *Maariv* some 90,000, of *Haaretz* 50,000, *Davar* 30,000 and the *Jerusalem Post* 20,000 (estimates based on information provided by Israeli journalists; further details in Wolffsohn, 1983a: 617).

The English-language *Jerusalem Post* is not directly party-affiliated, but does maintain close ties with the Labour Party and is partly owned (26%) by the Histadrut. *Al-Hamishmar* is the Mapam newspaper; *Hamodia*, the PAI party organ; and *Shearim* belongs to AI. *Hazofeh* is the NRP party newspaper.

Haaretz is the paper of the educated elite. (For data on newspaper readership see Wolffsohn, 1983a: 618 f.)

Rakah (NCL) publishes the most widely read Arab daily, *Al-Etihad*. The Histadrut also publishes a daily in Arabic, *Al-Anva*. The various newspapers which appear in East Jerusalem have gained a following among Israeli Arabs. These include the leftist *Al-Fagr*, which supports the PLO, *Al-Shaab*, which also supports the PLO but is non-socialist, and the generally pro-Jordanian *Al-Kuds* (details in Wolffsohn, 1983a: 625 f.).

Table 21   Israel's Independent Daily Newpapers

Newspaper	Political Tendency	Weekend Circulation (1985)	Weekday Circulation (1985)
Maariv	Right of centre	135,000	90,000
Jediot Aharonot	Right of centre	360,000	180,000
Haaretz	Left of centre	65,000	50,000
Jerusalem Post	Labour bloc	20,000	30,000
Davar	Histadrut/ILP	30,000	30,000

Source: A. Schweitzer, *Haaretz*

Table 22   Israel's Party-Affiliated Newspapers

Newspaper	Party
Davar	Histadrut/ILP
Al-Hamishmar	Mapam
Hazofeh	NRP
Shearim	AI
Hamodia	PAI
Al-Etihad (Arabic)	NCL

(b) RADIO AND TELEVISION

The radio and television networks in Israel are publicly owned and operated institutions. During the epoch of Mapai/ILP dominance as well as since 1977, especially once the Likud began to really 'take charge' in 1981, a number of undisguised attempts at politicizing these media have been made (see Wolffsohn, 1983a: 622 ff.). Only since 1969 has Israel operated a television network of its own. The IDF military network is extremely popular and has become increasingly controversial in its political views since 1977.

(c) QUALITY OF REPORTING

Those newspapers with the widest and largest circulation such as *Maariv* and *Yediot Aharonot* are, in comparison with the sensationalist mass circulation boulevard press of many European countries, surprisingly factual and informative. The level of the journalism in these dailies is comparable to that of the more reputable regional and national papers in Europe. *Haaretz* is Israel's best paper in terms of breadth of coverage and balance.

(d) FOREIGN-LANGUAGE NEWSPAPERS

Because it is so frequently quoted by foreign correspondents, the *Jerusalem Post* is certainly the best-known of Israel's foreign-language newspapers, but it is only one of many. In Israel it is possible to find a newspaper published in nearly every major language of the world, if not a daily, then often a weekly paper.

(e) REPORTING ON MILITARY AFFAIRS

The Israeli media exercise a kind of self-imposed censorship in their reporting on military affairs. This is institutionalized in the 'Publishers' Committee', the name given to the gatherings of the chief editors of the largest newspapers and the country's leading journalists with representatives of the military and the government in order to exchange confidential information. (For a detailed treatment, see S. Rosenfeld in *Jerusalem Quarterly*, no. 25: 100 ff.) This arrangement functioned well as long as a basic consensus on matters of military policy obtained. Since the War in Lebanon (1982/3), however, relations between the military and the press have become more strained.

FURTHER READING

Yitzhak Galnoor, *Steering the Polity. Communications and Politics in Israel* (Beverly Hills, Calif., and London: Sage, 1982).

Dina Goren, *Secrecy and the Right to Know* (Ramat-Gan: Turtledove, 1979).

Yariv Ben-Eliezer, 'Television in Israel', PhD thesis, New York University, 1978.

G. Kressel, *A Guide to the Hebrew Press* (Zug, Switzerland: Interdocumentation Company, 1977); a general survey.

Avraham Wolfenson, 'Party newspapers in the political process', PhD dissertation, Hebrew University, Jerusalem, 1979.

V
Foreign Policy

1 *RELATIONS WITH THE UNITED STATES OF AMERICA*

The support of the USA in Israel's struggle for independence was, beyond a doubt, a decisive factor on the political and diplomatic fronts, but not militarily, as the weapons which saved Israel during the 1948/9 War of Independence were supplied not by America but by the Soviet Union via Czechoslovakia. Until well into the 1960s in fact, the US role as a weapons supplier for Israel was virtually negligible. It was not until after the 1967 Six Day War – to be exact, after President de Gaulle's imposition of an embargo on the delivery of French arms to Israel – that an intense partnership developed between the United States and Israel in matters of security.

Large-scale American economic support for Israel also developed at a much later date than is generally assumed. Although US economic aid had been flowing to Israel for many years previously, the 1973 Yom Kippur War marked a quantum leap in the level of capital imports (as well as transfer payments in general) to Israel originating with the US government.

Until into the late 1950s, in its Cold War era search for allies in the Middle East, the Eisenhower administration tended to regard Israel more as a strategic liability than an asset. The very fact of Israel's existence made it difficult to construct a system of strategic alliances with the West in this region.

The Sinai Campaign in October and November of 1956 marked a period of considerable tension between Israel and the United States. Together with British and French troops, the Israeli army had defeated the Egyptians. Israeli troops had conquered the Sinai peninsula and reached the Suez Canal. Only after the application of massive pressure by the United States was Israel persuaded to withdraw its forces from the occupied areas in March 1957. Among other measures, the Eisenhower administration had requested the Federal Republic of Germany temporarily to suspend its reparation payments to Israel. This proposal, however, met with scant favour on the part of West German Chancellor Konrad Adenauer.

Even in the 1960s the United States preferred to deal with Israel through intermediaries in certain areas. The secretly arranged deliveries of West German arms to the Jewish state are a good example. This was one way for the USA to keep Israel supplied with weapons and yet to avoid alienating the Arab states. Only after news of these arms deals was publicized in late October 1964 and the Israelis insisted that the deliveries continue did the USA step into the breach in order to spare the Federal Republic of Germany even more political embarrassment.

On the eve of the Six Day War the United States also hesitated in its support. In connection with Israel's withdrawal from the Sinai in 1957 it had promised Israel it would guarantee free passage through the Straits of Tiran in the future, but when Egypt's President Nasser ordered his artillery to close this vital sea-lane ten years later the USA chose not to act. Once war broke out, the United States was not prepared to accept a total military victory on the part of Israel, nor was it willing to tolerate the incorporation of the territories conquered during the Six Day War. Only the idea of minor border adjustments met with a warmer response from Washington.

One factor, however, had changed by 1968: the United States was now Israel's most important source of arms.

In the 1969/70 War of Attrition along the Suez Canal both the United States and the Soviet Union sought to prevent an Israeli military 'victory'. While the Egyptians, in direct contravention of the truce agreement of August 1970, continued to push their air defence lines forward to the Suez Canal, in particular by erecting numerous new SAM missile batteries, Israel was pressured into holding back.

During the October 1973 Yom Kippur War the United States conducted an extensive airlift to supply Israel with vital military supplies. This massive resupply by air was undertaken because, during the first days of the fighting, it seemed that Israel's very existence was at stake, and the prospect of Israel's being overrun could not and would not be tolerated by any US administration. Later, when the tables were turned and it appeared that Israel would win an overwhelming victory, American diplomacy under Nixon and Kissinger sought to prevent Israel from achieving 'total victory' over Egypt and Syria.

Following the Yom Kippur War, Secretary of State Henry Kissinger began his odyssey of 'shuttle diplomacy', negotiating the first Sinai disengagement agreement between Israel and Egypt in January of 1974 and arriving at an Israeli–Syrian disengagement agreement for the Golan Heights in May. The real strength of the United States in Middle East diplomacy now became manifest. In contrast to the Soviet Union, the USA possessed open channels of communication to both Arab governments and Israel and began to play an indispensable role in the negotiation and execution of agreements. Kissinger's shuttle diplomacy achieved a second Sinai disengagement agreement between Israel and Egypt in September 1975. At the same time, the United States pledged not to negotiate (officially) with the PLO until the Palestinian organization was prepared to recognize Israel's right to exist.

The initiative undertaken by Egypt's President Sadat in opening the Egyptian–Israeli peace dialogue was undertaken without the foreknowledge or assistance of the United States, but its role soon became essential in the difficult negotiation process. Not until the active participation of the Carter administration was the groundwork laid for the Camp David Agreements (17 September 1978), in which the territorial issues between Israel and Egypt were solved and the framework was sketched for continuing negotiations towards an (intermediate) solution with regard to the West Bank and the Gaza Strip. American support and involvement also proved indispensable on the road to the peace treaty between Egypt and Israel of 26 March 1979.

The Carter administration vehemently criticized the Begin government's settlements policy but was not able to prevent the intensified schedule of new settlement construction. Despite Israel's enormous military and economic dependency on the United States, the ability of the USA to 'steer' the Jewish state proved limited indeed, as President Reagan was also to experience. If even informed at all, he was unable to prevent the destruction of the Iraqi nuclear reactor near Baghdad by Israeli air force planes on 6 June 1981. Events in Lebanon from the beginning of 'Operation Peace for Galilee' were initiated and directed primarily by Israel; the role of the United States, insofar as it played any active part at all, was limited to damage control. The Reagan Plan of September 1982, which foresaw a key role to be played by Jordan and in the final analysis revealed the American president's opposition to the incorporation of the West Bank and Gaza into the Jewish state, was torpedoed by the Israeli government. A modified revival of the Reagan Plan seemed possible in mid-1985, when Jordan indicated its willingness to serve as a bridge to moderate Palestinians. Israel's national unity cabinet, however, was split over this issue.

The difficulties the USA has experienced in influencing Israel can be easily explained in structural terms. First of all, Israel has traditionally been able to rely on solid support in Congress, particularly in the House of Representatives. This is traceable to the high degree of political organization and activity among the American Jewish community. Second, there is the widespread conviction, especially on Capitol Hill and in the Pentagon, that Israel represents America's sole reliable long-term ally in the Middle East. Although not uncritical of Israel with regard to specific issues, the American public shares the general view of Israel as a 'strategic asset'. Third, the American military establishment has profited from Israel's experience in deploying American weapons in battle and also from the Soviet hardware Israel has captured as a result of its military victories and passed on to the USA. There is little likelihood that any of these structural advantages which Israel enjoys in the United States will change in the foreseeable future.

One reservation must be appended: the support of the American Jewish community has crumbled somewhat since 1977. The reasons for this development are partially related to events and personalities and are partly structural in nature. The Sadat initiative succeeded in winning a significant degree of sympathy among American Jews, whereas the behaviour of the Begin government was not infrequently described as obstinate. In addition, the policy practised by Israel with regard to settlements in the occupied territories since 1977 met with intense criticism from American Jewish organizations and the sharp differences of opinion within Israel over the War in Lebanon also spilled over into the American Jewish community, which became just as divided over this war as Israeli society itself.

These developments served to accelerate a structural process which set in during the 1970s and which can be characterized as a growing independence on the part of the Jewish Diaspora, that is, of those Jews living outside Israel. Following the Holocaust and the founding of the State of Israel, the claim of the Jewish state to the leadership of world Jewry was largely unquestioned. This had not been the case historically, as Zionists had previously formed a distinct minority among the Jews of the world. Once the existence of Israel became an accepted fact of life and its political behaviour began to draw criticism from within the Jewish community, the process of the 're-emancipation of the Diaspora' began.

Another important inner-Israeli structural factor here may be the increasing 'Orientalization' of Israel's society, which over the long term will lead to some degree of alienation between the more and more Oriental population of Israel on the one hand and the non-Oriental Ashkenasi Jews of the United States and Western Jews all over the world on the other. This, too, will contribute to the 're-emancipation of the Diaspora', in the United States and elsewhere.

2   RELATIONS WITH THE UNION OF SOVIET SOCIALIST REPUBLICS

The Soviet Union's agreement to the plan for the division of Palestine in late 1947 and thus to the foundation of a Jewish state came as a surprise to the international community and most especially to Zionist politicians. Until that time relations between Zionism and Soviet communism had been characterized by a pronounced enmity, which was due to more than just the large numbers of Jews who had been counted among Stalin's opposition in the USSR. The root causes are closely connected to internal structural problems of the Soviet Union.

First, numerous Russian Jews were to be found among the veterans of the Russian socialist movement and later of the Communist Party. Not infrequently, the loyalties of these Jewish Soviet citizens were divided between communist internationalism and Jewish nationalism. In other words, they proved less than totally immune to the 'virus' of Zionism. In any case, there were forces favouring a greater autonomy for the Jews of the Soviet Union and this, even if presupposing the best of intentions, confronted the Soviet leadership with a problem inherent in the structure of the Soviet multi-national state. If the Jews had been granted a greater degree of autonomy, that is, of self-government in communal affairs, this would have set off a virtual avalanche of similar demands on the part of other nationalities and ethnic groups in the Soviet Union. This, in turn, would have eventually undermined the position of the central government in Moscow and, most especially, the authority of the Communist Party.

The policy of the Soviet Union towards Israel is therefore to be seen in the context of the internal problems with the nationalities of the USSR, a condition which, of course, also applies to the issue of emigration permits for Russian Jews. If all Soviet Jews were to be permitted to leave the country at will, this would likely prompt a flood of applications on the part of other groups, the Volga Germans, for one example. From the Soviet viewpoint it was better policy to let the most irritating activists leave in order to achieve greater peace and quiet on the domestic front. The Soviet leadership has responded in a similar manner in the case of emigration visas for Soviet citizens of German extraction.

The emigration issue cannot, however, be interpreted solely in terms of domestic politics, as this does not suffice to explain the unusually large numbers of Soviet Jews permitted to emigrate in the period from the late 1960s to the mid-1970s. These were the years in which the United States had insisted upon a liberalization of the Soviet Union's emigration policy with regard to its Jews as a price for the relaxation of tensions in the era of détente. This, in turn, confronted the USSR with another problem in foreign relations, namely, the potential affront to the sensibilities of the Arab states. In fact, angry Arabs accused the Soviets of allowing precisely those persons to emigrate who would later turn up as Israeli soldiers fighting against the Arab states. The Kremlin leadership was thus forced to thread its way through a series of obstacles.

The history of diplomatic relations between Israel and the Soviet Union also cannot be separated from long-term structural conditions. It may be that in the autumn of 1947 the Soviet leadership hoped to use Israel in order to gain a toehold in the Middle East. Moscow may have also believed that through the influence of the, if not socialistic, at least social democratic Republic of Israel the traditional feudal systems of the Middle East could be transformed into a 'progressive' region. In any case, it was the arrival of Soviet (again, not American) weapons that proved instrumental in securing Israel's existence during the 1948/9 War of Independence.

Within the first few months after the establishment of diplomatic relations, however, the Soviet leadership learned that the risks in terms of domestic structural and international superpower politics outweighed the regional political advantages of relations with Israel. In Moscow, Soviet Jews gave the newly arrived first Israeli ambassador, Golda Meir, a triumphal welcome and the idea of Israel electrified Russian Jews. The potential consequences with regard to other national and ethnic groups in the USSR were not to be overlooked and by the winter of 1948/9 the Soviet government had already imposed stricter controls on Jewish activists and the leaders of other nationalities. These measures gave rise to the first serious tensions in Soviet–Israeli relations. The ill feelings were further exacerbated as Stalin proceeded to eliminate those veteran communists in the Eastern bloc nations whose power was based on their own local organizations and who were thus not solely dependent upon Stalin and the Soviet Union. Suspected, like communist Russian Jews, of dual loyalties, the entire 'founding father' generation of communists in the Eastern bloc countries was persecuted and stripped of power or even liquidated in the late 1940s and early 1950s. Many of these veteran communists were also Jews.

Relations between Israel and the Soviet Union together with its Eastern bloc satellites visibly worsened. On 11 February 1953 the USSR broke off diplomatic relations with Israel. The pretext was furnished by a bomb explosion at the Soviet embassy in Tel-Aviv two days before, but the deeper reasons are to the seen in the described structural contingencies.

Stalin died on 5 March 1953, and the climate of relations improved under his successors. Diplomatic relations were already re-established on 21 July 1953, but the atmosphere of close cooperation which prevailed in 1947 and in the first Arab–Israeli war was never achieved again.

The Soviet leadership now steered towards Egypt and Syria in its search for a Middle Eastern beachhead. This became apparent in September 1955 when the Soviet Union and Egypt announced that Czech (read: Soviet) weapons would be supplied to Egypt.

The Soviet Union played a part in the overture to the Six Day War by informing the Egyptian and Syrian governments of supposed Israeli troop concentrations along their borders. Egypt and Syria felt compelled to undertake countermeasures, thus setting the spiral of information, misinformation, calculations and miscalculations into motion that led to the outbreak of hostilities. In order to document its solidarity with the Arab world the Soviet Union once again broke off diplomatic relations with Israel. At the time of writing, formal relations have not been restored. The only Eastern bloc country not to follow suit was Romania.

With its decision to rely exclusively on its 'Arab card' the USSR in the end gambled away its chances of playing a winning hand as Middle East mediator. By thus isolating itself, the Soviet Union remains in the position of the spoiler, able to block any solution not to its liking, but not capable of bringing a solution about. The United States has profited from this situation and, despite numerous reversals, the USA remains indispensable in its role as mediator or conduit for communications in the Middle East.

3 RELATIONS WITH THE UNITED KINGDOM

After independence, Israel's relations with the former Mandate power, Great Britain, were understandably not free from tensions. An important change in Israeli–British relations came about after Egyptian President Nasser nationalized the Suez Canal in 1956. The British and French reaction to this seizure of their assets was to ally themselves with Israel and to unleash a joint attack on 29 October 1956.

Nevertheless, relations between Britain and Israel continued rather on the cool side. This may be in part ascribed to the fact that, for Israel, relations with Great Britain, as with most other European states, carry a lower priority than its partnership with the USA. Moreover, a number of rebuffed approaches on Israel's part have led the Israeli government to assign relations with Britain a low priority on its foreign policy agenda. When, for example, Israel attempted to diversify its sources of crude oil following the cut-off of deliveries by Iran and the end of Israel's exploitation of the Sinai oil fields (both in 1979), Britain refused to help Israel fill the gap. Repeated efforts to reverse this decision have thus far all failed.

Nevertheless, Great Britain remains an important commercial partner for Israel, indeed its most important Western European trading partner in most years. Only West Germany has 'competed' with the United Kingdom in this respect, but the latter has almost outdistanced it.

As a rule, British–Israeli relations have tended to be more cordial with the Labour Party in power in Westminster than under Conservative governments. The Thatcher government, however, represents something of an exception, as the prime minister herself was a member of the British–Israeli parliamentary group and numerous Jews reside in the London constituency represented by Mrs Thatcher. Nonetheless, the British prime minister lent her active support to the European Community's Venice Declaration of June 1980 (see below) and also imposed a (largely symbolic) arms embargo on Israel after it initiated the War in Lebanon in 1982. By mid-1985 this embargo had not yet been lifted.

4 RELATIONS WITH FRANCE

France played a doubly important role in the early phase of Israel's foreign policy. In the early 1950s Paris was the focus of at first indirect and finally direct contacts between representatives of Israel and the Federal Republic of Germany. An era of close military cooperation between France and Israel began in 1954 and France remained Israel's most important weapons supplier until 1967. This cooperation included nuclear research and technology. Israel's first nuclear reactors were supplied by France and the foundation of Israel's military nuclear potential was also laid at this time.

In the first years of General Charles de Gaulle's presidency, however, France gradually began to edge away from its very close and one-sided relationship with Israel. The Six Day War thus furnished a pretext for, rather than the cause of, the French break with Israel. The French president accused Israel of having unnecessarily initiated hostilities. De Gaulle believed that he had offered a solution which would have prevented the war and blamed Israel's leaders for not having followed his advice. In a press conference in November 1967 the French president severely criticized Israel's policy and announced the imposition of an embargo on French arms deliveries to Israel. While these restrictions were tightened in the following years, the rise in French arms exports to the Arab world, particularly to Libya, under de Gaulle's successors led to a further worsening of French–Israeli relations.

In the early 1980s France came to the realization that it had manoeuvred itself into a dilemma similar to that of the Soviet Union with regard to the Middle East. France, too, had placed all its bets on its 'Arab card' and thus lost political influence in the region. Elected in 1981, the new French president, Mitterrand, was able to correct his nation's lopsidedly 'pro-Arab' political course with relative ease, as he had always been counted among the 'pro-Israel' forces in France. Mitterrand became the first French president to visit Israel while in office and followed a much more balanced approach to the Arab/Palestinian–Israel conflict.

5 RELATIONS WITH THE FEDERAL REPUBLIC OF GERMANY

As seen from Jerusalem, bilateral relations between Israel and the Federal Republic of Germany are second in importance only to its partnership with the United States. The history of West German–Israeli relations can be divided into seven phases:

(a) the reparations question (up to 1953);

(b)   the difficulties surrounding the establishment of diplomatic relations (up to 1965);

(c)   the beginning of routine relations (until late 1969);

(d)   between 'Ostpolitik' and the Middle East (the era under Brandt and Scheel);

(e)   the Palestinian question and the oil crisis (1973–7);

(f)   under Begin's shadow (until the autumn of 1983);

(g)   seeking a full-fledged partnership with the United States (since the autumn of 1981).

Granted that it is quite possible to set other accents and thus other chronological limits, the division into the seven phases listed above is followed here because it provides a convenient and workable framework for description. There is, of course, some overlapping of phases, but the divisions are maintained for the sake of clarity.

(a) THE REPARATIONS QUESTION (1949–53)

As early as 11 November 1949, in an interview with the publisher of the *Allgemeine*, the weekly publication of the Jewish community in Germany, Konrad Adenauer, who had been elected the first chancellor of the newly created Federal Republic of Germany on 15 September of that year, declared that his government was prepared to make reparation payments to the Jewish victims of the National Socialist regime. In January 1951, in the face of enormous financial difficulties, the Israeli government decided to undertake indirect negotiations with the Federal Republic. On 12 March 1951, Israel presented a formal note to the four allied powers demanding the sum of 1 billion dollars from West Germany and 500 million from East Germany. While the Soviet Union neglected to reply to the note, the Western powers insisted on direct German–Israeli talks. Chancellor Adenauer smoothed the way for negotiations with his statement to the Bundestag (the West German parliament) of 27 September 1951. In January 1952 the Knesset voted by a margin of 60 to 51 to conduct direct talks with the FRG. This decision followed a tumultuous debate in which the anything but non-violent protests both inside and outside the Knesset were initiated by the Herut Party led by Menachem Begin.

The reparations negotiations, which began in Wassenaar (near The Hague in the Netherlands) on 21 March 1952, led to the Luxemburg agreement signed in the capital of the duchy on 10 September. Over a period of twelve years the state of Israel was to receive the sum of 3 billion German Marks and the Conference on Jewish Material Claims against Germany 450 million Marks. This latter organization represented those Jewish victims who were not citizens of Israel. The agreement was ratified by the Bundestag on 18 March 1953. Without the support of the 125 opposition deputies of the Social Democrats (who voted unanimously for the agreement) the government could have suffered an embarrassing defeat, as only 84 of the deputies in Chancellor Adenauer's own CDU/CSU faction voted for the treaty, whereas 4 voted against it and 39 (including the Finance Minister Fritz Schäffer and Bavarian leader Franz Josef Strauss) abstained.

In 1953 the West German government was quite prepared, even anxious, to assume full diplomatic relations, but the Israeli government hesitated.

After 1955, and even more so after the events of 1956/7, it was Israel's turn to press the issue and Bonn's to side-step so as not to damage West German interests in the Arab world. Most important, the Federal Republic had tied its own hands with its so-called 'Hallstein doctrine', according to which the FRG would not maintain diplomatic relations with any country recognizing the German Democratic Republic (East Germany). The fear in Bonn was that the Arab states would respond to the assumption of diplomatic relations between the FRG and Israel by recognizing the GDR.

(b) THE DIFFICULTIES SURROUNDING THE ESTABLISHMENT OF DIPLOMATIC RELATIONS (1955–65)

In addition to the issue of formal diplomatic relations, three further questions dominated German–Israeli relations in this phase: (1) arms deliveries, (2) National Socialist criminals and the statute of limitations and (3) the activities of German rocket experts in Egypt.

In March 1956 the rumour was still floating about that West Germany and Israel were about to take up diplomatic relations, but this was finally denied in April. The same cycle repeated itself in July 1957.

In the autumn of 1956, Chancellor Adenauer had resisted pressure from the Eisenhower administration temporarily to suspend reparations payments to Israel as a means of forcing an Israeli withdrawal from the territories occupied during the Suez Campaign. The manner in which Bonn stood up to Washington deeply impressed the Israeli government, which subsequently approached the Federal Republic with a weapons shopping list (Shimon Peres's overture to F. J. Strauss, for example). The majority of the Israeli cabinet approved these moves in a vote taken on 15 December 1957, the exception being the ministers of the socialist parties Mapam and Ahdut Haavoda, which wanted nothing to do with arms from Germany. On 24 December Prime Minister Ben-Gurion declared before the Knesset that only the Federal Republic of Germany could be relied upon as a long-term supplier of weapons, which Israel needed in any case. On 27 December the West German government declared that it would, as a matter of principle, refrain from delivering weapons to 'areas of tension'. As a result of the internal struggles in his cabinet on this issue, Ben-Gurion resigned on 31 December.

In its 24 June 1959 issue the German weekly *Der Spiegel* revealed that the Federal Republic had for some time been buying 'Uzi' machine guns as well as other light weapons made in Israel. This revelation precipitated a cabinet crisis in Israel, as, in the view of Ahdut Haavoda, exporting weapons to Germany was even worse than importing German arms. Meeting in New York, Adenauer and Ben-Gurion nevertheless reached an agreement on German military aid to Israel on 14 March 1960. A secret treaty was signed on 8 June 1962. The United States, Great Britain and Italy lent a hand in carrying out the provisions of this agreement, which was favoured by West German Defence Minister F. J. Strauss but opposed by Foreign Minister Schröder. The secret arms deliveries were uncovered by the *Frankfurter Rundschau* on 26 October 1964. On 12 February 1965 Chancellor Ludwig Ehrhard stated that the Federal Republic would no longer deliver arms to nations in 'areas of tension'.

Bonn's anger over East German leader Walter Ulbricht's visit to Egypt (24 February to 3 March 1965) was followed by Kurt Birrenbach's special mission to Israel, which led to the decision to establish diplomatic relations. These were approved by the West German government on 5 May and assumed formally on 12 May 1965.

Tensions arose between Israel and West Germany over the activities of German rocket technicians in Egypt made public in March of 1963 but actually having already been conducted for a considerable time under cover. The Bonn government solved this problem by drawing the specialists back to Germany with attractive job offers at home.

The controversial issue of the application of the statute of limitations to Nazi criminals had placed a burden on Israeli–German relations which first became visible in November 1964 (but which had also been growing for some time behind the scenes). A compromise acceptable in both Bonn and Jerusalem was arrived at in March 1965. The statutory limit for prosecutions was extended an additional five years. This rational solution had become politically much more difficult since the fourteen-week Eichmann trial in 1961 had once again stirred up memories and emotions from the past. As early as 1959, anti-Semitic graffiti had damaged the image of the new Germany in the eyes of the Israeli public.

(c) THE BEGINNING OF ROUTINE RELATIONS (1965–9)

On 12 May 1966, the Federal Republic and Israel formalized an economic agreement including low interest annual loans of 130 million German Marks to Israel (later raised to DM 140 million).

The Six Day War unleashed a wave of sympathy for Israel among West Germans. Pro-Palestinian demonstrations on the part of the just-budding new left at German universities proved, however, a sign of things to come. During the war the Bonn government remained officially neutral, although 20,000 gas masks were supplied for the use of the civilian population. Their delivery was opposed by Defence Minister Schröder. Foreign Minister Willi Brandt declared that the strict neutrality of the government of the Federal Republic of Germany did not mean 'moral indifference or lassitude of the heart'. In other words, the Bonn government sided with Israel.

(d) BETWEEN 'OSTPOLITIK' AND THE MIDDLE EAST (THE ERA UNDER BRANDT AND SCHEEL)

Even though the governing coalition in Israel was led by the social democratic ILP, the Israeli response to the assumption of power in Bonn by the West German Social Democrats under Willi Brandt in 1969 was muted. The Golda Meir government feared that the new coalition in Bonn might sacrifice West Germany's special relationship with Israel on the altar of its 'Ostpolitik'. Jerusalem was especially suspicious of the new West German foreign minister, Walter Scheel (of Brandt's coalition partner, the Free Democrats).

In the winter of 1969/70 a series of lectures by Israeli ambassador Ben-Nathan at West German universities was repeatedly, and sometimes violently, disrupted by leftist student groups demonstrating their sympathy for the Palestinian cause.

In February 1970 Abba Eban became the first Israeli foreign minister to visit the Federal Republic. His visit was reciprocated by his West German counterpart, Scheel, in July 1971. While in Jerusalem, Scheel defended the paper on the Near East adapted by the foreign ministers of the European Community in May, in which Israel was called upon to withdraw from all of the territories occupied in 1967.

During the Munich Olympic Games in September 1972, members of the PLO murdered Israeli athletes. A few weeks later these terrorists were released in exchange for the hostages seized in the hijacking of a Lufthansa airliner by the PLO.

In June 1973 Willi Brandt became the first chancellor of the Federal Republic to visit the Jewish state. His Israeli hosts repeatedly emphasized that bilateral relations were not 'normal'. On 23 October 1973, a few days before the end of the Yom Kippur War, the Bonn government advised the United States that it would no longer be permitted to use German ports for the transshipment of war material to Israel. Additional ill-feeling was created in Israel by the declaration of the foreign ministers of the European Community of 6 November 1973 (see below).

(e) THE PALESTINIAN QUESTION AND THE OIL CRISIS (1973–7)

In November 1974 the Federal Republic of Germany became the first member state of the European Community to call for the self-determination of the Palestinian people before the United Nations General Assembly. As economic considerations came to dominate Bonn's foreign policy, the differences of opinion with Israel grew.

In July 1975 Yitzhak Rabin became the first Israeli prime minister to visit the Federal Republic. Rabin invited Chancellor Helmut Schmidt to a return visit, which failed to take place before the 1977 Knesset elections turned Rabin and the ILP out of office. Schmidt subsequently avoided a meeting with Rabin's successor, Menachem Begin.

(f) UNDER BEGIN'S SHADOW

On 29 June 1977 the European Council more or less openly endorsed the right of self-determination for the Palestinian people. Increasingly, the Middle East policy of the European Community became dominated by the Paris–Bonn partnership between French President Giscard d'Estaing and West German Chancellor Schmidt. This included the EC Declaration of Venice (13 June 1980) which Israel regarded as one-sidedly pro-Palestinian. Israel's anger grew over what it viewed as inadequate European support for the Egyptian–Israeli peace process (the Camp David accords of September 1978 and the peace treaty of 1979). Bonn was reproached for hiding behind the back of the French.

In its 5 January 1981 issue *Der Spiegel* reported that the Bonn government was planning to sell Leopard-2 tanks and other advanced German weaponry to Saudi Arabia, which played host to Chancellor Schmidt the end of April. The growing Saudi Arabian–West German economic and political relationship and especially an interview given by Chancellor Schmidt on the German ARD television network (30 April 1981) aroused the ire of the Israeli government. Prime Minister Begin's response took the form of a political frontal attack. Begin spoke of the collective guilt of the entire German people for the crimes of the National Socialist era and stated that Helmut Schmidt, who had been a Wehrmacht officer in the Second World War, carried part of the burden of war crime responsibility. On 25 May 1982 Chancellor Schmidt announced that no German tanks would be sold to Saudi Arabia.

(g) SEEKING A FULL-FLEDGED PARTNERSHIP WITH THE UNITED STATES (SINCE 1981)

Since the early 1980s, regional turbulence and the inability of the Western European countries to influence, let alone steer, events in the Middle East have impelled the West German government to adhere more closely to the American line. This process, which can be described as the Americanization, even as the Reaganization of Germany's Middle East policy, was accelerated after the change of government in late 1982, with the Christian Democrats taking over the reins of power as the major partner in the new governing coalition.

In January 1984 Chancellor Helmut Kohl travelled to Israel with the aim of making good the reluctance of his predecessor to visit the Jewish state. In contrast to its predecessor, however, the Kohl government was willing to sell arms (except for the Leopard-2 tank) to Saudi Arabia. This created an unfavourable climate for Kohl's trip, and the atmosphere was further worsened by what Israelis viewed as the Chancellor's lack of historical sensitivity.

6 RELATIONS WITH THE EUROPEAN COMMUNITY

The problems of the Middle East became the prime focus of attempts to coordinate a common foreign policy among the nations of the European Community. As early as May 1971 the EC foreign ministers adapted a paper that was sharply criticized in Israel. Not only did this European position paper call for an Israeli withdrawal from all the territories occupied in the 1967 Six Day War; particularly irritating for Israel was the proposal that Jerusalem be placed under international administration. Israel was also angered by the suggestion that the Palestinians be given a 'free choice' between a phased return and resettlement with compensation in other countries.

The next, even greater wave of ill-feeling was unleashed by the declaration of the EC foreign ministers of 6 November 1973, exactly one month after the outbreak of the Yom Kippur War. The actual aim was less to criticize Israel than to secure Europe's oil supply in the face of the Arab oil embargo against 'pro-Israeli' states. The main bone of contention was once again the demand for the turnover of occupied territories as well as the 'recognition' that a just and lasting peace must take the 'legitimate rights of the Palestinians' into consideration. In 1977 the nine member nations of the EC declared that the conflict in the Middle East could only be settled by giving the 'legitimate right of the Palestinian people to an effective expression of its national identity' concrete form, whereby the 'necessity of a homeland for the Palestinian people' must be considered. In other words, the goal was the creation of a precursor for a Palestinian state, a concept Israel rejected categorically.

The Camp David accords and the Egyptian–Israeli peace treaty received a reserved reception in the European Community. France in particular sought to push the EC into distancing itself still further from Israel. Jerusalem, however, also blamed the West German government for not only going along with the French but also accelerating the change in course.

The 13 June 1980, Venice Declaration of the European Council (of the heads of state and government of the European Community) provoked the most angry response in Israel to date. In addition to repeating already known EC positions, the Community now called for the 'association' of the Palestinian Liberation Organization in the solution of the Palestinian problem.

The Declaration of Venice was at least in part designed to place a certain distance between the European Community and the United States concerning Middle Eastern politics and thus to obtain for Europe a greater freedom of movement in the Middle East. The EC attempted to set its sights on a solution beyond the limits of the Camp David process.

After the assassination of Egyptian President Sadat (6 October 1981), however, the European Community more closely followed the American lead with regard to the Middle East. EC countries participated in manning the peacekeeping force sent to the Sinai following the Israeli withdrawal in April 1982, and France, Italy and Great Britain dispatched troops as part of the Multinational Force in Lebanon in 1982/3, all of this with the assent and support of the Bonn government, which is prevented by law from sending troops abroad.

Israel's reaction to the EC positions was restrained by an important economic consideration: about 40% of Israel's foreign trade is conducted with the European Community (see section C/XVI). For its part, however, the EC can little afford to tighten the screw on Israel too much for fear of provoking American domestic reactions and a worsening of US–European relations. The European Community is thus forced constantly to strike a balance between its American and Middle Eastern priorities.

7 RELATIONS WITH THE THIRD WORLD

(a) ASIA

Israel has found itself in a most difficult position with regard to many Asian nations. Because of their Moslem populations, especially Pakistan and Afghanistan, as well as India and Indonesia, but even Malaysia and the Philippines were not inclined to entertain (at least publicly) any sort of close contacts with Israel. On the other hand, in the 1950s Israel did succeed in establishing good relations with Burma, Thailand, and later with Singapore as well as Iran during the era of the Shah.

Relations with Turkey were characterized by well-meaning mutual restraint. Both Iran and Turkey were able to afford better relations with Israel, as they are Islamic but not Arab countries whose governments followed a strictly secular course, one which eventually backfired on the domestic front. The 1979 revolution in Iran which overthrew the Shah and led to the founding of the Iranian Islamic Republic also brought about an abrupt and total reversal in Israel's relations with Iran. Israel's relations with Turkey have also been virtually frozen by the Ankara government. Certainly the domestic resurgence of Islamic fundamentalism was one factor. The economic considerations involved included the hope of attracting more Arab aid and investment without the sort of strings that were increasingly being attached to money from the European Community, particularly with regard to human rights. In addition, Turkey sought to woo the Arab nations diplomatically in order to head off the possibility that the growing Greek–Arab friendship might lead to an Arab tilt towards Athens on matters such as the Turkish occupation of northern Cyprus.

With both nations sharing a degree of international isolation, Israel has long maintained close military contacts with Taiwan, although their commercial relations have not been extensive. In 1984 and 1985 increasing note has been taken of Israel's delivery of weaponry to the People's Republic of China, although the intensity of the contacts has remained largely invisible to the public. To date, China has shown no inclination to assume diplomatic relations with Israel.

Israel maintains good and stable relations with Australia and New Zealand. Japan, not willing to place its considerable trade relations with the Arab world at risk, has kept a friendly distance.

Despite Israel's political isolation and the economic necessity of maintaining good relations with the Arab world, there are areas in which Asian nations have proven reluctant to renounce the agricultural and military knowhow offered by the Jewish state. India and Indonesia have provided examples, and especially Sri Lanka, where the Singhalese central government has gladly made use of the anti-guerrilla expertise of the Israeli military in its struggle against Tamil rebels.

(b) AFRICA

Israel's development aid was particularly welcome in Africa during the 1960s. In 1973, however, the Arab states successfully pressured the majority of African nations into breaking off diplomatic relations with Israel. The only exceptions were Malawi, Lesotho and Swaziland. It was only at this time that relations between Israel and South Africa intensified, leading to the exchange of ambassadors in 1974/5.

A change of course was to be noted among some African nations by the early 1980s. Zaire and Liberia have re-established diplomatic relations with Israel, and the contacts with Kenya and Nigeria are more than merely commercial. The degree of cooperation with Kenya could be seen in 1976 when the Israeli commando team which freed the hostages in Entebbe (Uganda) was permitted to make a stopover in Nairobi. The team's rescue of the hostages would have been impossible without Kenyan logistical support. The underlying cause of this careful re-approach towards Israel may be seen in the disappointment of the African states over the promises of Arab financial aid that failed to flow in the hoped for amounts.

Many African states cannot afford more cordial relations with Israel for domestic social and religious reasons. In Africa, too, Islam is an extraordinarily important factor. The rebellion inspired by Islamic fanatics in northern Nigeria is just one example. The disturbances among the Moslem populations of Senegal and Gambia in the early 1980s, encouraged by Libyan leader Gaddafi, are more recent cases. What contacts there are between Israel and such African states where strong Islamic religious and social structures obtain are therefore likely to remain behind the scenes.

Occasionally a tip of the iceberg of invisible relations peeks out. In 1984, for example, it was learned that Israeli secret agents had assisted the government of Nigeria in kidnapping and returning a member of the Nigerian regime deposed in 1983 from his exile in London. The abduction and the Israeli–Nigerian cooperation behind it were discovered by accident. In order to avoid complications at home with its own Islamic population and abroad with the Arab world, the Nigerian government affirmed its sympathies for the PLO and heavily emphasized its visible relations with the Arab world. Nevertheless, the nature of relations between Israel and Nigeria, as well as with the rest of black African nations, the quiet cooperation below the official political surface, is not likely to change in the near future. Israel continues to lend valued assistance in the development of the local infrastructure and agriculture, as well as military aid, especially in techniques for combatting internal resistance. The President of Zaire, Mobutu, is one of the recent beneficiaries of such Israeli assistance. It should also be mentioned that France and the United States work closely with Israel in the black nations of Africa.

The largely Christian country of Ethiopia remains a special case on the African continent. There have been deep traditional, including religious ties between Ethiopia and Jews. Until the fall of Emperor Haile Selassie in 1974 Ethiopian–Israeli relations had been very close. For two reasons Israel continues to maintain a special interest in Ethiopia.

The first of these reasons are the Falashas, a group of Ethiopians whose identity is Jewish, who know and respect the Old Testament but have no connection to the Talmudic tradition. In other words, the Falashas represent a form of Judaism dating back more than 2,000 years. No one knows exactly where and how the Falashas originated. They tend to resemble more their Ethiopian environment than, for example, Ashkenasi or Oriental Jews. Even the question of their identity as a part of religious Judaism is a matter of controversy among leading rabbis in Israel. What is certain, however, is the fact that in Ethiopia the Falashas are regarded as Jews, identify themselves as Jews and have also been persecuted as Jews in the course of their turbulent history. The situation of the Falashas became extremely difficult after Emperor Selassie was deposed. In 1977 and 1978 Israel had sought for a means to bring the Falashas to Israel but failed. Nevertheless, in 1984 and especially in 1985 'Operation Moses' furnished headlines, as it became known that Israel had succeeded in organizing an airlift of some 10,000 Falashas to the Jewish state. The Ethiopian regime protested at this action, but the rumours of an Israeli compensation in the form of military aid against the Arab-supported Moslem Eritrean secessionists have not ceased.

The second reason for Israel's interest in maintaining relations with Ethiopia's government, independent of its ideological slant, is strategic in nature. Were Ethiopia to be ruled by a regime totally inimical to Israel, it, together with the already hostile People's Republic of (South) Yemen on the opposite side of the Red Sea, would be in a position to block the narrow eastern exit of the Red Sea through the Strait of Bab-el-Mandeb into the Gulf of Aden. Apart from further political, economic and even military conse-quences, the closing of this sea-lane to Israeli ships and to ships bound for Israel would economically cripple not only the port of Eilat, but the whole southern region of Israel as well. Sworn enemies of Israel on both sides of the Bab-el-Mandeb would confront the Jewish state with a situation not unlike those faced in 1956 and 1967 when Egyptian President Nasser closed the Straits of Tiran at Sharm-el-Sheik, except that the much greater distance between Israel and Bab-el-Mandeb would pose significantly more daunting military and political problems.

The extraordinary geo-political importance of Ethiopia for Israel has led to the most unusual of political associations. Thus, in its 1978 campaign against Somalia, Ethiopia received aid not only from the Soviet Union, Cuba and Libya but from Israel as well.

Israel's relations with the Republic of South Africa is the second special case on the African continent. Again, as with Taiwan, a major reason for South Africa's close contacts with Israel can be found in their common fate of international political isolation. Relations have grown cordial despite the fact that religiously motivated anti-Semitism is not uncommon among the Boer majority. The degree of cooperation between the two nations in the economic and technological spheres (and, it is rumoured, in the field of military nuclear research) is not to be underestimated. Nevertheless, the dimensions of the partnership are as easily exaggerated (see the statistics on Israel's export structure in C/XVI/4).

(c) LATIN AMERICA

Latin America has tended to play a relatively minor role in Israel's foreign policy. Most Latin American states have been traditionally pro-Western and have tended to follow the lead of the United States in foreign affairs. This has proved of advantage to Israel, especially in vote counting at the UN General Assembly, where the attitudes of the Latin American nations have consis-tently proved more sympathetic than those of African and Asian countries. From Israel's point of view, the behaviour of the Latin American bloc even towards the UN anti-Zionism resolution of November 1975 was relatively well intentioned.

Although Mexico has proved a reliable source of crude oil for Israel, relations with established Latin American governments and political move-ments have been anything but uncomplicated. The heads of state and dominant political groups in these Catholic countries have generally sup-ported the Vatican's position with regard to Jerusalem, namely, that the capital of Israel ought to be placed under international administration. Problems arose soon after the close of the Second World War, particularly with Argentina, Brazil and Paraguay, as these nations offered shelter to fleeing Nazis. Adolf Eichmann was abducted from Argentina in 1960 and the infamous concentration camp doctor Mengele was presumed to have found a haven for many years in Paraguay and Brazil. These figures from the past thus placed a burden on Israel's interest in improving bilateral relations in present-day Latin America.

Israel's relations with Argentina have proved ambivalent. Apart from the issue of fugitive Nazi criminals, there was the issue of obviously anti-Semitic incidents directed against the large Jewish population in Argentina itself. Numerous Argentinian Jews were among those who offered political and sometimes armed resistance to the military junta which had replaced the Peronist government in 1976. The persecution of such individuals and their families as well as the more extensive 'settling of accounts' with larger Jewish groups as conducted by the Argentine military regime presented Israel with a serious dilemma. On the one hand, Israel pressed for an end to the harassment of Argentine Jews, whether resistance fighters or not. On the other hand, however, Israel did not wish to jeopardize its lucrative arms trade with Argentina. It is an open secret that Israel supplied the Argentine armed forces with weaponry, including airplanes and rockets, both during and after the Falklands War. This, in turn, considerably complicated Israeli–British relations in 1982–3.

The development of Brazil's nuclear programme is also a source of worry to Israel. Since the 1970s Brazil has cooperated closely with Iraq in matters of nuclear technology. Since the 1970s, and especially in the early 1980s, Brazil has played a major role as an arms supplier to Arab countries, again particularly to Iraq.

Many Latin American governments have been or are confronted with guerrilla-led rebellions supported not only by Cuba and the Soviet Union but also by the Palestine Liberation Organization. These governments have frequently sought the assistance of Israel in acquiring anti-guerrilla warfare tactics. In addition, they have purchased Israeli weapons.

Where, on the other hand, the rebels have been successful, as in Cuba and Nicaragua, Israel's stock has fallen dramatically. The political symbolism of revolutionary Nicaragua provides a pointed illustration. In Sandinista victory celebrations the Israeli-made 'Galil' rifle is frequently displayed as a symbol of the former oppressors. One such weapon was presented to Fidel Castro as a memento. Yasser Arafat was among the prominent guests in Managua on the first anniversary of the Sandinista victory. The PLO is known to support the rebels in El Salvador and in Honduras, while, on the other side, Israeli officers have been sent to advise the governments of these countries.

FURTHER READING

Michael Brecher, *Decisions in Crisis. Israel, 1967 and 1973* (Berkeley, Calif.: University of California Press, 1980).

Shlomo Aronson, *Conflict and Bargaining in the Middle East. An Israeli Perspective* (Baltimore, Md.: Johns Hopkins University Press, 1978).

Michael Brecher, *Decisions in Israel's Foreign Policy* (London: Oxford University Press, 1974); by the same author, *The Foreign Policy System of Israel. Settings, Images, Process* (London: Oxford University Press, 1972); these books are classics on this subject.

On Soviet–Israeli relations, Yaacov Ro'i, *Soviet Decision-Making. The USSR and Israel, 1947–1954* (New Brunswick, NJ: Transaction Books, 1980), excellent; by the same author, *From Encroachment to Involvement. A Documented Study of Soviet Policy in the Middle East, 1945–1973* (New Brunswick, NJ: Transaction Books, 1974).

For the subsequent period, Galia Golan, *Yom Kippur and After. The Soviet Union and the Middle East Crisis* (Cambridge: Cambridge University Press, 1979); for a Soviet perspective, cf. Y. M. Primakov, *Anatomy of the Middle East Conflict* (Moscow: Nauka, 1979).

On US–Israeli relations, Bernard Reich, *The United States and Israel. The Dynamics of Influence* (New York: Praeger, 1984); by the same author, *Quest for Peace. United States–Israel Relations and the Arab–Israeli Conflict* (New Brunswick, NJ: Transaction Books, 1980); Haim Shaked and Itamar Rabinovitch (eds.), *The Middle East and the United States. Perceptions and Policies* (New Brunswick, NJ: Transaction Books, 1980).

DOCUMENTS

For the years since 1947 see the *Documents on the Foreign Policy of Israel* edited by the Israel State Archives (a superb edition of sources; up to late 1984 three volumes had been published; the rest will appear annually).

The Ministry of Foreign Relations has also published five volumes of selected (sometimes selective) sources under the title *Israel's Foreign Relations.*

PART B
SOCIETY

VI

The Population

1 DEMOGRAPHIC DEVELOPMENTS AND STRUCTURES

(a) JEWISH–ARAB POLARIZATION

The modern demographic history of Palestine dates from the arrival of the first Zionist-motivated Jewish immigrants at the end of the nineteenth century. In 1845 there were 11,800 Jews living in Palestine. In 1882, on the eve of the first *aliya*, there were 24,000 (*Encyclopaedia Hebraica*, 1958: 674; Friedlander and Goldscheider, 1979: 14. These numbers are based on estimates by experts rather than on actual census counts.) On the eve of the First World War there were 85,000 Jews in Palestine; and there were 84,000 according to the census of 1922. By 15 May 1948 the Jewish population had reached 650,000, and it stood at 1,014,000 in December 1949 following the War of Independence.

The Arab population of Palestine grew from approximately 500,000 in the middle of the nineteenth century to some 600,000 by the beginning of the First World War (Friedlander and Goldscheider, 1979: 16; *Encyclopaedia Hebraica*, 1958: 707; Gerber, 1979).

At the time of the census of 23 October 1922, 668,000 Arabs were living in Palestine. By 1947 there were approximately 1,200,000 and on 15 May 1948, only 156,000 (see Table 23). These last two statistics are, however, not infrequently subject to misinterpretation as the figures for 1947 count the population of the entire region encompassed by the Mandate for Palestine, including the West Bank and the Gaza Strip, whereas the figures for 1948 count only the population within the borders of the newly founded State of Israel and exclude the West Bank and the Gaza Strip.

Nevertheless, the basic fact remains that even in the remainder of Palestine (excluding Transjordan) the proportional relationship between the Jewish and Arab populations had been so radically reversed between 1922 and 1948 that the once overwhelming Arab majority had, by 1948, been reduced to a minority.

The number of Jews living in Palestine in 1948 was roughly equivalent to the number of Arab residents in 1922, whereas the number of Arabs living within the territory of Israel in 1948 was approximately twice the size of the Jewish population of Palestine in 1922. That this massive shift entailed enormous political and psychological consequences for both sides is self-evident.

(The reader seeking geographical orientation is referred to the maps in

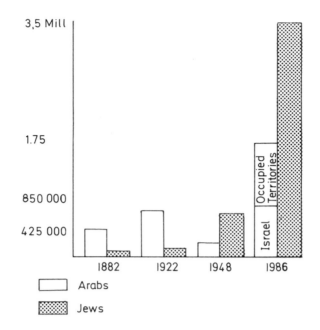

Figure 31   Arabs and Jews in Palestine and Israel, 1882–1982.

Figures 2–11. Figure 31 demonstrates the shifts in the Jewish and Arab populations.)

By the end of 1981 the number of Arabs living in Israel was approximately equal to the Arab population of 1948.

If Israel were to annex the occupied territories, the state would then include slightly less than 2 million Arabs, as opposed to 3·4 million Jews. Even if these Arabs were denied the right of participation in Knesset elections, the basic fact of a mixed Jewish and Arab population could not be ignored.

Even the 720,000 Arabs living within the pre-1967 borders represent a minority of sufficient size as to make it all but impossible to describe Israel accurately as 'purely' Jewish. Over the long term it will not be possible to escape confronting this most fundamental problem: the Jewishness of the Jewish state.

Of the average annual Jewish population growth of 9% in the years between 1922 and 1948, 75% was due to immigration, the remaining 25% to natural growth. The annual increase of 2·75% in the Arab population over the same period was almost entirely due to natural population growth and was not related to migratory movements (Friedlander and Goldscheider, 1979: 17 ff.). This finding is of historical-political significance, as it has often been claimed that the economic development of Palestine during this period had acted as a magnet attracting numerous Arabs from other states and territories (see Gottheil, 1975).

Table 23   Arabs and Jews in Palestine and Israel, 1882–1985 (figures for
           the population in thousands)

Year	Jews	Arabs[1]	Total
1882[2]	24	426	450
1914[2]	85	600	685
1918[2]	56	600	656
1922	84	668	752
1931	175	859	1,033
1935	355	953	1,308
1940	464	1,081	1,545
1945	554	1,256	1,810
1948*	650	156	806
1951	1,404	173	1,577
1954	1,526	192	1,718
1957	1,763	213	1,976
1961	1,932	247	2,179
1967	2,384	393	2,777
1973	2,845	493	3,338
1977	3,077	576	3,653
1981	3,320	658	3,978
1983	3,410	710	4,120
1985	3,510	740	4,250

Notes:
[1]   Designated as 'non-Jews' in official statistics.
[2]   All figures for these years are estimates
*   15 May 1948

Sources: Encyclopaedia Hebraica 1958: 503, 518, 674, 707; Friedlander and
           Goldscheider, 1979: 30; Gertz, 1947: 46 f.; Horowitz and Lissak, 1978:
           appendix 1; Statistical Abstract of Israel, various vols.; Haaretz, 18
           October 1983 with data from the Central Bureau of Statistics.

(b) INNER-JEWISH POLARIZATION

Figure 33 documents a process of increasing 'Orientalization', that is, the impressive increase in the proportion of Jews of Afro-Asian descent in Israel's population since 1948. This fundamental quantitative development has necessarily led to long-term qualitative changes, as discussed in section B/VI/2.

Whereas the Jewish society of Israel was almost exclusively Euro-American in character in 1948, it has since then become structurally polarized.

Statistics on immigrants' countries of origin for the various aliyot can be found in Friedlander and Goldscheider (1979: 38) and in the publications of the Israeli Central Bureau of Statistics (Immigration, 1975: tables 1 and 2).

Despite the process of Orientalization described above, it must be noted that even in 1981 the majority of voters were still of Euro-American descent.

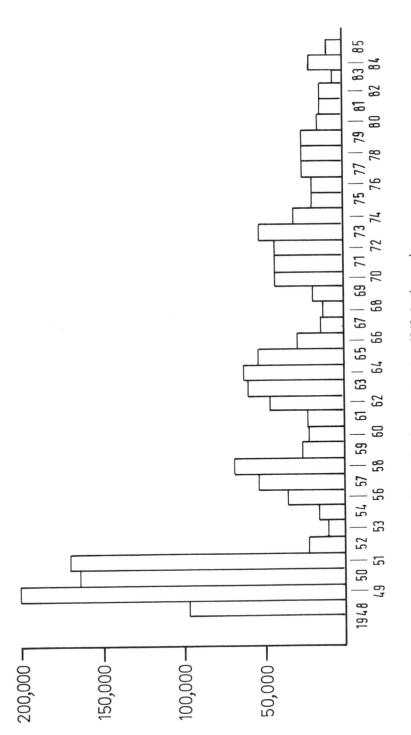

Figure 32   Immigration since 1948, in thousands.

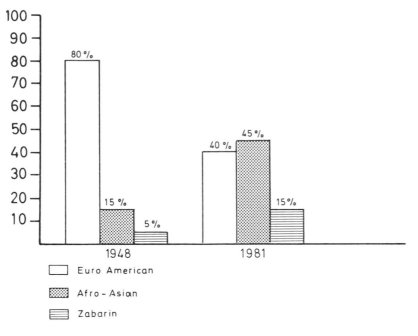

Figure 33   The Jewish population of Israel, 1948 and 1981.

In 1981, 50% of the voting-age population consisted of Ashkenasim, 45% were voters of Afro-Asian heritage and 5% were at least second-generation Sabras (data on paternal ancestry from Elections, 1981: XXIII).

(c) THE BASIC DEMOGRAPHIC STRUCTURE

Figure 33 also demonstrates when and how Israel's Euro-American society was transformed into one with a tripartite structure, the 'first' element consisting of the traditional, mainly Eastern-European groups that moulded the nation during the Yishuv, that is, the period before independence, as well as in the following phase of massive development, the 'second' element being the 'Oriental' Jews, that is, Jews who immigrated to Israel from the nations of northern Africa or western Asia and thus also designated as 'Afro-Asian', and the 'third' element representing Israel's Arab population with its religious diversity of Sunni Moslems, Druze and Christians.

(d) POLITICAL GENERATIONS AND *ALIYOT*

In accordance with Karl Mannheim, the term 'political generation' is understood here as an age-group whose political orientation is shaped mainly between the ages of 17 and 25 under the influence of the then current political events. Since the attitudes of a political generation tend to be formed by the same events, the individuals of that generation exhibit largely similar points of reference without being by any means identical (for further details see Wolffsohn, 1983a: pt. II). The political generations of the Yishuv and of

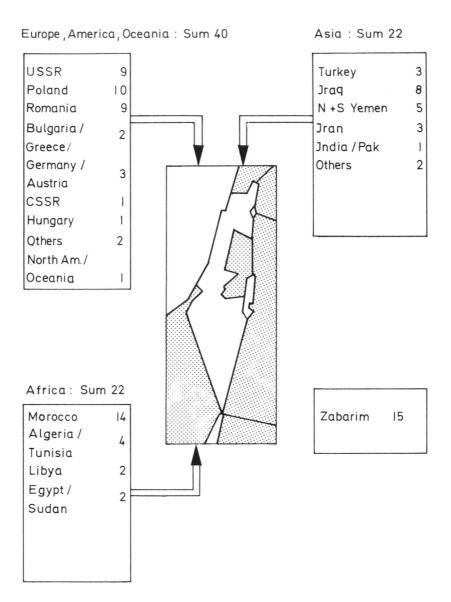

Europe, America, Oceania : Sum 40

USSR	9
Poland	10
Romania	9
Bulgaria / Greece/	2
Germany / Austria	3
CSSR	1
Hungary	1
Others	2
North Am./ Oceania	1

Asia : Sum 22

Turkey	3
Jraq	8
N +S Yemen	5
Jran	3
Jndia / Pak	1
Others	2

Africa : Sum 22

Morocco	14
Algeria / Tunisia	4
Libya	2
Egypt / Sudan	2

Zabarim	15

Figure 34   Jewish population by origin of father, 1981 in (%).

Israel can be easily identified along the lines of the various waves of immigration, to which the term *aliya* (plural: *aliyot*, literally: 'ascendance') is applied.

The *first aliya*, lasting from 1882 to 1903 and including 25,000 to 30,000 immigrants, proved to be of little consequence for the future political system. It was strongly influenced, but deeply disappointed by late nineteenth

Table 24   Political Generations

Political Generation		1st aliya 1882–1903	2nd aliya 1904–14	3rd aliya 1919–23	4th aliya 1924–31	5th aliya 1932–9
Chief effect(s) in Palestine/Israel		Agricultural settlements	Laid foundations of political and economic structures	Strengthening of leftist parties	Stronger organizations, 'bourgeois' tendency, religious moderation	Strengthened bourgeois tendencies religious moderation (PAI), political militancy
Create in Palestine/Israel			Socialist reform party: HPZ Socialist revolutionary: PZ *Kibbutzim*	Histadrut, communist groups Leftist-religious parties: HP, PAI		'New Immigration' Ezel
Political influences from	Palestine/ Israel					
	Orient					
	Germany					Ideology: private property and enterprise Events: Great Depression National Socialism
	Poland			As in Russia	Ideology: private property and enterprise Events: persecution	Ideology: private property and enterprise Events: as in Germany
	Russia	Ideology: liberalism Events: pogroms 1881 ff.	Ideology: socialist reformist, socialist revolutionary Events: pogroms 1903 ff. Russo-Japanese War, 1904–5 Russian Revolution of 1905	Ideology: socialist-communist Events: Russian Revolution, 1917 ff.	Ideology: communist and market oriented Events: Lenin's New Economic Policy	
mass immigration of Oriental Jews 1948 ff.		*5708*	*1956*	*1967* *Zabarim*	*1973*	*1977*	*1982*
Weakening of traditional ideologies, hardening of foreign policy positions		Pragmatic outlook, hawkish foreign policy views	As in generation of 5708	Predominance of territorial issues First groups of extra-parliamentary opposition	Polarization Protest groups: GE, DMC	As in generation of 1973 'Peace Now'	See 1973, soldiers refuse military service

Ideology: _haluziut_	Ideology: building the state	Ideology: state	Rising self-doubt	Issue of character of the state	
Events: struggle for independence	Events: Suez campaign	Events: Six Day War, PLO	Events: Yom Kippur War, political protests	Events: Sadat initiative, Camp David	Events: War in Lebanon

Ideology:
private property,
religion
events:
persecutions and
expulsions

century *Russian liberalism*, especially by the behaviour of Russian liberals during the pogroms of 1880–2.

Most of the immigrants of the first *aliya* were less interested in the establishment of political organizations than in securing their individual economic existence through agricultural enterprises. The traditions of the Russian agrarian revolutionaries were manifest among the more collectively oriented immigrants, for example, among the Bilu group. Such groups remained, however, a minority in the first *aliya*. The great majority regarded themselves simply as colonists and settlers and were, some twenty years later, often described as a 'planter aristocracy' more willing to hire acquiescent and cheap Arab labour than more revolutionary and expensive Jewish workers (see Table 24).

The initiative for the establishment of political institutions arose principally among the immigrants of the *second aliya*, especially among the socialists of this *aliya*, which produced, among other top politicians, two later prime ministers of Israel, Ben-Gurion and Eshkol, as well as Israel's second and third presidents, Ben-Zwi and Shazar.

This wave of immigration brought between 35,000 and 40,000 immigrants into Palestine between 1904 and 1914, especially in the wake of the Kishinev pogrom in Russia (April 1903) and the further persecutions of Jews there following the Russo-Japanese War (1904/5) and the failure of the Russian Revolution of 1905.

The agriculturally oriented social reformers of the second *aliya* founded Hapoel Hazair, while the social revolutionaries (among them, at this time, Ben-Gurion) created Poale Zion. As true Marxists, the members of Poale Zion believed in the revolutionary role of the proletariat, that is, of the industrial workers, of whom virtually none were to be found in the Palestine of the early twentieth century. It was thus the goal of PZ to stimulate the process of industrialization, in order to pave the way for the creation of a (Jewish) proletariat, which could then – oddly enough within the entirely Jewish setting – overthrow the (Jewish) bourgeoisie.

This wave of immigrants remained politically dominant for a long period, although they gradually lost much of their revolutionary zeal. In the course of the years, more and more of them became social democrats and reformers. (For further information and sources see Wolffsohn, 1983a: pt. II.)

The members of the second *aliya* were mainly from middle-class backgrounds but derived their ideology from the social reformers and revolutionaries of Russia and thus imported these variations of leftist ideology into Palestine.

For subsequent groups of arriving immigrants, the authority of these founding fathers of Poale Zion and Hapoel Hazair was, as even the highly self-confident Golda Meir confirmed, beyond dispute. (Meir herself was a leading representative of the third *aliya*.) Both politically and in purely personal terms, the leadership of the second *aliya* occupied – and effectively blocked – the key positions in the political, economic and cultural spheres for a long period lasting, in fact, well into the era following independence. (On the political elite of the Yishuv see Wolffsohn, 1983a: 223; Lissak, 1981: chs. 4 and 5, on the economy, and 6 on culture.)

Believing in the supreme importance of the organization as a prerequisite for successful development, the leaders of the second *aliya* launched economic enterprises with close ties to their parties and thus laid the decisive groundwork for the Histadrut as well as the later state sector of the economy. The network of links between party politics and the economy forged by the generation of the second *aliya* transcended its origins in the Labour bloc and became of central importance for the entire political and economic system in Israel since their achievements served as models for the efforts of the non-socialist groups as well (see Eisenstadt, 1973: 39).

The first *kibbutzim* were also organized by members of the second *aliya*. Contrary to some characterizations, the men and women who founded the *kibbutzim* were not Marxian socialists. Had they been true Marxists, they would have turned their activities to the organization of the industrial proletariat rather than becoming agricultural pioneers.

The immigrants of the *third aliya* (1919–23) belonged to the political generation shaped by the events of the Russian October Revolution. This was the true 'Bolshevist' political generation. More precisely, they were the Bolshevists of the early phase of the revolution who, although not seeking 'democracy for all', at least hoped to establish democracy for one 'class', namely, for the proletariat, rather than a party dictatorship. The 'working class' was to be the ruling class, but it was to be democratic, at least in its internal structures.

This ideological and organizational concept proved significant for the founding of the Histadrut. The third *aliya* was not agrarian. It was instead urban in its outlook and thus more strictly Marxian in that it believed in the revolutionary potential of the industrial proletariat. The only problem was that this proletariat did not yet exist.

The third *aliya* contributed both the ideology and the membership basis for the more leftist parties such as the Poale Zion Left, the Socialist Workers' Party and later the Communists.

The third *aliya* was also of importance for the religious bloc. The development of the leftist-religious parties (Hapoel Hamisrahi and Poale Agudat Israel) was closely related to the influence of basically socialistic (one could also say, egalitarian, justice-seeking) but non-materialistic ideals among Orthodox Russian and Polish Jews.

Many of the immigrants of the *fourth aliya* had experienced the period of Lenin's New Economic Policy in the Soviet Union. This form of modified 'free market' economics within a socialist framework served as a model which the socialists among the immigrants of the fourth *aliya* hoped to introduce into Palestine. Their efforts considerably strengthened the then rather weak economic enterprises sponsored by Ahdut Haavoda and the Histadrut. Furthermore, their having experienced the creation of a powerful party apparatus in the Soviet Union also served in the long run to strengthen the parties they joined in Palestine, even though the socialists of the fourth *aliya* were for a long time forced to accept relatively minor positions in the party hierarchy and had to content themselves mainly with offices on the local level.

Quantitatively, however, middle-class ideology and backgrounds dominated in the fourth *aliya*, which for the first time provided a recruiting ground for non-socialist groups and thus represented a threat to the domination of the Labour bloc. The extent to which the fourth *aliya* turned the political current against the parties of the left is demonstrated by a comparison of the results of the elections to the Delegates' Assemblies of 1920 and 1925 (see Figure 13).

The fact that the Orthodox immigrants of the fourth *aliya* arriving from Poland in the early 1920s had experienced the wave of anti-Semitism then raging in their native land led to a more moderate stance among Agudat Israel supporters with regard to Zionism, although only gradually and over the long term (Wolffsohn, 1983a: 158 ff.; Friedmann, 1977: chs. 10–12).

The 'modernization' of the Orthodox part of the Yishuv was significantly affected by the immigration of religious German Jews arriving with the *fifth aliya* (Marmorstein, 1969; Schiff, 1977: ch. 3; Friedmann, 1977: ch. 14). These German Jews, both strongly Orthodox and at the same time 'modern', tried to combine Torah (i.e. religious) and Derech Eretz (i.e. secular) concerns in a functional and technical approach. More important, having experienced the rise of National Socialism at first hand, the German immigrants had come to realize the important contribution Zionist organizations were making to the very survival of the Jewish people. Their resistance to Zionism was thus already overcome. This was also true of numerous Polish immigrant supporters of Agudat Israel as well, who owed their survival to the Zionists who helped to secure the all-important immigration visa to Palestine. This process of 'modernization' and the subsequent more moderate attitude towards and even cooperation with Zionism provoked in turn a split within the Orthodox membership of Agudat Israel. The most strictly Orthodox believers rejected any form of compromise with Zionism, broke away from the AI and founded Neture Kartha (Guardians of the City). They continue to live in the Mea Shearim quarter of Jerusalem and their rejection in principle of the State of Israel even extends to cooperation with the PLO.

During the fifth *aliya*, the generation of the Great Depression and of National Socialism made its impact felt among the Labour parties. The socialist part of this political generation believed that the collapse of capitalism was imminent and was filled with a revolutionary impatience which manifested itself most particularly in the increasingly leftward movement of Hashomer Hazair.

Among the parties of the middle class, the fifth *aliya* led to the foundation of the liberal-bourgeois New Immigration Party (later known as the Progressive Party/Independent Liberals), the political fate of which remained closely tied to the maturity and ageing of its generation of predominantly bourgeois German immigrants (see Wolffsohn, 1983a: ch. 27 for data).

The most important development which the fifth *aliya* brought for the middle-class parties was the arrival of militant young Poles, members of the Revisionist youth organization Beitar. Their militancy can be explained as a reaction against the rising tide of anti-Semitism which they had experienced in Poland. Once in Palestine, they demanded an 'active' policy against the Arabs and the Mandate authorities. Without these young militants Ezel would probably not have been founded, nor would it have made itself independent of the Revisionists.

Due to their predominantly bourgeois composition, the fourth and fifth *aliyot* also led to an increase in the prestige of such 'middle-class' professions as medicine and law.

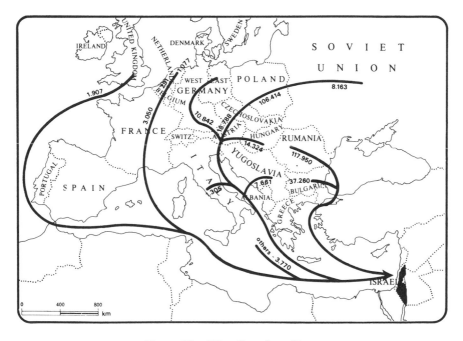

Figure 35   The aliya *from Europe.*

Source: Carta, 1977: 28.

At first, Sabras of all political blocs and persuasions were only able to continue along existing lines, and not to go off in new directions. Again and again the polls have established that the Sabras are more pragmatic than the 'founding fathers' and identify less with Mapai/ILP or the left in general. For a long time it was possible to apply the simple formula: the younger, the more to the right. (See Tables 18 and 19, and for further data Etzioni-Halevy and Shapira, 1977: 58 f.; Arian, 1979: 81, and 1978: 81; Wolffsohn, 1983a: 166 ff.)

The gradual shift to the right is therefore closely connected to the structural 'Sabraization' of Israeli society (see also C/XII/4). It must also be noted that 'Oriental' Israelis have a higher birth rate, so that the growth in the numbers of Sabras means at the same time an increase in the proportion of 'Orientals'. 'Sabraization' and 'Orientalization' are intertwined processes.

During the Yishuv and in the first years of the new state of Israel, the only channels to political power open to Sabras led through the ranks of the various party militias and later Zahal (see Wolffsohn, 1983a: 169 ff. for examples and further literature).

The generation of Sabras born in the 1920s did not attain real political power until the installation of the Rabin government in 1974. This group is known as the Generation 5708, the political generation whose soldiers fought for and achieved the independence of Israel in the year 5708 of the Jewish calendar (1948/9). Sabras are now in the process of taking over in most of the parties.

In the National Religious Party the pragmatic generation of the 1930s (Education Minister Hammer and his followers among the NRP 'young guard') has gradually assumed power since 1968, this precipitating an ideological as well as generational and ethnic crisis within the NRP. These ageing youngsters are also of Ashkenasi origin.

To continue the practice of naming political generations according to significant formative events, this is the political generation of the Sinai Campaign.

The political generation of the Six Day War was the first ever to experience the new political-geographical dimensions of Eretz Israel (i.e. Greater Israel) with the occupied territories. Nevertheless, its organizational (but not its ideological) impact appears to be less than that of the political generation of the Yom Kippur War with its protest movements and demands for greater political participation, activism and more 'democracy'. This is also the same political generation which sought either to promote (Peace Now) or to prevent (Gush Emunim) the peace-making process with Egypt by means of extra-parliamentary activities, and it is at the same time the political generation in which significant numbers of individuals have for the first time refused to follow military orders, as for example in the occupied territories and in Lebanon.

The political trend towards the right, involving a shift away from the ideals of the *halutzim*, the agricultural pioneers, in particular, as well as a decreasing emphasis on ideology in general, was not only strengthened by the arrival of the Afro-Asian immigrants of the late 1940s. It was also encouraged by the traditional parties themselves in their attempts to 'buy' political allegiances. Considerable efforts were undertaken to provide services in all areas of life for the newly arrived immigrants in the hope of influencing their later behaviour at the polls. The fact that Oriental, especially Moroccan, immigrants remained at a disadvantage led to their gradual move away from the party of the 'founding fathers', Mapai/ILP, to the Herut/Gahal/Likud bloc.

Since this shift clearly involves a protest reaction, the Likud could easily lose the support of Oriental Israelis if it fails materially to improve their situation. Up to and including the Knesset elections of 1984, however, this had not happened – at least not yet. If on some future election day, Oriental voters decide once again to register a protest at the polls, it will go against the

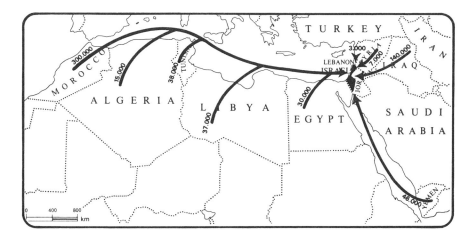

Figure 36   The aliya *from Arab countries.*

Source: Carta, 1977: 27.

leadership of the Likud and other rightist parties like Tehiya, which is, after all, an almost exclusively Ashkenasi organization. A purely ethnic but corrupt list like Tami may not be their preference. An ethnic Orthodox party like Shass, which obtained four Knesset seats in 1984, may be more attractive. A more far-reaching Orientalization of the Herut rank-and-file as well as its leadership may prove the most promising possibility. The already at least partially completed 'takeover' of Herut may be one reason why Oriental Israelis did not abandon their allegiance to the Likud in 1984 despite economic setbacks and what appears to have been their original intention to 'punish' the ruling party, at least if we are to believe the pre-election polls.

In principle, a government steering a hard course on foreign policy issues in general and in relations with the Arabs and the occupied territories in particular seems to meet with the general understanding and support of younger Sabras and Oriental Jews. (See also section B/VI/2/e.)

(e) POPULATION POLICY

From the beginning of the Mandate in 1922, and especially after 1939, the British allowed only limited numbers of Jews to immigrate to Palestine. The Zionist parties had argued in vain for an 'open door' policy and were forced to accept immigration quotas, which they then divided up in a manner which was anything but non-political.

The Zionist parties, which were dominant at first only in the Yishuv but later also in the entire WZO, distributed the precious immigration permits mainly to their own supporters (for data see Horowitz and Lissak, 1977: 257; Friedlander and Goldscheider, 1979: 71 ff.). It must nevertheless be noted that the socialist Zionists of that time evidenced the strongest dedication to the work of building a Jewish society in Palestine. However politicized and immoral this immigration policy many have been, it did prove advantageous to the establishment of the later state. Individual and collective interests clearly collided in this case.

After achieving independence, Israel immediately opened its doors to all immigrants and in 1950 passed the Law of Return, Article 1 of which states that 'every Jew has the right to immigrate to Israel' and thus to attain Israeli citizenship.

The mass immigration of the years 1948 to 1951 confronted the new state with enormous economic and social problems, as Oriental immigrants often arrived with little or no vocational training to qualify them for jobs in a modern industrial economy.

In November 1951 *'selection criteria'* for immigrants were established by the Jewish Agency (Friedlander and Goldscheider, 1979: 98 ff.). In practice, these guidelines gave preference to immigrants from Europe or America. By that time, however, the number of immigrants from these continents was steadily declining. In the early 1950s upper-class Jewish emigrants from North Africa preferred to immigrate to France (ibid.: 102). The new regulations thus had little effect on the composition of the immigrant groups.

'The Orientals were not Israel's first choice, but there was no other alternative than to accept them' (Smooha, 1978: 86.) It is said that Nahum Goldmann even suggested sending some 100,000 Jews from Morocco and Iraq back to their native lands in 1952 but that Ben-Gurion resisted the proposal. (Minutes of a meeting between the Israeli government and the WZO cited in a book by S. Ben-Simchon, *Haaretz*, 2 August 1983. I have thus far not been able to substantiate the truth of this claim.)

Reparations payments by the Federal Republic of Germany contributed to the improvement of Israel's economic situation beginning in 1954, when a phase of significant economic growth set in (see section C/XIII). The policy of immigration quotas for North African Jews was, however, continued, thus opening an apparent gap between ideological pronouncements and political reality. This led to domestic political controversies in Israel, Herut condemning the restrictions on immigration most sharply and drawing parallels to the policies of the British Mandate (Friedlander and Goldscheider, 1979: 104 ff.). This may, indeed, have been the beginning of the Orientalization of Herut supporters, a process which was to prove a decisive factor in the 1977, 1981 and 1984 elections.

The predominance of immigrants from Europe and America since 1967, as well as the stream of Soviet immigrants, mainly between 1971 and 1973, were phenomena closer to the economic, cultural and social ideal. The reluctance of the Jewish upper classes from Iran to immigrate to Israel after the Iranian Revolution was registered with disappointment. That this was so nevertheless fits the general pattern established since the beginnings of Zionist immigration to Palestine.

(f) EMIGRATION

Even among the highly motivated members of the second *aliya*, which began in 1904, only some 6,000 of the original 37,000 immigrants still remained in Palestine by 1918 (Gorni, 1970: 205 f.). In 1927 and 1928 more Jews emigrated from than immigrated to Palestine.

After independence as well, the numbers of Jews turning their backs on

Israel were significant. The not always uncontroversial figures of the Central Bureau of Statistics list some 390,900 Israeli citizens as 'not yet returned' (*Statistical Abstract of Israel*, 1983: 125, also with annual statistics). In the summer of 1984 a controversy arose over the exact number of *yordim* (the somewhat pejorative Hebrew word for emigrants). A study prepared for the Ministry of Immigrants Absorption claimed that 252,000 Israelis had left the country between 1948 and late 1983. The Central Bureau of Statistics, on the other hand, gave a figure of some 350,000 (G. Alon, *Haaretz*, 30 August 1984). Most of these emigrants live in the United States. The numbers were particularly high for 1980 (31,000), 1981 (32,400) and 1982 (90,800), although it must be noted that the time elapsed between the date of departure and the present is also the shortest. The most recent figures can, therefore, be expected to decrease after some time (see *Statistical Abstract of Israel*, 1982: 121, and 1983: 125).

Up until 1973 the annual figure for Israeli citizens 'not yet returned' was well under the 10,000 mark, the highest contingent (7,100) having been recorded in 1967. Table 25 shows the data for the period since 1973.

Table 25   Israeli Citizens 'Not Yet Returned', 1973–1983

1973	11,500
1974	12,900
1975	10,400
1976	13,500
1977	12,600
1978	8,100
1979	11,200
1980	24,400
1981	18,400
1982	33,300
1983	89,200

Source: *Statistical Abstract of Israel*, various vols.

It is also of significance that approximately 70% of the Jewish immigrants who were allowed to leave the Soviet Union in the 1970s decided to remain in various Western countries rather than proceed to Israel (data in Wolffsohn, 1983a: 399).

Yerida, that is, emigration, enjoys about the same prestige in Israeli Jewish society as a four-letter word. The *Talmud* (*Bava Batra* 91a) admonishes that Jews may leave Eretz Israel, the Land of Israel, only in case of emergencies and also states that 'everyone' (i.e. every Jew) 'who lives outside Israel acts like an idolater' (*Ketuvot* 110b).

What do the polls reveal? in April 1974, shortly after the Yom Kippur War, a survey conducted by the Israel Institute of Applied Social Research found that 9% of those questioned did 'not desire' or 'not desire very much' to remain in Israel, whereas 40% intended to continue on living there 'by all means'. Some 21% wanted to do so 'very much', 13% 'wanted' to, another 7% chose the response 'more or less' and 10% 'not very much' (Levy and

Gutmann, 1974: 36). Although only 9% expressed clearly 'negative attitudes' concerning their desire to stay in Israel and a total of 74% wanted to remain 'by all means', 'very much' or just 'wanted' to, the latter figure is certainly not impressively high for a country which wishes to act as a magnet for immigrants.

Moreover, the number of younger Israelis between the ages of 20 and 29 willing to leave is higher than among their elders. On the one hand, this must be seen within the context of a generally higher mobility among young people. On the other hand, it could also be argued that this indicates a weaker spiritual bond with Israel. The latter argument is strengthened by a PORI poll conducted in June 1980. Among its findings was that 36·1% of all Israelis between the ages of 18 and 29 approved of *yerida* (emigration), as opposed to 23·4% among the overall population (*Haaretz*, 8 July 1980). Here, too, origin was an important intervening factor. The desire to remain in Israel was stronger among Ashkenasim than among Oriental citizens (Levy and Gutmann, 1974: 43). *Yerida* was also approved of by more Oriental than Ashkenasi Israelis (PORI poll, loc. cit.).

Four years later, in March 1984, PORI conducted another survey on the subject and found that only 15% approved of emigration and 75% 'didn't approve'. In other words, the approval rate decreased from about 23% in 1980 to only 15% in 1984 (*World Opinion Update*, vol. VII, no. 5, May 1984: 71 f.).

At the same time, 28% of the interviewees stated that they personally knew people who were 'planning emigration' and 20% knew of actual emigrants or persons firmly intending to leave Israel. The interviewees nonetheless overwhelmingly rejected the idea of *yerida* for their own persons. Asked whether they considered themselves a 'potential emigrant', 90% replied they did not, and only 5% answered affirmatively (loc. cit.).

There is an undeniable gap between the position or attitude assumed by the interviewees and the actual behaviour of their environment.

(g) AGE STRUCTURE

Table 26 shows that Israel's population is extraordinarily young. However, the average age of the Jewish population steadily increased until 1981, whereas that of the non-Jewish, that is, Arab population declined during the period 1955 to 1970 and then remained constant until 1981. In 1982 the average age of both the Jewish and non-Jewish groups once again declined.

The extent to which the increasing youthfulness of the population is simultaneously a growing Orientalization is demonstrated by the 1982 statistics for children up to the age of 9, of which there were 134,800 among Sabras of Euro-American backgrounds, 148,900 among Sabras where the father is of North African heritage and 108,600 among Sabras where the father is of Asian extraction. This makes for a total of 257,500 among Jews of Afro-Asian origin. The 304,500 Sabras whose fathers were already born in Israel partially restored the balance, although with a shift in favour of the Oriental groups (*Statistical Abstract of Israel*, 1983: 61). But here, too, we find a cross-current. The number of babies (children under the age of 1) was highest among Sabras with a father born in Israel, and there are more children between the ages of 1 and 4 whose fathers were born in Israel than

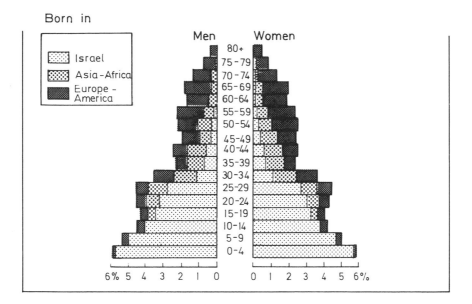

Figure 37a   The Jewish population: age, sex and origin, 1978 (%).

Source: Karmon, 1983: 66.

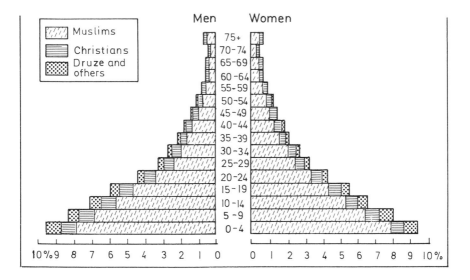

*Figure 37b   The non-Jewish population: age, sex and religion, 1978
(%).*

Source: Karmon, 1983: 66.

Table 26   The Population of Israel, 1948–82: Age Structure

Age cohort as
percentage of total: *0–4   5–14   15–19 20–24 25–34 35–44 45–64   65+   average age*

Jews:

		0–4	5–14	15–19	20–24	25–34	35–44	45–64	65+	average age
8 Nov.	1948	12·2	16·5	8·4		43·9		15·0	4·0	28·9
	1955	13·6	20·3	7·4	7·6	14·8	13·2	18·4	4·7	27·9
	1970	10·7	19·4	10·4	10·0	12·0	10·7	19·6	7·2	30·1
	1981	10·7	19·9	8·0	8·2	16·7	9·9	16·9	9·7	30·7
	1982	10·5	20·2	8·0	7·9	16·6	10·4	16·9	9·5	30·2

Non-Jewish:

		0–4	5–14	15–19	20–24	25–34	35–44	45–64	65+	average age
	1955	18·7	27·0	10·5	8·0	12·0	7·5	10·9	5·4	23·0
	1970	19·5	30·2	10·1	7·4	12·3	8·0	8·6	3·9	21·1
	1981	17·2	29·6	11·8	9·4	12·2	8·2	8·6	3·0	21·1
	1982	16·7	29·8	11·7	9·0	12·5	8·2	8·7	2·8	20·7

Source: *Statistical Abstract of Israel*, 1983: 56 f.

in Africa, Europe, America or Asia. The latter group is by far the smallest (loc. cit.). Among Sabra fathers, however, we may assume a significant number with Oriental origins. Nevertheless, the 'performance' of the ethnic groups seems to indicate an 'Ashkenization' of Orientals in terms of child-bearing.

The lowest average age among the Arab population groups is to be found among the Moslems (19·5 years), followed by the Druze (20·7) and the Christians (26·8) (*Statistical Abstract of Israel*, 1983: 57). This is closely related to the more 'modern' life-styles among the Christian Arabs (see section B/VI/3).

(h) OTHER DEMOGRAPHIC DATA

The divorce rate (per 1,000 of the average population) was 1·7 from 1950 to 1954, 0·9 from 1965 to 1969 and 1·3 in 1982 among the Jewish population. The divorce rate among Moslems was 0·7 from 1955 to 1959, 0·4 from 1965 to 1969, 0·7 in 1981 and 0·5 in 1982. The estimates for the Christian Arabs remain at about 0·1 between 1955 and 1981. Among the Druze the numbers were 1·0 from 1955 to 1959, 0·5 from 1965 to 1969, 0·6 for 1981 and 0·8 for 1982 (*Statistical Abstract of Israel*, 1982: 75 ff.).

The infant mortality rate for the Jewish population sank from 38·8 for the period 1950/4 to 11·6 in 1982, among Moslems from 60·6 for 1955/9 to 22·1 in 1982 (a dramatic decline but still nearly double the rate for the Jewish population), among the Christian Arabs from 46·1 to 12·2 (significantly less than the rate for the Moslems and only slightly higher than that for the Jews!) and among the Druze from 54·3 to 18·9 (*Statistical Abstract of Israel*, 1983: 76 ff.).

The gross reproduction rate between 1955 and 1959 was 1·73 for the Jewish population, 3·98 for the Moslems, 2·24 for the Christian Arabs and 3·47 for the Druze. The figures for 1982 were 1·35 among Jews, 2·68 among

Moslems, 1·13 among Christian Arabs (the lowest rate of all!) and 2·91 among Druze (ibid.: 98).

The general fertility rate for Jewish women was 121·8 in 1951, 90·7 in 1981 and 92·4 in 1982. For Sabras the rate was 107·9 in 1951, 101·8 in 1981 and 102·7 in 1982. For Afro-Asian woman it was 199·7 in 1951, 81·0 in 1981 and 80·9 in 1982 ('modernization'!). The rate for Euro-American women was 90·8 in 1951, 73·0 in 1981 and 77·5 in 1982. The fertility rates for Moslem mothers were 241·0 in 1955 (earliest available statistics) and 173·2 in 1982 (a much more modest 'modernization'). The decrease in the fertility rate for Christian Arab women was dramatic: from 147·3 in 1955 to 76·0 in 1982. The rates for Druze women were 202·7 in 1955 and 169·1 in 1982 (ibid.: 99 f.). The overall trend is towards fewer children, most especially among Euro-American Jews and Christian Arabs, and to a lesser but still observable extent among Moslems and Druze.

In all of these areas the patterns for Christian Arabs and Euro-American Jews on the one hand and Moslems and Druze on the other are remarkably similar.

The average life expectancy for 1971 was 72·8 years for Arab women and 68·7 for Arab men, 73·8 for Jewish women and 70·6 for Jewish men. The data for 1980 were 73·3 years for Arab women and 70·8 for Arab men, 76·2 for Jewish women and 72·8 for Jewish men (ibid., 1982: 110 and 1983: 114).

(i) REGIONAL DISTRIBUTION

The shifts in the percentage of the overall Israeli population residing in the various districts of the country are shown in Table 27. These figures show a clear shift to the southern region as well as a certain, although incomplete, reduction in the concentrations around Tel-Aviv and the Central District. It is noteworthy that the shift has been to the south, and not to Jerusalem, despite the prime ideological and political status of the nation's capital. The population increase of the Jerusalem District has, in fact, remained very limited. The strong development of the south is related to the settlement of Oriental immigrants there as well as to the 'challenge' of the Negev. In 1982

Table 27   Israel's Population Distribution by Region, 1948 and 1982 (%)

1948	1982	District
35·7	24·8	Tel-Aviv
14·3	20·4	Central District (including Petach Tikva, Ramlah, Rehovot and the Plain of Sharon)
16·8	15·4	Northern District (incl. 0·5% in the Golan Heights in 1982)
20·5	14·2	Haifa
2·5	12·2	Southern District
10·2	11·5	Jerusalem
—	0·5	'Judaea and Samaria'

Source: Statistical Abstract of Israel, 1983: 33.

1% of the total population lived in the occupied territories (including the Golan Heights).

One means employed to relieve the congestion of the central areas was the founding of 'development towns' in which numerous new citizens of Oriental heritage have been settled since 1948. Among the better-known of these new centres are (from south to north) Mitzpe Rimon, Jeruham, Dimona, Beersheba, Arad, Ofakim, Netivot, Ashkelon, Ashdod, Javneh, Kiryat Gad, Bei-Shemesh, Afula, Upper Nazareth, Tiberias (formerly an Arab city) and Kiryat Shmonah (see Figure 38).

For the sake of electoral geographers it should be noted that many of these new towns delivered large majorities for the Likud in the elections of 1977, 1981 and 1984 (on regional inequalities see Gradus, 1983).

As was already the case at the time of the War of Independence, the Jewish population in 1982 was largely urban (90·2%). The Arab population, too, was becoming increasingly urbanized. Whereas 30–35% lived in the cities during the Mandate period, 55·4% did so in 1972 and 69·8% in 1982. At the same time, the proportion of the rural Arab population dropped from 44·6% to 30·2% (data compiled from various sources for the Mandate period and from the *Statistical Abstract of Israel*, 1983: 43).

2   THE 'SECOND ISRAEL': ORIENTAL JEWS

Oriental Israelis, that is, those Israelis whose roots lie in North African and West Asian countries, particularly those of Moroccan and perhaps least of all those of Iraqi heritage, tend to be more 'proletarian', more religious (Goldscheider and Friedlander, 1982: 10 ff.; Bar-Lev and Kedem, 1984; Shokeid, 1984) and more nationalistic than Israelis of European or American backgrounds. Furthermore, a significant socio-economic gap exists between these two groups.

(a) SOCIO-ECONOMIC DATA: THE INNER-JEWISH GAP

While the following statistics demonstrate an undeniable improvement in the quality of life for Oriental Israelis, the data also show that their development has nevertheless lagged behind that of Euro-American Jews in Israel.

1   Education

The proportion of Oriental Israelis in junior high schools (grades 6 to 8) and in high schools has risen dramatically (see Table 29). Table 40 indicates a continuous growth in the numbers of Oriental Israelis born outside Israel enrolled in higher education, but the proportions remain below those for students from European and American backgrounds.

Much more revealing are the data for the second generation, the Sabras of the various ethnic groups. Here the statistics show that proportional enrolments of Oriental Jews increased in the period up to 1974/5 but have been dropping since 1977/8. Both the time frame (the election of 1977 and the subsequent change in governments) and the political-psychological perspective are significant; the overall situation improves, hopes rise, the trend falters, disenchantment grows. In this case the trend was even backwards. It

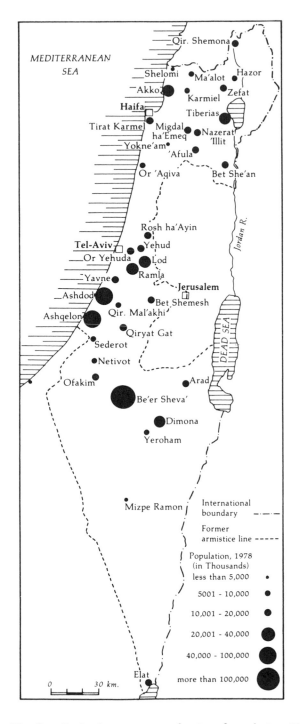

Figure 38   Israel's development towns, by size of population, 1979.

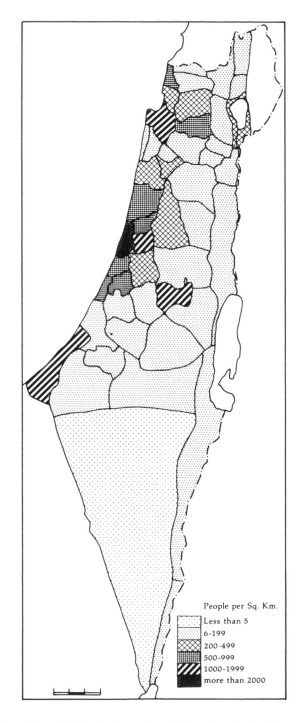

Figure 39 The distribution of population (population density by natural regions).

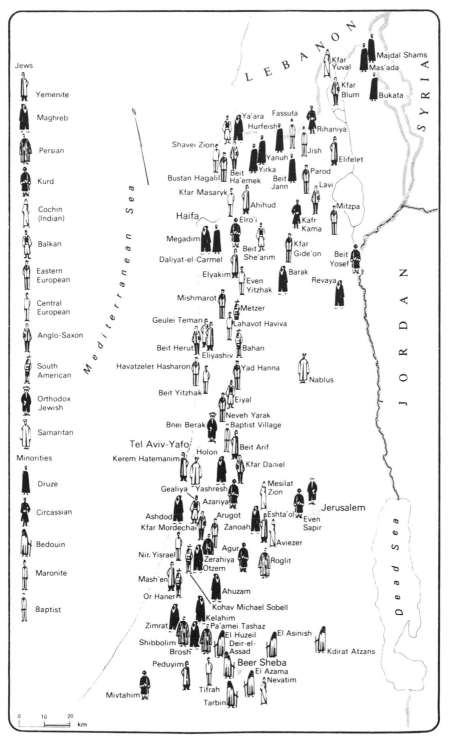

Figure 40   Israel's population and communities.

Table 28   Israel's Arab Population. Distribution by Region, 1948 and
           1981 (%)

1948	1981	District
58·1	47·2	Northern District
17·6	15·7	Haifa
10·3	9·6	Central District
9·9	7·9	Southern District (mainly Bedouins)
2·3	1·6	Tel-Aviv
	18·2	Jerusalem (incl. East Jerusalem)

Source: Statistical Abstract of Israel, 1983: 34.

must be noted, however, that the drop in the proportion of students among
Sabras of Euro-American backgrounds was even greater, as the demand for
university graduates had declined on the Israeli job market. (For further
information on the ethnic problem and education, see E. Peled, 1984;
Steinitz, 1984; Yossi Shavit, 1984; Shokeid, 1983; Yuchtman-Yaar and
Semyonov, 1979.)

Table 29   Jewish Secondary Students Ages 14–17, 1966/7 to 1981/2 by
           Parental Origin (number of students per 1,000 of appropriate
           population group and ratio of Euro-American to Afro-Asian
           groups)

Year	Euro-Americans	Afro-Asians	Ratio
1966/67	686	379	1·81
1969/70	775	442	1·75
1976/77	797	637	1·25
1979/80	809	710	1·14
1980/81	817	734	1·11
1981/82	828	758	1·09

Sources: Bernstein and Antonovsky, 1981: 11; Statistical Abstract of Israel,
           1982: 275, 291 and 1983: 298 f., 311.

2   Occupational Structures

The economic and intellectual elites of the Oriental Jews, most especially of
the Moroccan (and least of all the Iraqi) emigrants did not come to Israel.
For the most part the elite opted to immigrate to France instead.

The majority, that is, somewhat more than half of those who became
Israeli citizens, belonged to the traditional middle classes in their native
lands, that is to say, they were largely artisans and merchants (Friedlander
and Goldscheider, 1979: 42 f.).

In Israel the new immigrants found employment mainly in 'proletarian'
occupations, a situation which became even more pronounced among the

Table 30   Jewish Students Ages 20–29, 1964 to 1980/81 by Origin of
            Father (% of all Jews of the appropriate age cohort, approx.
            75% of all students in 1978/9)

Origin	1964/65	1969/70	1972/73	1974/75	Average 1977/78 and 1978/79	1980/81
Israel						
Total:	8·1	9·9	9·8	9·5	7·5	7·2
Father from:						
Israel	5·2	7·5	8·6	10·0	11·3	
Africa/Asia	1·6	2·5	2·8	3·0	2·6	
Europe/America	10·7	12·6	13·8	14·0	12·7	
Africa/Asia	0·8	1·6	2·0	2·1	2·1	2·8
Europe/America	5·3	9·8	9·3	8·4	9·8	9·1

Sources: Council for Higher Education, 1982: 14; *Statistical Abstract of Israel*,
            1982: 629, and 1983: 657.

Sabras of the second (Sabra) generation than was the case for the immigrant
generation (Bernstein and Antonovsky, 1981: 15).

In 1978, 50·5% of the immigrant generation and 57·4% of second-
generation Sabras were blue-collar workers. Among Euro-American immigrants to Israel this trend was reversed: 34·4% were blue-collar workers in
the first generation and only 28·2% in the second. In 1982, 36·6% of Oriental
immigrants and 34·5% of the second generation were to be found in blue-
collar occupations. Among Euro-American immigrants 25·2% of the first
generation were blue-collar workers and only 13% of the following generation born in Israel. Despite the remaining gap, an improvement for the
second generation of Oriental Jews is recognizable. (See 'Jewish employed
persons by occupation, contingent of birth, period of immigration and sex',
in *Statistical Abstract of Israel*, 1983: 370 f.)

In 1982, 25·3% of Oriental Sabras and 15·9% of the immigrant generation
were employed as white-collar workers ('clerical and related'). The proportions for the Euro-American groups were 18·7% and 25·4%, first and second
generations respectively. This can be viewed as a recognizable improvement,
provided clerical work is to be considered as such. The proportion of
professional and technical workers rose from 9·0% (immigrant generation) to
12·0% (second, Sabra generation) among Oriental Israelis, but rose among
Ashkenasim from 15·5% to 24·7% (loc. cit.).

In the scientific and academic professions the gap was enormous: 15·2% of
Ashkenasi Sabras were occupied in these professions in contrast to only 2·6%
of Oriental Sabras. In the immigrant generations 13·8% of the Ashkenasim
as opposed to 3·0% of the Orientals fell into this category. For Oriental
Israelis this meant that there had been no improvement at all from one
generation to the next (loc. cit.).

In 1954, 43·2% of Oriental Israelis were employed in construction or in industry. This fell to only 31·9% among Oriental immigrants by 1981 and to 31·4% among Oriental Sabras, a pronounced downward trend overall, but one showing little difference between the generations. The proportions declined among Ashkenasim from 35·2% to 22·8% in the immigrant generation and to 13·2% among Sabras during the same period. The gap thus remained (Smooha, 1978: 291 f.; *Statistical Abstract of Israel*, 1982: 348 f.).

3   Income and Housing

Table 31 includes data on income since 1930 and shows a clear decline in the transition period from the Mandate to the first years after independence and an improvement during the 1970s as well as the continuing gap between Ashkenasim and Oriental Jews. Despite this gap, however, the overall economic improvement is impressive – a development which can easily lead to exaggerated expectations all too difficult to fulfil (see Semyonov and Krauss, 1983).

The gap operating in favour of second-generation Oriental Jews in the area of housing in 1980 should also be noted.

4   Composition of the Oriental Population

Neither the differences in the composition of Israel's Oriental population before and after independence nor the fact that this group represented a very distinct minority up to 1948 should be overlooked. Only 4·7% of the third *aliya* came from Western Asia or North Africa. In the fourth *aliya* the proportion was 11·8% and in the fifth 9·0%. From 1939 to 1945, 18·3% and from 1946 to 1948, 4·0% of the immigrants were Orientals, whereby the numbers of West Asians greatly exceeded those from North Africa (Friedlander and Goldscheider, 1979: 38).

5   Income Distribution

The data in Table 31 also indicate a significant leap forward economically for Oriental Israelis in the period from 1970 to 1975. A slight backward trend set in in 1977 (change of governments) and continued through 1980. In 1981 there was a slight improvement, which certainly was not without effect on the election results (see section C/XIII/2). The setback in 1982 was minor.

A study of the regional distribution of income reveals that the new 'development towns' in which mainly Oriental immigrants have been settled since 1948 rank well below the national average in income (Ginor, 1979: 109). This fact is significant for understanding the geography of Israel's election results.

6   Poverty

Poverty will be defined here as having an income ranking among the lowest 10% on the scale. While Ginor (1979: 175) registered an increase in poverty among Oriental Jews from 59·9% to 67·3% in the period from 1968/9 to 1975/6, her data also registered a concurrent drop in poverty among Ashkenasim from 33·2% to 22·2%.

Table 32 includes data for the period from 1975/6 to 1979/80. These

Table 31 The Jewish Population, 1930–1984
By Origin, Income and Living Conditions

| | Income/Oriental Family (% of Euro-Am.) | Persons/Room | |
		Euro-Am.	Afr.-As.
1930	70	2.5	3.5
1946	78	2.7	4.5
1956/57	73	2.1	3.2
1965	72		
1968/69	72	1.6	2.0
1970	74		
1975	82		
1977	81	1.0	1.6
1980	80		
1981	81	2.5* (3.4)	4.0* (3.4)
1982	80		
1983	82	3.1*	4.5*
1984	78	3.1*	4.5*

*Persons per household
( ) Second generation

Sources:
Ginor, 1979:106; *Statistical Abstract*, various vols.

figures illustrate a dramatic improvement in the economic situation of Oriental Jews (as well as Israeli Arabs). This is especially true in the case of the more recent immigrants, where a gap has opened in favour of the Oriental Jews.

The index of relative equality is defined as the average monthly income of Oriental Israelis in IL (Israeli pounds) or – since 1980 – in shekels, divided by the average monthly income of the Ashkenasi population then multiplied by 100. This index has risen from 73 in 1956/7 to 82 in 1975, 87 in 1977 and 92·3 in 1979/80 (Smooha, 1978: 282; *Statistical Abstract of Israel*, 1978: 297, and 1983: 295).

(b) THE SOCIAL GAP: ATTITUDES AND BEHAVIOUR

Apart from short-term emotional waves of mutual solidarity (for example, during the wars of 1967 and 1973 and the Lebanon incursion of March 1978), attitudes towards ethnic relations among Jewish Israelis have remained fairly stable (see Figure 41 and Table 33). Following every outbreak of hostilities, up to and including the Lebanon incursion of 1978, polls revealed that ethnic feelings were consistently perceived as more harmonious than immediately before the fighting began. The outbreak of the War in Lebanon in 1982 represents an exception to this pattern. Failing to generate even a passing wave of emotional unity, the War in Lebanon only contributed to the deterioration of the social consensus in Israel.

In July 1981 a PORI survey found that 69·2% of Oriental Jews expressed

Table 32   Poverty in the Jewish Population, 1975/76 to 1979/80 (income in lowest 10%)

	1975/76	1979/80
Jews in total	82·5	96·3
Afro-Asians in total	55·5	31·0
Veterans	34·8	21·5
New immigrants	20·7	9·5
European-Americans in total	18·3	57·9
Veterans	11·1	31·8
New immigrants	7·2	26·1
Israel	8·7	7·4
Non-Jews	17·5	3·7

Source: Statistical Abstract of Israel, 1977: 266 f., and 1983: 302 f.

the belief that they were not being discriminated against, an opinion which was shared by 50% of the Ashkenasim and 65% of the Likud voters but only 52·9% of the Maarah voters. Among the population as a whole, the percentage of those perceiving discrimination fell from 64% in 1971 to 58·7% in July of 1981 (Haaretz, 5 August 1981).

The surveys conducted by Ben-Rafael (1982: 147) in 1978 and 1979 revealed that Israelis of Moroccan and Yemenite backgrounds viewed the ethnic polarization as significantly sharper than that between 'rich' and 'poor', 'left' and 'right' or 'religious' and 'secular'.

A striking phenomenon continuing from the 1950s to the present is that North African Jews are much more likely to seek the company of Ashkenasim than is the case the other way around (details in Wolffsohn, 1983a: 410 ff.; Ben-Rafael, 1982: 137, 167). The latter apparently view such contacts as a step down, the former as a step up the social ladder. It would seem equally manifest that Oriental Jews have come to assume the dominant European-American value-structure and prefer 'integration' to the kind of 'pluralism' Smooha (1978: 14) defines as 'cultural diversity and social division'.

The acceptance of intermarriage (among Sabras) is greater among Oriental Jews than Ashkenasim, although here, too, the polls indicate an increasing willingness to enter into mixed marriages (Peres, 1976: 91; Levy and Gutmann, 1976a: 297).

Surveys of attitudes may be very revealing, but actual behaviour is a more valid indicator. Let us therefore examine the data on intermarriage. An intermarriage or 'endogamy' index is calculated by Israel's Central Bureau of Statistics. The lower the index is, the more frequent are the cases of intermarriage. This index was 0·81 in 1955, 0·73 in 1965, 0·64 in 1975, 0·62 in 1979 and 0·60 in 1980. This indicates that the greatest progress in mutual acceptance was made between the 1950s and the 1960s and continued into the 1970s but that conditions have remained relatively unchanged since then. (On the offspring of ethnic intermarriages, see Yogev and Jamsky, 1984.)

In a study of acquaintance networks, Weimann (1984) found that these are also impinged upon by ethnic distinctions.

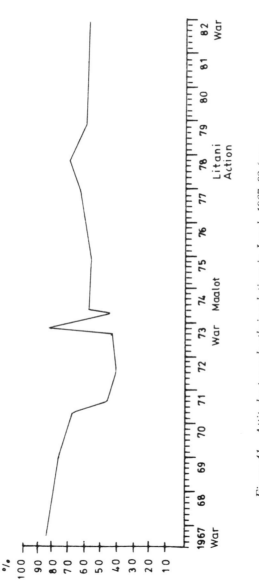

Figure 41   Attitudes towards ethnic relations in Israel, 1967–82 'very good' or 'good'.

Table 33   Attitudes towards Ethnic Relations in Israel, 1967–82 (%)

Period	% of respondents replying 'very good' or 'quite good'
June 1967	84
Up to April 1969	Between 84 and 74
March–April 1971	65 (beginning of 'Black Panther' activities)
June–July 1971	47
May–June 1972	40
July–September 1973	43
October 1973	80 (Yom Kippur War)
April 1974	47
May 1974	57 Maalot
Summer 1975 to Autumn 1977	Between 55 and 61[*]
Summer 1978	68 (March: fighting in Lebanon against PLO)
March 1979	59
July–August 1982	58 (polarization after 1981 elections, War in Lebanon

[*]Only a slight drop up to the May elections.

Sources: Etzioni-Halevy and Shapira, 1977: 201 ff.; Stone, 1982: 286; Ben-Sira, 1983: 85.

It must also be noted that Oriental Jews seem to prefer an increasing political compartmentalization, as evidenced by a growing trend in favour of the small parties in their voting behaviour from 1977 to 1984. In addition, they have established more strongly ethnic parties in the religious camp. Thus Tami was founded in 1981 and achieved notable success, only to lose in 1984, whereas Shass, formed in 1983, did well in 1984. On the other hand, there was also a trend towards rather than away from Herut.

(c) UNDERREPRESENTATION

Smooha (1978: 39 ff.) has drawn up an impressive collection of data on the underrepresentation of Israeli immigrants from Islamic countries, and the present author has supplemented the collection (Wolffsohn, 1983a: 413 ff., 432, 503).

Although Oriental Jews remain undeniably underrepresented in Israeli society, a certain improvement cannot be overlooked. Nevertheless, the rule of thumb still holds: the lower the political rank, the better the representation of Oriental Israelis.

This can be observed particularly well on the level of local politics. In 1957, for example, only 20·9% of the general secretaries in the local Histadrut workers' councils were of Oriental heritage. The percentage had risen to 56·9% by 1973 (Smooha, 1978: 318).

There are also hopeful signs to be noted in the upper echelons of the political system. Oriental Jews have become judges in the Israeli Supreme Court; Israel's chief of staff in 1984, Moshe Levy, was an immigrant from

Iraq; and the man who became secretary general of the Histadrut in 1984, Israel Kessar, is from Sanaa in Yemen.

Apparently, Jews from the Arab states of Asia are at an advantage in comparison with Jews from North Africa. It must not, however, be overlooked that David Levy, an immigrant from Morocco (and therefore not a Sabra) was defeated by a relatively narrow margin in the September 1983 ballot of the Herut Central Committee to choose the party's candidate for the post of prime minister. The winner was Yitzhak Shamir, who is of Polish extraction.

The increase in the number of Oriental MKs representing religious parties in the Eleventh Knesset (1984) was striking. Seven out of the thirteen members from religious parties were Oriental Jews. These included all four of the Shass deputies, two of the four NRP parliamentarians and Tami's only delegate, Abuhatzira.

Finally, the very low number of Jews of African or Asian descent to attain high rank in the military (major general or troop commander) ought to be mentioned. Between 1948 and the end of December 1978, 105 of the officers who had attained such a rank were of European or American ancestry and 82 were Sabras – most of these, in turn, were Ashkenasim and only 7 were of Oriental heritage (compiled from data provided by the IDF spokesman). Chief of Staff Levy therefore represents an exception illustrating that the factor of ancestry can serve as an impediment to the larger group but presents no bar to advancement for the particularly industrious and able individual. In the case of equal accomplishments, the disadvantages become fewer. These are socio-economic rather than individual in nature.

(d) POLITICAL ATTITUDES AND BEHAVIOUR

The political consciousness of Israelis of Oriental heritage is much more pronounced in the second generation than in the first (Shoked and Deshen, 1977: ch. 12, and 1982: 155 ff.; Levy and Gutmann, 1976a: ch. 7; Lehman-Wilzig, 1981: 188).

At the same time, the polls have shown that Sabras of Oriental backgrounds stand more to the 'right' politically than their parents. (See Etzioni-Halevy and Shapira, 1977: 57 for polls on the 'left' and 'right' as well as religious issues.)

Over the long term this meant that it was the growing numbers of Sabras of African and Asian heritage which caused the political pendulum to swing, first in favour of Gahal/Likud and the NRP (up to 1977) and then also to Tehiya and Tami in 1981 as well as Shass and Rabbi Kahane in 1984. This has been especially evident in the 'development towns' since 1965 (see Tables 18 and 19 as well as Wolffsohn, 1983a: 188 f. and 326–30).

According to polls conducted by Hanoch and Rafi Smith (*Jerusalem Post*, 3 August 1984), 51·1% of Israel's Oriental Jews voted Likud in 1977, 51·6% in 1981 and 52·3% in 1984. Tehiya got 1·3% of the Oriental vote in 1981 and 3·2% in 1984. Rabbi Kahane received 2·5% of the votes cast by Oriental Jews in 1984. Their overall vote for the religious parties dropped from 17·9% in 1977 to 15·7% in 1981 and 15·3% in 1984 (17·8%, however, including Kahane's Kach). To sum up: since 1977 roughly 70% of the Oriental Jewish vote has gone to the Likud and to religious parties; conversely, 'only' about

60% of Euro-American Jews have voted for Labour and its allies since 1977.

Despite the measurable, 'objective' improvement in the socio-economic situation of Oriental Jews, the heightened political consciousness of the younger generation has brought the recognition that possibly even more can be accomplished by means of protest votes. One anti-establishment step could be taken by merely voting Herut/Gahal/Likud, which maintained its non-establishment image through the elections of 1981 and even in 1984, at least as far as its 'Oriental' touch was concerned. In the early 1970s some of the highly impatient founded the party of the 'Black Panthers', which has since undergone numerous splits and remained ineffective. Tami (established in 1981) and Shass (in 1983/4) proved relatively successful anti-establishment ethnic lists.

Figure 42 illustrates the increasing preference of Oriental Jews, especially Sabras, for Gahal/Likud (see Arian, 1983: 96; Peres and Shemer, 1984).

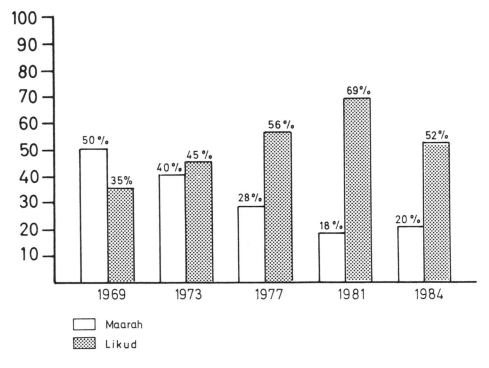

Figure 42   Party preferences of Oriental Jews, 1969–85.

In 1977 and 1981 Oriental Israelis decided the outcome of the elections and were also a key factor in the 1984 stalemate. In 1981 and in 1984 the Likud was the bloc chosen most often by Oriental Jews, and the Maarah was the choice of Ashkenasim.

Diskin (1982a), however, has demonstrated that Oriental Israelis are more prepared to stick with the Likud through good times rather than in bad, their electoral loyalty depending on concrete economic promises and measures. It was as a result of the well-timed measures of Finance Minister Aridor in 1981 that the turnabout in public opinion in favour of the Likud came about.

But why, then, did they still cast their votes for the Likud in 1984, when the economic outlook for the average Oriental Israeli was less bright than it seemed in 1981? Was it because the short-lived election-time economic bubble which rose in early 1984 brought them back over again? This seems unlikely, as there was only a minor improvement in the rating given the economic policy of the Likud-led government by the general public between December 1983 and July 1984. The approval rate increased from 11% to 18% (Smith polls, *Jerusalem Post*, 17 July 1984), but the overall gap between Labour and Likud grew ever narrower (Smith polls, *Jerusalem Post*, 19 June 1984).

One explanation is that the party identification of Oriental Likud voters has in the meantime intensified. About 30% of the general Israeli public claims to make its choice at the polls for reasons of identification with or support for a specific party or its leadership team rather than because of the party's positions on economic or social policy (Smith polls, *Jerusalem Post*, 29 June 1984). Despite the vacillation which can be observed in the polls taken between the elections of 1977 and 1981 as well as in the period between the 1981 and 1984 Knesset elections, Oriental Jews apparently returned to Likud at the polling station, making their decision even as late as on election day itself, as Diskin claimed in 1984 (*Haaretz*, 5 August 1984). Apart from some cyclical volatility, there now seems to be a stronger identification with the Likud among Oriental voters than has previously been assumed.

Upon further consideration, however, a qualification must be made with regard to this theory. It would appear that this party identification has proved highly susceptible to election-time 'gifts'. We have already observed this phenomenon between January and June 1981 as well as between June and July 1984. In both cases, timely measures taken by the Likud-led coalition led within four weeks to a dramatic improvement in the government's image in the eyes of the public. Approval of the government's economic performance (as 'successful' or 'fairly successful') rose from 12% in June to 18% in July 1984, approval of its social policies from 29% to a sensational, ethnically accentuated 46%, approval of its defence policy from 40% to 46%, and of its handling of foreign affairs from 38% to 45%. Finally, public approval of the government's overall performance rose from 25% to 34% (H. and R. Smith, *Jerusalem Post*, 17 July 1984). This data would seem to cast serious doubt on the theory of increased party identification and to suggest that a better explanation might be found in the mechanics of electoral manipulation, both in 1981 and 1984.

Without the predominantly Moroccan Tami Party, the Likud victory among Oriental Jews would have been even more clear-cut in 1981, and if it had not been for Shass, the Likud might have won a slightly greater share of the vote in 1984. Tami and, to an even greater extent, Shass represent the most successful purely Oriental political groupings to date, although it must be added that this success appears much more modest when viewed from a larger perspective, especially with regard to Likud's ethnic results. This is due in part to the fact that Oriental Israelis have, in principle, always sought to improve their situation within the framework of the traditional established parties. (For further details and literature, see Wolffsohn, 1983a: 418 ff.)

Table 34   Selected Findings Presenting the Dynamics of Public Opinion
within Different Subgroups (%)

	Between the wars of 1967 and 1973	Between Sadat's visit and October 1980
Subdivision by Country of Origin		
Percentage assessing that Israeli Arabs' loyalty is diminishing		
1) Israel born of European origin	15–23	34–61
2) Israel born of Asia-Africa origin	8–31	23–45
3) European born	23–36	45–69
4) Asia-Africa born	23–27	36–64
Percentage ready to become friendly with Israeli Arabs		
1) Israel born of European origin	25–41	66–75
2) Israel born of Asia-Africa origin	20–23	52–60
3) European born	27–37	60–69
4) Asia-Africa born	19–21	55–61
Percentage of those claiming that Arabs are not inferior to Jews		
1) Israel born of European origin	40–44	70–71
2) Israel born of Asia-Africa origin	23–31	58–60
3) European born	33–49	68–75
4) Asia-Africa born	24–25	41–49

Source: Peled, 1983: table 3.

Despite all of the above, we must look for still further reasons to account
for the preference of Oriental Israelis for the Likud. In doing so, let us turn to
the issues of relations with the Arabs and of settlements in the occupied
territories.

(e) ATTITUDES TOWARDS THE ARABS AND THE OCCUPIED TERRITORIES
The polls have shown time and again that Israelis of European and Ameri-
can origin at all educational levels are more willing to form friendships with
Arabs than Jews of Oriental ancestry belonging to the same sociological
groups (Peled, 1972: 62; Peres, 1976: 91 ff.; Levy and Gutmann, 1976a: 277;
Zemah,1980; Peled, 1973).

Whereas all the other data referred to in this section (as well as in all other
studies on the subject) present a momentary picture, Table 34 shows the
results of the longitudinal research Peled (1983) has carried out together with
her colleagues in the Israel Institute of Applied Social Research (IIASR,
Jerusalem) since 1967.

Oriental Jews are more optimistic as to the loyalty of Israeli Arabs than their Ashkenasi counterparts, who may see things more realistically. In general, the first as well as the second generations of Oriental Israelis have remained less willing to establish friendly personal relationships with Israeli Arabs than Ashkenasim. The latter also less often considered Arabs to be inferior than did Orientals. Nevertheless, a comparison between the data for the period between 1967 and 1973 with the figures for the years 1977 to 1980 will show an overall moderation among all groups.

While 50% of the immigrants from Europe and America were interested in social contacts with Arabs, only 41% of the immigrants from Africa and Asia expressed similar interest. In the second generation the relationship was 51% to 39%, an even wider gap (Zemah, 1980: 45 f.). Since, in contrast to their parents, the younger generation has grown up in Israel and thus has had no direct negative experience in Arab countries, this result must be viewed as a product of their political education in Israel. It is possible that they have merely assumed the attitudes of their parents, but it is also imaginable that they have, as members of an underprivileged group themselves, sought another group to which they might feel superior. If such an attitude already existed in principle, it was certainly reinforced by the political confrontation with the Arab states and the PLO.

This data is doubly important, first because further reverberations in the Israeli–Arab/Palestinian conflict cannot be excluded as it becomes ever more difficult for the political parties in Israel to 'sell' a dove-like policy, and second because of the effects on the Arabs living in Israel proper.

In all polls conducted by IIASR since 1967, far more Oriental Israelis than Ashkenasim have said they felt 'hate' for the Arabs (Levy and Gutmann, 1976a: 277; Z. Peled, 1979: 8, and 1980).

In September 1979, 70% of all Jewish Israelis responded that they believed their Arab fellow-citizens did 'not hate' them (Peled, 1980: 15 f.). Peled does not give any figures with regard to ethnic differences, but this clear majority opinion would not have been possible without Oriental Israelis. It must be noted on the other hand that, according to a poll conducted by Zemah (1980: 37) in January 1980, 51·6% of Jewish Israelis believed that the native Arabs did, in fact, 'hate' them. These numbers must therefore be interpreted with great caution. It is a noteworthy fact that Israelis of the older generation in Tel-Aviv and in the other 'older' cities expressed this pessimistic opinion much more frequently (totals ranging from 57% to 63%) than inhabitants of the newer development towns (21%) with their large Oriental majorities. On the other hand, 52% of the latter believed that Israel's Arabs had not yet accepted the existence of the Jewish state and 60% agreed with the statement that their Arab fellow citizens were 'happy' to see Israel suffer setbacks (Zemal, 1980: 89 f.).

According to a PORI poll, industrial workers (mainly Oriental Jews) are 'more' likely (exact figures not given) to favour deporting 'Arabs who promote disturbances in the West Bank and Gaza Strip' (general population: 45·9% in favour, 39·7% against, Haaretz, 3 July 1981). Of the Israelis polled, 55·5% denied any responsibility on the part of their country for the September 1982 massacre of Palestinians in Beirut, and here the proportion of Oriental Israelis was 'substantially higher' (PORI poll in Haaretz, 3 November 1982).

Support for settlements in the occupied territories was stronger among

Oriental than Ashkenasi Israelis in both the 1974 and 1979 polls conducted by the IIASR (Bach *et al.*, 1974: 10; Levinsohn, 1979: 10). By the end of 1982 the enormous costs of the government's settlements policy had sparked controversies within the parties – including Herut – as to whether or not an active settlements policy and social welfare programmes were mutually exclusive (see, for example, *Haaretz*, 24 November 1982 and 23 December 1982). For the first time, the grass-roots Peace Now movement was able to organize demonstrations with more than just a symbolic handful of Oriental Jews participating (*NZZ*, 18 January 1983; L. Galili, *Haaretz*, 26 September 1982). Apart from these individual points of agreement, however, public opinion surveys showed that Israelis of Oriental heritage rejected 'the tactics' of Peace Now in far greater numbers than the 53·8% of the (not further defined) general public which did so in July 1983 (M. Segal, *Jerusalem Post*, 16 August 1983). What is more, dovish parties made poor showings in Oriental neighbourhoods in the 1984 Knesset elections.

It is both an oversimplification and inaccurate to state that Israelis of Oriental heritage prefer the Likud only because of its hawkish positions. Just a brief look at the correlation between the data on public satisfaction with the economic policy of the government and its overall popularity is sufficient to reach the conclusion that this is a highly important, if not the decisive, factor. Using various polls, Diskin (1982a: 58) clearly demonstrated that the disenchanted Likud voters of 1977 began to return to the fold after newly appointed Finance Minister Aridor began to introduce his policy of election-time concessions (see also Figure 56). The reversal of the trend in public opinion in February 1981 was a result of economic policy, not of the rocket crisis in Lebanon, which did not flare up until April, nor of the destruction of the atomic reactor outside Baghdad, which took place on 7 June. (See Wolffsohn, 1983a: 700 f. for literature and data to 1978; Stone, 1982: 228 ff. for data to the fall of 1979; Peretz and Smooha, 1981 for the period from July 1977 to June 1981. The data are for the general population.)

The pattern was slightly different, however, in 1984. Once again the Likud tried the tactic of election gifts, but the general public remained dissatisfied with the economic policies of the government, despite the improvement in its economic performance between June and July. The voters did, however, respond more positively to the social policies of the Likud government. Between December 1983 and June 1984, 11–12% – and in July, 18% – judged that the government had 'succeeded' or 'largely succeeded' in the economic sphere, whereas 28–29% – and in July, 46% – expressed the same judgement on the government's social policy. The opinion of Oriental Israelis was the decisive factor here (Smith poll, *Jerusalem Post*, 17 July 1984). In 1981 the ultra-hawkish voters of the Tehiya Party were much more 'western', that is, Ashkenasi, than the voters of the Likud (Levy and Gutmann, 1981: 9 ff., esp. table 4; Elections, 1981: esp. tables 4, 5 and 18). This same pattern was recognizable in 1984, when only 3·2% of Oriental voters chose Tehiya-Zomet and 5% of the Ashkenasim did so (Smith poll, *Jerusalem Post*, 3 August 1984).

Tehiya was, of course, able to garner more support among the second generation of Oriental Israelis, the Oriental Sabras, than among the immigrant generation. Nevertheless, the proportion of Oriental Israelis voting

Tehiya remained consistently below that of Ashkenasim in every population group (Levy and Guttman, loc. cit.). Tehiya is mainly a party of Sabras of European and American backgrounds.

To confuse things even further, it must be noted that Rabbi Kahane's super-hawkish and extremely anti-Arab Kach list got only 0·4% of the Ashkenasi but 2·5% of the Oriental vote in 1984 (Smith poll, *Jerusalem Post*, 3 August 1984). Kahane himself is an immigrant from the United States, as are many of the members of his party. Altogether, 69% of Oriental Jews voted for hawkish parties in the 1984 Knesset elections (compiled from the Smith poll, loc. cit., for the Likud, Tehiya-Zomet, Kach, NRP, Morasha, Shass).

Nevertheless, there are many examples for the neutralization of security and territorial issues by economic policy factors. While Oriental Israelis formed a large majority of the 40·9% of Israelis who found the War in Lebanon justified (PORI poll in *Haaretz*, 3 March 1983), the same institute reported that the Labour bloc succeeded in overtaking the Likud in the polls in April. The main causes of the dissatisfaction with the governing coalition were its economic policy and the muddled situation in Lebanon (*Haaretz*, 6 May 1983). In April as well, 50·7% of the Israelis surveyed said that their monthly incomes were not sufficient to meet current expenses. On the basis of the known socio-economic data it can be concluded that Oriental Israelis were certainly overrepresented in the groups most directly affected by the economic difficulties. At the same time, 53% of the Israelis polled judged the economic policy of the government negatively, as opposed to only 39% in December of 1982 (*Jerusalem Post* quoted in *FAZ*, 9 May 1983).

In other words, 'bread and butter' issues appear to be more important to Oriental Israelis than policies towards the Arabs or the occupied territories. If at some point forced to choose between the alternatives 'settlements' and 'social welfare', the possibility of their opting for the latter cannot be dismissed. In fact it would seem likely. If a government is able to couple its settlements policy with a programme of subsidies for housing construction and purchases for lower income groups, it may well then succeed in escaping the either/or alternative and thus master the art of squaring the circle. The Likud, together with the other hawkish parties, especially Tehiya, seems to have achieved just that. Despite their dismal economic performance, they were able to both establish settlements and, as the above-mentioned polls suggest, to burnish their popular image on social policy as well.

3 THE 'THIRD ISRAEL': THE ISRAELI ARABS

(a) TERMINOLOGY AND POLITICS

The population group under discussion here is frequently described in terms other than the one chosen in the heading above. Since language often either consciously or unconsciously involves politics, it is necessary to draw attention to the various terms employed, each with its own emphasis and value-judgement.

The subject of this book is Israel, the existence of which is taken for granted and viewed as legitimate. The term *Israeli Arabs* is therefore employed here.

The term *Palestinians in Israel* shifts the emphasis to the Palestinians without necessarily calling Israel's legitimacy into question. Nevertheless, this term implies that the prime reference group for these people is the Palestinians, not the Israelis, and that these 'Palestinians' are more or less strangers to Israel rather than part of that state. The description *Palestinians living under Israeli occupation* is one which casts serious doubt on Israel's legitimacy, as it presumes that Israel 'occupies' the land belonging to the Palestinians – and not to the Jews. This becomes clearer if it is recalled that the Arabs being referred to here live within the pre-1967 borders of the Jewish state. The characterization *Arabs living under Zionist occupation* is one which totally denies the legitimacy of Israel.

(b) SOCIO-ECONOMIC DATA

Table 26 illustrates the youth of Israel's Arabs. In 1955, 64·2% were not older than 24, and in 1981 and 1982 the figure was 68%. Moslems remain a clear majority among Palestinian/Israeli Arabs. Figure 43 and Table 35 illustrate the data for various years.

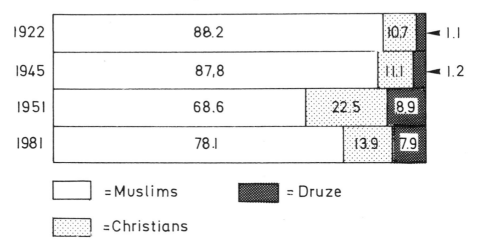

Figure 43   The Non-Jewish population of Israel, 1922–82.

Some 2,500 Circassians live in Reihaniya and Kfar Kama, two small villages in Galilee. The Circassians are Sunni Moslems who fled to the Middle East from their original home in the Caucasus region between 1861 and 1864 in the face of the Russian invaders.

The Bedouins live mainly in the southern part of Israel, in the Negev (see data on the regional distribution of Israel's population in Figure 49).

The development of the Arab sector is illustrated dramatically in the field of education (see Mar'i, 1978). In 1948/9 there were only fourteen Arab students enrolled in secondary schools in Israel. In 1969/70 there were 8,050 and in 1982/3 there was a total of 28,326 in all three types of secondary schools (*Statistical Abstract of Israel*, 1983: 653).

Table 35   The Non-Jewish Population of Israel, 1922–83 (%)

	Moslems	Christians	Druze and other
1922	88·2	10·7	1·1
1945	87·8	11·1	1·2
1951	68·6	22·5	8·9
1981	78·1	13·9	7·9
1982	76·9	13·6	9·5
1983	77·0	13·5	9·5

Sources: Friedlander and Goldscheider, 1979: 34; *Statistical Abstract of Israel*, various vols.

The number of Arab university students rose from 511 in 1969/70 to 1,281 in 1974/5 and 1,740 in 1978/9 (Council for Higher Education, 1982: 15). It must not be overlooked that the number of Israeli Arabs with a higher education is still extremely small on the whole, but nonetheless too high in relation to the employment opportunities available to Arab graduates. It is noteworthy that, in contrast to the Jewish population groups, the numbers of Arab students did not drop in the late 1970s.

Table 36   Arab Student Enrolments

1) Secondary Students (total number)

1949	14
1970	8,500
1982	26,814
1983	29,426
1985	32,006

2) University Students (total number)

1970	511
1975	1,281
1979	1,740

3) University Graduates (total number)

1949	193
1960	1,237
1970	5,566
1983	9,891

Among Arabs over the age of 14, 49·2% did not continue their education in 1961, but only 18·0% failed to do so in 1981; 28·2% of all women were in this category and only 7·8% of the men (*Statistical Abstract of Israel*, 1982: 617). In other words, the status of women in Arab Israeli society remains inferior to that of men.

The employment structure among Israel's Arabs has undergone drastic changes, that is, 'modernization'. Under the Mandate, approximately two-thirds of all Arabs were employed in agriculture. This fell to 49·8% in 1955, to only 11·8% in 1981 and to 11·1% in 1982 (*Encyclopaedia Hebraica*, 1958: 709; Harari, 1976: 15; *Statistical Abstract of Israel*, 1982: 333, and 1983: 355).

In 1955, 26·3% were employed in industry (including the electrical sector) and construction. The figures for 1981 and 1982 were 45·2% and 42.5% respectively. Only 15·8% were to be found in the tertiary sector (commerce, transport and services) in 1955. This rose to 42·9% in 1981 and 46·3% in 1982 (*Statistical Abstract of Israel*, 1983: 355). The development from a traditionally structured agrarian economy via the growth of first the secondary (industrial) sector and then the tertiary sector to a 'modern' economy is apparent (see Figure 44 and section B/VI/3/e).

Urbanization is a further sign of 'modernization'. In 1948, 76·4% of non-Jewish Israelis lived in rural settlements, and only 23·6% in cities or urban surroundings, that is, communities with a population greater than 10,000 as well as non-Jewish towns with a population of between 5,000 and 10,000 in which less than half of the inhabitants were engaged in agriculture (*Society in Israel*, 1976: 5). The figures for 1974 present a completely different picture: 41·7% resided in rural settlements, 58·3% in urban settings (loc. cit.). In December 1980, 32·1% were living in rural areas and 67·9% in urban areas, and the figures for July 1983 were 29·1% rural to 70·9% urban (Jerusalem not included; *Statistical Abstract of Israel*, 1982: 41, and 1984: 41). Parallel to this, an urbanization of the villages and towns also took place. In 1951 Taibe had 6,350 residents, but a population of 16,800 by 1981 (Harari, 1976: 7; *Statistical Abstract of Israel*, 1982: 50; for further examples see Wolffsohn, 1983a: 196 f., as well as Figure 45).

Traditionally, Christian Arabs have been regarded as the most 'modern' in the sense of the criteria applied above. However, the Moslem Arabs, including the Druze, but the Bedouins only to a lesser extent, have also become much more 'modern' (see section B/VI/1/h).

(c) THE JEWISH–ARAB GAP

Despite their indisputable accomplishments, the progress Israel's Arabs have been able to achieve is only of modest proportion in comparison with the advances made by the Jewish population of the country. Jewish Israelis are better educated, hold many more jobs in the service sector and fewer which could be described as 'proletarian', earn more money and live in less crowded housing (data in Wolffsohn, 1983a: 205 ff.; Lustick, 1980: ch. 5).

The average gross monthly income of Israeli Arabs fell from 61·1% of that of Ashkenasi Israelis in 1970 to 59·1% in 1981 and then rose modestly to 63·9% in 1982), while the income of Oriental Israelis rose continuously. In 1975, however, the Arabs' 86·9% topped the Oriental Jews' 82·2% of the average Ashkenasi income (*Statistical Abstract of Israel*, 1982: 291, and 1983: 311). The proportion of Arabs in the lowest income groups has decreased significantly and the gap has, therefore, considerably narrowed.

The Arab income structure does not present a unified picture, as there are differences between Israeli Arabs and Arabs living in the occupied territories, many of whom work in Israel proper (see section B/VI/3/e). In the period from 1969 to 1981 the annual rise in income was higher when the workers from the occupied territories were excluded than when their incomes were included in the average, although the differences were not overly large

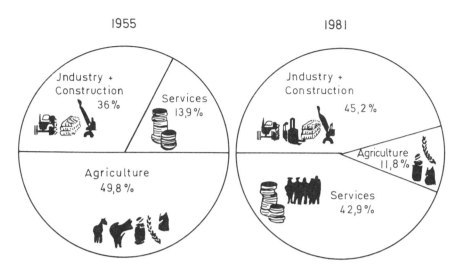

Figure 44   Employment structure of the Arab population.

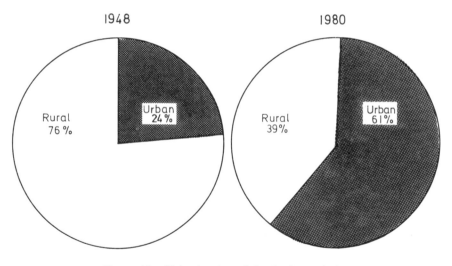

Figure 45   Urbanization of the Arab population.

(*Statistical Abstract of Israel*, 1982: 369). This nevertheless indicates that Israeli Arabs tend to be better paid than Arabs from the occupied territories.

By way of contrast, the unemployment rate for the Arab population has remained constantly below that of the Jewish population over the last decade (ibid.: 355; for information on the material standard of living see section C/XIII/6).

(d) SOCIAL ATTITUDES AND BEHAVIOUR

A certain 'natural' separation, that is, geographic distance, exists between the Jewish and the Arab populations of Israel as a result of their geographic distribution (see section B/VI/1/i). From the beginnings of Zionist immigration as well as after independence, Jews tended to found their own settlements separate from the existing Arab communities. The deliberate separation carried out during the foundation of Tel-Aviv beginning in 1909 is a particularly striking example. The goal was clearly to create a Jewish city apart from the Arab city of Jaffa, rather than as a part of the same community.

This had nothing to do with 'racism' or 'hatred'. The Zionist pioneers were determined to totally and completely reform their people, and they were so possessed by this ideal that it led them to ignore and neglect their non-Jewish environment. If one is to make value-judgements, this highly intensive preoccupation with their own group was clearly the 'fault' of the Zionists, but is this not understandable from the point of view of Jewish history? On the other hand, why should the Arabs have to assume the burden for the consequences of the actions of non-Jewish Europeans? There is more grey between Arabs and Jews than most black-and-white analysts can imagine.

Most Israeli Arabs live in central and western Galilee, in the 'Big Triangle', mainly in and around Nazareth. In 1948, 62·9% of the residents of the Northern District were non-Jewish, as compared to 48·6% in 1981 (*Statistical Abstract of Israel*, 1982: 37). In the Yesreel Valley subdistrict the non-Jewish population formed a slight majority in 1981 and in the Acre subdistrict a clear majority. A further concentration of Arab population is to be found north-east of Tel-Aviv in the so-called 'Little Triangle'. In the cities of mixed population – Acre, Tel-Aviv, Jaffa, Haifa, Lod and Ramla (Jerusalem, occupied in 1967, presents a special case) – the Arabs are clearly in the minority. There are also smaller concentrations of Arabs to the east of Beersheba and near Haifa.

The geographic distance only serves to illustrate the social distance. As in the section dealing with the attitudes of Oriental Jews towards the Arabs (B/VI/2/e), the longitudinal survey elaborated by Peled (1983) is deserving of special attention here.

The first item of Table 37 shows that Jewish Israelis have given an increasingly lower evaluation of the loyalty of the Arabs to the (Zionist) state in the period between 1967 and 1980. Arab Israelis have been viewed with increasing favour relative to Arabs from the territories (item 2). Clearly, fewer and fewer Jews claim that Arabs are inferior (item 3). If the willingness to get acquainted with the Arab language can be taken as an indicator, the trend has been to a greater open-mindedness towards learning about the culture and mentality of the Arabs (item 4). Apart from this inter-group data, the inter-personal responses of the Jewish public have also demonstrated more moderation and even better matter-of-fact relations (visits in Arab homes or having had Arabs as guests, items 8 and 9).

On the inter-state level as well, more moderation has been reflected by the interviews. A growing number of Jewish Israelis have come to the conclusion 'that Arab states are ready for peace' (item 10).

What follows below are some momentary 'snapshots'.

In June 1967, 31% of Jewish Israelis declared they were 'unconditionally

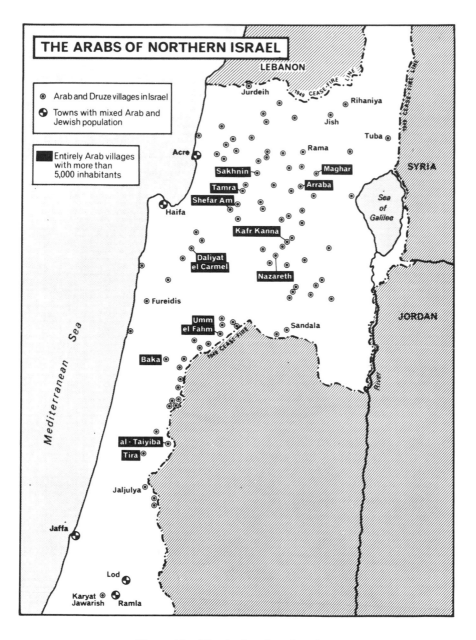

Figure 46   The Arabs of northern Israel.

Source: Gilbert, 1974: 57.

Table 37   Selected Findings Presenting the Dynamics of Jewish Public
           Opinion in Israel on the Topic of Jewish–Arab Relations in
           Israel (%)*

	Between the wars of 1967 and 1973	Between the 1973 war and Sadat's visit	Between Sadat's visit and up to Oct. 1980 (incl.)
Inter-group level			
1) Percentage assessing that the loyalty of the Israeli Arabs is diminishing	17–33	13–54	36–70
2) Percentage preferring Israeli Arabs to those of the territories	21–42	**	57–68
3) Percentage claiming Arabs are not inferior to Jews	40–42	**	51–56
4) Percentage supporting introducing Arabic in obligatory school curriculum	46–56	**	65–67
Inter-personal level			
5) Percentage ready to become friendly with an Arab (with no reservations)	26–32	37–38	59–64
6) Percentage ready to live in same building with Arab family (with no reservations)	24–28	**	38–44
7) Percentage ready to live in same neighbourhood with Arab families (with no reservations)	19–21	**	35–41
8) Percentage who visited an Arab home	42–45	**	54–56
9) Percentage who had Arabs visiting in their home	26–27	**	37–44
Inter-state level			
10) Percentage who think that now Arab States are ready for peace	8–34	19–50	33–83

 * The figures in the table represent the range of the percentages as obtained
   in *different surveys* within the said periods.
** The question was not asked.

Source: Peled, 1983: 22.

prepared to be friends with the Arabs' and 66% gave the same reply in December of 1979 (Peled, 1980: 20; further data and literature in Wolffsohn, 1983a: 420 ff.).

The image of Jews among the Arabs also improved in this time period (Peled, 1979; Benyamini, 1981).

Surveys conducted by Mar'i (1978) and Smooha (1980) registered a mutual willingness to establish contacts with the other population group, but according to Smooha (1980: 62 f.) this readiness was considerably greater among Arabs than among Jews.

Apart from impersonal business contacts, however, actual contacts remained few in number (loc. cit.), although increasing slightly from 1967 to 1978 (Peled, 1979: 9). In June 1967, 73% of Jewish Israelis had never had an Arab guest in their homes, which was true of 56% in November 1978. The proportion of those who had never visited an Arab at home sank from 58% to 46% (loc. cit.).

The willingness to overcome barriers decreases among Jewish Israelis to the extent that they identify the Arabs as Palestinians. The same is true of the Arabs to the extent that they are not prepared to accept the basic situation of their group within the Jewish state (Peled, 1979: 10, and 1980: 21; but for the most extensive data see Smooha, 1980: 148. Data on the attitudes of Oriental Jews towards the native Arab population can be found in section B/VI/2/e.).

Recent data, however, indicate that young Jewish Israelis are highly prejudiced against Arabs and are also unwilling to grant them equal rights (Hoffman and Nager, 1985; Zemach and Zin, 1984).

(e) AREAS OF TENSION

Apart from the influences of the inter-state Arab–Israeli conflicts, four domestic problem areas have repeatedly led to tensions between Jewish and Arab Israelis: (1) the issue of citizenship (see section A/I/2), (2) the military administration, (3) the acquisition of Arab land by Jews and (4) the relative cheapness of Arab as compared to Jewish labour.

The military administration, which had greatly restricted the Arabs in their freedom of movement, was ended in December 1966.

Conflicts over the purchase of land began at the outset of Zionist immigration to Palestine. After the founding of Israel the issue was the 'Judafication' of areas populated by Arabs (especially in Galilee). The government claimed Arab land for Jewish development projects, first to improve the infrastructure of the country, and second to 'implant' more Jews in areas heavily populated by Arabs.

In 1976 this policy led to the 'Land Day' confrontation. On 30 March 1976, a bloody clash took place, in the course of which seven Arabs were shot by Israeli police. A short time later the Israeli government, led by Prime Minister Rabin, told Arab representatives in unequivocal terms that Israel was, and would remain, Jewish (*FAZ*, 21 June 1976).

When discussing the question of cheaper Arab labour, it must not be forgotten that this problem had, during the Yishuv, already led not only to Jewish–Arab tensions, but to inner-Jewish conflicts as well, some of which were violent in nature (Giladi, 1973: 164 ff.). Not all Jewish employers in either the agrarian or the industrial sectors complied with the Zionist, Labour Party and union 'Jewish labour' (*Avoda Ivrith*) demands. Such employers set their commercial interests above Zionist ideology and profited from the fact that Arab workers were not only 'cheaper' but also less politicized and aggressive. The perspective of an eventual bi-national, functional coexistence thus opened by this development came to an end between 1936 and 1939 when the Arab Revolt led to a practical economic separation (see Horowitz and Lissak, 1978: ch. 2).

Following independence Jewish Israelis, especially Ashkenasim, exhibited an increasing unwillingness to perform tasks involving hard labour, preferring instead to set their ideological qualms aside and to hire Arab labourers. Since 1967 the supply of willing and inexpensive Arab labour from the occupied territories has grown ever larger. In 1970, 20,600 labourers, or 11·9% of the total workforce in the occupied territories, were involved. In 1981 the figures were 75,800 workers, or 35·1% of the total Arab labour force in the occupied territories, and 79,100, or 34·7% of that workforce, in 1982 (*Statistical Abstract of Israel*, 1982: 754, and 1983: 780). Most of these workers were employed in construction: 54·3% of all residents of the occupied territories working in Israel in 1970 and 51% in 1980. In 1970, 24·4% were employed in agriculture, as were 12·7% in 1981 and 12·8% in 1982 (loc. cit.).

(f) ARABS AND PARTY POLITICS

The fact that it never came to the foundation of a purely 'Arab' political party following the creation of the state of Israel can be explained (among other factors) by the shock of the sudden transformation of the Arab community from the large majority in Palestine into a minority in the new Jewish state, a shock which crippled all political activity. In addition, the remaining Arabs were left with little motivation to undertake political initiatives in the wake of the experience of the total failure of their traditional political leadership, which had largely deserted them during the War of Independence (see Landau, 1971: 90 ff.).

Until 1977 increasing numbers of Israeli Arabs voted for the Communist Party because it pursued Arab interests in the political arena, including the Knesset, and because the Communists were non-Zionist, although not anti-Zionist. The decision to vote for the Communists was not and is not a decision for 'communism' but rather a protest, and as such fits within the framework of Israel as a state. Israel's existence is not rejected either by the old Communist Party or by the NCL, which accepts Israel's existence but aims to create another, bi-national rather than Zionist, i.e. exclusively Jewish, Israel.

In the long run, all of those Arabs who are not prepared to accept the existence of Israel, either as a Zionist or as a bi-national state, will have to form an organization of their own. Such a move, however, would probably not be acceptable to Israel's 'armed democracy' (in the original Zionist sense of the term), as was the case in the period 1958/65 in connection with the Arab-nationalist al-Ard Movement.

In November 1964 the Supreme Court of Israel ruled that is was possible to permit political parties which did not accept the status quo, but not parties like al-Árd which did not recognize or which sought to undermine the state (Landau, 1971: 1160 f.; similarly the ruling of October 1965, discussed in Rubenstein, 1974: 246 and in Wolffsohn, 1983a: 425 ff.).

In 1984 the Central Elections Committee disqualified an Arab-Jewish party, the Progressive List for Peace (PLP). Resembling the NCL (but without its communist ideology), the PLP accepted the existence of Israel but aimed to transform it into a bi-national, non-Zionist, i.e. not exclusively Jewish state, which the PLP conceived of as coexisting alongside a Palestinian state in the West Bank and Gaza Strip. Israel's Supreme Court struck down the disqualification by the Central Elections Committee, which had also banned Rabbi Kahane's extremely anti-Arab Kach, and allowed both parties to run for the Knesset. Both succeeded in overcoming the 1% hurdle, Kach receiving one and the PLP two Knesset seats.

The Yom Kippur War served to heighten the political consciousness of Israel's Arabs, particularly among the youth, some of whom had already organized themselves as the Sons of the Village on the local political level in 1972/3 and did very well in the local elections of 1973 and 1978, but achieved a more modest success in 1983.

Like the Sons of the Village, the National Progressive Movement (NPM), founded by Arab intellectuals at the end of the 1970s, is closer to the more radical rejectionists of the PLO than to the more moderate al-Fatah. Running under different names, the NPM met with significant success in the local elections in November 1978, especially in the 'Little Triangle' north-east of Tel-Aviv, after attracting a great deal of attention as a result of its success in the Council of Arab Students at Hebrew University since 1977/8 (for details see Wolffsohn, 1983a: 216 ff.).

A third purely Arab organization is also worthy of note. The Moslem Youth also favours a radical pan-Arab approach to Palestine, but is not a secular party in the normal sense of the term. With its rather fundamentalist religiosity, the Moslem Youth can, with all due caution in making such a comparison, be seen as something like a Sunni–Arab–Israeli equivalent to Shi'ite 'Khomeinism'. Characteristically, it sprang up in the late 1970s and became more visible after the Iranian revolution.

As soon as one or more of the above-mentioned organizations attempt to become active on the national level they will be confronted by the same normative, institutional and judicial barriers encountered by the al-Ard Group.

In 1958/9 al-Ard presented a serious challenge to the Communist Party, as it was first and foremost an Arab-nationalist group and only second a party of the 'left', an attribute it chose not to define precisely. The al-Ard also supported Egypt's President Nasser, who was then the pan-Arabian idol, whereas the CP, riding Moscow's coat-tails, had cast its lot with Nasser's rival, Iraqi President Kassem.

The only traditional party which made the effort to be both Jewish and Arab was the Communist Party. It hoped to neutralize the 'national' aspect by stressing the socio-economic 'class' factor – and failed. The national existence of two peoples in one party remained a 'myth' (Greilsammer, 1978: 346 ff.).

In 1984 the Progressive List for Peace (PLP) presented a truly Arab–Jewish list for the first time in the nation's history. The PLP was founded in 1983 by Arab intellectuals from the Nazareth branch of the New Communist List, who broke away from that party to form an at first purely Arab, non-communist organization in order to pursue the goal of a bi-national Israel. They gave themselves the name Progressive Movement for Peace (not to be confused with the radical National Progressive Movement) and were soon joined by a number of former al-Ard members. The newly established party won one-quarter of the seats on Nazareth City Council in the 1983 local elections.

In early 1984 the party turned Arab–Jewish when former Shelli founders Uri Avnery and Matityahu Peled, together with other former Shelli members and other non-Zionist (but not anti-Israel) Jews joined. All of them favoured direct negotiations with the PLO. The new bi-national character of the party was not accepted by all of its Arab founders, some of whom refused to join in the new configuration.

Campaigning as the Progressive List for Peace, the new party competed with the NCL for the endorsement of the PLO in order to attract as many Arab voters as possible in the 1984 elections. Among Arab voters the NCL came in first in 1984, and the PLP in third place (see Figure 47), but Jewish support was negligible.

Mapam opened its ranks to Arab citizens in 1954, but these remained a distinct minority. Despite its intensive efforts to attract Arabs, the Shelli Party, founded in 1977, met with no success and failed to receive a single Knesset seat in 1981. The Matzpen group, which attacks the Zionist, i.e. the exclusively Jewish character of the State of Israel, on principle (Bober, 1972: 4), managed to achieve an Arab membership of about 10% (Yuval-Davies, 1977: 48).

Mapai/ILP had traditionally relied on its allied Arab minority lists (led by the heads of the Arab clans) to maintain political contacts with the Arab population. In 1969 membership in the ILP was opened to Druze and in 1973 to other Arabs. There had already been Druze members in Herut since the 1960s, as this party, despite its Zionist-nationalist character, maintained from the beginning the position that all Israeli citizens should enjoy equal rights. In Herut the effective barrier was a different one: ideology and policy (further details and literature in Wolffsohn, 1983a: 427 ff.).

(g) ARABS IN THE MILITARY

As early as 1948 there were already some Circassians fighting on the side of the Israelis. After independence some young Druze began to serve as volunteers in the army. On 3 May 1956 the first Druze unit consisting of draftees was created, the initiative for this step have been taken by the Druze leadership in Israel. The gradual 'Arabization' of the Druze in Israel, as well as tensions between Israeli authorities and Druze on the Golan Heights and the prolonged War in Lebanon, which found Israel fighting alongside the Lebanese Christians (who were, to put it mildly, the traditional rivals of the Druze), served to erode the loyalty of some younger Druze soldiers to Israel. Some of them (albeit not many) even deserted Zahal to join their religious and ethnic brothers in Lebanon.

Bedouins are not subject to the draft, but are allowed to serve as volunteers, a smattering of whom are to be found in Zahal. In late 1984 the ranks of Zahal were also opened for some two hundred volunteers from 'Arab villages' (i.e. non-Bedouins; A. Mantzur, *Haaretz*, 18 December 1984).

(h) UNDERREPRESENTATION

Smooha (1978: 351 f.) has put together an extensive documentation of the political underrepresentation of Israel's Arabs in relation to their proportion of the total population. It need only be updated in the area of local politics.

Table 38 shows the number of Arab deputies in the various Knessets. The numbers in parentheses refer to the total of members elected to the Knesset via the Arab minority lists.

Table 38 Arab Members of the Knesset, 1949–84 (number of MKs from minority lists in parentheses)

1949	1951	1955	1959	1961	1965	1969	1973	1977	1981	1984
3(2)	8(5)	7(5)	7(5)	6(4)	7(4)	7(4)	6(3)	7(1)	5	7

(i) POLITICAL ATTITUDES AND BEHAVIOUR

As a result of the heightened political consciousness among Israeli Arabs, encouraged and conditioned by their improved educational status, protest attitudes and actions in the form of votes cast for the only non-Zionist party in the country, the Communists (and NCL from 1965 on), increased significantly, as shown in Figure 47 and Table 39. The success of the Progressive List for Peace in 1984 fits into this pattern, which also documents the desire of many Israeli Arabs for bi-national institutions neither Zionist nor Communist in character, but instead 'pluralistic' in the sense of rejecting exclusivity and demanding mutual tolerance.

The Communists' losses in 1959 were related to the already described rivalry with the al-Ard Group. The losses in 1981 were less indicative of a renewal of willingness to cooperate with the Zionist parties than of resignation.

Overall participation in 1981 was considerably lower than for the local elections of November 1978, in which the Sons of the Village and the National Progressive Movement were allowed to run. While voter participation reached 80% in 1973, it fell to 76% in 1977 and to only 70% in 1981 (Elections, 1981: XXIV, 2). The participation in Moslem communities was lower than in Druze areas (loc. cit.), which is a further indication of protest behaviour, as the Druze have traditionally been better disposed towards the state. Except for the 1949, 1977, 1981 and 1984 Knesset elections, Arab voter turnouts have been higher than for Jewish voters. Despite the increase in the participation of Arab voters from 70% in 1981 to 76% in 1984, the pre-1973 levels were not reached. This continuing gap may indicate a certain resignation on the part of those for whom it does not make sense to vote for bi-national, let alone Zionist, parties. The non-voters may, therefore, consist of basically uninterested and fatalistic eligible Arabs as well as rejectionists. Figures on the latter remain open to speculation – or polls, which, to this author's knowledge, are unfortunately lacking.

Nevertheless, the NCL remained the party with the single largest bloc of voters among Israel's Arabs in 1981. The Labour bloc received the most

SOCIETY

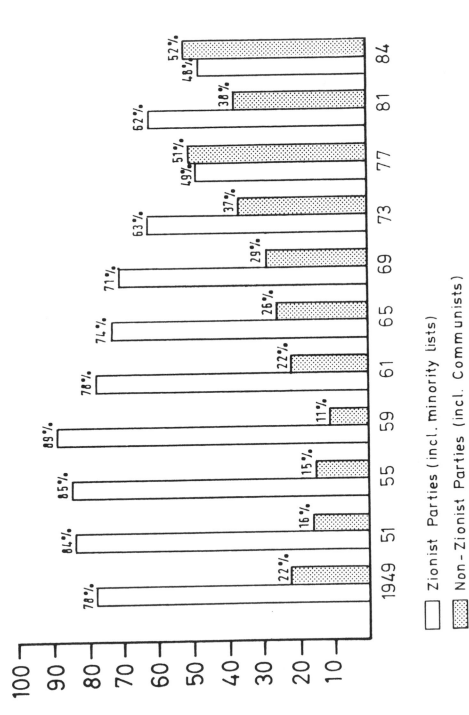

Figure 47   Arab voting patterns in Israel, 1949–84.

Table 39   Arab voting patterns in Israel, 1949–84

Elections	Arab Voters	Participation (in %)	Zionist Parties	Minority Lists	Communists	PLP
1949	24,000*	79	26·1	51·7	22·2	—
1951	69,000*	86	28·9	54·8	16·3	—
1955	70,827	90	26·6	57·8	15·6	—
1959	75,155	89	30·2	58·5	11·3	—
1961	80,454	86	32·0	45·6	22·5	—
1965	92,505	87	33·1	40·8	23·1	—
1969	105,948	85	29·7	41·0	29·5	—
1973	119,627	80	27·1	36·0	36·9	—
1977	132,684	76	27·9	21·5	50·7	—
1981	168,000	70	48·7	13·4	37·9	—
1984	199,968	76	50·0	—	32·0	18·0

* Estimates (rounded) by Harari, 1978: 12 and, similarly, Landau, 1971: 167, 172).

Sources: Landau, 1971: 165 ff.; Harari, 1978: 12, 14; Elections, 1981: XXVI; Cohen, 1984: 24.

votes among Bedouins, with 50% in 1981 (Elections, 1981: XXXI). In Druze communities the minority lists were the largest vote-getters, followed by the Labour bloc and the NCL (ibid.: XXVII).

The 1984 elections demonstrate the first real upheaval among Israeli Arabs. The rejection of the Zionist parties (including their affiliated Arab minority lists) was more decisive than in the previous record year, 1977. Overall, slightly less than 50% of the vote was cast for Zionist parties in 1977. This dropped to a total of 48% in 1984 and, for the first time, there was a truly bi-national alternative. Looking at the results for the individual parties, the setback for the Communists (NCL/Rakah) was relatively modest, namely, a 3% drop (from 1981) to 35%. The Alignment came in second with 23% in 1984, compared with about 29% in 1981, but in the earlier election the Arab minority lists linked to the Maarah had attracted another 13% of the vote. It is thus safe to say that the support for the Alignment among Arab voters was cut almost in half (from a total of 42% in 1981 to 23% in 1984).

The undisputed winner among Israel's Arabs was the Progressive List for Peace, which got 18% of the Arab vote. The results for the other parties in 1984 were 6% for Ezer Weizman's Yahad, 5% for Shinui, 3% for the Likud and 8% for the other coalition parties (data from Y. Litani, Haaretz, 27 July 1984; A. Mantzur, Haaretz, 30 July 1983; H. and R. Smith, Jerusalem Post, 3 August 1984).

It is practically self-evident that the developments described above have led to an 'Arabization' of the Communist voters. In 1955 Arabs cast only 27·8% of the total votes for the CP, whereas they contributed 80–83% in 1981 and 98% in 1984 (Wolffsohn, 1983a: 194; Elections, 1981: XXVII; and author's calculation for 1984).

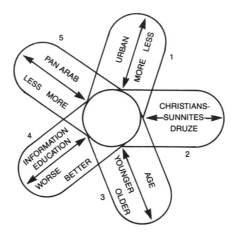

Figure 48   Likelihood of radical attitudes and behaviour among Israeli Arabs.

Notes:
1) Urban–Rural: the more urban, the more radical.
2) Christian–Sunnite–Druze–(Bedouins): Christians Arabs are more radical than Sunnites. These are more radical than Druze and the latter are more radical than Bedouins.
3) Old–Young: the younger the Arabs, the more radical.
4) Formal education and media exposure: the better educated and the more exposed to (Arab) media, the more radical.
5) Pan-Arab influence: the more influenced by pan-Arab ideas the more radical.

We can also call this process one of 'radicalization' because it shows the gradual but steady erosion of the 'roots' (Latin *radix*, thus English 'radical') of the Jewish State of Israel among its Arab population. This development demonstrates an active, not just passive, alienation and thus an increasing unwillingness to accept the predominantly Jewish character of the state. The 'carrot' of the bread-and-butter issues which had long attracted Arab votes to the Labour parties can no longer compensate for the Jewish, i.e. Zionist, 'stick'. This radicalization could be observed first among Christian Arabs and later among Moslems, Druze and finally Bedouins (for data see Wolff-sohn, 1983: 198 f.). Again, this is a 'radical' and not an 'extreme' trend. It does not threaten the existence of the State of Israel, but rather its predominantly Jewish substance. Israel's Arabs apparently desire a different Israel, not necessarily its destruction, or, if they had wanted to destroy it, they have come to a realization that its transformation remains the only realistic alternative.

The following can be said of Israeli Arabs: the younger, the more urban, the better educated, especially if Christian, or (Sunni) Moslem, and less so if Druze or Bedouin, and the more exposed through the media of radio and TV to the influences of the neighbouring Arab states, the more 'radical', that is, likely to vote for non-Zionist parties such as the Communist NCL and PLP or, as in 1981, deliberately not to vote at all. (see Figure 48 and, for more details, Wolffsohn, 1983a: 203 ff.)

The increasingly important role of the 'Palestinian' element in the political consciousness of Israeli Arabs is documented in the surveys conducted by Peres (1976: 185 f.), Tessler (1977: esp. 317), Meari (1978: 56) and Smooha (1980: 58 f.). The results, with the exception of Smooha, can also be found in Wolffsohn (1983a: 211 ff.).

In opinion polls the Arabs have been offered more than just the Zionist or bi-national alternative which they find at the ballot box. In order to get a more differentiated view, let us therefore examine some of the more revealing polls. The Arabs of Israel are divided over the issue of Israel's right to exist, which was accepted by 40% in 1974/5, and by a further 35% 'with reservations' (Tessler, 1977: 318). In Smooha's 1976 poll (1980: 42), 49·8% responded positively, 28·7% 'with reservations' and 21·5% negatively. Three years earlier, Tessler had already received 25% negative responses. In 1976, 64% of all respondents considered Zionism a 'racist movement' (Smooha, 1980: 42).

Whereas 63·1% of the Druze accepted Israel's legitimacy in 1976, 57·1% of the Bedouins, 44·3% of the Christians and 47·9% of the Moslems did so (Smooha, 1980: 44).

A comparison of Jewish and Arab attitudes concerning individual aspects of the Israeli–Palestinian conflict is made possible by the collected results of the surveys conducted in 1980 by Smooha and Peretz (1982). The pollsters found that Israeli Arabs contradict the Zionist consensus on the following points: (1) the national character of the Palestinians, (2) the borders of 1967, (3) recognition of the PLO as the representative of the Palestinian people, (4) the creation of a Palestinian state on the West Bank and in the Gaza Strip, (5) the annexation of East Jerusalem and (6) the right of the Palestinian refugees to return. On the other hand, Israeli Arabs do not accept the ideology of the 'rejectionist front', which seeks to replace Israel with a 'democratic and secular state in the whole of Palestine'. In other words, most of the polls, and especially the last one discussed, confirm our previous statement concerning the process of 'radicalization': Israel's Arabs do not reject Israel's existence but rather its predominantly Jewish substance.

4   SOCIAL-DEMOGRAPHIC ASPECTS OF CRIME STATISTICS

The purpose of the data presented here is not to prove that criminal acts are determined by socio-economic or demographic factors, but these certainly cannot be entirely excluded from the consideration of the motives behind criminal acts.

Among adults convicted of criminal offences (men over the age of 16 and women over 18), Arabs were clearly overrepresented. Table 40 shows the percentage of Arab convicts followed in parentheses by the percentage of Arabs in the overall population for the given year.

Until 1970 about one-third of criminal acts were directed against property,

Table 40   The Arab crime rate relative to population, 1955–82,
           (1) Arabs as % of Total Convicts, (2) Arabs as % of Total
           Population

Year:	1955	1960	1965	1970	1979	1982
1)	36·3	34·4	28·0	25·8	23·6	23·4
2)	12·5	12·5	13·0	17·0	19·0	17·0

Sources: Statistical Abstract of Israel, various vols.; Society, in Israel 1975: 167.

another third against persons and about a quarter involved violations of 'public order' (i.e. transgressions against state institutions or norms). This last proportion increased to 32% in 1979 but fell again to 27·9% in 1981 (Society in Israel, 1975: 167; Statistical Abstract of Israel, 1983: 624). The political implications are self-evident.

In 1979, 80% of Arab criminals were Moslems, 12% Christians and 8% Druze. The proportions remained nearly the same in 1981 (Statistical Abstract of Israel, 1982: 597, and 1983: 624).

In 1982 about one half of all juvenile offences were committed by Arabs, as reported by a special investigative committee (Jerusalem Post, overseas edition, 10–17 June 1984). A quarter of these crimes was carried out by youngsters who had come to Israel from the occupied territories. The proportion of juvenile offences committed by Arabs rose from 29% in 1978 to 49% in 1982 (loc. cit.).

In the criminal statistics for Jews, criminals of African descent were the most numerous, followed by Sabras, who pushed Jews from Asian countries into third place in 1970. By 1979 Sabras were actually leading the statistics when the background of the father was not taken into account (Statistical Abstract of Israel, 1982: 597, and 1983: 624; Society in Israel, 1975: 169).

While 80–85% of all crimes committed by Jewish adults in the period from 1960 to 1974 were against property (Society in Israel, 1975: 169), this proportion sank to 29% by 1979, at which level it remained in 1981. As in the case of Arab adults, 32% of crimes committed by Jewish adults in 1979 were against 'public order', whereas this percentage had been only 7% in 1974 (loc. cit.). This is a dramatic change which can hardly be understood in non-political terms or without reference to 'socio-economic' motives.

FURTHER READING

GENERAL WORKS

Ernest Krausz (ed.) Studies of Israeli Society, 2 vols. (New York: Praeger, 1980, 1983).

Dov Friedlander and Calvin Goldscheider, The Population of Israel (New York: Columbia University Press, 1979).

Fanny Ginor, Socio-Economic Disparities in Israel (New Brunswick, NJ: Transaction Books, and Tel-Aviv: Tel-Aviv University, 1979).

S. N. Eisenstadt, Israeli Society (London: Weidenfeld & Nicolson, 1964); 'the' classic.

POLITICAL GENERATIONS

Unfortunately, the in-depth analyses of the political generations of the founding fathers have been written in Hebrew. Therefore the reader will have to consult histories of the Zionist movement and parties. Nevertheless, one may get a general, though journalistic, picture by reading:

Amos Elon, *The Israelis–Founders and Sons* (New York: Bantam Books, 1971).

On American Jews who immigrated to Israel, see:

Kevin Avruch, *American Immigrants in Israel* (Chicago: University of Chicago Press, 1981).

Aaron Antonovsky and Abraham D. Katz, *From the Golden to the Promised Land* (Jerusalem: Academic Press, and Darby, PA: Norwood, 1979).

On American and Soviet immigrants, see:

Zvi Gitelman, *Becoming Israelis. Political Socialization of Soviet and American Immigrants* (New York: Praeger, 1982).

On Oriental Jews, see:

Sammy Smooha, *The Orientation and Politicization of the Arab Minority in Israel* (Haifa: The Jewish-Arab Centre, Institute of Middle East Studies, 1980);

Marc L. Robbins, 'The strategy of innocence: political resocialization of Oriental Jews in Israel', unpublished PhD dissertation, Princeton University.

On German-Jewish immigrants who were less decisive for the political system, see:

Shlomo Erel, *50 Jahre Immigration deutschsprachiger Juden* (Gerlingen: Bleicher, 1983);

David M. Elcott, 'The political resuscitation of German Jews in Palestine, 1933–1939', unpublished PhD dissertation, Columbia University, New York;

Gerda Luft, *Heimkehr ins Unbekannte* (Wuppertal: Peter Hammer, 1977);

Eva Beling, *Die gesellschaftliche Eingliederung deutscher Einwanderer in Israel* (Frankfurt am Main: Europäische Verlagsanstalt, 1967).

ORIENTAL JEWS

Eliezer Ben-Rafael, *The Emergence of Ethnicity. Cultural Groups and Social Conflict in Israel* (Westport, Conn., and London: Greenwood Press, 1982).

Moshe Shokeid and Shlomo Deshen, *Distant Relations. Ethnicity and Politics among Arabs and North African Jews in Israel* (New York: Praeger, 1982).

Sammy Smooha, *Israel. Pluralism and Conflict* (Berkeley, Calif. University of California Press, and London: Routledge & Kegan Paul, 1978); a classic, but a polemical one.

ARABS

Alouoh Hareven (ed.), *Every Sixth Israeli. Relations between the Jewish Majority and the Arab Minority in Israel* (Jerusalem: Van Leer Foundation, 1983).

Tsiyona Peled and David Bar-Gal, *Intervention Activities in Arab-Jewish Relations: Conceptualization, Classification and Evaluation* (Jerusalem: Israel Institute of Applied Social Research, 1983).

Ian Lustick, *Arabs in the Jewish State. Israel's Control of a National Minority* (Austin, Texas: University of Texas Press, 1980).

Sammy Smooha, *The Orientation and Politicization of the Arab Minority in Israel* (Haifa: University of Haifa, The Arab-Jewish Centre, Institute of Middle East Studies, 1980).

Jacob M. Landau, *The Arabs in Israel. A Political Study* (London: Oxford University Press, 1971).

See also the sections on Elections (A/I/3) and Oriental Jews (B/VI/2).

VII
Religion

1 THE RELIGIONS OF ISRAEL

Israel was founded as a Jewish state which, in its Declaration of Independence, assured the faithful of all other religions full religious freedom. This guarantee was translated into practice by the Ministry for Religious Affairs, which granted the various religious groups far-reaching internal autonomy (see also the section on the issue of citizenship and religion, A/I/2/c). The great majority of non-Jews belong to the Arab population, which is composed mainly of Suni Moslems, Christians and Druze (data in section B/VI/3/b).

The followers of the Bahai faith, now persecuted in the country in which their creed originated, Iran, maintain their world headquarters in Haifa.

Some 12,000 Karaites live in the area of Ramla, in the vicinity of the international airport at Lod. They recognize only the Bible as binding and reject the tradition of rabbinical interpretation.

Some 300 Samaritans live in Holon near Tel-Aviv and another 300 in Nablus on the West Bank near their holy place, Mount Gerisim.

Figure 49 shows the regional distribution of the various religious groups in Israel.

2 THE POLITICAL FUNCTION OF THE JEWISH RELIGION

Without the Jewish religion neither Zionism nor the State of Israel would have been conceivable, although it must be stressed that for the Orthodox, Zionism was and still is regarded as near, if not total, blasphemy. The reason for this is that the Orthodox view history, and therefore the struggle to found a Jewish state, as dependent on the will of God, and thus not in need of the 'helping hand' of man. When and if God wills, He will provide for the return of the Children of Israel from the Diaspora.

We have already mentioned (see section A/II/5/b) that approximately 25% to 30% of Israeli Jews describe themselves as 'religious' or 'traditional'. Once again, of course, the polls reveal certain subjective perceptional biases on the part of the interviewees. In the 1974/5 poll conducted by Goldscheider and Friedlander (1982: 7), 55% described themselves as 'very religious' or 'religious', and 45% said they were 'not religious' or 'not at all religious'. But when measured by six 'religiosity indices' (such as maintaining separate sets of dishes and utensils for dairy and meat products, attending synagogue, not driving on the Sabbath, etc.) only 14% still qualified as 'religious' by all six measures and another 14% were 'moderately religious' (ibid.: 9).

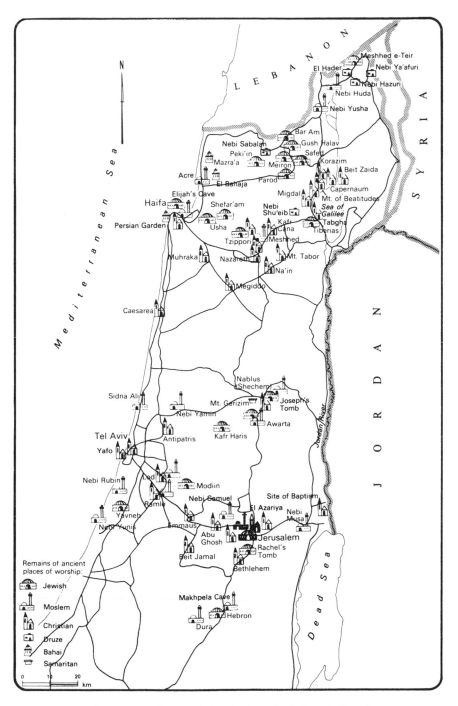

Figure 49   Regional distribution of religions in Israel.

It can therefore be said that, among secular Israeli Jews, their Israelism (a term never clearly defined) is much more pronounced than their Judaism. To a certain extent, this confirms traditional Orthodox arguments against Zionism. The adherents of the Orthodox Agudat Israel (not to mention the members of Neture Kartha) have maintained time and time again that Zionism would de-Judaize the Jewish people. As Goldscheider and Friedlander (1982: 22) concluded on the basis of their polls, 'In general, it may be argued that the greater the exposure [of immigrated Jews] to Israeli society, the lower the level of religiosity' (see A/II/1 and A/II/5/b; Marmorstein, 1969; Schiff, 1977; Wolffsohn, 1983c).

Polls conducted by Seligson and Caspi (1983) indicate a correlation between religiosity and ethnicity on the one hand and increasing intolerance *vis-à-vis* Arabs on the other hand. The political function of religion for some of the more fanatic West Bank settlers of Ashkenasi origin can be clearly seen among Gush Emunim and Kach (Rabbi Kahane) activists. For these settlers the Bible serves as a political argument (the Land of Israel as a country granted exclusively to the Jews) as well as a political atlas (which, of course, includes the West Bank in the Land of Israel).

Despite all this, the 'hawkish' function of the Jewish religion in Israel is not entirely one-sided. There are also the religious peace activists of (the albeit numerically marginal) Oz Veshalom. There are also National Religious politicians, such as Abraham Melamed, for whom the Jewishness of Tel-Aviv is of greater significance than the Israeli flag flying in Jericho. Since 1982 the War in Lebanon has given rise to numerous discussions within the MRP over the problems that hawkish policies have created for Judaism in Israel. In addition, the Orthodox view of man's role in history makes Agudat Israel a basically dovish party. Orthodox Jews believe that God determines the course of events and view man's role in history as rather limited. Moreover, a truly Orthodox Jew will not ascend the Mount of the Temple in Jerusalem for fear of treading on the place where the Holy of Holies once stood, where only the High Priest was permitted to enter and which can no longer be located with certainty. (For further examples of the polarizing rather than harmonizing function of the Jewish religion in the Jewish state see Wolffsohn, 1978, and Abramov, 1976.)

It has already been mentioned (see section A/II/5/b) that only about half of the voting potential of the total of 25% to 30% of religious Jews in the country has been mobilized by the religious parties in Knesset elections. Again, we observe a discrepancy between professed attitudes and actual behaviour. This fact also demonstrates the capacity of Mapai/ILP and even more so of Herut/Gahal/Likud to attract religious voters. Diskin (1980: 21 ff.) has demonstrated that since 1949 the voters of the religious parties have consistently preferred Herut/Gahal/Likud over any other party or bloc as a second choice. Here, the political function of religion can be seen in the indisputable trend to the political right, a trend observed among the voters long before it became a determining element for the national government in the formation of the 1977 coalition.

Although Oriental Jews are more often religious than Israelis from Ashkenasi backgrounds (see section A/II/5/b and Goldscheider and Freidlander, 1982: 10 ff.), this trend in attitudes has led to mixed political reactions on the behavioural level. Table 18 and 19 show that most of the supporters of the religious parties have not been Oriental Israelis, who have increasingly turned to the Likud. In relative numbers, nevertheless, greater proportions of Oriental Jews have voted for religious parties than has been the case among their Ashkenasi counterparts. In 1977, 18% of Oriental Israelis voted for religious parties, and only 12% of the Ashkenasim did so. The proportions were 16% and 10% respectively in 1981 and 15% vs 10% in 1984 (figures rounded off from the data provided by H. and R. Smith, *Jerusalem Post*, 3 August 1984).

3   RELIGIOUS INSTITUTIONS

The separation of the institutions of religion in Israel, that is, the maintenance of differing legal codes regulating matters of personal status for Jews, Moslems, Druze and Christians, has its historical origins in the legal system of the Ottoman Empire (the Millet system). In Israel it is also closely related to the strong political position of the religious parties.

The religious courts are concerned mainly with questions of marriage and divorce, support payments and the execution of wills. The judges serving in the religious courts are state civil servants, although the religious institutions are autonomous in their practice. Since its Declaration of Independence defines Israel as a Jewish state and at the same time grants its citizens freedom of conscience and religion, an institutional autonomy for the various religions represents the only possibility to defuse the inherent potential for conflict (see Rubinstein, 1974: 105; Wolffsohn, 1983: 626 f.).

The inner-Jewish agreement concerning the status quo, the document in which Mapai, Misrahi and the General Zionists promised the Orthodox Agudat Israel far-reaching concessions, has proved extraordinarily dynamic, working occasionally to the advantage of the secular public, but mostly (and particularly since 1977) favouring the religious elements of the Jewish population. In the agreement reached on 19 June 1947, it was promised that public institutions would observe Jewish religious holidays, that a distinction would be made between dairy and meat products and that the operation of public transport as well as cinemas and theatres would be prohibited on the Sabbath (i.e. from Friday night to Saturday night). Moreover, the regulation of marriage and divorce was to remain the exclusive domain of the religious institutions.

The Chief Rabbinate has historical roots dating from the Ottoman period but was not formally established until under the Mandate and has increasingly evolved into a religious service organization. This development was encouraged as a result of the composition of the committee which selects the two Chief Rabbis, as this panel includes not only rabbis but secular party politicians as well. The two Chief Rabbis, the one a Sephardic (Oriental) and the other an Ashkenasi rabbi, are the highest religious judges in the land. Because their position depends less on their religious-metaphysical authority than on their secular political power base, the Chief Rabbis are consequently neither recognized nor in fact even taken seriously by the strictly Orthodox AI, not to mention Neture Kartha. But from the viewpoint of the non-religious population, on the other hand, they are often enough a thorn in the flesh. It ought to be mentioned that the founder of the Orthodox-religious Shass Party, Rabbi Ovadia Joseph, was a former Sephardic Chief Rabbi who failed to be re-elected as a result of NRP and AI resistance and who subsequently took his revenge by turning to the political arena in 1983.

The highest religious authority for AI is the Council of Torah Sages. Its members are selected on the basis of their religious knowledge and merits rather than being politically elected. Their religious authority is therefore unchallenged. This also holds true for the highest religious body of Shass, the Council of Torah Scholars. (For further information see Friedmann, 1977: *passim*; Wolffsohn, 1983a: 629 ff.; Abramov, 1976: esp. 167 ff.; Schiff, 1977: 154 ff.).

The religious councils, which organize and supervise religious affairs on the local level, are service organizations without a shimmer of religious authority and are staffed by 'religious bureaucrats' whose appointments are made according to highly politicized and secular procedures (Wolffsohn, 1983a: 633 f.).

4   RELIGIOUS MOVEMENTS WITHIN JUDAISM

In Israel, and in the Diaspora as well, there are three major divisions or movements within Judaism, consisting of Orthodox, Conservative and Reform Jews.

The Orthodox parties (NRP, AI and PAI) have consistently used their considerable political influence to prevent the recognition of the Conservative and the Reform movements. As a result, religious acts performed by Conservative and Reform rabbis, including marriages, are not recognized under Israeli law (see Tabory, 1982).

'Who is a Jew?' Those persons whose mothers are Jews or who have converted to Judaism have been formally recognized as Jews. Few problems have arisen in connection with the maternal principle, as it corresponds with the *halacha*, the Jewish religious laws. With regard to conversion, however, there have been political problems, which the Orthodox define as religious in nature.

The issue of conversions to Judaism carried out under the guidance of Conservative or Reform rabbis has repeatedly led to political controversy. The key question of deciding who is a Jew is one which the Orthodox demand the right to resolve alone, particularly when it comes to conversions. Immigrants from the USA are most frequently affected, as about two-thirds of American Jews belong to one of the more 'modern' Conservative and Reform movements.

Repeatedly, Mapai/ILP has indicated its desire, and sometimes even promised, to end the discrimination against Reform and Conservative Judaism in Israel. The ILP did so again before the 1984 Knesset elections. But in its search for possible coalition partners after these elections, Labour soon vowed to preserve the religious status quo, including the significant material and organizational gains attained by the religious parties since 1977, and thus demonstrated that it could not be counted upon to support Reform and Conservative Jews. Shulamit Aloni's Citizens' Rights Movement has remained their most faithful ally on this issue.

FURTHER READING

Charles S. Leibman and Eliezer Don-Yehiya, *Civil Religion in Israel. Traditional Judaism and Political Culture in the Jewish State* (Berkeley, Calif.: University of California Press, 1984).

Simon N. Herman, *Jewish Identity. A Social Psychological Perspective* (Beverley Hills, Calif., and London: Sage, 1977).

Zalman S. Abramov, *Perpetual Dilemma. Jewish Religion in the Jewish State* (Rutherford, NJ: Fairleigh Dickinson University Press, and London: Associated University Press, 1976).

Salomon Poll and Ernest Krausz (eds.), *On Ethnic and Religious Diversity in Israel* (Ramat-Gan: Bar Ilan University, 1975).

VIII
Interest Groups

1 TRADE UNIONS

(a) HISTORY AND ORGANIZATION

Israel's largest trade union, the Histadrut, was founded in December 1920 as the workers' organization of the leftist socialist parties. From the beginning the Histadrut was not merely a union, but an organizational and ideological trail-blazer in the development of national institutions. Since all the collective settlements (*kibbutzim*) and cooperatives (*moshavim*) founded by the Labour parties also belonged to the Histadrut, which, in turn, itself became a sponsor of economic enterprises (see section C/XII/2), the Histadrut had, by 1948, become the real centre of political and economic power in the Yishuv. At first Ahudat Haavoda (founded in 1919), then Mapai/ILP were politically dominant, although the results of the Histadrut elections since 1920 show evidence of a continuous undermining of the socialist and social democratic power base even in this bastion of the Labour parties (see Wolffsohn, 1983b: 292 f.).

Figure 51 and Table 41 demonstrate on the one hand the pre-eminence of the Maarah and its predecessors in the Histadrut, and on the other the relatively massive decline of this predominant position. Recently, this trend has stabilized.

The voting procedures employed in the elections to the National Convention of the Histadrut are similar to those governing Knesset elections. They include voting for party lists as well as the principle of proportional representation and the 1% barrier. In the course of the years the Histadrut has been opened to the non-socialist parties, so that all of the important national parties and groups with the exception of the religious parties now offer lists in Histadrut elections.

The double role of the Histadrut, representing both employer and employee (the latter through the huge Histadrut holding company Hevrat Ovdim with its numerous affiliated firms), has led to alienation between the membership and the union leadership. In addition, the interwoven personnel structures of the Histadrut and the dominant Mapai/ILP up until 1977 made any confrontation with the government over economic policy extremely difficult.

To this day not a single member of Herut/Gahal/Likud has ever belonged to Vaada Merakeset, the Histadrut 'cabinet'. From 1977 to 1981 this 32-member executive consisted of 22 members from the ILP, 5 from Mapam, 2 representatives of local worker's councils, 1 'Religious Worker' (an ILP faction), 1 Independent Liberal and 1 Arab (who stood close to the ILP; *Haaretz*, 9 December 1977). The structure of the 'cabinet' formed in 1981 was not significantly different. (For data on the Histadrut during the Yishuv see Shapiro, 1976: 265; and for the period 1949 to 1969 see Smooha, 1978: 338 f.)

Ten general secretaries have been elected to lead the Histadrut: David Ben-Gurion (1921/35), David Remez (1935/45), Joseph Sprinzak (1945/9), Pinchas Lavon (1949/50 and 1956/61), Mordechai Namir (1950/6), Aharon Becker (1961/9), Yitzhak Ben-Aharon (1969/73, the only general secretary from the former Ahdut Haavoda, which merged with Mapai and Rafi in 1968), Jeruham Meshel (1974/84) and Israel Kessar (since 1984). The latter, born in Sana'a (Yemen), is the first Oriental Jew to become general secretary of the Histadrut.

Figure 50 presents a schematic overview of the multiplicity of the Histadrut's activities. It could have included many other areas in which the Histadrut also maintains organizations of its own, as, for example, in sports the Hapoel clubs, or the *kibbutzim* and *moshavim* (most of which are affiliated to the Labour parties and therefore to the Histadrut), or the media, where one of Israel's major dailies (*Davar*) is among the many publications owned and run by the Histadrut, to mention but a few of the many further areas of interdependence.

The parties represented in the Histadrut General Assembly (its 'parliament') profit from proportional financial subsidies. Large numbers of Histadrut and Hevrat Ovdim employees have also been members of the Labour parties, mainly of Mapai/ILP. Some 60% of Histadrut membership dues flow into the coffers of its health insurance organization, Kupat Holim, the services of which are available to the members of the national religious Hapoel Hamizrahi Union as well as to the members of Poale Agudat Israel.

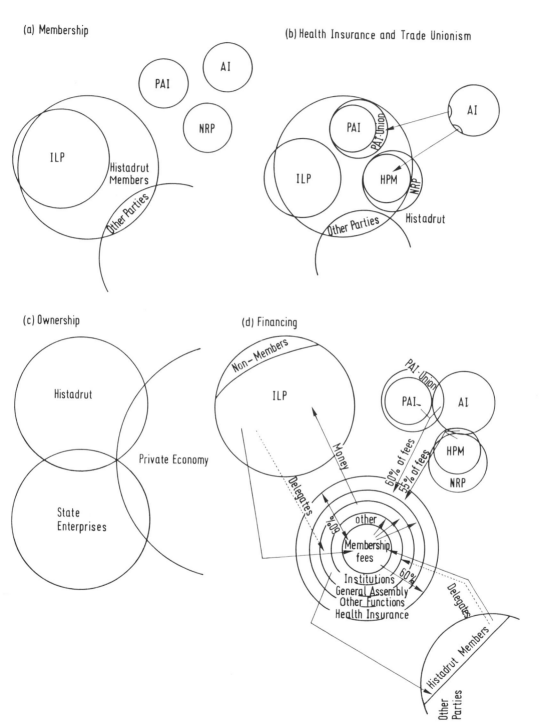

*Figure 50   Interdependence of Histadrut, political parties, private
economy and state economy.*

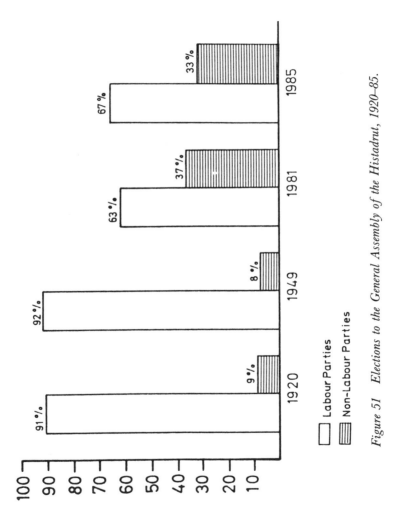

Figure 51   Elections to the General Assembly of the Histadrut, 1920–85.

Table 41   Elections to the General Assembly of the Histadrut, 1920–85 (%)

	1920	1923	1927	1933	1942	1944	1949	1956
Labour; later Maarah	90·9	83·9	91·6	97·7	96·3	92·1	91·5	84·8
Later: Likud								3·8
Others	9·1	16·1	8·4	2·3	3·7	9·7	8·5	11·4

	1960	1966	1969	1973	1977	1981	1985
	86·3	77·5	65·2	62·6	57·1	63·0	66·7
	3·5	15·2	22·8	22·7	28·2	26·9	21·4
	10·2	7·3	12·0	14·7	14·7	10·1	11·9

This is a result of cooperative agreements signed with HPM in 1927 and with PAI in 1953. There are also members of Agudat Israel who belong to the trade union department of the (NRP-run) Hapoel Hamizrahi in order to enjoy the benefits of Kupat Holim. Fifty-five per cent of HPM membership dues go to Kupat Holim, the rest to HPM and the NRP. Sixty per cent of PAI membership dues are transferred to the health insurance organization, the other 40% remain for the PAI party and union.

In certain areas, Histadrut enterprises are linked to the private and state sectors as a result of joint property ownership.

Ben-Meir (1982) describes the 'four pillars' of the Histadrut: first, the trade union; second, the cooperative economic enterprises; third, the social services (such as health insurance); and fourth, the educational organizations (see also B/IX/1) and cultural activities (see A/IV). The organizational interconnections between the Histadrut and other institutions of the polity, economy, society and culture of Israel are therefore extraordinarily diverse.

The National Labour Federation (NLF) was founded by the Revisionists in 1934 as a rival to the Histadrut. In 1965, however, Herut decided it could work much more effectively from within the Histadrut rather than against it. This decision led to a split in the NFL, the more pragmatic wing joining the Histadrut. The traditional wing continued the independent NFL organization and later founded the Independent Centre Party. By 1984, however, this division had become a dead issue and the chairman of the Independent Centre (which had meanwhile changed its name to Laam), Eliezer Shostah, led his organization in joining the Histadrut movement.

From its inception in 1922, Hapoel Hamizrahi (HPM) was a political party, trade union, settlement organization and economic enterprise all in one. This was also true of Poale Agudat Israel (PAI), an organization of Orthodox workers. In 1950 HPM joined the trade union division of the Histadrut as a partner in collective bargaining and was followed in 1953 by PAI. Both HPM and PAI continue to maintain their independence as trade unions and as political parties but their members are entitled to the services of the Histadrut-operated health insurance organization Kupat Holim. This is the largest medical insurance programme in Israel, insuring some 70% of the total population.

(b) MEMBERSHIP

The membership of the Histadrut was 4,433 or 5% of the Jewish population of Palestine in 1920, reached 23% of the total population in 1933 and rose to 27% in 1939 (Horowitz, 1973: 36).

It must be noted that women and children (under the age of 18) are also included in the membership figures. Accordingly, 61·7% of all Israelis over the age of 18 belonged to the Histadrut in 1977, this figure including the Israeli Arabs as well. Four years later the proportion was 60·2% (computed from the numbers of persons eligible to vote for the Histadrut National Convention as given in Harel, 1981, and population statistics from the *Statistical Abstract of Israel*).

In accordance with the statutes of the Histadrut, 'every worker over the age of 18 who makes his living without exploiting others' is eligible for membership. Nowadays, persons who do not employ more than five other workers (especially artisans) as well as housewives are permitted to join.

The member joins the central organization of the Histadrut rather than an individual union. In 1980 the Histadrut included 49 industrial unions and professional organizations, to which members were assigned by the central offices. The individual unions are organized like the parent body and also hold general elections. In many of these elections HPM, PAI and even the National Labour Federation may and do compete, thus giving the member unions a somewhat more pluralistic character than that of the central organization.

HPM counted around 100,000 members in its last tally in 1966. The NLF also had some 100,000 members in 1980 (dependants not included), and PAI reported 47,000 members in the early 1970s.

(c) COLLECTIVE BARGAINING

In wage negotiations with management the Histadrut, HPM, PAI and AI have for years cooperated in presenting a common position representative of their joint membership. This collective union power must be viewed in the context of the traditional pioneering role of the Histadrut in the economic development of the state as well as in combination with the Histadrut's interlacing network of personal and political interconnections with the AH/Mapai/ILP, representing the core of every governing coalition from the 1920s until its fall from power in 1977. As a consequence of this combined union network, it has proved all but impossible to carry out any economic policy measure against the collective will of the unions. In addition, Israel, as a nation of immigrants – or at least as a nation which regards itself as a land of continuing immigration – can hardly afford to project the image of a nation riven by labour strife or plagued by unemployment.

The agreements obtained as a result of Histadrut-led collective bargaining have, for the most part, also been extended to include the NLF membership.

Up to 1977 both the major party in the governing coalition and the Histadrut belonged to the same political camp and their interlocking relationships made coordination with the public sector in its role as employer easier than it has proved to be since 1977. There had, of course, been internal disputes in the period before the change of power, but a basic consensus was always obtainable. The existence of such a large public and Histadrut sector in Israel's economy places certain limits on the principle of free collective bargaining. (See Medding, 1972, on the zenith of Mapai dominance and Reshef, 1983/4, on the period 1973–83. For data on the sectors of the economy, see sections C/XII, XIII and XIV.)

2 EMPLOYER ORGANIZATIONS

The Manufacturers' Association, founded in 1923, was at first basically Zionist in its orientation but remained independent, avoiding the political embraces of the Revisionists and maintaining what is generally recognized to be a non-partisan stance in the post-independence period, although its members occasionally ran for the Knesset as candidates of the Liberals, the Progressive Party, Herut, Rafi, or DMC. (For information on the *Yishuv* period see Giladi, 1973: 246; Wolffsohn, 1983a: 63 ff.)

During the Mapai/ILP dominated epoch the Manufacturers' Association became so accustomed to state subsidies that it rejected the new market-oriented direction of economic policy introduced by the Likud government in October of 1977. The manufacturers later even vehemently opposed these measures, launching particularly strong attacks on the financial policies introduced by Minister of Finance Aridor in 1981 (Wolffsohn, 1979).

Even in terms of membership, the Manufacturers' Association is by no means a truly 'capitalistic' organization, as it has been joined by Kibbutz Industries as well as by enterprises run by religious and bourgeois parties, thereby making it a pluralistic organization.

Over the years, the Manufacturers' Association has maintained a more or less neutral stance in party politics. Its flirt with the bourgeois parties during the Yishuv failed dismally (Giladi, 1976: 246 ff.) and Revisionist offers were turned down (Shapiro, 1977: 117 f.; Shavit, 1978: 168, 198, 258; Wolffsohn, 1983a: 583 ff. on the period since independence).

(a) COLLECTIVE BARGAINING

The smaller employer organizations from the different branches of the economy meet with the Manufacturers' Association to discuss their bargaining positions in the Coordinating Committee, in which the latter organization has the greatest influence.

(b) ACCESS TO THE LEVERS OF POWER

Besides being basically non-political (at least as far as party politics are concerned), employers in Israel have enjoyed only limited access to the levers of political power, especially in the face of the long Labour-Histadrut dominance in the state and economy prior to 1977. In addition, a policy of confrontation with a Labour coalition which had been entrenched in power for so long could have been suicidal for employers who, besides, had become accustomed to their state subsidies. In fact, when the Likud (under Minister of Finance Ehrlich) attempted to change the course of economic policy between October 1977 and October 1979, the manufacturers torpedoed the effort. For their part, the Labour-led governments were interested in maintaining subsidies to industry for reasons of general economic policy, as such support encouraged exports and helped at least in part to limit the balance of trade deficit.

As the major governing party since 1977, Herut depended on its voters in the lower economic strata and was thus hardly likely deliberately to alienate its base of support by steering a political course friendly to business and industry. To launch a frontal attack on the principle of state subsidies to the economy would have been tantamount to political suicide, as not only producers but Israeli consumers as well have been among the beneficiaries. One of the first acts of Finance Minister Aridor as the first Herut politician to hold this office was to affirm the policy of subsidies (in January 1981).

3 ARTISANS AND RETAIL MERCHANTS

(a) POLITICAL HISTORY

During the Yishuv period the Artisans' Association maintained close ties with the General Zionists, but then gravitated towards Mapai after independence (see Medding, 1972: 54 f.). The same is true of the Retailers' Association, which, like the former organization, had presented its own candidates in the elections to the Constituent Assemblies of the Yishuv.

As a result of internal controversies in the 1950s the Retailers' Association once again tilted more to the GZ/Liberal Party, but has experienced problems with the economic and especially the tax policies of the Liberal Party since 1977. Although dissatisfied, the Retailers nevertheless remained loyal to the Liberals.

(b) POWER

The representatives of the artisans and retailers have no real political 'power' in the sense of effective political influence or the potential to carry out threats. Unlike the Histadrut, they are not in a position to mobilize any significant numbers in terms of membership, would themselves be most hurt by any 'strike', and have thus far found no access to key positions of political leadership, either during the Mapai/ILP epoch or under the Likud since 1977, as they have not even been able to count on finding a sympathetic ear in 'their own' party, the Liberals.

4 KIBBUTZIM

Kibbutz (plural: kibbutzim) is the name applied to a type of collective settlement which has existed in Palestine since 1909. The first kibbutz was Degania, just to the south of the Sea of Galilee. The key word to any description and to the self-image of the kibbutz was community. A further keyword was equality: all members were to hold equal shares of the community property (which, in the beginning, was very little) and no one was to be privileged in work or position. Parents were not to be allowed to transfer their social advantages to their children, and education thus played a singular role in the community. Children slept, not with their parents, but in special children's houses.

A further principle which was, at least in the beginning, put into practice held that everyone was to take turns doing all of the required kinds of work in rotation. Decisions were to be made only in meetings of the membership. These meetings, however, were more and more sparsely attended.

The *kibbutz* was to prepare the way for the new Jewish community, which was to be agriculturally oriented. The ideal, the model for what the whole society was to become, was the *halutz*, the agricultural pioneer, in contrast to the Diaspora Jew, who was to be found typically in the retail or service sectors of the economy. In short, the 'new Jewish man' was to be a creation of the *kibbutz*.

The beginnings of the *kibbutz* movement had their roots in anarchism and were anything but dogmatic or party-oriented, let alone Marxist (Meier-Cronemeyer, 1969; Darin-Drabkin, 1967; Ben-Avram, 1976; Ophir, 1973; Margalit, 1971; Wolffsohn, 1983a).

(a) KIBBUTZ ORGANIZATIONS

The *kibbutzim* (collective settlements), like the *moshavim* (cooperative settlements), are not easy to classify as 'interest groups', as they fall somewhere between the usual definition of a party faction and that of an interest group. A number of *kibbutz* organizations have been founded:

Hever Hakvutzot was created in 1925 and favoured the smaller forms of the *kibbutz*. It was the *kibbutz* organization of Hapoel Hazair, relatively pragmatic in nature, which attempted to reduce the confrontation with the Revisionists during the Yishuv.

Kibbutz Hameuhad, founded in 1927, preferred the large *kibbutz*, which it saw as the pioneer form of the larger national community. It eventually became the core of the newly organized Ahdut Haavoda in 1944, tended to the left on social issues but was activist (i.e. on the 'right') in defence policy. There were close interconnections in personnel between Kibbutz Hameuhad and the Palmach, the pioneer troops of the Hagana.

In 1951 the Mapai membership of the above organization split off to form Ihud Hakibbutzim, which was joined by Hever Hakvutzot in October of the same year. Kibbutz Hameuhad thus became identical with AH and Ihud a part of Mapai.

In 1979 Ihud and Kibbutz Hameuhad merged to form the United Kibbutz Movement, but have continued to maintain their individual organizational identities.

Kibbutz Haartzi, founded in 1928, remained closely tied to Hashomer Hazair and its successor, Mapam.

In 1938 Hapoel Hamizrahi founded the first national religious *kibbutz*. The Orthodox Poale Agudat Israel followed in 1944 and the left-liberal Progressive Party founded its first *kibbutz* soon thereafter. (On HPM *kibbutzim*, see Fishman, 1975 and 1983.)

By the end of 1982 the United Kibbutz Movement was the largest organization of its kind with 158 settlements, followed by Kibbutz Haartzi with 81, the national religious HPM with 16, the Zionist Workers (Independent Liberals) with 5 and the Orthodox PAI with 2 (*Statistical Abstract of Israel*, 1983: 45; for earlier data see Wolffsohn, 1983a: 348).

(b) KIBBUTZ VOTING BEHAVIOUR

In the first years following independence the *kibbutz* membership generally voted as a block for the party of 'their' organization, but these ties had become somewhat loose by 1977. (For details on the voting patterns of the individual *kibbutz* organizations in the period 1947 to 1977 see Wolffsohn, 1983a: 595–7.)

In 1981 the *kibbutzim* with connections with the Labour parties supported the Labour bloc almost as solidly as before, although Ihud continued to be somewhat 'undisciplined' (delivering 'only' 91%). In 1981, just as in the immediate post-independence period, there were hardly any differences between the *kibbutz* organizations: all again voted for 'their' party (see Table 51).

In 1984 the results from both the United Kibbutz Movement (UKM) and Kibbutz Haartz settlements proved a disappointment for the Labour parties. Again, the support shown by the latter organization for the Alignment (85%) exceeded that demonstrated by the voters of the former (82%), but the Maarah had lost about 10% of its former support in both organizations.

Most of the remainder of the UKM votes did not, as had been expected, go to Lova Eliav, general secretary of the ILP from 1970 to 1972, Eliav had left the party because of what he interpreted as Labour's estrangement from its pioneer past and because of its hawkish positions. Instead, Shulamit Aloni's left-liberal Citizens' Rights Movement picked up the bulk of the remaining 20%. Due to the surplus vote agreement between the Alignment and the CRM, these votes were thus not lost for Labour (Y. Oked, *Jerusalem Post*, 4 August 1984).

That any political shift took place at all has to do with the change of generations in the *kibbutzim.* The 'second generation', those born and raised

---

Table 42   Votes for the Labour Bloc from *Kibbutz* Organizations of the Labour Movement, 1949–84 (%)

	Mapam K. Haartzi	Mapai Ihud	UKM	AH K. Hameuhad
1949	99·6	96·7*		98·0
1951	99·4	97·8*		96·0
1955	99·6	98·2		98·3
1959	99·7	98·1		98·6
1961	98·3	96·8		95·4
1965	97·8	97·4		96·9
1969	93·9	89·5		96·6
1973	87·0	86·6		92·0
1977	83·7	68·1		82·3
1981	94·7	91·1		93·7
1984	85·0		82·0	

---

* Hever.Hakvutzot.

Sources: various election statistics prepared by the Central Bureau of Statistics; *Haaretz*, 25 July 1984.

in the *kibbutz*, failed to develop the same strong ties to the *kibbutz* and its political party or parties as did the 'pioneer' first generation. This was one of the most important findings made by Rosner (1978) and his colleagues in their survey of numerous *kibbutzim* in 1969 (polls, explanations and further literature in Wolffsohn, 1983a: 353 ff.).

In a follow-up study in 1976, Rosner and Ovnath (1979) came to the conclusion that the ties to the 'general ideology' and to the 'basic values' of the *kibbutz* had further loosened in comparison with 1969.

The opinions expressed in these two polls merely served to confirm what had been observed earlier on the behavioural level in terms of voting in the 'new' *kibbutzim* founded since 1948. There, the members tended to defect much earlier from the labour parties than those of the collective settlements dating from before independence. The newer the *kibbutz* and the younger its members, the more manifest was the shift away from the labour parties. (Data in the various elections analyses of the Central Bureau of Statistics in Elections, as well as in Wolffsohn, 1983a: table 105, pp. 595 ff.)

(c) CHANGING ATTITUDES WITHIN THE *KIBBUTZIM*

Although the 'basic values' and the 'general ideology' of the *kibbutz* may have experienced a decline in the second and following generations, the spirit of patriotism and of volunteerism, the willingness to become involved, actually increased between Rosner's first and second surveys. Ichilov (1981) encountered the same phenomenon in her poll of 17- and 18-year-olds in *kibbutzim* and in the cities (apparently conducted in the late 1970s, but no precise date is given by the author). Among the youth of the *kibbutzim*, 68% considered 'loyalty to the state' 'very important', as opposed to a mere 7·4% of city youth; 60·2% of the *kibbutz* youth said they were interested in the current affairs of the country, as against only 8·4% in the cities (ibid.: 311). Earlier polls also confirmed that this more collective and community-oriented spirit of volunteerism and involvement in public affairs is more frequently found in *kibbutzim* than in Israeli cities (see Antonovsky and Arian, 1972: 143).

This is one side of the coin. On the other side, the signs of crisis are unmistakable. Some examples follow.

A new study by the Zahal Institute for Behavioural Studies comparing the youth of draft age in 1966 and 1976 with those in 1980/1 has shown that youth from the *kibbutzim* are much less willing voluntarily to assume extra duties in the military or to apply for officer candidate courses than youth from the cities. In 1966 and 1976, that is, during the Mapai/ILP era, *kibbutzim* youth had shown a much higher motivation than their urban contemporaries (*Haaretz*, 13 May 1983. The IDF spokesman was unwilling to release more details to the author.) Ironically, under policies of the super-nationalistic Herut-led coalition since 1977 the interest and public involvement of *kibbutzim* youngsters in public affairs has diminished. This may, however, be too far-reaching an interpretation. After all, a certain general lassitude had already set in earlier, during the Mapai/ILP era. 'Basic values' had already been called into question and it stands to reason that the impetus to become involved should also have suffered a consequent decline.

Younger *kibbutznikim* display little willingness to give up the easier life in the established communities in order to participate in the founding of new settlements. This is very worrisome to the *kibbutz* organizations (H. Hand-werker, *Haaretz*, 31 May 1983).

What is more, 41% of the Kibbutz Haartzi youth and 45% in Ihud were prepared to give up life in the *kibbutz* and to choose another way of life (Orchan and Samuel, 1981: 403). In 1983 the United Kibbutz Movement complained that 'over 40%' of their second-generation members wanted to leave the *kibbutz* (J. Canaa, *Jüdische Rundschau*, 30 June 1983; see earlier statements in *Haaretz*, 13 December 1979). One qualification to the general statement is necessary: the desire to leave seems less widespread in the religious *kibbutzim* (J. Ariel, *Haaretz*, 13 February 1980).

(d) CHANGING ATTITUDES TOWARDS THE *KIBBUTZIM*

In the meantime, the general public has come to view the *kibbutzim* as settlements of a 'planter aristocracy' (see Sherman, 1982). Feelings of 'sympathy' for the *kibbutzim* among the Jewish population of Israel rose from 59% in 1976 to 63% in 1978 but receded to 55% in 1981 and to only 52% in October 1983 (Leviathan, 1980: 233; Avnat and Leviathan, 1984: 2).

Given the fact that the *kibbutzim* are almost exclusively Ashkenasi, they enjoy far less approval among the Oriental population than among Israelis from European or American backgrounds. Among Oriental Sabras 45% expressed sympathy in 1976, and 55% in 1978. During the Likud era there was a decline to 49% in 1981 and to 47% in October of 1983 (Leviathan, 1980: 233; Avnat and Leviathan, 1984: 4). A simultaneous decline could also be observed among Sabras with an Ashkenasi background. Nevertheless, their sympathy for the *kibbutzim* remained well above the average (67% in 1976, 70% in 1978, but only 62% in 1981 and 59% in 1983; ibid.).

Not only attitudes and sympathies but behavioural patterns as well give indications of the split and disputed image of the *kibbutzim*. A particularly striking example for observers of the Israeli political and social scene was given by the events of 1981 in and around Kiryat Shmonah in the north of Galilee, where the Likud was able to muster vehement, sometimes even violently anti-Labour, that is, anti-*kibbutz* sentiments in the campaign for the Knesset elections. This was possible because of the fact that many residents of this development town inhabited by Oriental Israelis commuted to jobs in the *kibbutzim* of the surrounding area, where they felt deprived, or at least less privileged, in comparison with the Ashkenasi *kibbutznikim* whose 'dirty work' they were hired to carry out.

Whether objectively valid or not, this sentiment is politically and socially relevant. It is as indicative of 'ethnic' tensions as of the fundamental change which has taken place in the *kibbutzim* themselves. In their pioneer period it was considered tantamount to a sacrilege to hire outside labour. However, not only was this done, but it led to social tensions between 'socialist' employers and their workers, who, in a logical gesture of protest, demonstrated and voted in favour of the 'bourgeois' (more correctly: populist, but definitely non-socialist) Likud. Viewed in this perspective, the decline in the public's sympathies for the *kibbutzim* between 1978 and 1983 may be more than just a cyclical and temporary tendency. It may indicate a structural, that is, long-term, decline of the image of the *kibbutz* in Israeli society in general and in the Oriental Israeli society in particular.

In view of the fact that younger Israelis expressed less sympathy towards *kibbutzim* than their elder countrymen, this structural trend appears all the more plausible. In all the opinion surveys conducted by Leviathan and Avnat (1976, 1973, 1981 and 1983) the sympathy expressed by the youngest age cohort was always well below the average. For the age group 18 to 30, the rate was 52% in 1976, 55% in 1978, 44% in 1981 and 42% in 1983. (Compare these figures with the rates for the total sample given above, Avnat and Leviathan, 1984: 4.)

Although the *haluzic* ideal of the agricultural pioneer is regarded as the perfect image of the founding fathers, the proportion of *kibbutz* and *moshavim* members was and remains a minority of the total Jewish population of Palestine and Israel (see Table 43). Furthermore, the gap between the ideological ideal and its realization was evident from the beginnings of Jewish settlement in the Land of Israel. The 'rightism' and 'materialist value orientations' which Gottlieb and Yuchtman-Yaar (1983) analysed in their 1980/1 poll thus have historical roots.

The high social prestige of *kibbutzim* was and is anything but unfounded. Especially in the crisis years of the Yishuv, during the Arab Revolt, the *kibbutzim* performed pioneer work in creating numerous new settlements as defensive villages. The data on the foundation of settlements between 1936 and 1941 speak a clear language. The Zionist movement was always able to

Table 43   The Populations of the *Kibbutzim* and *Moshavim* as a Percentage of the Total Jewish Population, 1914–83

Year	Kibbutz Residents	Kibbutz Residents as % of Jewish Population	Moshav Residents	Moshav Residents as % of Jewish Population	Shitufi Residents	Shitufi Residents as % of Jewish Population
1914	180	0·2				
1922	735	0·9				
1927	3,909	2·6				
1931	4,391	2·5	3,400	1·9		
1936	16,444	4·4	10,000	2·5		
1941	72,738	5·8				
1947	47,408	7·5				
1948	53,700	7·8	22,900	3·3	1,500	0·2
1960	78,000	4·1	115,100	6·1	3,600	0·2
1965	80,600	3·5	119,600	5·2	4,700	0·2
1970	84,900	3·3	122,300	4·8	5,500	0·2
1974	94,000	3·3	129,000	4·5	6,100	0·2
1977	101,600	3·3	134,500	4·4	7,100	0·2
1981	113,700	3·4	144,000	4·4	8,400	0·3
1983	115,500	2·9	140,800	3·5	9,100	0·2

Sources: *Statistical Abstract of Israel*: various vols.; *Society in Israel*, 1976: 4 f.; *Encyclopaedia of Social Sciences*: various vols.; Horowitz and Lissak, 1977: 343.

rely on the *kibbutzim*, and the *kibbutznikim* were ever ready to follow up their words with deeds and, if need be, with sacrifices. The *kibbutzim* were really the vanguard of the Zionist enterprise and, in a way, they still are, despite the symptoms of crisis (or merely 'change'?) just described. Here are some data to give substance to this statement.

At present approximately 40% of Israel's agricultural production comes from the *kibbutzim*. Industrial production there rose by 87% in the 1970s, which means that industrial and agricultural production are now nearly equal (A. Gai, *Haaretz*, 6 September 1982). Eighty per cent of the industrial production of the *kibbutzim* is in metals, plastics, food processing, wood and furniture (Gai, loc. cit.). Of Israel's total exports, 6% were from *kibbutim* in 1980 (A. Lewin, *Haaretz*, 1 August 1980, and on *kibbutz* industries in general see Daniel, 1976: 55 ff.). In 1979/80 the *kibbutzim* accounted for 40% of Israel's total acreage under grain cultivation (and again in 1981/2), 18% of the citrus crop (13% in 1981/2) and 69% of the cotton crop (80% in 1981/82; *Statistical Abstract of Israel*, 1982: 390 ff., and 1983: 416 ff. See Figure 59 and section C/XIII/1,2,3.)

Seen in this light, the *kibbutzim* are also 'overrepresented' in terms of output and proved accomplishments. These 'quantities' represent 'quality' on the one hand and in turn a most considerable political 'quantity'. It is therefore not surprising that the Labour parties have turned to the *kibbutzim* again and again for leadership recruits. The *kibbutzim* can thus be found to be 'overrepresented' in the factions of the social democratic and socialist parties when their representation in the Knesset is compared to their portion of the total voting age population, which is, in any case, a problematical and not a very useful yardstick (data in Wolffsohn, 1983a: 362. On indicators for representativity see Caspi, 1976.)

5   MOSHAVIM

In 1921 a group of persons whose aim it was to hold fast to the *halutzic* agricultural pioneer ideal but who were not so extremely enamoured of the goals of collectivism and rigorous equality and who also did not reject the concept of private property left various *kibbutzim* to found Nahalal in Galilee, the first *moshav*. Among these was Shmuel Dayan, Moshe Dayan's father.

All members of a *moshav* (plural: *moshavim*) receive on lease equally large parcels of land, which they are free to work as they see fit. Purchasing and marketing are undertaken largely in common, which makes it possible to describe the *moshav* as a cooperative venture.

In contrast to the *kibbutzim*, the *moshavim* were, from the very beginning, viewed by the leftist socialist parties (with the exception of the more pragmatic and moderate Hapoel Hazair) as a kind of step-child, as not quite 'part of the family' (see Wolffsohn, 1981: 610 ff.). The relative lack of interest, if not to say neglect, evidenced in the approach of the 'mother' organizations, that is, the socialist parties, to the *moshavim* also proved to be the structural weakness of this settlement movement. Unwillingly, relatively late, and really only in order to keep up with the other parties did Ahdut Haavoda (founded in 1919) begin to found *moshavim* in the 1920s.

The quantitative development of the *moshavim* following Israel's independence was much greater than that of the collectivist *kibbutzim*, which failed to attract Oriental immigrants. The figures on the numbers of *moshavim* founded since 1948 (called *moshavim ovdim*) are clear proof (data in Wolffsohn, 1983a: 347).

There was a total of 405 *moshavim* in 1983, 244 of which belonged to Labour's Tnuat Hamoshavim, 67 to HPM, 46 to Ihud Hachaklai (see below), 17 to the Zionist Workers (IL), 6 to PAI, 13 to Herut, 5 to Hitachdut Haikarim and 7 independent *moshavim* (*Statistical Abstract of Israel*, 1983: 44). The *moshavim* of the national religious Hapoel Hamizrahi and Mapai were particularly active in the integration of Oriental immigrants.

A third form of settlement known as the *moshav shitufi*, combining elements of both the *kibbutz* and the *moshav*, should also be mentioned. On the *moshav shitufi*, production and marketing procede collectively, as in *kibbutzim*, but consumption remains the exclusive sphere of the individual household, as in *moshavim*. The land is worked by all and is not parcelled out to individuals.

A *kfar shitufi* is a village in which production and marketing are carried out on a cooperative basis. (In the case of the *moshav*, production and marketing as well as consumption are all private.) In late 1982 there were 41 *kfarim shitufiim* (*Statistical Abstract of Israel*, 1983: 45; for earlier data see Wolffsohn, 1983a: 349).

It is characteristic of all four forms of settlement that the land is held in common and is leased out rather than sold to individuals, and that each member has a house of his own (Viteles, 1966–8, vol. 4: 3).

The 'step-children' of the settlement movement have had their revenge, however, having turned their backs on the various sponsoring parties much earlier than the members of the *kibbutzim*. This is true of the *moshavim* founded by the labour parties as well as for those affiliated with 'civic' and 'religious' parties.

Table 44   Elections in the *Moshavim*, 1949–84 (%)

	1949	1951	1955	1959	1961	1965	1969	1973	1977	1981	1984
Mapai/ Maarah	60·9	61·3	53·4	51·6	51·9	41·3	50·9	45·7	31·1	42·6	56·4
Herut/ Gahal/ Likud	2·4	1·7	4·7	6·3	5·5	9·8	11·8	22·8	28·6	28·3	21·8
Others	36·7	37·0	41·9	42·1	42·6	48·9	37·3	31·5	40·3	29·1	21·8

Table 44 strikingly illustrates the great discrepancy between political generations in terms of political behaviour, and thus also in attitudes. The younger members (i. e. from *moshavim* founded after 1948) proved much more likely to turn away from the Maarah. What is more, these settlements are inhabited mainly by Oriental Israelis (data in Wolffsohn, 1984: 183).

It can be thus demonstrated that not only the urban 'proletariat' of Oriental heritage, but that rural workers as well tended to vote in fewer numbers for the labour parties and chose with surprising frequency the Likud instead.

The election results for 1981 reveal that the founder generation (of the older *moshavim*) returned to the Maarah, but that the increase in the more recently founded *moshavim* was only patchy. The attractiveness of the Likud for Oriental settlers in the newer *moshavim* increased, and 'the' Oriental party, Tami, also achieved better than average results in the predominantly Oriental new *moshavim*.

A settlement-by-settlement analysis of the unofficial results of the 1984 Knesset elections shows no change in the pattern prevailing since 1977 (see *Haaretz*, 25 July 1984). Once again the Alignment received less support in the newer *moshavim* founded since 1948 and largely inhabited by Oriental Jews.

6 OTHER AGRICULTURAL ORGANIZATIONS

During the Yishuv period, the Hitachdut Haikarim (Farmers' Federation, FF), the organization representing the interests of the private *moshavot*, had broken with the principle of 'Jewish work' and had hired less organized, less demanding and thus cheaper Arab labour. This led to violent inner-Jewish disturbances in 1927.

The *moshavot* ran their own 'Farmers'' list in the elections to the Delegates' Assemblies. The FF was founded in 1923 and was later close to the General Zionists/Liberals. A total of seven agricultural settlements were run by the FF in 1958 and five in 1982. The Minister for Agriculture, Grufer, in 1983/4 was a member of the FF as well as of the Liberal Party. The *moshavim*, not to mention the *kibbutzim*, felt that their concerns were being neglected under Grufer.

The Agricultural Union (Ihud Haklai) was once close to the Progressive Party, but after independence it also opened itself to influences from Mapai. The Agricultural Union counted 37 member settlements in 1958, compared with 43 in 1981 and 46 in 1982. (Various volumes of the *Statistical Abstract of Israel*; for data and a bibliography on these organizations see Wolffsohn, 1983a: 605 ff., also containing Knesset elections results in these settlements.)

FURTHER READING

HISTADRUT

Dov Ben-Meir, *Histadrut* (Bonn: Neue Gesellschaft, 1982).

Abraham Daniel, *Labour Enterprises in Israel*, 2 vols. (Jerusalem: Academic Press).

Joseph Glatt, 'The historical development of Histadrut', PhD dissertation, Columbia University, New York, 1973.

Walter Preuss, *The Labour Movement in Israel* (Jerusalem: R. Mass, 1965).

Noah Malkosh, *La Histadrouth* (Tel-Aviv: Institut Afro-Asiatiques, d'études syndicales et cooperatives, 1963).

KIBBUTZIM AND MOSHAVIM

Paula Rayman, *The Kibbutz Community and Nation Building* (Princeton, NJ: Princeton University Press, 1981).

E. Baldwin, *Differentiation and Co-operation in an Israeli Veteran Moshav* (Manchester: Manchester University Press).

Maxwell I. Klayman, *The Moshav in Israel* (New York: Praeger, 1970).

Dov Weintraub, Moshe Lissak and Yael Azmon, *Moshava, Kibbutz and Moshav* (Ithaca, NY: Cornell University Press, 1969).

Harry Viteles, *A History of the Co-operative Movement in Israel* (London: Vallentine, Mitchell, 1966 ff.).

Haim Darin-Drabkin, *The Other Society* (New York: Harcourt, Brace & World, 1963).

IX
Education and Recreation

1 SCHOOLS

During the Mandate and in the first years following independence, Jewish schools could be grouped according to the four differing trends or directions of educational and political philosophy they followed, each closely associated with a party movement: (1) the 'general trend', which was close to the General Zionists; (2) the 'worker's trend' of the Histadrut; (3) the '(National) Religious trend'; and (4) the schools of the Orthodox Agudat Israel, which were not subject to the control of the institutions of self-government of the Yishuv (Schoneveld, 1976: chs. 4–6; Wolffsohn, 1983a: 533 ff. with data and literature).

On the eve of independence the 'general trend' was attended by 50·1% of all pupils and was thus clearly ahead of the schools sponsored by the national religious Mizrahi (with 25%) and the Histadrut (with 24·8% of the total enrolment), but in 1952/3 43·4% of all pupils in Israel were enrolled in Histadrut schools, 27·1% in the 'general trend', 19·1% in the Mizrahi schools and 8·3% in those run by the AI (Schiff, 1977: 179).

Since 1953 only two types of school have existed: state schools (non-religious), and state religious schools.

The schools of the *kibbutzim* have been allowed to retain a great measure of independence, and the schools of Agudat Israel (the so-called 'independent trend') are autonomous, although they receive state support payments which amount to nearly the total of their budgets. Since joining the Likud-led coalition in 1977, AI has been singularly successful in channelling money into its schools. The Poale Agudat Israel sponsored schools have merged with the state religious institutions. The relationship between attendance at religious and non-religious schools has worked out to a proportion of approximately 30 to 70.

Jewish and Arab schools are largely separate from one another, the curricula being identical in some areas and differing in others, especially in history, where the accent is either Jewish or Arab, or in religion, where the emphasis is either Jewish, Islamic, Christian or Druze. A particular bone of contention has been the issue of instruction in the Old Testament (details in Mar'i, 1978; Zarzur, 1982).

(a) THE STRUCTURE OF THE PRESENT EDUCATIONAL SYSTEM

Israel's system of education has four levels.

(1) Pre-school education is offered to children between the ages of 3 and 6. Pre-school classes are obligatory beginning at the age of 5.

(2) Until 1968 primary education included grades 1 to 8. A reform measure then shortened the primary school period to six years.

(3) At least four years of post-primary education were required up until 1968. A minimum of three years is now obligatory. Pupils in grades 7, 8 and 9 attend an intermediate school (middle or junior high school). The grades 10 to 12 form the second part of post-primary education and the appropriate schools are officially known as 'secondary schools'.

(4) Higher education in Israel encompasses the universities as well as other post-secondary institutions.

Table 45   The Patterns of Education in Israel

(1) Up to 1968: 8 years primary school
                 + 4 years secondary education
(2) Since 1968: 6 years primary school
                 + 3 years intermediate secondary
                 + 3 years secondary education

A primary goal of the intermediate school is to improve the chances for Oriental Israelis to attend an upper level secondary school. There are no entrance examinations at this level. In order to bridge socio-economic differences, Oriental and Ashkenasi students are often brought together into integrated schools by bussing students from different quarters of the city or from other areas. This bussing policy continues to be a subject of intense controversy. First, the time and distance involved in getting the students to their schools have become longer. Second, educational 'transplantation' has led to social isolation. Third, better educated parents were afraid of the 'levelling' effect of 'mixed' classes.

(b) SECONDARY SCHOOLS

There are three types of secondary schools in Israel today.

(1) The general academic type leads to the *bagrut*, the final secondary school examination which entitles its holder to attend a university, provided he or she passes the entrance examinations there. *Bagrut* examinations are

administered centrally for the whole country by the Ministry of Education.

(2) The vocational type emphasizes practical education, preparing the student for the job market as well as for technical or engineering studies at the post-secondary level.

(3) The agricultural type leads to a diploma, but not to the *bagrut*.

In 1981/2 general academic secondary schools were attended by almost as many Oriental pupils (30·7%) as students of European-American backgrounds (31·2%). Among the children of Sabras, however, the Euro-Americans were probably overrepresented. Nevertheless, the first figure does indicate that immense efforts at more formal equality are being made. In the vocational schools the proportions of the ethnic groups attending correspond more to expectations. With 64·5% the Oriental pupils were clearly dominant, compared with 21·2% for Euro-Americans and 14·3% for the children of Sabras. The same Oriental overrepresentation was to be found in the agricultural schools, in which 61·9% of the students attending had an Oriental father, 19·4% an Ashkenasi, and 18·7% a Sabra father (*Statistical Abstract of Israel*, 1983: 661). The overrepresentation of Orientals in the agricultural schools has much to do with the fact that many Oriental Israelis live in the newer *moshavim* (those established after 1948). These parents tend to send their children to the agricultural schools, which are both nearer and easier. The result is that the educational gap between Orientals and Ashkenasim is widened and perpetuated.

Special variations of the three general types of secondary schools just described include:

kibbutz schools, which have maintained a certain degree of independence, as they are allowed to modify required curricula and the grading system (see M. Kerem, in Ackermann et al., 1982, vol. 2: 9 ff.);

yeshivot, which are schools emphasizing study of the *Talmud* (the commentaries on religious law and oral traditions) and the *Torah* (the Pentatuch) for students with religious interests and motivation. These schools combine religious and secular subjects and also lead to the *bagrut*, which thus formally opens the way to university studies for the graduates of *yeshivot*.

The popularity of the *yeshivot* has significantly increased in the course of the years. In 1949/50 these schools were attended by 4,862 students. This rose to approximately 30,000 in 1978/9 (see M. Bar-Lev, in Ackermann *et al.*, 1982, vol. 1: 507 for further data).

(c) ATTENDANCE REQUIREMENTS

Until 1968 Israeli students were required to attend at least eight years of school. Since then the requirement has been raised to a minimum of ten years (in addition to pre-school instruction).

(d) FINANCING

Some 70% of the costs of operating the school system is assumed by the central government (see data on government expenditures in section C/XV/3). About 13% of the burden is carried by city or local authorities, who have, as a result of their generally difficult financial straits, been forced to pass on as much of their financial obligations as possible to the state. Remaining costs are covered by donations.

(e) TUITION

Nowadays, education from the pre-school through the upper secondary level is virtually free of cost. Up to 1978 tuition was required at the secondary level. Since January 1984 a monthly fee of approximately US $10 has been levied. According to plans announced by the government formed in September 1984, an annual tuition fee of about US$900 was to be instituted at the university level (*FAZ*, 14 September 1984).

Yeshivot are financed by the sponsoring institutions and, since 1977, to an increasing extent by the Ministry for Religious Affairs. Several times the NRP and AI have been able to press the coalition to adopt financing measures for the *yeshivot*.

(f) SUPERVISION

The supervision of schools is mainly the duty of the Ministry of Education and Culture, although other ministries are also involved in certain areas, especially the Ministry of Labour and Social Affairs, the Defence Ministry (in the primary education of draftees) and the Ministry of Agriculture (for the agricultural schools).

Local authorities support and run numerous secondary schools, including many of the best, and also operate approximately half of all pre-schools. Like some other public institutions (i. e. the Histadrut, Women's Zionist Organization and IDF) they also operate vocational secondary schools.

The *yeshivot* are supervised by their sponsoring institutions. or parties (the NRP and AI, for instance). Those *yeshivot* which also lead to the *bagrut* coordinate their curricula with the central authorities.

2 UNIVERSITIES

Israel has seven universities: the Technion (Institute for Technology), founded in 1912; Hebrew University, founded in 1925; the University of Tel-Aviv (on a small scale beginning in 1935 and on a large scale since 1956); the national religious Bar Ilan University in Ramat-Gan near Tel-Aviv, opened in 1955; the University of Haifa, since 1963; the Institute for Higher Education opened in Beersheba in 1965 and renamed Ben Gurion University in 1973; and the Weizmann Institute of Technology in Rehovot, which opened its doors for postgraduate studies in 1934 (see Figure 52).

A veritable explosion in the student population took place in these educational institutions, as in the Western nations, in the 1960s and 1970s.

In 1948/9 there were 957 students attending Hebrew University, but by 1982/3 its enrolment had reached 15,475. At the Technion there were 678 students in 1948/9 and 8,040 in 1982/3. The numbers for Tel-Aviv were 616 students in 1959/60 and 17,530 in 1982/3. Tel-Aviv has thus become Israel's largest university in terms of enrolment. Bar Ilan was attended by students in 1959/60 and 9,830 in 1982/3. The enrolment at Haifa was 2,839 in 1969/70 and 6,100 in 1982/3. Ben Gurion University had 1,315 students in 1969/70

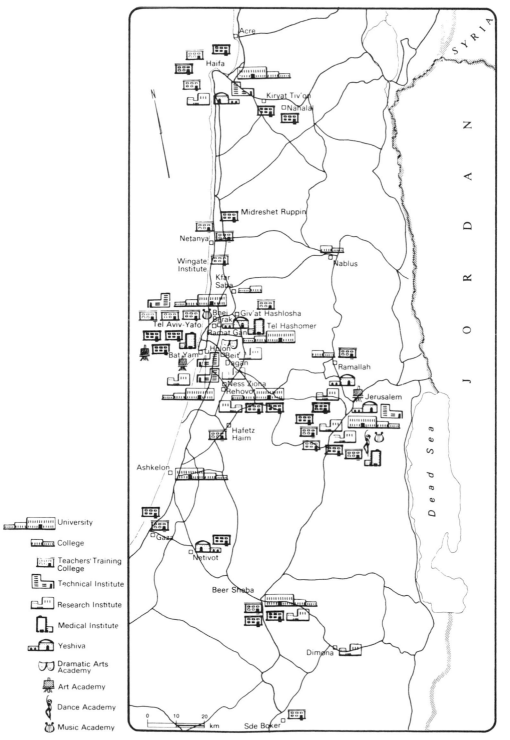

Figure 52 Post-secondary educational institutions.

Table 46 Membership of Youth Organizations, 1960–82

	1960[1]	1963	1971/2	1982
Learning and Working Youth (Histadrut)	68,000	99,037[2]	100,000[3]	100,000
Boy Scouts[4]	13,000	20,132	20,000	55,000
Bne Akiva (NRP)	11,000	18,615	18,000[5]	30,000
Hashomer Hazair (Mapam)	11,000	12,054	12,000[7]	16,000
Rel. Working Youth (HPM)	7,500	11,658	11,000	15,000
National Working Youth (once Revisionist, now tends to Likud)	*	8,394	8,300[7]	10,000
Makabi Youth (GZ)	5,000	6,934	6,999	7,000
Mahanot Olim (AH)	2,500	4,545	4,500[8]	4,200
Beitar (Herut)	3,600	3,623	4,200	3,500
Ezra (PAI)	2,500	3,209	3,200	4,200
Zionist Youth (Progressives/IL)	1,000	1,777	1,700	2,000
AI-Boys	*	1,600	*	*
AI-Girls	*	1,400	*	*
Halutz, Arab Youth (Histadrut)	*	1,388	*	*
Total	124,500	194,316	189,800	247,200
Total Number of (Jewish) Students	430,200	511,200	501,700[9]	673,010
Members of Youth Organizations in %	29%	38%	37%	37%

Notes:
* No data available.
[1] Histadrut estimates (loc. cit.: 701).
[2] 37,010 of these belonging to the 'Working Youth'.
[3] 100,000 also given for 1975.
[4] 25,000 in 1975.
[5] 2,680 of these as 'Arab Boy Scouts', 34,000 in 1975.
[6] 12,000 in 1975.
[7] 15,000 in 1978 (letter to the author from the Information Office of the National Workers' Organization, 4 September 1978).
[8] 4,000 in 1975.
[9] Excluding AI elementary schools for which no data are available.

Sources: Histadrut, 1965: 699 ff.; Shapira et al., 1979: 124; Youth Movements, 1972; Bentur/Weigert, 1976: 36; Statistical Abstract of Israel, various vols.; H. Handwerker, Haaretz, 14 February 1982.

and 4,920 in 1982/3. The Weizmann Institute was, and remains, much more exclusive, having had 419 students in 1969/70 and 470 in 1982/3. It is a research institute in which mainly scientists from natural sciences teach and study on the postgraduate level (all data from the *Statistical Abstract of Israel*, 1983: 675 f.).

Table 47   Israel's Universities

1) Hebrew University, Jerusalem
2) University of Tel-Aviv
3) Bar Ilan University, near Tel-Aviv
4) Technion (Technical University), Haifa
5) University of Haifa
6) Ben Gurion University, Beersheba
7) Weizman Institute, Rehovot

Israel's universities are financed largely by the government and the Jewish Agency. Their contributions totalled 82·9% of the total budgets in 1973/4, sank to 69% in 1977/8 and rose again to 74·4% in 1980/1. Tuition and fees covered 7·4% of the universities' budgets in 1973/4, made up 11·3% in the period 1975/6 to 1977 and 4·2% in 1980/1. The remaining percentages were made up by donations and 'other sources' (Council of Higher Education, 1982: 57).

3   YOUTH ORGANIZATIONS

During the Yishuv and in the early post-independence period the youth organizations, as a rule closely tied to the political parties, were important components in the political education and formation of the Jewish youth (see Wolffsohn, 1983a: 544 ff. for further details and literature). Over the years, the ideological rigidity of the Labour youth organizations has lessened, with the possible exception of Mapam's Hashomer Hazair. The religious youth movements still remain very strict, but popular (see Table 46).

The popularity of the Histadrut youth organization continues to stagnate, while that of the much less political Boy Scouts has risen, and the popularity of the national religious organization Bne Akiva has increased even more in recent years. The ideological purity of the Bne Akiva has, however, recently suffered due to the splits in the National Religious Party. The foundation of Rabbi Druckmann's Morasha was a serious blow, as it won over some of Bne Akiva's leaders, including Joseph Shapira. The polarization between religiously motivated doves and hawks has also affected Bne Akiva, which has become more hawkish in recent years.

FURTHER READING

Walter Ackermann *et al.* (eds.), *Erziehung in Israel*, 2 vols. (Stuttgart: Klett-Cotta, 1982); by far the most comprehensive anthology, unfortunately in German.

Peled Elad, 'The hidden agenda of educational policy in Israel: The interrelationship between the political system and the educational system', PhD dissertation, Columbia University, New York, 1979.

Mordechai Peri, 'The responsiveness of the Israeli national educational policy-making system to demands for change, 1973–1975', PhD dissertation, University of Oregon, 1977.

Doris Bensimon-Donath, *L'Education en Israel* (Paris: Anthropos, 1975); an introduction.

Max Rauch, 'Higher education in Israel', PhD dissertation, University of California, Los Angeles, 1971.

R. L. Braham, *Israel: A Modern Educational System* (Washington, DC: Government Printing Office, 1966); somewhat outdated but still useful.

Joseph S. Bentwich, *Education in Israel* (London: Routledge & Kegan Paul, 1965); outdated but important for the earlier periods.

YOUTH MOVEMENTS

Joseph W. Eaton, *Influencing the Youth Culture: A Study of Youth Organizations in Israel* (London: Sage, 1970).

X

Israel and World Jewry

The World Jewry possesses an (albeit limited) institutional voice in Israel in the *Jewish Agency* (JA), which is composed of the members of the Executive Council of the World Zionist Organization and an equal number of representatives from non-Zionist Jewish organizations.

On issues concerning immigration, agricultural and settlement policy the JA contributes its advice, and its money. The general direction of policy is, of course, set by the Israeli government (details, including information on the Diaspora activities of the Zionist parties, in Wolffsohn, 1983a: 377 ff. and 383 f.). The JA also engages in economic enterprises of its own, for example, Bank Leumi, which is Israel's largest financial institution.

Israel's financial support from the Jewry, is often made a matter of mystery. The actual figures can be found in section C/XVII (Figures 73–75 and Table 71).

Polls on the relations between Israel and the Diaspora have demonstrated time and again that Israelis feel strong ties to the Jews of the world, although this was less true of Israelis with Oriental backgrounds, especially Sabarim.

The tendencies are somewhat contradictory. On the one hand Sabarim consider themselves a part of the Jewish people, but on the other hand, they believe less strongly than their parents that they share a common fate with the Jews of the world outside Israel. Due to Israel's international isolation, however, it seems unlikely that the Sabras would willingly abandon their close contacts with the Diaspora, especially with the Jews of the United States (see Herman, 1977: 174; Levy and Gutmann, 1971: 87, 1976a: ch. 5, and 1976a: 42; Wolffsohn, 1983a: 385 f.).

The original self-image of Zionism is of fundamental importance here, as it conceived of itself in Rousseauian terms as the embodiment of the 'General Will' of the Jewish People: 'We are of the opinion that Zionist thought meets the needs of the Jewish People and therefore regard the Zionist Movement as truly democratic, totally independent of whether Zionist thought is shared by the majority of the People or not' (Moshe Beilinson, a Zionist socialist founding father, quoted in Gorni, 1973: 177).

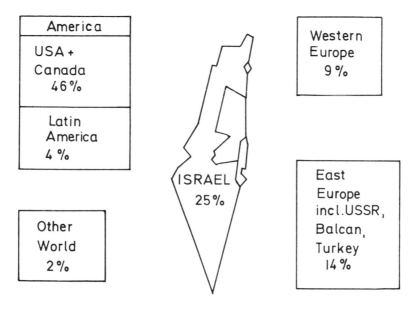

Figure 53 Distribution of Jews in the world, 1983 (%).

Source: American Jewish Yearbook, 1983.

This self-image was necessary for Zionism's self-justification previous to the Holocaust, as most Jews who left their native lands in those years did not immigrate to Palestine, and many who actually came did not remain (see Wolffsohn, 1983a: 398 f. for further data and literature, as well as section B/VI/1/f).

After the Holocaust and the founding of the state of Israel, the onus of self-justification shifted from the Zionists to those Jews who chose to remain in the Diaspora, as both sides adopted the view that history had proved

Zionism right, that the persecution of the Jews would continue always and everywhere.

One way for the Diaspora Jewry to salve its conscience was to contribute to the financial support of Isarel (see Figure 53).

Since the beginning of the Sadat peace initiative in 1977 and the intensification of the settlements policy under Begin, a policy anything but uncontroversial in the eyes of World Jewry, especially in the USA, a gradual polarization of the Diaspora Jews can be observed. The identity of the one camp continues to be oriented to Israel and its followers are prepared to support any action taken by the Israeli government. The other side has assumed a certain basically well-meaning but critical distance and derives its identity in the Diaspora to a lesser degree from Israel or not at all (see Sheffer, 1984; S. Cohen, 1983). In general, the leaders of Diaspora Jewry became much more dovish than the Israeli government between 1977 and 1984. The rank-and-file is somewhat less dovish, but still basically supports the approach of its leadership (ibid.).

FURTHER READING

Sam N. Lehman-Wilzig and Bernard Susser (eds.), *Public Life in Israel and the Diaspora* (Ramat-Gan: Bar Ilan University Press, 1981).

Moshe Davis (ed.), *World Jewry and the State of Israel* (New York: Arno Press/New York Times Company, 1977).

Charles S. Liebman, *Pressure without Sanctions. The Influence of World Jewry on Israeli Policy* (Rutherford, NJ: Fairleigh Dickinson University Press, and London: Associated University Press, 1977); by far the most informative book on this subject.

PART C
THE ECONOMY

XI

Basic Framework

The following basic factors drastically limit the manoeuvrability of decision-makers with regard to any innovations in economic policy in Israel.

(1) Israel's double economy, that is, the existence of separate Jewish and Arab economic sectors (including the occupied territories), will persist for the foreseeable future.

(2) The three-tiered structure, consisting of the government sector (including the Jewish Agency and the local authorities), the Histadrut sector and the private sector, is permanent. The dimensions of these three sectors may change but it can hardly be assumed that the Histadrut economy will be dissolved, as the political barriers appear virtually insurmountable, even with bourgeois majorities in the Knesset. The proportions of the net domestic product produced by the different sectors have averaged 40% for the government and Histadrut sectors together and 60% for the private sector.

(3) Jewish labour is not likely to become any cheaper in the immediate future. This is partly due to the traditional and, albeit reduced, still very effective political power of the Histadrut, a factor which makes it very difficult to discharge employees. It is also traceable to the continued application of Zionist ideology, which is immigration-oriented and thus unwilling to discourage would-be immigrants by tolerating unemployment.

If nothing else, considerations of political legitimacy dictate what can be described in purely economic terms as a policy of 'living beyond one's means'. The alternative might be an even lower rate of immigration and possibly even higher numbers of emigrants. On the other hand, if the state were to become insolvent the government might be forced to impose a 'belt-tightening' policy similar to those which failed in 1980 and 1983/4.

(4) The service sector is traditionally inflated, and this not least of all for political reasons. By expanding the bureaucracy the government can more easily cover up unemployment. In addition, it is a time-honoured method of maintaining the loyalty of the parties' and Histadrut's political clientele. Party functionaries and union officials are given a literally vital interest in the continuance of the prevailing political and economic structures by creating for them a solid economic basis in the form of attractively paying jobs in the service sector. This phenomenon was already observable during the Yishuv.

(5) Israel is poor in natural resources. Water resources are particularly scarce and a source of contention with Israel's neighbours, as for example in the dispute over the waters of the Jordan river in the early 1960s (see Brecher, 1974: ch. 5), the struggle over water rights on the West Bank, the planned canal from the Mediterranean to the Dead Sea and the rumours

that, following the invasion of Lebanon, Israel is planning, or has already begun, to divert water from the Litani River and other sources in southern Lebanon. These rumours have thus far been categorically denied by Israeli government spokesmen. (On the politics of water rights see Karmon, 1983: 99 ff.)

(6) The size of Israel's domestic market is severely limited. What is more, access to the geographically closest markets, the Arab states, is largely blocked for political reasons. In addition, the Arab League seeks to inhibit Israel's foreign trade by means of its 'black list'.

(7) Defence expenditures will continue to place an extraordinary burden on Israel's budget for the foreseeable future. The peace treaty between Israel and Egypt has, over the short and middle term, led to a considerable acceleration in monetary circulation as new military installations were constructed to replace those given up in the Sinai. Furthermore, it is scarcely possible to imagine any fundamental reduction in levels of armament as long as Syria, Iraq, Libya and the PLO continue to pose a military challenge to Israel, or at least are perceived as doing so by Israel's politicians. Jordan and Saudi Arabia, the latter building an air force base at Tabuk, only twenty minutes by air from Eilat, could also be pulled into a military confrontation,

(8) Independent of the political stripe of the government, the public sector continues to funnel capital imports into the economy, that is, income from state loans and donations from abroad, especially the funds originating with the Jewish Agency, the World Zionist Organization, the National Fund (Keren Kayemet Leisrael), or the Keren Hayessod (in the USA the United Jewish Appeal). The government also controls the economic and military aid from the United States. As long as Israel remains financially dependent on outside sources of support, the role of the government in the economy can hardly be expected to diminish in importance.

(9) Israel's foreign trade has become very heavily oriented to the European Community. As a result, Israel's decision-makers, whether they like it or not, will have to continue to at least partly adapt themselves to the political views of the EC in questions of foreign policy and security issues.

(10) Economic planning is extremely difficult in Israel, as it is, for example, rarely possible to reliably predict when, from where, and how many Diaspora Jews may want to come to Israel, or may, in the case of Soviet Jews, be allowed to leave. Political developments in the Middle East continually produce surprises, not only for layman. Military confrontations and coups occur frequently and without warning. For example, the fall of the Shah of Iran, Israel's main oil supplier, made it necessary to find substitute sources. The willingness of American Jews to give money to Israel and the extent of US economic and military aid cannot be planned on a middle- or long-term basis, as economic developments in the United States as well as the climate of public opinion there are factors which are of great importance but which are anything but easily predictable. Finally, the volume of direct private investments from abroad cannot be forecast accurately, as such decisions are strongly influenced not only by economic developments, but by political events in the Middle East as well. Even tourism, an important source of income for Israel, depends on foreign economic and political developments,

as well as on the conduct of Israel in such cases as wars or verbal attacks on
foreign political leaders such as those on West Germany's Helmut Schmidt
and France's Valéry Giscard d'Estaing in 1981. (On planning see Bilski,
1980.)

XII
Social and Political Ramifications
of Economic Policy

1 PARTIES AND THE ECONOMY

Political-economic activities on the part of Israel's parties are traceable to the
socialistic and social democratic second *aliya*, and especially to Ahdut
Haavoda (AH, founded in 1919). It was the goal of the leftist parties to work
from a position of economic strength so as to care for their members 'from the
cradle to the grave', as well as to gain and maintain a political leadership
role.

The religious parties, led by Hapoel Hamisrahi (HPM), adapted the
organizational patterns established by the leftist parties.

The economic policy of the British Mandate authorities, although inadequate in the eyes of the Yishuv and therefore in need of being supplemented by inner-Jewish economic activities, also led to entrepreneurial
activities on the part of the parties. What is more, there was no public
financing of elections or party activities, so that the parties were forced to
find their own financial resources. In order to serve the welfare of their
members, the parties first had to take care of themselves (cf. A/II/4).

Mapai/ILP controls not only real estate, but also printing plants and
publishing houses (details in Wolffsohn, 1983a: 562 f.). But since ownership
of capital goods is not necessarily equivalent to ready cash, the ILP experienced financial difficulties following its losses at the polls and the resulting
reductions in its public subsidies.

The (new) AH (since 1948) and Mapam are largely supported by the
'financial empires' of their *kibbutzim* organizations, which are not only
involved in agriculture but in industry as well. They also own considerable
tracts of real estate. The HPM/NRP, Progressive Party/IL and PAI also rely
on their own *kibbutzim* and *moshavim* organizations as sources of income.

The Progressive Party/IL was also active in the construction industry, providing party members with housing, especially during the fifty-year period of mass immigration. In addition, the IL had ties with agricultural marketing cooperatives.

The General Zionists/Liberal Party was involved in construction and in credit financing. Herut was active in real estate. In its early years the party overextended itself, launching enterprises in the furniture and auto service industries, a refrigerator plant, electrical appliance wholesalerships, an import-export firm, an insurance company and a travel agency. Together with its trade union, the National Labour Federation, Herut was also active in the construction industry. Most of these enterprises proved unprofitable and were subsequently closed down.

The Communists have financed their work mainly through their own publishing house, as well as through an import-export company specializing in trade with Communist bloc nations (Greilsammer, 1978: 339).

The NRP owns real estate, apartments, factories, numerous industrial cooperatives and five larger multifunctional funds. The centrepiece of the NRP enterprises is the United Misrahi Bank, which took over the stock of the formerly state-owned Tefahot Bank in 1978. Both the AI and PAI operate their own banks, and AI also owns a construction company (details in Wolffsohn, 1983a: 562 ff.).

It can be said that the economic enterprises of the parties are concentrated mainly in construction (housing), in printing and in banking (special-term credit financing).

Since party enterprises have not been exempt from general economic downturns, public financing offered the parties welcome financial security. Furthermore, partisan distinctions proved difficult to maintain in a market economy, where both management and consumption were oriented to economic rather than partisan political considerations (see Wolffsohn, 1983a: 568 ff.).

2   THE HISTADRUT ECONOMY

With the Histadrut the Labour parties built up a significant additional economic base, beginning with the forming of Hevrat Ovdim (Workers' Society) in 1923 (Daniel, 1976: vol. II; Ben-Meir, 1982: 219 ff.).; Wolffsohn, 1983a: 560 ff.). From this modest start grew a holding company of major dimensions, embracing both the industrial and service sectors. In contradistinction to the cooperative and agricultural sector of the Histadrut, this area is known as the Histadrut 'institutional economy' (Daniel, 1976: vols. I and II).

Every member of the Histadrut automatically belongs to Hevrat Ovdim. The Histadrut National Convention and National Council are the highest organs; the Histadrut National Council appoints the Secretariat of Hevrat Ovdim and its Executive Committee is chosen by the Histadrut Executive Committee. The secretary general of the Histadrut is simultaneously the chairman of Hevrat Ovdim.

Here are some data on the size of the Histadrut sector. In 1960 the 'institutional economy' employed 35,580 workers. The number of employees rose to 42,240 by 1966 and 55,100 by 1973. This amounted to 22·8%, 22·7% and 23·0% of the total of gainfully employed workers in the respective years. This proportion fell to 'only' 22·2% in 1976 and was 22·3% in 1980 (Aharoni, 1976: 185; Histadrut, 1977: 25; Daniel, 1976: 160; Ben-Meir, 1982: 220). As a proportion of the various sectors of the economy, the total Histadrut sector accounted for 79·1% of total employment in the agricultural sector, 21% in the industrial sector (excluding diamonds), 27·1% in the construction sector, 25·9% in the transportation sector and 18·6% in the commercial, banking and service sectors (Ben-Meir, 1982: 220).

The development of the Histadrut economy as a proportion of net domestic production is shown in Tables 48 and 49.

Table 48   The Histadrut Sector as a Proportion of Net Domestic Product, 1953–80 (%)

1953	20·3
1955	18·0
1957	20·6
1960	20·4
1964	23·4
1970	19·5
1980	23·0

Sources: Horowitz, 1973: 52; Daniel, 1976, Vol. II: 196; Ben-Meir, 1982: 220.

Table 49   The Histadrut Sector as a Proportion of Other Economic Sectors, 1970 and 1977 (%)

	1970	*1977*
Agriculture	72·0	69·8
Industry	16·6	22·0
Construction	22·4	25·0
Transport	20·3	16·1
Commerce and finance	16·9	15·4

Source: Ben-Meir, 1980: 143.

The largest individual enterprises within the Histadrut are as follows.

Koor, an industrial conglomerate founded in 1944, accounted for 14·4% of all Histadrut employees in 1970 (Daniel, 1976, vol. II: 44) and 20·3% in 1976 (Histadrut, 1977: 25).

Soleh Boneh, founded in 1923, is the largest construction company in the nation and employed 22,600 workers in 1976 or 26·2% of the Histadrut total (Histadrut, 1977: 25; *Statistical Abstract of Israel*, 1977: 301).

Bank Hapoalim, which for a long time was the second largest bank in the country (after the Bank Leumi), is currently attempting to overtake its rival.

Teus was founded in 1958 as a holding company by a collection of seventeen individual enterprises and specializes in the construction of factories in the new development zones.

Shikun Ovdim, a housing corporation, is owned by Hevrat Ovdim, as is Hassne, the largest insurance company in Israel (founded in 1924).

Histour, a travel agency, is also a Hevrat Ovdim enterprise. The list can be extended at length. (see Figure 65 and Table 61 on the number of firms and their employees in the Histadrut economy.)

Illegal contributions by Histadrut companies to the Labour parties have been more often suspected than proved. A case which attracted particular attention was that of Asher Yadlin, who was nominated by the Rabin government to become president of the Central Bank, but was shortly thereafter accused and later convicted of having transferred large sums of money to the ILP, especially during election campaigns, while serving as an officer of the Histadrut (see Wolffsohn, 1983a: 561 for details and, for his version, Yadlin, 1980).

3   THE STATE ECONOMIC SECTOR

The state economic sector consists of the national government, the local communities and the 'national institutions', that is, the Jewish Agency, the ZWO, Keren Kayemet Leisrael (National Fund) and Keren Hayessod (the United Jewish Appeal in the USA).

The national institutions are mainly responsible for securing capital imports from abroad. These organizations also distribute funds in coordination with the government, the Jewish Agency, for example, for the creation of new settlements and the National Fund for agricultural projects.

The public sector has always accounted for an extraordinarily large proportion of total economic activity, averaging between 20 and 25% of the GNP (Horowitz, 1973: 52; Safran, 1978: 112). The commercial enterprises run by the government produced 6·5% of the GNP and 13·2% of the total income of the state (including tax revenues as well as foreign loans and grants) in 1979/80 (*Statistical Abstract of Israel*, 1982: 162, 569 f.; see Table 63). The national airline El Al, the railways, electrical utilities, postal system, telegraph, telephone, radio and television and other areas of the economy are under direct control of the state (see Shimshoni, 1982: 234 f.).

Investment in Israel is encouraged by the state sector of the economy to an unusual degree. During the period of massive immigration in the early 1950s the funds invested by the state made up approximately two-thirds of total investments. From 1962 to 1966 the proportion was 43%, which rose to 46% in 1967 and has since, with some deviations both up and down, averaged around 40% (various *Annual Reports of the Bank of Israel*). As a percentage of the GNP state investments averaged 5% from 1960 to 1972, rose to 6% in 1973/4 (due to the increase in military spending during and after the Yom Kippur War), returned to the 5% level from 1975 to 1979, dropped to an average of 3% from 1980 to 1982, and reached 4% again in 1983. The drop in state investments was particularly dramatic in 1980 – a reduction of

10·7% in comparison with the previous year, which was followed by a further decrease of 6·1% in 1981 (*Annual Report of the Bank of Israel*, 1982: 80 and 1983: 82).

Between 1960 and 1965, 21% of total employment was in the public sector. This rose to 25% in 1973/4, to 27% in 1978 and 30% in 1982 (various vols. of the *Statistical Abstract of Israel*). The increase under the Likud government is striking, as in 1977 the Likud was still campaigning for a reduction of the state's role in the economy.

Concerning the relationship between taxes and GNP see section C/XV/2.

4 IDEOLOGY AND THE ECONOMIC ORDER

Since 1962 polls conducted by the IIASR have shown a decrease in the popularity of 'leftist' positions and a corresponding increase in 'rightist' ideology as well as a renewed upswing of the 'centre' (see Figure 54 and Table 50). It is revealing that even among the voters of the Labour bloc 23% considered themselves part of the political mainstream, 13% as right of centre and only 34% as belonging to the left in 1969 (Arian, 1972a: 197).

By way of contrast, however, the numbers of those stating they preferred a

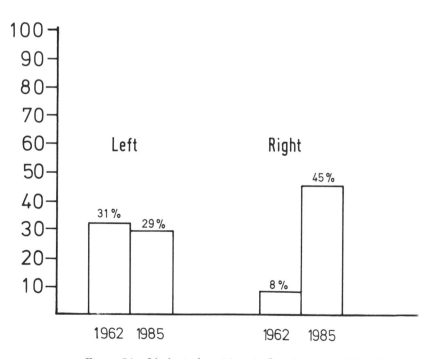

Figure 54   Ideological positions in Israeli society, 1962–85.

Sources: Arian, 1981: 14; PORI.

Table 50   Ideological Positions in Israeli Society, 1962–85 (%)

	1962	1969	1973	1977	1981	1985
Left	—	6	3	4	4	29
Moderate left	31	19	19	14	13	
Centre	23	26	33	29	27	—
Right	8	16	23	28	35	45
Religious	5	6	7	6	6	—
No answer	33	27	15	19	15	—

Sources: IIASR data in Arian, 1981: 14. Arian and Shamir, 1983: 26th
PORI poll. For 1985, *Haaretz*, 14 May 1985 (left and right only).

'socialistic' or 'more socialistic' economic order did not decrease, remaining
instead constant at around 60% (see Figure 55 and Table 51).

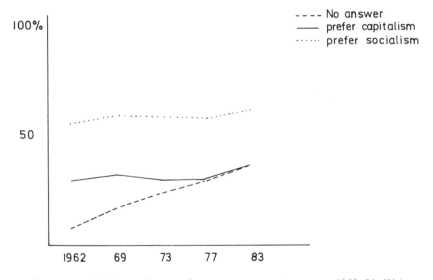

Figure 55   Public preferences for various economic systems, 1962–81 (%).

   Politicians desiring to reduce the role of the state in the economy ('socialism') must therefore reckon with considerable resistance, and for this reason
alone any undertaking aimed at diminishing the role of the state in the
economy may prove extremely difficult. The data in section C/XII/3 would
indicate that the Likud did not succeed in fulfilling the promises made to this
effect in the campaign of 1977.
   The contradiction between the ideological positions and the economic
philosophy of (Jewish) society in Israel is apparent. Moreover, a nationalist
orientation is prevalent in Israel's society (see Gottlieb and Yuchtman-Yaar,
1984).

Table 51   Public Preferences for Various Economic Systems, 1962–81 (%)

	1962	1969	1977	1981
Capitalist	10	7	11	10
More capitalist	19	24	18	25
More socialist	39	38	31	40
Socialist	15	19	25	20
No answer	20	9	15	5

Source: IIASR data in Arian, 1981: 14.

5 THE STAGES OF ISRAEL'S ECONOMIC HISTORY

1948 to 1953. These were the years characterized by the War of Independence of 1948/9 and the massive immigration which continued until 1951. The government attempted to master its problems by means of drastic economies, rationing and price controls, but inflation and unemployment nevertheless soared.

The new economic policy, initiated in 1952, marked the first significant economic policy shift. The measures included a large devaluation of the Israeli pound, which fell to half of its former value against the dollar, restrictive policies with regard to the budget and monetary policy, and a partial lifting of price controls (see Michaely, 1975: chs. 1 and 2; Halevi and Klinov-Malul, 1968: ch. 1; Lerner and Ben-Shahar, 1975: 68 f.). Michaely (1975: 23) contends that from this time on the process of *liberalization* of Israel's foreign trade policy (in the traditional sense of a liberal, i.e. free market oriented policy) has continued almost without a break. It may be said that this has been true of Israel's economic policy in general (see Horowitz, 1973). From 1977 to 1979 the Likud government tried in vain to accelerate the trend but abandoned its attempts by 1981 under Finance Minister Aridor.

1954 to 1965. These years were characterized by continuous growth, accompanied and stimulated in no small degree by the initiation of German reparations payments to Israel. Efforts aimed at a redistribution of population were undertaken in order to shift the centre of population concentration away from Tel-Aviv and its environs towards the north and south. With the creation of the new development towns the construction industry acted as the motor of an economic upswing.

In February of 1962 a (second) 'new economic policy' was introduced. Israel's currency was once again devalued and an attempt was made to unify the three-tiered currency exchange system. More important, all export subsidies were eliminated – but reintroduced in 1966. In 1962 most import duties were simultaneously reduced. A considerable gap developed, however, between the declarations of intent and their realization. From the beginning the agricultural sector was exempt from this new policy of liberalization (Michaely, 1975: 24).

1966 to 1967. These two years were marked by a recession due, among other factors, to the reductions in public spending initiated in 1964. A programme to stimulate the economy was being planned when the Six Day War broke out.

1967 to 1973. The phase from the Six Day War to the War of Attrition (followed by the Yom Kippur War) was characterized by high growth rates (although these remained below those of the 1954–65 phase). Unemployment fell, defence expenditures rose, and economic ties began to grow with the occupied territories, the West Bank and Gaza Strip. High government spending produced a spurt of inflation and the trade deficit also rose.

1973 to 1977. The psychological shock of the *Yom Kippur War* resulted in an increased defence budget and thus a further rise in public spending. Before the war 6 billion Israeli pounds were projected for the 1973/4 budget, but 16·6 billion were actually spent (Shimshoni, 1982: 239). The Israeli pound was devalued from 4·2 to 6 to the dollar. In order to slow inflation, indirect taxation as well as the capital gains tax and import duties were increased, public loans were raised on both a voluntary and involuntary basis, subsidies on basic necessities were reduced and the prices for public services increased. Despite all of these measures the inflation rate was barely slowed. The official devaluation of the Israeli pound was followed by a gradual downward trend which brought the exchange rate for the US dollar to 10·3 by the autumn of 1977.

1977 to the summer of 1984. In contrast to its junior partner in the Likud, the Liberals, Begin's Herut Party was largely uninterested in economic questions. The post of finance minister was taken by the leader of the Liberal Party, Simcha Erlich. In October of *1977* Erlich introduced the (third) 'new economic policy', abolishing all currency controls overnight and allowing the Israeli pound to float. The intention was also to eliminate export subsidies as well as other subsidies, especially those for basic foodstuffs. Apart from the liberalization of the currency exchange policy and the sale of a few state-owned companies (two banks), the Likud-led government was able to realize very little of its widely proclaimed 'liberalization' policy, which proved as hard to sell to employers as to employees (see Wolffsohn, 1979a). Later, even the liberalization of the currency exchange policy was diluted.

Rather than being reined in, inflation instead began to gallop out of control. The reasons were as follows. In 1978 the foreign trade deficit reached a quarter of the gross national product. Inflation was on the rise worldwide and especially affected countries dependent on the import of raw materials, Israel included. Public expenditures, particularly in the defence sector and for education and social welfare, rose and thus increased the budget deficit. Private demand, especially for imported goods, proved impossible to curb and consequently further widened the trade deficit. As that part of the national debt owed to foreign creditors rose, additional financing had to be secured in order to meet payments on the debt. The peace treaty with Egypt necessitated the creation of a new military infrastructure in the southern part of the country. The policy of indexing wages and salaries further contributed to the inflationary spiral. In addition, the entire system of tax collection was inefficiently organized.

The rises in both inflation and the cost of living (as a result of the reduction of subsidies for basic foodstuffs) affected mainly the lower economic strata in Israeli society, particularly the Likud voters of 1977.

Erlich's position as finance minister became untenable, and he was replaced on 7 November 1979, by Yigael Hurvitz, who attempted to cut government spending and to combat inflation.

These efforts at restoring the financial health of the public sector by means of a general belt-tightening policy were instituted with a view towards a foreign policy goal as well: to make Israel less vulnerable to American pressure. Hurvitz, considered a hawk on foreign policy, was suspicious of and opposed to peace negotiations with Egypt. His reasoning was that Israel's economic dependence on the United States would also increase its political dependence and eventually make it impossible to pursue an independent foreign policy.

Neither the cabinet nor the Israeli public could be convinced of the necessity of a drastic belt-tightening. By February 1980, only about six weeks after the announcement of the policy, 42% of the Israelis polled expressed the opinion that the government was expecting 'too great' a personal sacrifice from them, but 48% considered the measures to be 'correct' and 10% as 'too little' (Kahanman and Levinson, 1980: 3). The government did not succeed in making use of this latter political potential, however. This failure was partly due to substantial opposition within the cabinet to reductions in the defence budget, the proposed freeze in publicly financed construction, cuts in the ranks of public employees and reductions in subsidy payments. Such measures simply could not be adopted by a cabinet already looking to the next year's elections.

On 18 January 1981, Hurvitz was replaced by Yoram Aridor, who became the first Herut finance minister in the Likud government (Hurvitz was the leader of Laam/Rafi). The decisive change was with regard to financial subsidies for basic necessities. In the face of the approaching elections the aim was to regain the favour of the lower-class Likud voters of 1977. The polls demonstrated that this goal was accomplished. In January and February 1981 only 9% expressed satisfaction with the economic policy of the government. By the end of June this proportion had risen to 39% (Peretz and Smooha, 1981: 508, IIASR data). Real net income rose by 16·2%, after having fallen by 1·6% in the previous year (*Bank of Israel*, 1982: 2). Direct and indirect taxation was lowered. As a result, consumption rose and the inflation rate accelerated accordingly. The devaluation of the currency (the shekel since 1980) was slowed, thus increasing available income. This in turn led to a rise in the demand for imported goods and further weakened domestic industries. (For detailed analysis of economic policy since 1976/7 see the chapters on Israel in various issues of the *Middle East Contemporary Survey*.)

By *1981/2* the public and private spending spree could not be continued without grave risk, especially since the economy was forced to assume the burden of the War in Lebanon beginning in July 1982. It became necessary to increase taxes and to force compulsory loans. In the period from 1981 to 1982 alone the total tax burden was increased by 80% (*Bank of Israel*, 1982: 91). In addition, subsidies for basic products were further reduced and the creeping devaluation of the shekel slowed. In short, the Israeli economy in 1981 and 1982 was subjected to alternate hot and cold showers which apparently did it little good, nor did they serve to increase the popularity of the government's economic policy. In 1982 growth was only 1·2% and real income fell by 2·9%, but private consumption rose by 7·5%, which was only possible with the help of an inflationary increase in private indebtedness. Imports exceeded exports by 4·7% and debts to foreign creditors rose by 15·5% (all data from *Bank of Israel*, 1982).

By the autumn of 1983 foreign indebtedness had reached 21·5 billion dollars, the inflation rate 160%, and 50% of the citizens polled stated that their monthly income was insufficient to meet current expenses (*Haaretz*, PORI poll of 5 October 1983).

On 11 October 1983, nearly six years to the day after the proclamation of Erlich's 'new economic policy', the new government under Shamir announced a programme of economic reforms as its first official measure. A 23% devaluation of the shekel, an equally large rise in gasoline prices and a 50% reduction in subsidies for basic foodstuffs were announced. Aridor had planned a devaluation of 36% as well as a 75% cut in subsidies but was unable to get the approval of the cabinet. In the end, Aridor's back was broken politically by his proposal to introduce the US dollar as an official second currency. All other aspects of the economic misery notwithstanding, this was a measure incompatible with Israeli national pride, and the now unpopular Aridor was forced to resign. His replacement, Yigael Cohen-Orgad assumed office on 10 October 1983.

Cohen-Orgad had criticized the open-handedness of his predecessor, Aridor. In fact, one of the reasons for his nomination as the new minister of finance was that he had identified the chief economic ills: too many subsidies, exorbitant government expenditures and an overvalued shekel. The new finance minister announced what he considered to be a necessary series of austerity measures and it was expected that he would be able to push them through the cabinet.

Nevertheless, within the five months from October 1983 to March 1984 a new record sum in printed money was pumped into the economy (A. Tal, *Haaretz*, 14 March 1984; N. Strassler, *Haaretz*, 22 March 1984). Undaunted, Cohen-Orgad attempted to give austerity another chance when he introduced his 1984/5 budget. It included higher taxes and lower government expenditures, mainly on welfare, investments and defence. In order to cure the country's economic ills, the finance minister was even willing to let the standard of living drop by about 7% and unemployment reach 100,000 (see A. Temkin, *Jerusalem Post*, international edition, 3 March 1984; N. Strassler, *Haaretz*, 1 March 1984).

The political obstacles turned out to be both innumerable and insurmountable. The proposed cuts in the defence budget and for settlements in the West Bank were criticized by the hawks in the coalition (a group to which Cohen-Orgad had himself belonged). Apart from the criticism, reductions in defence spending were simply not realistic as long as the IDF remained in Lebanon. Deputy Premier David Levy feared that reductions in subsidies would alienate the poorer Oriental strata of Israeli society and thus cut into Likud's support in future elections. Abuhatzira's Tami Party made use of the proposed economic guidelines as one of their arguments for breaking up the coalition and demanding premature elections.

With new elections (to which he had been opposed) set for July 1984, Cohen-Orgad reversed directions and began to resurrect some of Aridor's successful 1981 tactics. Economic benefits for traditional supporters of the coalition partners (mainly Likud) were introduced (see S. Maaz, *Haaretz*, 31 May 1984). Groups that were neglected, or thought they were, tried to blackmail the government by initiating strikes. By mid-July 1984 the government had already exceeded its budget in the areas of subsidies, salaries and social welfare services (BBC Summary of World Broadcasts: Middle East, Africa and Latin America, 17 July 1984, quoting the Histadrut daily *Davar* and the NRP daily *Hazofeh*).

In protest over these election presents, two top officials of the Finance Ministry resigned in mid-June 1984; one was the director general of the ministry, the other a personal aide to Finance Minister Cohen-Orgad. At the same time, the general public, expecting a drastic currency devaluation after the elections, started a new run on the US dollar. Once again the individual citizen was to be made to believe that as long as only the state went bankrupt he could go on enjoying life as before. Obviously, many citizens did not believe this (see election results and section B/VI/2/d and e).

In the wake of the 23 July 1984 elections new foreign currency regulations were, in fact, introduced. So were reductions in food subsidies in late July, but the outgoing government failed to present the expected emergency measures and negotiations over the formation of a new coalition proved long and difficult. Meanwhile, Israel's foreign currency reserves had dropped to the 'red line', that is, less than the value of three months' imports (see M. Merhav, *Jerusalem Post*, international edition, 18 August 1984). 'Extreme' measures were called for and expected from the new government.

The newly formed national unity cabinet pushed through a number of budget cuts, imposed wage and price freezes and raised taxes, but the continuously raging controversies over how much to cut and where served to neutralize somewhat the general effort towards austerity and economic recovery. As had been the case under the previous government, each minister touted budget reductions primarily in those areas of government activity for which he was not responsible. The disputes cut across the party lines and were thus not traceable to the division between Likud and Labour members of the government.

The Reagan administration in Washington was also less then pleased with the economic policy of the new government. None of the major parties in the national unity cabinet was willing to abandon its basic convictions with regard to social policy in favour of a brand of 'pure' economics deemed politically dangerous for the Jewish society (see section C/XI). Moreover, the May 1985 Histadrut elections loomed over the party horizon and no one wanted to risk imposing any additional, unpopular austerity measures.

On 1 July 1985, however, on a split vote of 17 to 5, the cabinet invoked the emergency provisions of the Law and Administration Ordinance in order to impose a slate of drastic economic austerities. The shekel was devalued by 19% and sharper foreign currency rules were imposed. Dramatic slashes in public spending, to total some 1·5 billion dollars, were announced, including heavy cuts in the subsidies on basic foodstuffs and the elimination of 10,000 civil service jobs. Price freezes and wage reductions were imposed, and the practice of indexing wages to inflation was to be ended, thus permitting a drop in real income for Israeli workers. At the time of writing it still remains to be seen whether the ILP can, for its part, persuade the Histadrut to accept the emergency measures, and how long the Likud can risk allowing its vital constituency of lower income voters to bear the burdens of austerity.

6   PUBLIC SATISFACTION WITH ECONOMIC POLICY

(a) POLLS

The popularity of the economic policies of the various governments since 1971 is illustrated by Figure 56 (data from IIASR, see Wolffsohn, 1983a: 705 f.; Stone, 1982: 229, 235; Peretz and Smooha, 1981: 508).

Apart from the fact that the government's defence policy, despite considerable upswings and downturns (during the 1973 Yom Kippur War and afterwards), has always been substantially more popular than its economic policy, it is possible to follow the sinking popularity of the Rabin government up to the elections of 1977. The new economic course of the Likud government at first enjoyed extraordinary favour, but this was rapidly followed by disillusionment. It was not until well into the first half of 1981 that Aridor succeeded in reversing this trend, which, together with the destruction of the atomic reactor near Baghdad, led to the Likud election victory (Diskin, 1982b).

In the course of 1982, and especially during 1983, the popularity of the government's economic policy and of the finance minister decreased steadily. In March 1983, 28·4% of the (Jewish) Israelis polled still considered Aridor the best-qualified man to head the Finance Ministry; in May it was 23·4% and in June 20·3% (M. Segal, *Jerusalem Post*, 2 August 1983; further IIASR data in this area are not available at the time of writing).

According to Hanach and Rafi Smith (*Jerusalem Post*, 17 July 1984) the economic performance of the government was rated very low by the public between December 1983 and June 1984. In December 1983 and April 1984 the proportion of those giving their approval ('successful' or 'fairly successful') was 11%. In June 1984 it was just 12%, but was already 18% in July (elections on the 23rd). As economic and social policies are interrelated, it is worth examining the evaluation of the latter on the part of the Israeli general public. The approval rate was 28% ('successful' or 'fairly successful') in December 1983 and 29% in April and June, but soared to 46% by the election month, July (ibid.).

'The only way you can explain it is by the economic laws that the government passed a couple of weeks ago, which are designed to guarantee individual savings [against inflation] and provide loans for soldiers leaving the Army. [Younger Israelis are more likely to vote Likud.] And there is the $100 million that the government reportedly spent over the past few weeks to keep down the prices for subsidized goods,' explained pollster Hanoch Smith (*Newsweek*, European edition, 23 July 1984: 48). In other words, we can observe almost the same pattern in 1984 as in the 1981 election campaign.

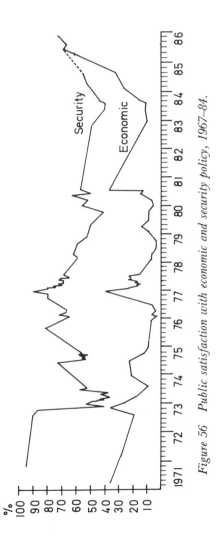

Figure 56   Public satisfaction with economic and security policy, 1967–84.

It is worth mentioning that the economic policies introduced by the national unity cabinet in late 1984 were evaluated as 'bad' or 'very bad' by 45% of the public in December 1984 (PORI poll in *Haaretz*, 20 December 1984).

Strikes and lockouts can also be taken as an index of satisfaction with economic policy, at least of the willingness to compromise on economic decisions (see Table 52).

(b) STRIKES

The incidence of strikes, especially since the beginning of the 1960s, indicates a lack of basic agreement in economic questions. In the crisis years of 1965/6 the willingness to seek confrontation increased, but fell dramatically in the war year 1967 (due to the fact that many reservists were called up but also to the prevailing atmosphere of 'national unity'). The number of conflicts increased until 1972, but 'combat fatigue' prevailed in the war year 1973 and in the years following the shock of the Yom Kippur War. The increase from 1975 to 1977 was again dramatic, but the number of strikes fell in 1978, only to increase again in 1979 and 1982, whereas the rate of strikes in 1980 was equal to the drop in 1978 (as well as to the average of the years following independence).

Table 52   Strikes and Lockouts in Israel, 1949–83

Year		*Year*		*Year*	
1949	53	1966	286	1976	123
1950	72	1967	142	1977	126
1951	76	1968	100	1978	85
1952	94	1969	114	1979	117
1953	84	1970	163	1980	84
1954	82	1972	168	1981	90
1955	87	1973	96	1982	112
1960	135	1974	71	1983	93
1965	288	1975	117	1984	149

Source: *Statistical Abstract of Israel*, various years.

XIII
Selected Economic Data

1 GROSS NATIONAL PRODUCT

Figure 58 presents a statistical outline of the economic developments described in the previous section. The gross national product began to grow in spurts beginning in 1954 and continued to do so until the middle of the 1960s. The economic crisis of 1966/7 can be easily recognized, as well as the enormous growth which set in in 1968 in the wake of the Six Day War. This phase of growth continued through the 'golden early seventies', but after the Yom Kippur War growth rate fell back significantly, reaching record lows in 1976 and 1977. These data thus make the background of the change in governments in 1977 more understandable. Since 1978, however, growth rates have remained rather modest when compared with earlier decades.

In 1982 growth in the gross national product reached the second lowest level since the founding of the State of Israel. According to the Central Bureau of Statistics, the growth rate for 1983 was 1·8% (*Bank of Israel*, 1983: 2).

(a) EXPENDITURES FOR PRIVATE CONSUMPTION

From 1954 to the economic crisis of 1966/7 Israelis demonstrated that they were able and avid spenders (see Figure 57). In 1968 and 1969, the years following the Six Day War, the nation made up for its earlier restraint in consumption, although the increases in spending then receded up to 1977. The first two years under the new government witnessed larger increases in spending, but the policy of spending cuts in 1980 led to a reduction in consumption. This drop was more than made up for in the following election year 1981, when the annual rate of spending increased by 11%. Thus it was only in 1980 that expenditures for private consumption dropped in comparison to the previous year. In 1981 private spending rose by 10·9%, in 1982 by 7·2% and in 1983 by 7% (*Bank of Israel*, 1983: 2). While the state teeters on the brink of bankruptcy, the individual consumes.

(b) EXPENDITURES IN THE PUBLIC SECTOR

Reductions in public spending in comparison with the previous fiscal year took place in 1952 (policy of spending cuts), 1957 (following the Sinai Campaign in the autumn of 1956 and the American pressure which led to Israel's withdrawal from the conquered territories), 1972 (in an attempt to apply the brakes to inflation, only to be followed in 1973 by a gigantic increase in public expenditures due to the costs of the war) and in 1976 and 1977, the years immediately before the fateful elections. Under Finance

Minister Erlich the voters were thanked in the form of increased public spending, which, however, was reduced by 8·7% the following year. The lack of success of Finance Minister Hurvitz's programme of spending cuts is attested to by the rise of 9·1% in public spending in 1980, whereas his successor, Aridor, financed campaign 'gifts' to the voters by easing import restrictions rather than through increases in public expenditures (see Table 54). In 1982 government expenditures were reduced, this despite the War in Lebanon. There was also a reduction in spending in 1983 (*Bank of Israel*), 1983: 2).

2 PRICE DEVELOPMENTS

The history of the annual rate of inflation and of the price index as shown in Table 53 demonstrates the permanence of the phenomenon inflation in Israel. Despite the complaints, then, it can be seen that the inflation rates of the 1960s were relatively low in comparison with those of later years. The economic upturn of the early 1970s made itself felt more than previous growth surges in terms of upward pressures on prices. The Yom Kippur War accelerated this development, which in 1977 the Likud government pledged to reverse. The opposite proved to be the case, however, and in 1980 Israel held the world record for inflation at 131%. This record was broken in 1983 with an inflation rate of 191% and smashed in 1984, with an overall annual rate of 447% (Heinrich, *FAZ*, 23 January 1985). In its seven years in office, the Likud had managed to let the rate of inflation skyrocket by a factor of more than ten – from an initial 40% to over 400%.

Table 53   Annual Inflation Rates, 1949–84 (%)

Annual average change in level of price index (Dec. against Dec. of previous year)

1949	1·0	1970	6·1
1950	20·4	1971	12·0
1951	44·9	1972	12·9
1952	21·6	1973	20·0
1953	2·9	1974	39·7
1960	2·3	1975	39·3
1961	6·7	1976	31·3
1962	9·4	1977	34·6
1963	6·6	1978	50·6
1964	5·1	1979	78·3
1965	7·7	1980	131·0
1966	8·0	1981	116·8
1967	1·6	1982	120·3
1968	2·1	1983	145·7
1969	2·5	1984	373·8

Sources: Halevy and Klinov-Malul, 1975: 211. *Statistical Abstract of Israel*, various vols. *Bank of Israel*, various vols.

Table 54   Selected Economic Data, 1951–85

	Gross National Product[a]	Private Consumption[a]	Expenditures of Central Government[a]	Consumer Price Index[b]	Average Employee Wage[c]	Number of unemployed[d]	Money Supply[e]	Electric Refrigerator[f]	Private Car[g]
1951	29·7	22·6	20·2	97		6,337			
1952	4·7	7·5	-3·9	153		9,413	136		
1953	1·9	3·5	5·1	196		17,680			
1954	19·9	15·0	17·0	220		13,455	184		
1955	13·9	8·1	15·9	233		10,733	100		
1956	9·2	9·1	43·7	248	4·2	12,290			
1957	8·6	7·0	15·8	264	2·0	12,513			
1958	7·1	10·2	3·1	273	7·7	9,328		34	
1959	12·7	9·8	4·0	100·6	5·7	7,377			
1960	6·6	6·9	6·7	102·9	3·9	6,042	205	47	
1961	10·2	10·9	17·1	109·8	4·0	5,143			
1962	10·1	10·5	10·5	120·2	5·4	4,602			4
1963	11·4	10·0	11·2	128·1	4·8	4,032			
1964	9·8[h]	10·7[h]	2·8[h]	134·7	6·9	3,399			
1965	9·1	9·0	10·4	107·7	9·1	3,200	458	78	8
1966	0·8	1·9	11·0	116·3	10·2	7,930			
1967	2·2	2·3	38·3	118·2	-1·2	13,525			
1968	15·5	13·4	9·1	120·7	1·1	5,709			
1969	12·7	10·2	16·6	123·7	2·6	2,395			
1970	7·9	3·0	26·3	106·1	2·3	1,595	793	89	15
1971	11·1	5·8	1·3	118·8	3·1	938	960		
1972	12·7	10·1	1·5	134·1	0·7	744	1,248		
1973	4·1	8·3	45·3	160·9	6·1	879	1,560		
1974	5·2	7·7	2·8	224·8	-2·4	844	1,880	94	26

Table 54   Selected Economic Data, 1951–85

	Gross National Product[a]	Private Consumption[a]	Expenditures of Central Government[a]	Consumer Price Index[b]	Average Employee Wage[c]	Number of unemployed[d]	Money Supply[e]	Electric Refrigerator[f]	Private Car[g]
1975	3·6	0·3	10·2	313·1	-2·1	1,000	2,526		
1976	1·9	4·8	-9·7	411·2	1·4	1,396	3,212		
1977	2·3	4·8	-13·4	134·6	10·6	1,484	4,457		
1978	3·5	8·0	8·4	202·7	1·5	1,361	6,464		
1979	4·1	7·9	-8·7	361·4	9·5	1,477	8,438		
1980	3·2	-2·9	9·1	834·9	-3·2	9,077	16,681		
1981	4·4	10·8	6·9	216·8	10·4	11,577	29,748	99	34
1982	-0·4	7·4	-8·1	477·7	-0·4	10,958	62,810		
1983	1·4	7·5	-5·7	1,173·5	6·1	9,728	146,036		44
1984	-0·3	-6·3	6·8	5,560·4	-0·4	13,128	660,631		
1985	2·0	-0·4	3·8						

Notes:

[a] Percentage change over previous year at constant prices.

[b] Base 1950=100 until 1958; base 1959=100 from 1959 to 1964; base 1964=100 to 1969; base 1969=100 to 1976; base 1976=100 to 1980; base 1980=100 since 1981.

[c] Percentage change over previous year at constant prices; workers from West Bank and Gaza Strip included; new series since 1969.

[d] Daily average of persons unemployed.

[e] Annual average, base 1950=100 from 1950 to 1954; base 1955=100 since 1955.

[f] Percentage of all households owning an electric refrigerator.

[g] Percentage of all households owning a private car.

[h] New series since 1964.

Sources: *Statistical Abstract of Israel,* various vols. *Bank of Israel,* various vols.

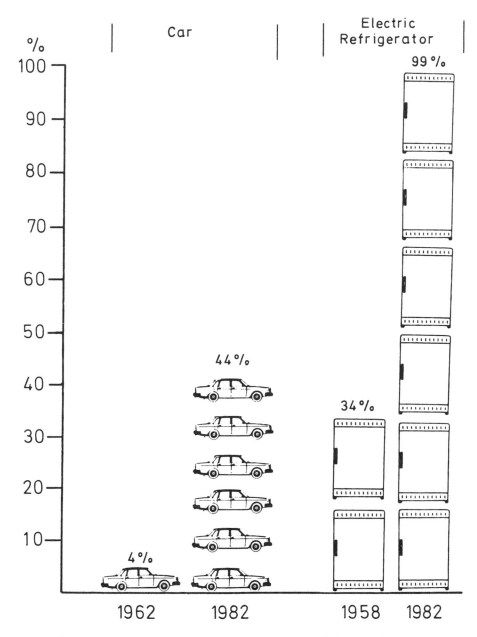

Figure 57   Percentage of households owning cars and electric refrigerators.

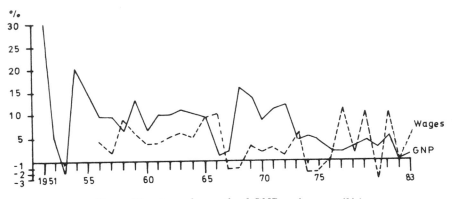

Figure 58   Annual growth of GNP and wages (%)

3   WAGES AND SALARIES

The increases in employees' wages and salaries were particularly significant in the crisis years of 1965 and 1966 and fell back only in the years 1967 (consequences of the recession), 1974 (following the war), 1975, 1980 and 1982. In the election year 1977 demands for wage increases were more readily yielded to, but in 1979 as well the weak leadership of the government, which remains a very large employer, became once again apparent in this area. This was in contrast to the reduction of 3·2% in real wages under the influence of Finance Minister Hurvitz in 1980, a drop which more than compensated for by the rise of 10·4% in the election year 1981. The year 1982 saw incomes drop by 0·4%, but 1983 followed with an increase of 6%.

The developments in wages and salaries among the various sectors of the economy are presented in Figure 59 and Table 55.

That wage developments are anything but apolitical is also illustrated by the wage agreements reached in the public service sector in the election years 1977 and 1981. On this issue the Labour and Likud blocs have little ground for mutual accusations, although the raises in 1977 far exceeded the rate of overall economic growth, where in 1981 the increases were 'merely' at the same level. The public sector fell behind the general trend of economic developments in 1976, 1978, 1980 and 1982. In 1983 it led once more, just in front of the credit sector, which was kept particularly busy and generated new jobs because inflation made additional banking services necessary.

The private sector exceeded the general level of wage increases in the years 1976, 1978, 1980 and 1982. It remained below the average in 1983.

Agricultural income exceeded the average increase only in the years 1978, 1980 and 1982. Incomes in the industrial sector were above the average rise in 1976, 1978, 1980, 1981 and 1982. Developments in the construction industry are particularly revealing because of the large numbers of Arab and Oriental workers. In 1976 wage increases were significantly above, but in 1977 even more significantly below, the average, which was also true for 1978 and 1979. From 1980 to 1982 wages in this sector rose at rates above the average, but fell below it in 1983. Generalizations of political import are thus

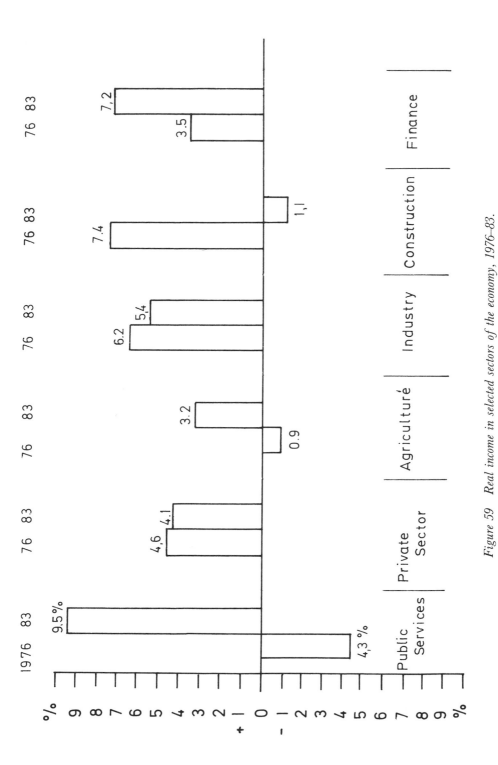

Figure 59   Real income in selected sectors of the economy, 1976–83.

Table 55   Income in Selected Sectors of the Economy, 1976–85

Sector	1976	1977	1978	1979	1980
All sectors	1·4	10·6	1·5	9·5	−3·2
Public services	−4·3	16·9	−0·8	15·6	−8·4
Private sector	4·6	6·9	2·9	5·9	−0·3
Agriculture	0·9	4·6	3·3	5·8	−1·7
Industry	6·2	6·3	2·9	6·2	−0·4
Construction	7·4	−1·1	0·5	6·7	−0·9
Finance	3·5	11·6	−0·8	5·6	1·5

	1981	1982	1983	1984	1985
	10·4	−0·4	6·0	−2·5	−6·9
	10·4	−4·7	9·5	−0·8	−12·4
	10·4	2·1	4·1	−3·2	−4·4
	7·6	2·0	3·2	−2·6	−6·0
	11·8	2·1	5·4	−0·2	−5·3
	8·9	4·8	−1·1	−6·5	−7·2
	9·7	−0·9	7·2	−9·0	−3·2

Source: *Bank of Israel*, various vols.

hardly possible here. In any case, it cannot be said that wage 'exploitation' is taking place. This politically important statement is also supported by a comparison of wage developments at constant prices in the construction sector with other branches of the economy (see the vols. of the *Statistical Abstract of Israel*).

4   UNEMPLOYMENT

The highest number of unemployed was registered in 1953, and the decline in unemployment in the following years took place at a relatively slow pace (see Table 54). The economic crisis of 1966/7 inevitably also affected employment. The large numbers of unemployed workers and the resulting surplus on the labour market probably explain the decreases in wages and salaries in these years. Until the end of the 1970s unemployment remained unusually low and only rose rapidly in the wake of the budget cuts and layoffs under Finance Minister Hurvitz. The popularity of the economic policies of the government in 1981 – despite higher unemployment – is thus astounding.

The unemployment rate increased from 2·9% in 1979 to 4·8% in 1980 and 5·1% in 1981, fell back to 5% in 1982 and was reduced in the following year to 4·5% (*Bank of Israel*, 1983: 70). The economic indicators for 1984 signalled a renewed increase in unemployment to about 6%. The rise was due most particularly to the recession in the construction industry. Nevertheless, the coalition partners were not 'punished' severely by the voters in 1984.

Historically, the average monthly total of job seekers has constantly exceeded the number of unemployed. In the crisis year 1953 the government employment offices registered a total of 42,180 persons seeking employment. This record was not surpassed until 1967, when the total reached 55,788. The average monthly total dropped below 20,000 for the first time in 1971, but then climbed again, surpassing the previous high with a monthly average of 20,290 in 1979, rising to 32,097 in 1980, 34,562 in 1981 and reaching 33,567 in 1982 (*Statistical Abstract of Israel*, 1983: 397).

5 MONEY SUPPLY

The steady rise in overall demand is documented by the data on the growth in the money supply contained in Table 54. Here, the Likud-led government exceeded the marks set by its predecessors, the government printers working harder than ever before.

6 MATERIAL STANDARD OF LIVING

The extent to which material living conditions in Israel have improved is illustrated by the fact that in 1982, 99% of all households possessed a refrigerator, as opposed to only 34% in 1958. The improvement is further documented by the rise in car ownership from 4% in 1962 to 44% in 1982. A great upswing in consumption took place during the 1970s (see Figure 57).

Ethnic background is an important factor in accounting for differences in the material quality of life among Israelis. In 1958 only 8·2% of Oriental Jews owned a refrigerator, whereas 51·4% of Ashkenasim did so. The proportions for each group reached 99·4% by 1981 (*Statistical Abstract of Israel*, 1982: 310), but a gap remains in the statistics on private car ownership. In 1965, 1·8% of the immigrants from Asia or Africa owned an automobile, as opposed to 9·9% of the European-American immigrants. The proportions for 1981 were 25% and 35·2% respectively (ibid., 1982: 311 and 1983:331).

Among the Arab population in 1965 only 8·2% of the households owned a refrigerator, whereas 90·8% did so in 1981. In 1970, 3·1% of the Arab population owned a private car and 13·3% did so in 1981. A significant detail is that the 11·5% level had already been reached in 1974 (ibid., 1982: 308 f.). A great increase in car ownership took place in the early 1970s, but the trend later flattened out in contrast to the growth in refrigerator ownership, which rose by approximately 40% between 1974 and 1981. It is thus only accurate to describe developments in this economic sector in a carefully differentiated manner.

XIV
Sectors of the Economy

1 NET DOMESTIC PRODUCT AT FACTOR COST

Figure 60 and Table 56 summarize the changes in net domestic product at factor cost for various sectors of the economy for the period from 1952 to 1982.

The role of agriculture shows the greatest overall decrease, and this is possibly a further explanation for the declining prestige of the *halutzic* agricultural pioneer ideal. One could also argue that the share of agriculture fell because of the decline of its prestige. People and governments were more interested in other sectors.

The proportionate share for commerce, including restaurants and hotels, has also greatly shrunk. Little change was evidenced in the shares of manufacturing, construction, electricity and water, transportation and the public service sector. In the public service sector, however, the role of public subsidies (in the form of government loans for domestic production and for exports), first registered in 1975, is of growing significance. The economic activity of the credit and insurance institutions has exhibited a growth nothing short of explosive. In 1982 agriculture grew slightly and services did even better, but the share of industry decreased.

The proportionate decline of agriculture in terms of its share of net domestic production also reflects the changes in the structure of Israel's exports (see section C/XVII/2).

2 OCCUPATIONAL STRUCTURE

The proportion of employees rose from 63·2% in 1955 to 78·1% in 1981 and 78·6% in 1982. That of employers remained relatively constant (3·7% in 1970 and 3·8% in 1982 after slumping to approximately 2·5% between 1974 and 1977). The proportion of self-employed fell from 22·6% in 1955 to 10·2% in 1982 (*Statistical Abstract of Israel*, 1983: 365).

The decreasing role of agriculture is further documented by the changes in the occupational structure (see Figure 61 and Table 57). In 1936, 44·9% of the total labour force in Palestine was still engaged in agriculture. After the Second World War only 32·1% remained in the agricultural sector (1945). Ten years after the independence of Israel, 17·6% of the nation's workforce was employed in agriculture. By 1970 this proportion had fallen almost by half to only 8·8%, and slid further to 5·7% in 1982. All the while public services and industry were growing significantly.

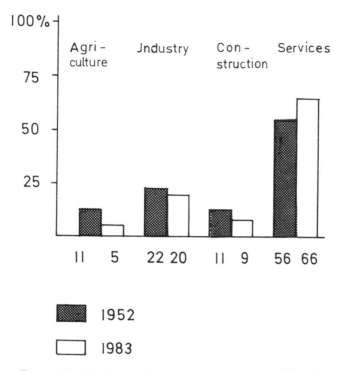

Figure 60   Net Domestic Product at factor costs, 1952–83.

The statistics for the Arab population demonstrate the gap between Jew and Arab as well as the general decrease in the role of agriculture. In 1936, 62% of the Arab population of Palestine worked in agriculture. The 50% who did so in 1945 already represented a considerable drop, and only 11·1% remained in the agricultural sector in 1982, when 18·1% of the Arab labour force was employed in industry, 24·1% in construction, 14·5% in commerce (including restaurants and hotels), 7·8% in transportation, 2·3% in finance and business services, 15·7% in the public service sector and 6·0% in private services (*Statistical Abstract of Israel*, 1983: 355).

In 1936, 19% of the Jewish labour force was employed in agriculture, as compared to only 10% by 1945 and 5·1% in 1982 (*Encyclopaedia Hebraica*, 1958: 731 f.; *Statistical Abstract of Israel*, 1983: 358 f.). The data in Halevy and Klinov-Malul (1975: 65) differ somewhat from the *Encyclopaedia Hebraica*. These authors give 21·4% as the proportion for 1936, 13·4% for 1945 and 10·3% for 1967.

The development of mining and manufacturing during the Mandate period from 1936 to 1945 was rather timorous, despite the demand generated by the war. The massive wave of industrialization following independence is evidenced by the jump from 15·5% of the labour force in this sector in 1945 to 22·4% in 1958. Since then the proportion has remained almost constant (see data in C/XIV). The construction industry was able to increase its share of the total workforce beginning in the 1930s and reaching a high of about 10%

Table 56   Net Domestic Product at Factor Cost for Major Economic Sectors, 1952–84; the figures are given as the percentage of net domestic product at current prices, before adjustment

	Agriculture, Forestry, Fishing	Mining and Manu- facturing	Construction and Utilities	Commerce, Restaurants, Hotels	Transport	Finance and Insurance	Real Estate	Public Services	Private Services
1952	11·4	21·7	10·9	22·7	7·4	2·5	5·2	18·2	—
1953	11·4	22·8	10·0	22·0	7·2	2·6	5·0	19·0	—
1954	12·1	22·4	9·7	21·6	7·6	2·6	5·0	19·0	—
1955	11·3	22·5	10·1	20·6	7·4	2·7	5·4	20·0	—
1960	11·7	23·8	9·5	18·6	8·0	3·8	5·9	18·7	—
1965	8·4	24·2	9·8	17·9	8·5	5·2	7·3	18·7	—
1970	6·5	24·1	12·1	11·0	8·9	8·9	6·1	19·1	3·3
1975	5·7	22·5	12·3	11·9	7·4	11·4 / −4·5[1]	8·6	18·3 / 3·5[2]	3·0
1981	5·0	23·1	11·6	11·1	6·4	13·7 / −5·8[1]	8·0	18·3 / 6·0[2]	2·5
1982	5·8	18·6	9·9	12·8	6·5	14·4 / −6·4[1]	7·8	22·4 / 5·2[2]	2·9
1983	5·2	19·7	8·8	12·7	7·1	13·5 / −6·2[1]	8·6	22·9 / 4·4[2]	3·2
1984	3·8	22·0	7·2	12·3	6·5	15·2 / −4·9[1]	8·5	22·4 / 4·3[2]	2·7

Notes:
[1] Imported bank service charges.
[2] Estimates of subsidies for various industries (since 1975).

Source: Statistical Abstract of Israel, various vols.

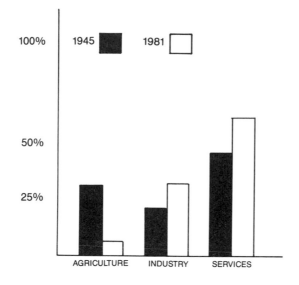

Figure 61   Employment in the major economic sectors, 1945 and
1981 (%).

in the 1960s, but its share fell to 6·2% in 1982 (*Statistical Abstract of Israel*, 1983: 336).

The division in the labour market between Jews and Arabs can be demonstrated in the construction industry. In 1982 only 4·5% of the Jewish labour force was engaged in this sector, as opposed to 24·1% of the Arab workforce (ibid.: 355 ff.).

It should be recalled that of the 75,800 workers from the West Bank and Gaza Strip employed in the Israeli economy in 1982, 52·8% were employed in the construction industry (ibid.: 780).

Figure 61 and Table 57 illustrate the massive growth of the service sector. Some 30% of all gainfully employed Israelis were to be found in the public service sector alone in 1982. In 1958 the proportion had been 'only' 21·9%. The share of the private service sector actually decreased from 7·6% in 1958 to 5·8% in 1981, but rose to 6·1% in 1982 (also compare wage levels in the various sectors, as shown in Figure 59 and Table 55).

The Jewish/Arab gap can also be easily recognized in the public service sector. Whereas 15·7% of the Arab labour force was employed in this sector in 1982, it comprised 31·3% of the total of gainfully employed Jews (*Statistical Abstract of Israel*, 1983: 355 ff.).

3   AGRICULTURE

The gradual shift away from agriculture in favour of industry and the service sector follows, of course, a worldwide pattern of economic development, this

Table 57   Distribution of Workforce by Economic Sector (%)

	Agriculture, Forestry, Fishing	Mining, and Manufacturing	Utilities	Construction (building and public works)	Commerce, Restaurants, Hotels	Transport, Storage, Communications	Financing, Business Services	Public and Community Services	Personal and Other Services	Total of Persons Employed (thousands)
1936	44·9	12·0		5·1	14·8			23·1		432
1944	32·2	14·5		5·3	15·6			32·3		545
1945	32·1	15·5		5·3	18·2			28·8		548
1958	17·6	22·4	2·2	9·8		6·2	12·3	21·9	7·6	655
1962	15·5	25·0	2·1	9·7		6·1	12·3	21·7	7·6	777·1
1967	12·6	24·6	2·2	7·6		7·3	13·5	24·1	8·1	835
1970	8·8	24·3	1·2	8·3	13·0	7·5	5·2	24·0	7·7	936·2
1975	6·4	24·8	1·0	8·1	12·3	7·3	6·7	27·3	6·1	1,112·6
1980	6·4	23·7	1·0	6·4	11·7	6·9	8·2	29·6	6·2	1,254·5
1981	6·1	23·4	1·1	6·2	12·0	6·7	8·8	30·0	5·8	1,280·1
1982	5·7	22·9	1·1	6·2	12·1	6·8	9·0	30·1	6·1	1,298·1
1983	5·5	22·8	1·0	6·5	12·8	6·5	9·5	29·5	5·8	1,339·4
1984	5·3	23·1	0·9	5·9	12·6	6·6	9·6	29·5	6·4	1,359·0

Notes:

1936–45:   Utilities included in industry.
            Transport, commerce and financing in a single category.
            Private and public services in a single category.

to 1970:   Commerce, restaurants, hotels and financing in a single category.

Sources: Encyclopaedia Hebraica, 1958: 731 f. Statistical Abstract of Israel, various vols.

despite the previously discussed central importance of the *halutzic* ideal of the agricultural pioneer for Zionist ideology. In the long run, this quantitative shift evidenced in the economic statistics necessarily led to a qualitative de-emphasis of certain aspects of the original ideology of development. Agriculture's reduced role in the overall economy also brought with it an unavoidable loss in its once so high social prestige, especially for the *kibbutzim*. The changes which have taken place within the *kibbutzim* and in their relations to Israeli society discussed in section B/VIII/4 must also be viewed against this background (see also A/I/3/g on the prestige of certain occupations).

Table 58 sketches some of the chief stations in the development of Israeli agriculture.

The total land area under cultivation rose from 1·65 million *dunam* (approximately 408,000 acres) in 1948/9 to 4·1 million *dunam* (roughly 1 million acres) in 1981/2. The greatest expansion took place in the 1950s. From the early to the mid-1960s the area under cultivation actually decreased and agricultural land use has risen only slightly since the beginning of the 1970s.

The cultivation of field crops is by far the leading activity. Fruit growing underwent an enormous expansion through the early 1960s, then experienced a phase of slow growth and finally a decline into the mid-1970s, only to undergo a further wave of rapid expansion into the 1980s.

Israeli agriculture is often inaccurately equated with citrus growing. Although the area under cultivation rose steadily until into the 1960s, it then stagnated until into the 1970s and has actually decreased since then.

The mechanization of Israeli agriculture is indicated by the statistics on the numbers of tractors in use. The greatest leap forward was registered in the 1960s and 1970s. The number of tractors in use doubled twice over in this period (see Figure 62).

The net capital stock in agriculture expanded significantly until into the 1960s, but the rate of expansion slowed into the mid-1970s and reversed direction in the early 1980s. The increase in complaints from the agricultural sector since the 1977 change in governments is thus apparently not only politically motivated, but also represents a reaction to a measurable and therefore 'objective' deterioration in this sector of the economy. In addition, agricultural production has been steadily rising in recent years, a factor which does not necessarily bode well for the farmer, as overproduction can lead to reduced profitability.

The crisis in Israeli agriculture since 1977 is also demonstrated by other indicators. Since 1977 the rise in the price index for agricultural goods on the input side has constantly exceeded the index for agricultural output (*Statistical Abstract of Israel*, 1983: 409). This represents an unmistakable reversal of the input/output price relation for the period from 1958/9 to 1976/7, during which the output price index was always higher.

That not only the *kibbutzim* but the cooperative *moshavim* are caught up in the crisis indicated by a comparison between the membership statistics for the years 1981 and 1970 (not to mention the levels of 1960). In contrast to the steady decline in *moshavim* membership, the *kibbutzim* have not done badly at all, even managing to increase the numbers of *kibbutz* members between 1970 and 1982 (see Table 59).

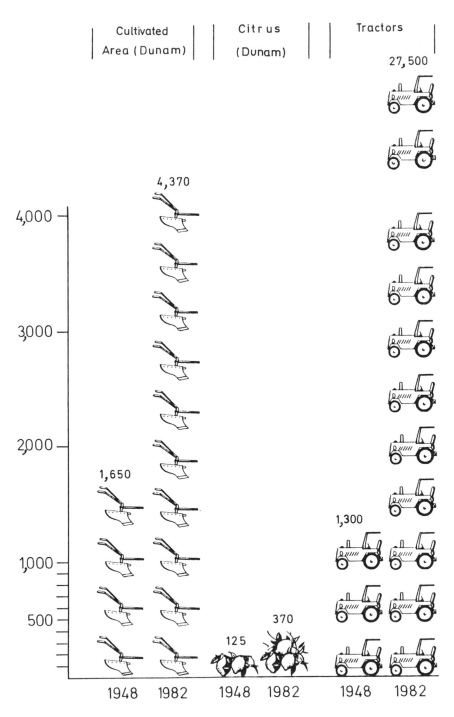

Figure 62   Agricultural development, 1948 to 1982.

Table 58   Agricultural Development, 1948/9 to 1982/3

	Cultivated area (in thousands of Dunam)					Net Capital Stock 1975/6 = 100	Net Agricultural Product 1967/8 = 100
	Total	Field Crops	Citrus Fruit	Other Fruit	Tractors (thousands)		
1948/9	1,650	1,094	125	230	1·3	—	—
1950/1	3,350	2,636	133	259	3·0	2509	24*
1955/6	3,685	2,681	213	323	4·8	44·1	38
1960/1	4,150	2,915	340	413	7·9	69·9	68
1965/6	4,032	2,648	416	426	12·1	81·3	82
1970/1	4,140	2,695	420	415	16·8	86·9	121
1975/6	4,250	2,845	430	392	21·1	100·0	166
1981/2	4,100	2,595	334	534	26·8	97·0	252
1982/3	4,370	2,500	370	560	27·5	96·6	274

Notes:
— No data available.
1* Data for 1951/2.

Source: *Statistical Abstract of Israel*, various vols.

The data reflect not only the extent of the crisis in terms of membership but the ideological crisis as well. From the very beginning the hiring of paid labour was regarded as irreconcilable with the ideal of the agricultural pioneer. If not from the very beginning, then at last from quite early on in the Yishuv period, however, the ideal was not adhered to. Although the number of wage employees in the agricultural sector fell between 1960 and 1981, it nevertheless remained nearly as high as the total combined figure for *kibbutz* and *moshav* membership. This can, of course, be explained in terms of 'economic necessities', but the gap between the demands of ideology and economic reality cannot be denied.

Even more objectionable from a Zionist-*halutzic* point of view is the rise in the numbers of Arab employees. What Table 59 does not show is that these are largely on the payroll of Jewish employers. What is more, the tendency has been not only to employ 'native' Arabs, but increasingly to 'import' them from the occupied territories.

In short, the data in Table 59 document the abandonment of the Zionist *halutzic* ideal. At the time of its inception in the nineteenth century, the *halutziut* goal was nothing short of the creation of a 'new Jewish man' in the guise of the independent farmer who would not rely on paid labour. The ideal has not been realized and no alternative has been developed.

Of the total value of agricultural production (at current prices) 95·4% was generated by the Jewish sector in 1975/6. The figure for 1981/2 was 95% (*Statistical Abstract of Israel*, 1977: 369, and 1983: 419). This data can only be properly interpreted in comparison with the numbers of Jewish and Arab agricultural workers (see Table 59).

Table 59   Employed Persons in Agriculture by Population Group and
           Employment Status; figures are given as the annual average in
           thousands

		1960	1970	1981	1984
All Israelis	Employers, self-employed and members of cooperatives (*moshavim*)	32·5	28·5	26·7	24·8
	Kibbutz members	21·0	15·5	19·4	20·9
	Unpaid family members	21·4	14·5	9·1	6·0
	Employees	46·2	31·3	31·5	33·9
Grand total:		121·1	89·8	86·7	85·6
Jews	Employers, self-employed, members of cooperatives, *kibbutzim* and unpaid family members	61·7	46·5	45·5	43·2
	Employees	36·1	18·0	15·7	17·1
Jews, total:		98·7	64·5	61·2	60·6
Non-Jews	Employers, self-employed, members of cooperatives and unpaid family members	13·2	12·0	9·7	8·2
	Employees from Israel:	10·1	13·3	15·8	16·8
	West Bank and Gaza Strip:	—	5·0	9·5	12·3
Non-Jews, total:		23·3	25·3	25·5	25·0

Source: *Statistical Abstract of Israel*, various vols.

The dependence of Israeli agriculture on exports grew from 27·7% in 1975/6 to 30% in 1979/80 and to 32% in 1981/2 (at current prices, the percentages of total production destined for export; ibid., 1977: 372 and 1983: 422).

Since 1948/9 the highest total crop value has consistently been obtained in field produce. Citrus produce ranked second and other fruits third, but in 1981/2 citrus production dropped to third place (ibid., 1982: 398 f. and 1983: 419). Again, this reflected the changes in Israel's agricultural sector.

4   INDUSTRY

The number of industrial establishments rose from 1,550 in 1937 to 2,500 in 1946, 4,662 in 1959, 6,325 in 1965/6, 5,857 in 1975/6 and 6,480 in 1979/80 (*Encyclopaedia Hebraica*, 1958: 901; Horovitz, 1973: 57; *Statistical Abstract of Israel*, 1982: 438). The growth in industrialization in Israel since independence is thus manifest. For the first time in many years, there was a drop in the number of industrial establishments in 1980/1, when the total fell to 6,079 – an indication either of concentration or of a crisis (*Statistical Abstract of Israel*, 1983: 464).

Figure 63 gives data on the size of the various branches of industry in Israel.

The food industry (including tobacco) has continued to account for the largest share of industrial production, but its proportion has fallen from 30·3% in 1951/2 to 18·8% in 1979/80. Metals products has in the meantime taken over second place, followed by oil and chemicals. The total share for machinery, electronic and electrical equipment adds up to about 12%, a drastic drop in comparison with the total of 27·4% in 1962/3. The overall share of the textile industry has also fallen.

(a) SIZE OF INDUSTRIAL ENTERPRISES

Most industrial establishments in Israel employ from one to nine persons. This was true of 72·2% of all firms in 1980 and 66·5% in 1982. However, it is also true that 46·3% of all industrial workers in 1980 and 43·3% in 1982 were employed by companies with payrolls of more than 300 employees (*Statistical Abstract of Israel*, 1983: 451). This constituted a sharp increase in comparison with 1976, when only 39% of the total industrial workforce was employed by large companies, despite the fact that in 1976 there was only one less firm in this category, namely, 153 out of a total of 11,916 (ibid., 1977: 396). In 1980 there were 154 such firms, or 1·4% of the total of 11,199. There were two fewer such large industrial enterprises in 1982, which shows that even the giants can disappear (ibid., 1983: 451).

(b) OWNERSHIP STRUCTURE

Figure 65 and Table 61 show the distribution in the ownership of Israel's industry, its relative weight and its impact on the labour market. The data do not, however, permit conclusions concerning the market position of individual enterprises.

As the figure and table indicate for the period 1976 to 1980, the number of establishments in the public sector has risen and more persons were employed in this sector as well as in the private sector in 1980 than in 1976. The Histadrut, on the other hand, apparently ran into problems in the period following the 1977 change in governments, although it subsequently recovered. In 1982 the numbers of private and public enterprises both dropped, whereas the number in the Histadrut sector actually grew. (For further details on the ownership structure see Shimshoni, 1982: 234 f.; Aharoni, 1976: *passim*; Wolffsohn, 1983a: 568 ff.)

(c) LOCATION: ECONOMIC AND SECURITY ASPECTS

A brief look at the geographic distribution of Israel's industrial enterprises suffices to recognize the traditional dominance of the Tel-Aviv and Central districts.

In 1979/80, 44% of the country's total industrial plants were located in the Tel-Aviv District alone and employed 27·6% of the nation's industrial workforce. In 1980/1 'only' 41·7% of Israel's total of industrial establishments (employing 27% of the entire industrial labour force) remained in the Tel-Aviv District, an insignificant reduction.

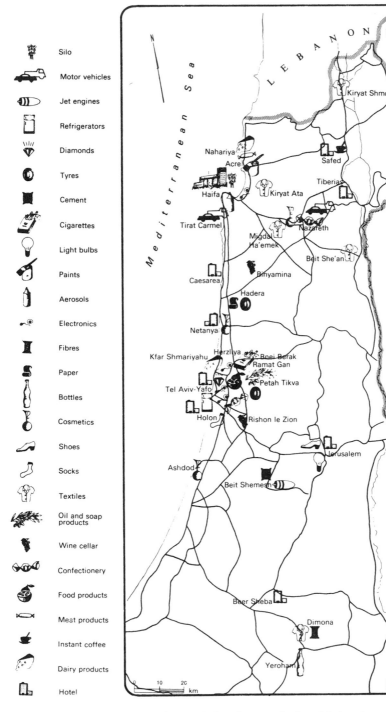

Figure 63 Regional distribution of selected industries.

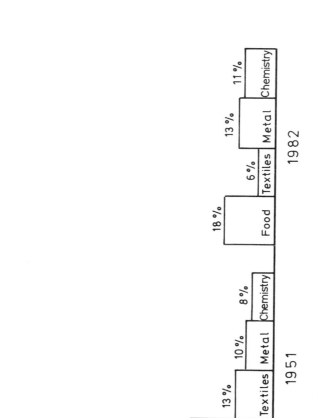

Figure 64   Developments in the industrial sector.

Table 60   Developments in the Industrial Sector

	% of Gross Output (at market prices)			Employed persons (thousands)	
	1951/52	1962/63	1979/80	1962/63	1979/80
Mining	1·6	2·4	2·7	5	5·1
Food	30·3	23·5	18·8	24	38·4
Textiles	12·7	11·2	6·2	22	21·0
Clothing	4·9	2·8	4·7	7	27·3
Leather	3·2	1·7	0·9	5	3·3
Wood	6·2	5·8	3·5	13	14·6
Paper	0·8	2·6	2·5	3	5·9
Printing	2·1	2·8	2·7	3	10·0
Rubber, plastics	1·5	3·6	5·1	8	11·4
Chemicals, oil	7·6	6·0	10·7	8	17·6
Non-metallic	7·9	7·3	4·3	3	10·6
Mineral products			3·5	7	6·3
Basic metal	10·2	9·0	13·0	13	42·0
Metal products			3·2	8	9·7
Machinery	5·1	27·4	9·2	4	30·0
Electrical equip.	1·9	6·7	7·1	7	21·3
Transport	1·5	1·2	1·9	17	6·3
Diamonds	2·6	5·4		11	

Sources: Klinov-Maul, 1975: 88. Horowitz, 1973: 59. *Statistical Abstract of Israel*, various vols.

In 1979/80, 16·3% and in 1980/1, 17·1% of the nation's industrial enterprises with (respectively) 23·8% and 24·3% of Israel's industrial workers were located in the Central District (including Sharon, Petach-Tikva, Ramla and Rishon Lezion).

A further 14·6% of the total plants employing 17·2% of the workforce in 1979/80 (and 15·6% of the plants with 17·6% of the workers in 1980/1) were located in the Haifa District.

The Northern District included 10·3% of the industrial firms (and 13·3% of the industrial labour force), the Southern District accounted for 8·2% of the plants (with 12·7% of the workforce) and the Jerusalem District had 7·1% of the enterprises (and 5·2% of the industrial workers) in 1980/1 (the data refer to establishments with five or more employees; *Statistical Abstract of Israel*, 1982: 436 f. and 1983: 466 f.).

Despite the clearly lopsided nature of this distribution, it has been possible to achieve a limited degree of balance in recent years. In 1975 the Tel-Aviv District still contained 52·6% of all the country's industrial plants, employing 33·2% of all workers in this sector (ibid., 1977: 399). In the same period, however, the Central District's share of the total rose from the 1975 level of 15·8 % of the firms (with 5·1% of the workforce).

The seemingly purely economic statistics point to a security problem of the first order. Whatever one's moral view of the matter may be, from an Israeli

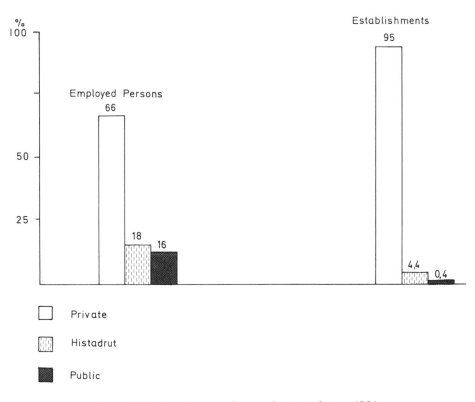

Figure 65   Distribution of ownership in industry, 1984

perspective the West Bank represents a vital geographic and military buffer zone protecting the industrial jugular vein of the nation. Apart from any dreams of aggrandizement, no Israeli politician is likely to agree to extensive territorial concessions concerning the West Bank. The question, of course, remains open as to whether 'security' can be defined solely in military-geographic terms to the exclusion of psychological-political factors.

The role of Israeli industry in relation to the country's exports is discussed in the section on foreign trade (C/XVI).

Table 61 Establishments and Employed Persons by Size and Sector

Sector	Employed Persons (% of total)			Establishments (% of total)			Employed Persons (1000s)			Establishments (number)		
	1976	1980	1984	1976	1980	1984	1976	1980	1984	1976	1980	1984
Private	69·6	71·5	66·3	95·6	96·6	95·2	193·3	197·1	200·0	11,386	10,815	10,269
Histadrut	16·4	11·6	17·9	4·1	2·8	4·4	45·6	32·1	54·2	494	314	475
Public	14·0	16·9	15·8	0·3	0·6	0·4	38·8	46·6	47·9	36	70	40

Source: Statistical Abstract of Israel, various vols.

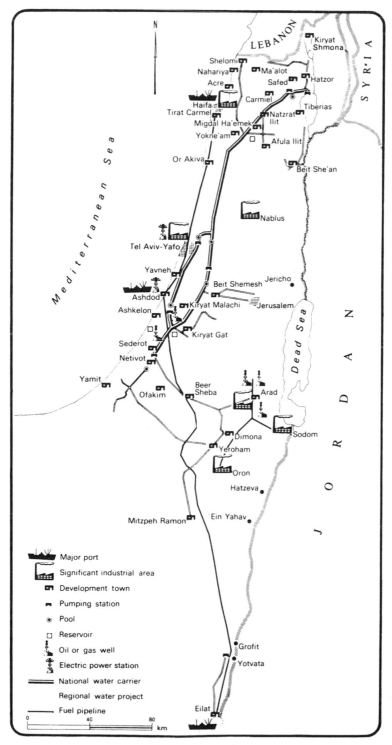

Figure 66 Economic regions.

XV

Budget and Taxes

1 DEFICITS

A comparison of revenues and expenditures in the annual national budgets shows deficits for fifteen of the thirty-four years since independence and cumulative deficits for twenty of these years (*Statistical Abstract of Israel*, 1983: 596). Government budgeting policies have thus added fuel to the inflationary fires. Table 62 contains information on the budget deficits.

The only periods without a cumulative deficit (i.e. deficits which could not be balanced by previously accumulated surpluses) were 1953–5, 1962–6, 1972/3, 1977–80 and 1981/2.

Table 62   Budget Deficits, 1949–83; figures are given in millions of shekels at current prices

	Income	Expenditures	Surplus or Deficit	Cumulative Surplus or Deficit
1949/50	9·3	9·4	−0·1	0·0
1951/52	19·6	20·9	−1·3	−1·2
1955/56	80·6	81·7	−1·1	−0·1
1956/57	97·8	105·0	−7·2	−7·3
1957/58	112·1	113·3	−1·1	−8·4
1959/60	148·1	151·5	−3·4	−3·9
1960/61	170·8	172·9	−2·1	−6·0
1964/65	365·5	367·6	−2·1	+17·7
1965/66	438·6	439·8	−1·2	+16·5
1966/67	447·2	485·6	−38·4	−21·9
1967/68	635·9	651·5	−15·6	−37·5
1968/69	742·7	786·2	−43·5	−81·0
1973/74	3,521·5	3,549·0	−27·6	−7·1
1974/75	4,721·7	4,752·1	−30·4	−37·5
1980/81	109,023·1	111,099·4	−2,076·3	−315·4
1981/82	254,904·1	246,305·7	+8,598·4	+8,283·0
1982/83	559,712·0	581,873·0	−22,161·0	−13,878·0
1983/84	1,891,924·0	1,848,735·0	+43,189·0	+29,311·0

Source: *Statistical Abstract of Israel*, various vols.

Without a doubt, both these statistics and the other economic data, especially the foreign trade figures indicate that the government was either incapable of initiating or unwilling to practise a policy of rigorous savings and that the country was thus 'living beyond its means' (see section C/XIII/1a).

2 GOVERNMENT REVENUE

Despite repeated complaints and criticism of the allegedly deficient capabilities of the tax collecting authorities, the main source of Israeli government revenue remains the tax system (see Lerner and Ben-Shahar, 1975: 188 ff.). As shown in Table 63, the share of tax revenues as a proportion of government income reached its high point during the early and mid-1960s at 64% of total revenues, then fell off until into the early 1970s, after which it briefly rose, only to 'settle down' at a level which has continued to hover near the 50% mark since the mid-1970s.

The percentage of taxes as a proportion of gross national product was approximately 25% until the end of the 1960s. This could not be considered particularly high, at least by Western European standards, where the levels generally fluctuated between 27% and 37% (Lerner and Ben-Shahar, 1975: 83). Since 1970, however, the share of taxes as a proportion of the Israeli gross national product has skyrocketed to the highest level in the world. The figures in Table 63 include the mandatory loans and war loans. The figure

Table 63   Taxes as a Proportion of Israel's GNP, 1968–83

1968–1972	38%
1973–1974	43%
1975–1978	48%
1978–1983	48%

Source: *Bank of Israel*, 1983: 96.

for the year 1982 alone, namely, 50%, is particularly noteworthy. That year, of course, marked the beginning of the War in Lebanon. The figure for 1983 alone was 51%.

The dominant share of tax revenues is derived from the income tax. Its share of total tax income was 37·6% in 1964, 44·5% in 1969, 44·3% in 1972, 39·5% in 1975, 55·6% in the budget estimates for 1982/3 and 46·2% in the estimates for 1983/4 (*Statistical Abstract of Israel*, various vols.).

The category 'other domestic income' includes revenues from the state-owned enterprises. 'Grants from abroad' are the reparation payments from the Federal Republic of Germany, whereas the contributions from the United States as well as the Diaspora Jewry cannot be distinguished from the loans in this compilation (for further details see section C/XVII).

During the mid-1950s, approximately 30% of all revenues came from abroad. This proportion dropped to 16% by the mid-1960s, then rose to just over 17% by the early 1970s, climbed to 24% during the mid-1970s and then

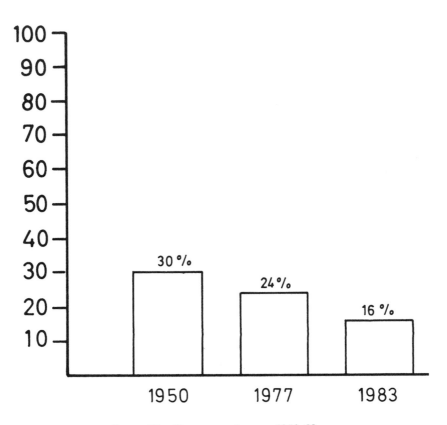

Figure 67   Government income, 1950–83.

fell again to an estimated 17% in 1982/3 and to an estimated 15% in 1983/4
(ibid., various vols.).

Domestic loans, often mandatory in character, as, for example, the war
loans intended to ease the financial burden of the state at the expense of the
individual citizen, ought for this reason to be counted as taxes. The proportion of such loans as a share of revenues rose rapidly in the wake of the Six
Day War and, although the levels have slowly dropped, they still remain
significantly above the pre-1967 levels.

3   GOVERNMENT EXPENDITURES

Figure 68 and Table 65 illustrate how the conditions of the basic political and
economic framework described in section C/XI limit manoeuvrability in the
area of financial policy.

Defence expenditures were at their lowest in 1966/7 on the eve of the Six
Day War and accounted for the largest share of the budget in 1970/1 during
the War of Attrition along the Suez Canal (March 1969 to August 1970).

Table 64   Government Income, 1949–84; figures are given as % of total

	Taxes	Other Domestic Revenue	Foreign Grants and Reparations	External Loans and Grants	Bank of Israel	Internal Loans
1949/50	42·3	0·6	5·9	24·2	19·1	7·8
1953/54	61·4	4·4	16·5	14·6	—	3·1
1956/57	53·7	10·0	11·8	13·2	7·0	4·2
1960/61	63·8	13·2	8·2	8·1	1·5	5·3
1964/65	64·4	10·2	3·8	14·9	—	6·7
1967/68	49·2	12·6	0·1	16·2	4·8	17·1
1970/71	48·8	8·9	—	20·1	5·9	16·3
1971/72	57·2	11·3	—	16·7	4·3	10·5
1976/77	46·0	16·0	—	24·0	3·0*	11·0
1982/83	48·5	16·7	—	15·7	7·7*	11·2
1983/84	39·6	5·7	—	16·3	27·9	10·5

Note:

* Advances from the *Bank of Israel*.

Sources: Horowitz, 1973: 77. *Statistical Abstract of Israel*, various vols.

Defence outlays have thus varied from 23·0% to 45·3% of total government expenditures. If we are to believe the statistics, the 1983/4 defence outlays were among the lowest in Israel's history. While it may, of course, be possible that statistical 'cosmetics' were applied, these may just as well have been used before. As it is impossible to know the intensity of the various 'treatments' we thus have a cumulative and therefore neutralized bias.

With the exception of the fiscal year 1952/3 a declining trend in defence expenditures set in following the War of Independence. This development was interrupted and reversed by the Suez Campaign (October and November 1956), after which, despite increases in some years, the general trend continued to be downwards.

Following the Six Day War, which demonstrated the superiority of the Israeli military, more money was spent on defence than before, but not a great deal more. The turning point came about as a result of the War of Attrition, the significance of which is often overlooked or underrated by observers outside Israel. Even the Yom Kippur War of October 1973 did not result in such dramatic rises in the level of defence outlays as the 1969/70 confrontation along the Suez Canal.

Many observers are completely surprised to learn of developments since the 1977 change in government. The share of the defence budget was actually reduced, despite the necessity of transferring and restructuring the military infrastructure from the Sinai to the Negev as a consequence of the peace treaty with Egypt. Moreover, it is surprising that the War in Lebanon did not end the downward trend in the relative role of defence expenditures.

Table 66 furnishes further details concerning defence outlays for the period since 1964. (The calculations by Glass, 1977: 84 produced figures which were in some cases lower, although they were also based on the data furnished by

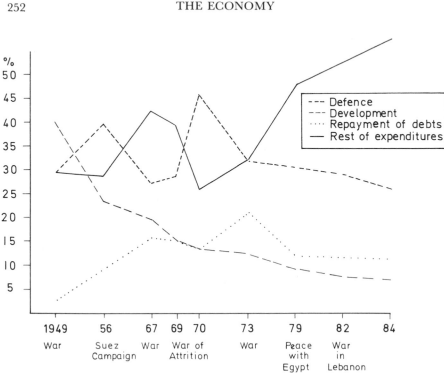

Figure 68   Government expenditures, 1949–84.

the Bank of Israel, which in turn is derived from the data gathered by the Israeli Bureau of Statistics.)

When considering total defence expenditures it is necessary to take not only immediate needs (col. 1) into account, but ensuing costs as well, which are sometimes incurred only after several years have elapsed, as is the case, for example, with payments on American loans for the purchase of defence goods abroad (col. 5).

The total defence burden was highest in the years 1973–5, in the period of the Yom Kippur War. This was due to large outlays for resupply and build-up. From 1975 to 1978, and even more so after 1978, defence needs dropped. Simultaneously, military grants from the United States were reduced, so that the total defence burden has increased since 1979 and in 1982 reached the level of 1970, thereby exceeding the costs of the period of the Yom Kippur War.

Following expenditures for the military and police, the second largest factor in the national budget is the Ministry of Culture and Education, which in 1979/80 and 1980/1 accounted for 6·3%, in 1981/2 for 5·9%, in 1982/3 for 6·6% (estimate) and in 1983/4 for 6% (projected) of the national budget (*Statistical Abstract of Israel*, various vols.). In 1976/7, the last fiscal year of the Mapai/ILP era, the share was 4·8%.

The rise in outlays for education and culture since the change in governments is due certainly in no small measure to the policy of free secondary education introduced by Education Minister Hammer (NRP).

Table 65   Government Expenditures, 1949–85; figures are given as % of total govt. budget

	Defence and Police	Development Budget	Debt Repayment	Rest of Budget
1949/50	29·5	39·8	2·3	28·4
1950/51	23·2	47·2	4·2	25·4
1952/53	29·6	37·4	5·2	27·8
1954/55	23·7	33·7	14·5	28·1
1956/57	39·5	23·8	9·3	27·4
1958/59	24·8	30·2	10·2	34·8
1962/63	25·2	21·9	19·9	33·0
1964/65	28·7	22·7	17·3	31·3
1966/67	23·0	19·6	15·3	42·1
1967/68	27·1	16·9	13·5	42·5
1968/69	28·4	15·2	18·0	38·4
1970/71	45·3	13·3	15·4	26·0
1971/72	40·0	15·7	16·0	28·3
1972/73	31·8	12·8	21·6	33·8
1974/75	35·7	10·4	7·9	46·0
1976/77	37·3	8·4	9·4	44·9
1977/78	31·9	7·6	13·2	47·3
1979/80	30·1	9·1	12·3	48·5
1980/81	29·1	7·9	16·9	46·1
1982/83	28·2	7·6	14·4	49·8
1983/84	23·8	5·5	11·4	59·3
1984/85*	17·9	4·6	30·0	47·5

* Estimates

Sources: Horowitz, 1973: 79. *Statistical Abstract of Israel*, various vols.

That expenditures for development would involve a smaller share of the national budget after the completion of the most important infrastructure projects and the absorption of the massive immigration of the early 1950s is self-evident.

Government expenditures for Jewish settlements in the West Bank ('Judea and Samaria') have remained one of the most controversial issues of fiscal (and territorial) policy. Exact figures are not available, but relying on figures computed by Meron Benvenisti, Ann Lesch (1983: 12 f.) estimates a sum between 200 and 300 million dollars annually in the Likud era. Zvi Sholdiner (*Haaretz*, 25 July 1980) gave an estimate of roughly 9% of the total national budget, but his base for the budget total did not include defence costs and payments on the national debt. Moreover, Zvi did not include infrastructural measures for the settlers such as synagogues and schools. According to then Minister of Finance Cohen-Orgad, the 1983/4 national budget provided for about $300 million for settlements. This would have amounted to 1·5% of the national budget (*International Herald Tribune*, 13 January 1984: 2). This figure roughly corresponds to the data gathered by Benvenisti and Lesch and is

Table 66 Defence Expenditures, 1964–85; figures given as % of gross national product at current prices

	Defence Demand	Net Defence Demand excluding military grants[1]	Net Defence Demand excluding all grants[1]	Domestic Defence Demand[2]	Domestic Defence Demand,[3] Foreign Exchange, Repayment of Loans	Wages in the Defence Sector
1964–66	10	10	9	6		5
1967	18	17	17	10		8
1968–69	19	19	19	12		8
1970	26	26	26	14	22	9
1971–72	22	20	19	13	19	8
1973–75	32	25	24	17	21	11
1976–78	26	22	17	14	19	10
1979–83	29	20	15	15	19	10
1979	21	16	10	14	17	10
1980	24	19	14	14	17	10
1981	26	23	19	14	17	10
1982	24	21	18	15	19	11
1983	20	19	13	15	19	10
1984	24	19	14	15	20	10
1985	24	14	5	14	19	9

Notes:
[1] Excluding grants from the United States.
[2] Gross domestic demand minus domestic sales.
[3] Repayment of loans, esp. US defence loans.

Source: Bank of Israel, various vols.

somewhat higher than an earlier estimate of $200 million in a study for the US Congress (see Mansour, 1983: 55). The Congressional estimate would have corresponded to the 1980/1 level of $140 million (or about 1% of the budget) as given by Seliktar (1980: 350). Kimmerling (1983: 178), who relies on Sholdiner's 1980/1 estimate of 8·7% (loc. cit.), but misinterprets the latter's data, adds the subsequent costs of these investments and thus reaches a total proportion of 12–15% of the national budget for 1980/1. Based on misunderstandings, this sum is obviously exaggerated. The actual proportion most likely lies somewhere in the middle of the estimates.

The main contributors to the settlements budget are the ministries of Agriculture, Housing, Religious Affairs, Defence and Education. Last but not least, the Jewish Agency also contributes (unspecified) sums, which are discretely imbedded in its general budget data.

The national debt rose steadily until the mid-1950s, dropped somewhat from 1956 to 1959 and then climbed to and remained at a high level up to 1973. The reduction of the debt factor during the years of the Rabin government (under Finance Minister Rabinovitch) is noteworthy. Since the Likud-led government assumed office, the national debt has once again risen.

XVI
Foreign Trade

1 THE BALANCE OF TRADE

Not least among Israel's political goals has been 'economic independence', if for no other reason than not to reduce even further the limits of the government's manoeuvrability in matters of foreign policy and to avoid a political-economic dependence that would leave the nation more vulnerable to pressures from abroad. Apart from these political reasons, the economic motives are obvious enough.

Figure 69 and Table 67 document the fact that it has not been possible for Israel to attain anything even resembling 'economic independence' since 1949.

Israel has been and remains dependent on imports, the costs of which cannot be met by the income from exports. To put it crudely: Israel has constantly lived beyond its means. This purely economic judgement cannot, however, remain the sole consideration. For political and psychological

255

reasons, no Israeli government has been able to apply a stronger brake to private demand for imported goods than that effected by the already high import duties. The government of a nation seeking to attract immigration, a government which requires its citizens to assume the burden of enormous defence costs, sees itself compelled for reasons both of state and of coalition politics to cultivate the kind of support and popularity obtainable by promoting consumption.

'Would you or wouldn't you agree that Israel should import consumer goods only to the same extent that she exports such goods?' was the question posed to the Israeli public in October 1983 by the PORI Institute. It might be recalled that this was the same month in which Minister of Finance Aridor was replaced and the economic crisis in the country was more evident to the public than ever before. Nevertheless, only 48% agreed with the statement in the poll, whereas 35% disagreed and the rest more or less vacillated (*World Opinion Update*, vol. VIII, no. 1, January 1984: 58). In other words, more than a third was determined to continue to consume, come what may, and about half of the public realized that it could not go on living as before. The poll, of course, only measured attitudes rather than actual behaviour. It is, therefore, open to speculation whether or not those who agreed with the statement would really be willing to live up to their stated conviction. The coalition partners were not overly optimistic. Otherwise they would not have introduced election-oriented economic policies beginning early in 1984.

A further reason for high levels of imports was the need for defence goods. This cannot, however, obscure the fact that private demand has contributed considerably to the negative balance of trade, particularly in the last few years. In 1980 (under Finance Minister Hurvitz's austerity policy) private imports decreased. In 1981 they remained stable, but increased again in 1982 (*Bank of Israel*, 1982: 167 f.). For the first time since 1972 imports in the private sector (in millions of US dollars at current prices) exceeded those of the public sector in 1979 and 1982, despite the large amounts of military goods imported by the government in these years (ibid., 1977: 47, and 1982: 171).

This very rough description of the balance of trade situation is in need of some polishing with details. Whereas exports covered only 11·3% of the costs of imports in 1949, this proportion had risen to 73·6% in 1981. Until the early 1960s the share of exports grew steadily and this upward tendency continued with some fluctuations from 1961 to 1966. A significant leap forward was made in 1967. This progress is not merely attributable to the acquisition of the occupied territories in the Six Day War, as the proportion of exports as a share of imports reached 68·3% excluding the figures for the occupied territories, and 70·1% when the latter were included (*Statistical Abstract of Israel*, 1982: 204 f.). Not until 1978 was the 70% level attained again. Following a setback in 1979 the 70% mark was finally exceeded in 1981, this despite the frenzy of imports and consumption that election year. In 1982 the share of exports dropped to 69·1% and again to 67·3% in 1983 (*Bank of Israel*, 1982: 2, and 1983: 2). Israel's first export surplus thus still remains a long way off.

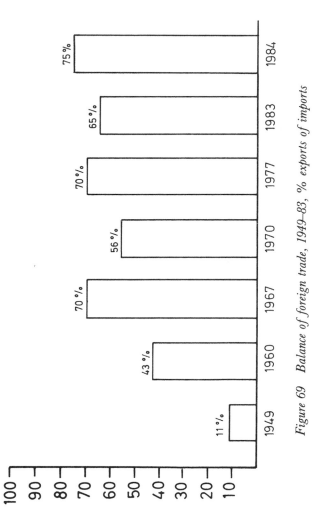

Figure 69   Balance of foreign trade, 1949–83, % exports of imports

Table 67   Balance of Foreign Trade, 1949–84; Figures are given in
           millions of US dollars excluding returned imports or exports,
           the West Bank and Gaza are included since 1967

	Imports	Exports	Excess of Imports over Exports	Exports as % of Imports
1949	251·9	28·5	223·4	11·3
1950	300·3	35·1	265·2	11·7
1955	334·4	89·1	245·3	26·6
1956	375·6	106·5	269·1	28·4
1957	432·8	140·2	292·6	32·4
1958	420·9	139·1	281·8	33·0
1959	427·3	176·4	250·9	41·3
1960	495·7	211·3	284·4	42·6
1961	583·9	239·1	344·8	40·9
1962	626·2	271·4	354·8	43·3
1963	662·0	338·3	323·7	51·1
1964	815·5	351·9	463·6	43·1
1965	814·5	406·1	408·4	49·5
1966	817·1	476·9	340·2	58·4
1967	758·9	531·8	227·1	70·1
1968	1,107·4	653·0	454·4	59·0
1969	1,318·2	756·6	561·6	57·4
1970	1,451·8	807·5	644·3	55·6
1971	1,841·9	1,017·5	824·4	53·7
1972	2,002·1	1,236·9	765·2	61·8
1973	3,035·2	1,586·1	1,449·1	52·2
1974	4,283·7	2,039·5	2,244·2	47·6
1975	4,230·3	2,202·2	2,028·1	52·1
1976	4,220·7	2,698·6	1,522·1	63·9
1977	4,914·4	3,425·0	1,489·4	69·7
1978	5,796·9	4,106·1	1,690·8	70·8
1979	7,568·3	4,810·8	2,757·5	63·9
1980	8,105·1	5,863·5	2,240·6	72·3
1981	8,135·0	5,990·4	2,144·6	73·6
1982	8,218·9	5,665·3	2,553·6	68·9
1983	8,730·9	5,602·6	3,128·3	64·2
1984	8,334·9	6,256·3	2,078·6	75·1

Source: *Statistical Abstract of Israel*, various vols.

2   EXPORT STRUCTURES BY ECONOMIC SECTOR

The structure of Israel's export trade has undergone a complete revolution.
Whereas in 1949, 64% of all export goods were produced in the agricultural
sector, farm produce accounted for only 11% of exports in 1982. On the other
hand, while industry had produced only 36% of all export goods in 1949, it

supplied 88·4% in 1982. The crisis in agriculture, especially in its traditional forms, is again illustrated by the drastic drop in the share of citrus exports from 63% in 1949 to 3·7% in 1982 (see Figure 70 and Table 68).

The diamond industry has been and remains an important export branch, although it is subject to strong fluctuations. Thus its overall share of exports in 1982 fell to 18%, thereby matching the level of 1949.

As has already been shown in other chapters, the developments in the export sector are evidence of the powerful influence of the wave of industrialization in Israel following independence and the subsequent effects on the guiding ideology of the agricultural *halutzic* pioneer ideal.

3   IMPORT STRUCTURES

Figure 71 and Table 69 document the changes which have taken place in the structure of Israel's imports.

Despite the often-heard accusation that Israelis suffer from a consumption mania, the share of imported consumer goods has actually fallen from roughly 32% in 1949 to 10% in 1982 (see the poll quoted in C/XIV/1). Of little surprise is the drastic rise in the overall share of imported oil.

4   IMPORTS AND EXPORTS BY REGION

The data in Figure 71 and Table 69 underline that Western Europe remains Israel's most important trading partner. In 1982, 42% of Israel's exports went to the European Community, which was the source of 37% of Israel's imports (*Statistical Abstract of Israel*, 1983: 226 f.). Although both exports to and imports from Europe were in the process of declining, the dominant role of the region for Israel's foreign trade is still indisputable. Due to this heavy orientation towards the European region, Israel's foreign trade balance could prove particularly vulnerable to politically motivated restrictions. Despite the fact that Europe, and the European Community in particular, is often scoffed at by the Middle Eastern states as the mouse that roared, or as a mere appendage of US policy (see Wolffsohn, 1983d, 1984 and 1985), it must not be overlooked that the extensive nature of the trade relations between Israel and the European Community constitutes an area of not only economic but also of political leverage to the advantage of the EC (see Figure 72 and Table 70).

In Asia, Israel's chief trading partners are Hong Kong and Japan. Under the Shah, Iran ranked third, both as a customer for Israeli exports and as a supplier of imports (oil). Figure 72 and Table 70 indicate that Israel's trade relations with South Africa are less extensive than political legend would have it.

The United States is Israel's second most important trading partner, at least in terms of the total cash value of goods exchanged. In 1982, 21·2% of Israel's exports went to the US and 19% of the nation's imports came from there (*Statistical Abstract of Israel*, 1983: 226 ff.).

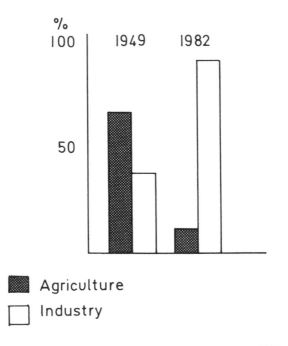

Figure 70   Structure of exports at current prices, 1949–1982.

Table 68   Export Structure, 1949–84

	1949	1955	1962	1967	1968	1969	1970	1971	1972	1975	1981	1982	1983	1984
Total	100%													
Agriculture	64	38	24	19	18	16	18	17	17	14	11	11	10	9
Industry	36	62	76	81	82	84	82	83	85	83	87	88	90	89
Citrus	63	36	18	15	14	13	12	12	10	9	4	4	3	2
Diamonds	18	23	30	28	36	35	27	29	35	28	19	18	24	21

Source: *Statistical Abstract of Israel*, various vols.

The sudden jump in the share of imports from and exports to 'unnamed countries' is a source of considerable speculation. It would certainly not be totally incorrect to suspect that these include those nations which trade with Israel (and not only in small volumes) but wish to remain 'unnamed' for political reasons. Since the volume of imports from is larger than that of exports to these countries, it may also be surmised that they include oil suppliers. Nonetheless, this can only be taken as speculation.

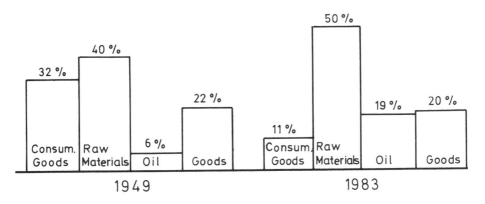

Figure 71   Import structure, 1949–83.

Table 69   Import Structure, 1949–84; figures are given as % of total
            imports at current prices

	Consumer goods	Raw materials	Crude oil	Investment goods
1949	31·7	40·1	6·0	22·2
1955	14·8	56·5	10·3	18·4
1965	10·1	61·9	6·4	21·6
1975	7·5	61·4	15·5	15·6
1981	9·5	51·9	25·7	12·9
1984	7·8	54·6	18·9	18·7

Sources: Halevy and Klinov-Malul, 1975: 116, for data to 1965. *Statistical Abstract of Israel*, various vols., for remaining data.

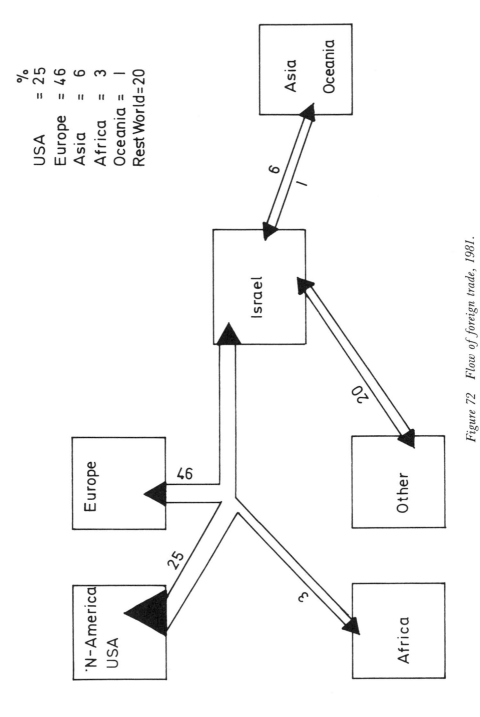

USA   = 25
Europe   = 46
Asia   = 6
Africa   = 3
Oceania   = 1
Rest World = 20

%

Asia
Oceania

6
1

Israel

Europe

46

25

'N-America
USA

20

Other

3

Africa

Figure 72   Flow of foreign trade, 1981.

Table 70   Flow of Foreign Trade, Export and Import Structure by
Region, 1950–84; figures in %, based on current prices in US
dollars

	Imports					Exports				
	1950	1960	1970	1981	1984	1950	1960	1970	1981	1984
Europe (total)	36·7	54·9	59·8	45·7	51·3	72·6	69·9	54·3	44·4	40·6
EEC	23·1	41·1	47·1	35·3	41·3	48·7	49·3	40·0	34·1	32·6
Asia	2·9	2·1	4·9	2·9	3·4	1·1	6·1	14·0	9·7	8·5
Africa	6·3	3·5	2·1	1·5	0·2	0·3	4·8	5·3	3·9	1·3
South Africa	—	1·3	0·7	1·3	2·0	—	0·9	1·4	1·7	1·8
America (total)	46·1	31·1	25·5	23·5	23·9	25·4	16·4	22·5	25·5	31·0
USA	35·3	29·1	22·2	20·4	21·1	23·6	13·6	19·1	21·6	28·2
Oceania	0·9	0·1	0·3	0·4	0·6	0·3	0·6	0·7	1·2	1·1
Unknown	7·2	8·2	7·5	25·9	18·7	0·3	2·0	2·2	13·7	18·5

Source: *Statistical Abstract of Israel*, various vols.

XVII
Economic Dependence on Foreign Suppliers

1 PAYMENTS TO ISRAEL AND CAPITAL IMPORTS

Figures 73–75 and Table 71 give a survey of Israel's chief sources of
imported capital. As a result of infusions of capital from foreign sources as
well as middle- and long-term loans, Israel has been able to at least in part
compensate for its recurring balance of trade deficits (shown in Figure 69 and
Table 67).

Three sources have been of particular significance in the course of the
years: World Jewry and the governments of the United States and of the
Federal Republic of Germany. All three have furnished grants to Israel (i.e.
sums not intended for repayment). In addition, the Jews of the world and the
US government have supplied middle- and long-term loans on easy terms of

credit. In the period from 1950 to 1955 the world's Jews effected 45·4% of all one-directional transfer payments to Israel. For the period between 1956 and 1960 this share was considerably less: 26·7%. In the period before and after the Six Day War (a period characterized by feelings of solidarity on the part of World Jewry with Israel) it was 43%. In the quiet years between 1971 and 1973 this share fell to only 24·3% and to 24% after the Yom Kippur War. (Was this due to the feeling that it was the responsibility of the US government to breach the gap opened by the oil shock?) In 1982 the share of World Jewry was 18·9%.

Despite the decline in the value of the US dollar, the real value of the World Jewry contribution for 1980 was only insignificantly higher than in 1974, and despite (or, perhaps, because of?) the War in Lebanon against the PLO, the payments in 1982 totalled less than in the previous year. It was not until 1981 that the Jews of the world sent more money to Israel than in the last year in which a Labour-led government was in office. Overall, a definite decrease in the willingness of World Jewry to contribute to Israel is unmistakable.

This lack of willingness can (although it need not necessarily) be explained in political terms. The economic developments which took place in the wake of the oil shocks of 1973 and 1979/80 naturally also influenced the ability to contribute. The polarization of World Jewry over the issue of the War in Lebanon in 1982 is, for example, an undisputed fact.

The importance of the United States as a source of capital imports (as well as of political support in general – not to mention defence goods!) can hardly be overemphasized. Especially since 1976, the share of one-directional capital imports from the USA has been overwhelming. In 1976 the proportion was 51·6% of all capital imports, in 1977, 47·2%; in 1978, 44·4%; in 1979, 49·4%; in 1980, 50·1%; in 1981, 45·7% and in 1982, 45·2%. In the face of these facts it is clear that any Israeli government cannot afford to strain its relations with the United States beyond a certain point, although this point has apparently not yet ever been really tested in any crisis. The economic and thus political leverage on Israel available to the US is very considerable, but it must be defined not only in terms of American foreign policy alternatives, but also in terms of US domestic politics. Here the limits of American abilities to pressure Israel become particularly visible. Nevertheless, if for political reasons the contributions of the Jews of the world (primarily American Jews) no longer flow as they once did, the US government might be presented with the opportunity to tighten the screws and demand that Israel pay greater attention to American interests.

Important as the reparation payments from the Federal Republic of Germany once were, especially from a political-psychological perspective, they must also be viewed in terms of the overall structure of non-repayable capital transfers. Until 1955 the German share of the total was 19·4%, payments having been instituted in 1954. Between 1955 and 1960 the proportion was 27·4% and from 1961 to 1965 11·5% (these figures including only payments to the Israeli government and not the reparations made to private individuals in Israel).

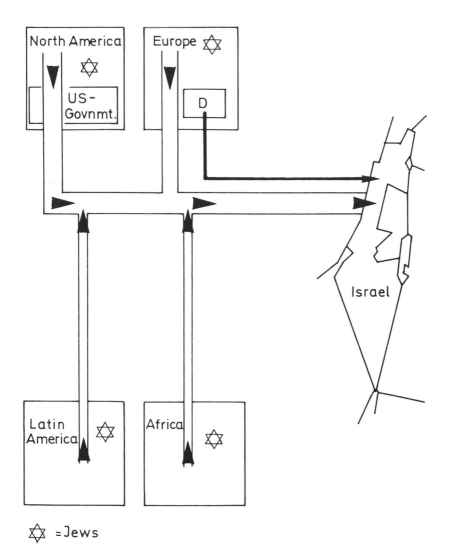

Figure 73   Capital imports to Israel, 1950–83.

2   *REGIONAL DEPENDENCY*

If the German reparation payments to private individuals are brought into the picture, it is easier to see how significant this financial support really was. The West German share of the total of non-repayable transfers for the period 1956 to 1960 was then 49·6%, for 1961 to 1965, 74·4%; for 1966 to 1970, 29·3% and for 1971 to 1973, 19·5%. Even in 1982 the total German contribution still amounted to 15·8%.

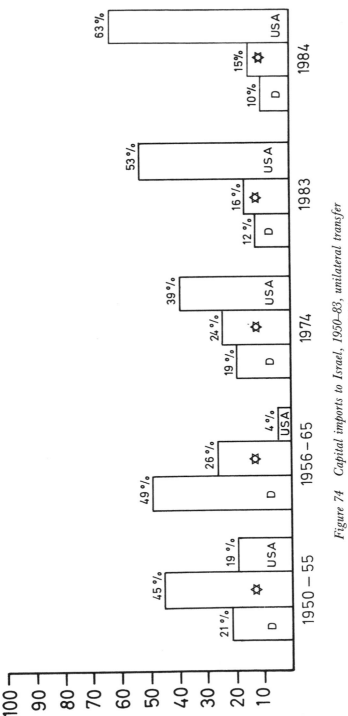

*Figure 74   Capital imports to Israel, 1950–83, unilateral transfer
payments (%).*

D = Federal Republic of Germany

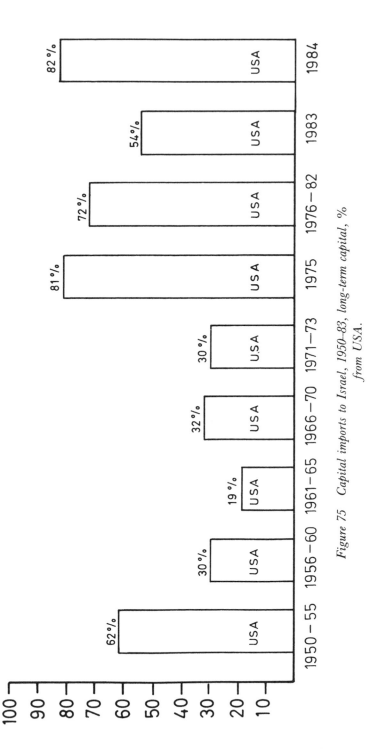

Figure 75 Capital imports to Israel, 1950–83, long-term capital, % from USA.

Table 71 Capital Imports to Israel, 1950–85; figures are given in millions of US dollars and exclude short-term loans

	1950–55	1956–60	1961–65	1966–70	1971–73	1974	1975–76	1977	1978	1979	1980–81	1982	1983	1984	1985
Excess of Imports over Exports	1,740	1,670	2,260	3,800	4,940	2,244	3,550	1,489	1,691	2,758	4,387	2,554	3,128	2,079	—
Total of unilateral transfer payments	1,080	1,350	1,740	2,420	4,000	1,718	4,050	2,060	2,356	2,943	6,219	2,788	3,068	3,398	5,212
West German reparations to Israeli govt.	210	370	200	—	—	—	—	—	—	—	—	—	—	—	—
Personal restitutions from West Germany	20	300	630	710	780	317	673	344	407	440	906	441	375	323	324
World Jewry[1]	490	360	440	1,040	970	413	1,051	466	424	453	1,149	528	507	507	568
United States govt. grants	210	70	40 }	670 }	2,250	672	1,818	977	1,046	1,453	2,978	1,259	1,619	2,123	3,937
Others[2]	150	250	430 }			316	508	273	479	597	1,186	560	567	445	383

Total of long-term capital imports[3]	530	400	1,070	1,530	2,300	541	2,478	583	1,061	1,151	2,118	1,058	1,634	940	−14
State of Israel bonds	200	190	150	460	720	165	301	174	186	80	230	157	152	94	212
US govt. loans	330	120	200	490	680	150	1,853	399	707	938	2,059	909	936	773	−110
Other loans and investments		90	720	580	900	226	321	10	168	133	−171	−8	546	73	−116

Notes:

[1] Includes only 'national institutions', i.e. United Jewish Appeal, Keren Hayessod, Keren Kayemet, Jewish Agency transfers to the government of Israel.

[2] Includes unilateral transfers by new immigrants accounting for about half of the total. This sum could be included with transfers from World Jewry, but the payments are to private persons rather than the government.

[3] Net totals excluding repayment of previous loans.

Sources: Lerner and Ben-Shahar, 1975: 77. Michaely, 1975: 200. Halevy and Klinov-Malul, 1975: 132 ff., 246. *Statistical Abstract of Israel*, various vols. *Bank of Israel*, various vols.

The payments from West Germany are the outgrowth of the politics of the past. The transfers from the United States and World Jewry have to do with the politics of the present (and future). In this respect the economic development of Israel is dependent on political factors. In other words, Israel's political freedom of action is limited by special economic conditions.

(a) FOREIGN LIABILITIES

Like most countries, Israel is restrictive when it comes to disclosing details concerning its foreign liabilities. In view of Israel's numerous loans from the United States, however, it is not too difficult to surmise that most of these liabilities will one day have to be repaid to Washington. Due to sometimes discreet and at other times less discreet hints and leaks, one may also assume that the Federal Republic of Germany is also an important creditor.

Once again, it can be seen that economic constraints, here in the form of long-term loans, may necessitate political concessions to the creditor nations. Their long-term political perspectives may differ from those of any Israeli government, and they may use the available economic leverage against Israel's policy. Up to now this has not been the case, but this fact does not constitute a permanent guarantee against the future. The data in Figure 76 and Table 72 underline the dramatic increase in Israel's foreign liabilities since 1977.

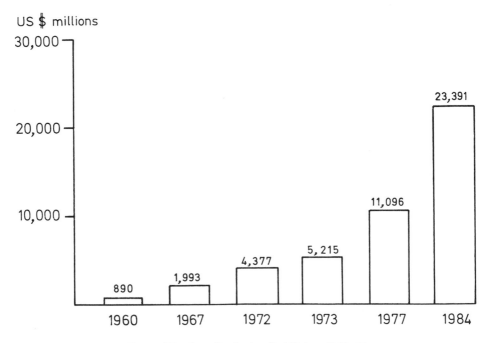

Figure 76   Israel's foreign liabilities, 1960–83.

Table 72   Israel's Foreign Liabilities, 1960–83; figures given as
end-of-year totals in millions of US dollars

	Grand total of liabilities 1	Total of foreign assets 2	Net liabilities (1 − 2)	Total liabilities of the economy*
1960	946	270	676	890
1961	1,094	365	729	1,009
1962	1,244	523	721	1,155
1963	1,399	656	743	1,299
1964	1,560	702	858	1,447
1965	1,804	825	979	1,673
1966	1,934	805	1,129	1,784
1967	2,180	1,036	1,144	1,993
1968	2,414	968	1,446	2,201
1969	2,816	744	2,042	2,504
1970	3,583	962	2,621	3,104
1971	4,761	1,585	3,176	3,944
1972	5,622	2,532	3,090	4,377
1973	6,919	3,890	3,029	5,215
1974	8,342	3,112	5,230	6,743
1975	10,151	3,487	6,664	8,257
1976	11,731	3,843	7,888	9,737
1977	13,604	4,782	8,822	11,096
1978	16,427	6,930	9,497	12,978
1979	19,595	8,460	11,135	15,284
1980	22,090	10,143	11,947	16,544
1981	24,505	11,153	13,352	18,213
1982	28,107	12,656	15,473	20,914
1983	29,313	11,573	17,740	22,592

*The Bank of Israel refers to this figure as the total liabilities of the economy,
which is calculated by deducting the assets of Israel's commercial banks
from the grand total (column 1) of Israel's liabilities.

Source: Statistical Abstract of Israel, various vols.

3   TOURISM

As a further aspect of the foreign trade picture, Israel's tourist industry is
dependent not only on the country's sun and beaches, but also on political
considerations. Until the early 1980s only the United States surpassed West
Germany in terms of the number of its citizens visiting Israel as tourists. In
comparison with the previous year, the stream of tourists from West Germany swelled by 17·7% in 1979 and by 17·3% in 1980, but then suddenly
dropped by 1% in 1981. What had happened? On 3 May 1981 Prime
Minister Begin had criticized West German Chancellor Helmut Schmidt
and 'the German people' with unusual vehemence and with reference to the

Nazi past. Even though 1981 was a year of worldwide recession and tourism from other nations to Israel declined as well, the sudden turnabout in the development of West German tourism to Israel can only be explained politically, and the complaints of the Israeli tourist agencies went precisely in this direction (*Statistical Abstract of Israel*, 1982: 126; *Bank of Israel*, 1982: 143).

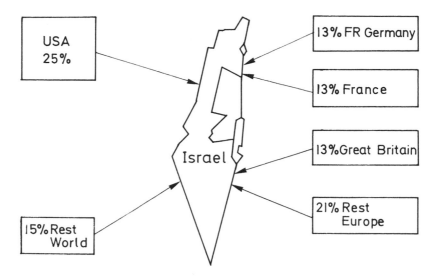

Figure 77   Tourism to Israel, 1980–82 (%).

Source: *Statistical Abstract of Israel*, 1983: 131.

FURTHER READING

Baruch Kimmerling, *Zionism and Economy* (Cambridge, Mass.: Schenkman, 1983).

Jacques Bendelac, *Les Fonds extérieurs d'Israel* (Paris: Economica, 1982).

Ira Sharansky, *Whither the State? Politics and Public Enterprise in Three Countries* (Chatham, NJ: Chatham House Publications, 1979); on Israel see pp. 67–105.

A. Daniel, *Labour Enterprises in Israel* (Jerusalem: Academic Press, 1976).

Abba Lerner and Haim Ben-Shahar, *The Economics of Efficiency and Growth. Lessons from Israel and the West Bank* (Cambridge, Mass.: Ballinger, 1975).

Michael Michaely, *Foreign Trade Regimes and Economic Development: Israel* (New York: Columbia University Press).

Economy, Israel Pocket Library (Jerusalem: Keter, 1973 ff.).

David Horowitz, *The Enigma of Economic Growth: A Case Study of Israel* (New York: Praeger, 1972); informative for the early period. (Written by one of Israel's most important fiscal policy-makers and later Governor of the Bank of Israel; see also his *The Economics of Israel*, New York: Pergamon, 1967.)

Carol S. Greenwald, *Recession as a Policy Instrument: Israel 1965–1969* (London: C. Hurst, 1974).

Howard Pack, *Structural Change and Economic Policy in Israel* (New Haven, Conn.: Yale University Press, 1971).

Nadav Halevy and Ruth Klinov-Malul, *The Economic Development of Israel* (New York: Praeger, 1968); probably the best introduction, though outdated.

Michael Heth, *The Legal Framework of Economic Policy in Israel* (New York: Praeger, 1967).

Perspectives: The Present as a Future Problem

To the fascination of observers of Israeli politics in the past decades, that nation has brought forth what certainly cannot be considered a dearth of charismatic – and anything but uncontroversial – political leaders, last but not least of whom was Menachem Begin, Israel's prime minister from 1977 until his resignation in 1983.

It would thus be easy enough to overlook the fact that Israel's present and future problems have less to do with individual personalities than with the identity of the Jewish state. Israel is in the throes of an identity crisis which has resulted in an unprecedented polarization within the Jewish state and, as a further consequence, within World Jewry (see Wolffsohn, 1983c). This identity crisis exhibits both an Arab-Jewish and an inner-Jewish facet.

In terms of recent developments concerning the Arab-Jewish aspect of this crisis, it was the War in Lebanon against the PLO, and most particularly the massacre in the two Palestinian camps near Beirut, which demonstrated more dramatically than any previous event the costs of Israel's success. For the Israelis, the issue thus joined involves not only the struggle against the PLO but the very goals of the Zionist enterprise. Is the suffering of the Palestinians to be the price for the existence of a Jewish state? Since the autumn of 1982 this question has been asked not only by fringe groups, but by a large portion of the mainstream Israeli public as well.

At the same time, the strategy of military hegemony was being called into question. The previous doctrine had been that it was necessary for Israel to possess such a preponderance of military might that the Arabs would never attain the capacity to destroy the Jewish state. Now, however, many Israelis have come to reflect that striving after political and military hegemony can lead to the devastation of one's opponent. Furthermore, the character of the War in Lebanon made it very difficult for Israelis to believe with a clear conscience in the 'purity of arms' (*tohar haneshek*) as the moral postulate of the Israeli army.

To simplify somewhat, it would appear that there are two schools of thought in Israel today. The one argues that it is not possible to come to terms with 'the Arabs' in general and 'the Palestinians' in particular. Its leading representatives include Menachem Begin and Ariel Sharon as well as General Eitan, Chief of Staff of the Israeli Defence Forces from 1978 to 1983. The other school of thought believes in compromise rather than confrontation and hopes to reconcile Zionist and Palestinian aspirations. What is decisive is that the lines between the two are by no means identical with the division between the two biggest political blocs, that is, Labour and Likud. In fact, the Labour Party seems to occupy a position somewhere between the two schools of thought.

Can it not be said that the developments since 1977 have nevertheless proved the 'hawks' right in allowing themselves to be guided by Jabotinsky's doctrine of the 'Iron Wall'? The underlying assumption here is that, although 'the Arabs' may never wax enthusiastic over the idea of a Zionist-Jewish entity in Palestine, they will in the end accept its existence if the experience of repeated military failures forces the realization that they would otherwise only continue to run up against the 'Iron Wall'. Is not the peace treaty with Egypt signed in March 1979, as well as the agreement with Lebanon negotiated in May 1983 (later abrogated by Lebanon), and even the indirect recognition of Israel by the majority of the Arab League at their summit meeting in Fez (September 1982), or the tactics adopted by Y. Arafat and 'his' Palestinian National Council in Amman (November 1984) confirmation enough of the correctness of this approach?

The doctrine of the 'Iron Wall' involves both defensive and offensive concepts. The defensive goal is solely to secure what has already been accomplished; the offensive aim, as was clearly demonstrated in the 1982 War in Lebanon, is to continue to push the wall forward and thus enhance the security of Israel proper. Instead of the basically defensive 'Iron Wall' one could even (as Dr Hans Maull of Munich suggested) borrow freely from Shakespeare's *Macbeth* and speak of an offensive 'iron woods' moving ever closer to the enemy's fortress.

At least one qualification must be made with regard to the image of the 'iron woods'. As already apparent in the case of retaliatory actions preceding, and especially since, the 1978 Israeli incursion into Lebanon, inept political and military actions undertaken on the Arab side have provided precisely the pretexts required for those whose aim it was to transform Israel's 'iron wall' into an 'iron woods'.

The inner-Jewish facet of the identity crisis is, of course, closely related to the Arab-Jewish aspect. What is at issue in the former is the determination of the substance of the Jewish state. To frame the question in starkly simplistic terms: is the Bible to be regarded as a moral compass or as a political atlas? In other words, should the West Bank be annexed (i.e. integrated into the territory of the State of Israel) because it was once part of the lands of Biblical Israel, or is it the task rather to live according to the teachings of the Bible?

For the hawks in the Begin government the War in Lebanon was part and parcel of the struggle over the Land of the Bible. For the members of the grass-roots 'Peace Now' initiative (including the son of then Interior Minister Burg of the National Religious Party injured in the grenade explosion in

Jerusalem on 10 February 1983) as well as for some leading politicians of the National Religious Party and of the Orthodox Agudat Israel, it is not the geography that is at stake, but rather the moral precepts of the Bible. Or is Numbers (33: 51–3) to be taken literally, wherein the Children of Israel are instructed to 'drive out all the inhabitants of the land' and to 'settle in it'? Shall the Bible be followed as a moral or as a political guide? Moreover, can religion and politics be kept strictly separate?

The bitterness of the military confrontation with the PLO brought out into the open a further dilemma for the Jewish identity of the Jewish state. Has Zahal, the Israeli Defence Forces, developed into an occupying army 'just like all the others'? And what is more, has the people of Israel in the meantime become a people 'just like all the others' (*kechol hagoyim*)? For conscientious Jews, to whom the theological concept of the 'chosen people' represents a moral challenge rather than a guarantee of self-righteousness, the very formulation of the question causes their blood to run cold.

In addition, an annexation of the occupied territories would, over the long term, unavoidably endanger the future of democracy in Israel. With a population that is only about three-fifths Jewish and two-fifths Arab it would be impossible to maintain an exclusively Jewish state in terms of both values and political leadership unless democracy were abandoned. Thus the question is posed: Zionism or democracy? This alternative has, in fact, been put forward publicly, not just by political fringe groups, but by mainstream politicians belonging mostly to the dovish wing of the Labour Party, to Mapam, the Citizens' Rights Movement and Shinui, as well as by 'Peace Now'. Since the proofs and quotations are legion there is no need to single out any here. Although there is a growing awareness of the problem, it is still far from being accepted as a matter of common wisdom.

The contrast in political styles between the Israelis of European and American backgrounds on the one hand and of Oriental origin on the other must also be mentioned. Today just over half of all Israelis come from Oriental backgrounds, and this Orientalization has altered the patterns of political behaviour. In Israel today one does not challenge one's opponent with arguments alone. Politics have become more 'Oriental', that is, more 'physical' and violent in nature. In Israel today one is attached not merely to institutions but to 'strong' and 'charismatic' personalities as well. From 1981 onwards one could hear the 'fans' chanting 'Begin, King of Israel', or 'Sharon, King of Israel'. Apart from the question as to whether the European tradition of 'rational politics' has ever been as strong in Europe itself as is often assumed, Israel is no longer, or no longer predominantly, the 'European bastion in Asia'.

As has been shown in the preceding chapters, most Oriental Israelis favour a harder line towards the Arabs and the Palestinians and approve of the increased pace of Jewish settlements in the occupied territories since 1977. (This is not to imply that there are no Oriental Israelis prepared to make compromises. Quite the opposite is true, but not for the political arena as a whole.) Oriental Israelis are less well off than Ashkenasim and thus demand a greater commitment to social welfare concerns. This, their compromise-seeking Euro-American compatriots usually reply, is only possible under the motto 'social welfare *OR* settlements' but not if the goal is to be 'social welfare *AND* settlements', as the already nearly bankrupt nation can little afford either, much less both.

The proponents of an accelerated pace of new settlements counter with the argument that it is only through a policy of state-subsidized housing construction in the West Bank that those groups in Israeli society who hardly dare to dream of a home of their own in the already settled parts of 'old' Israel could afford the purchase of a house or apartment in a new settlement. Therefore 'settlements *and* social welfare'?

At the moment, Israel's problems superficially seem to centre on questions of personality: Peres? Shamir? Navon? Sharon? Rabin? . . .

But the basic question remains: Zionism or democracy? Formulated in another way: territorial acquisitions or democracy? Instead of the 'either/or' alternative, an 'as-well-as' solution is still possible – but, of course, without territorial acquisitions.

And finally, what can and ought to be the guiding ideals of the Jewish state? Is the *halutzic* ideal of the agricultural pioneer, neglected as it was in daily practice even in the period before independence, still viable? Is the ideal to be found in the Jewish religion as seriously practised by only some 30% of the Jewish population of Israel? Is it perhaps to be Eretz Israel? Or can one preserve a sense of community and a willingness to make material sacrifices without being able to articulate one's ideals clearly?

Such questions present problem upon problem for a land already not lacking in problems.

FURTHER READING

GENERAL DATA

Statistical Abstract of Israel (Jerusalem: Central Bureau of Statistics, yearly); for practically *all* data on all fields.

Bank of Israel: Yearly Report; for economic data.

For events and processes as well as data since 1976–7, consult: *Middle East Contemporary Survey*, ed. Colin Legum *et al.* (New York and London: Holmes & Meyer, 1977 ff., yearly).

Opinion polls can be found in:

Russell A. Stone, *Social Change in Israel. Attitudes and Events, 1967–79* (New York: Praeger, 1982).

Eva Etzioni-Halevy and Rina Shapira, *Political Culture in Israel. Cleavage and Integration among Israeli Jews* (New York: Praeger, 1977).

Aaron Antonovsky and Alan Arian, *Hopes and Fears of Israelis. Consensus in a New Society* (Jerusalem: Academic Press, 1972); more general and older.

The best way to keep up with the more recent polls is by consulting:

World Opinion Update (Westport, Conn.: Greenwood Press, monthly), or *Index to International Public Opinion* (Westport, Conn.: Greenwood Press, yearly).

BIBLIOGRAPHIES

Books, *Kiryat Sefer*, bibliographical quarterly of the Jewish National and University Library, Jerusalem; slow but all-encompassing.

Articles, *Index of Articles on Jewish Studies*, bibliographical quarterly of the Jewish National and University Library, Jerusalem; also slow but excellent.

Assia Neuberg, *The State of Israel. An Annotated Bibliography*, 2 vols. (Jerusalem: The Centre for Public Libraries in Israel, 1969, 1977).

COMPREHENSIVE WORKS ON ISRAEL

The following works deal with more than the political topics:

Michael Wolffsohn, *Politik in Israel. Entwicklung und Struktur des politischen Systems* (Opladen: Leske, 1983).

Eli Barnavie, *Israel au XXe siècle* (Paris: Presses Universitaires de France, 1982).

Daniel Shimshoni, *Israeli Democracy. The Middle of the Journey* (New York: The Free Press, 1982).

Asher Arian (ed.), *Israel. A Developing Society* (Assen: Van Gorcum, 1980).

Richard F. Nyrop (ed.), *Israel. A Country Study* (Washington, DC: University Press of America, 1979).

Nadav Safran, *Israel. The Embattled Ally* (Cambridge, Mass.: The Belknap Press of Harvard University Press, 1978); includes an extensive analysis of US–Israeli relations.

Israel Pocket Library, 15 vols. (Jerusalem: Keter, 1974).

The following titles deal mainly with the political system:

Asher Arian, *Politics in Israel. The Second Generation* (London: Chatham House, 1985).

Itamar Rabinovich and Jehuda Reinharz (eds.), *Israel and the Middle East. Documents and Readings on Society, Politics and Foreign Relations, 1948 to the Present* (Oxford: Oxford University Press, 1984).

Claude Klein, *Le Système politique d'Israel* (Paris: Presses Universitaires de France, 1983); an institutional approach.

Robert O. Freedman (ed.), *Israel in the Begin Era* (New York: Praeger, 1982); limited in its time perspective but useful.

Itzhak Galnoor, *Communication and Politics. The Development of Israeli Democracy* (Beverly Hills, Calif., and London: Sage, 1982).

Gregory Mahler (ed.), *Readings on the Israeli Political System* (Washington, DC: University Press of America, 1982).

See also the volumes edited by Arian listed in the reference section, as these include much more than just election analyses.

For a comprehensive survey from a Russian perspective, see:

Galina S. Nikitina, *The State of Israel. A Historical, Economic and Political Study* (Moscow: Progress Publishers, 1973).

The Chief Dates in Israel's History:

A Chronological Table

1882   Beginning of Zionist-motivated immigration to Palestine, first *aliya* continuing to 1903

1897   Founding of the WZO with the goal of creating an internationally recognized 'homeland' for the Jewish people in Palestine

1904–14 Second *aliya*

1905   Founding of the first leftist Zionist parties in Palestine

1909   Founding of Tel-Aviv and the first *kibbutz*, Degania

1917   2 November: Balfour Declaration

1917–18 British troops occupy Palestine

1919–23 Third *aliya*

1920   April: first Jewish–Arab clashes, especially in Jerusalem
Founding of the Histadrut

1921   May: Jewish–Arab clashes, especially in Jaffa

1922   League of Nations confers Mandate for Palestine on Great Britain

1924–31 Fourth *aliya*

1929   Massacre of Jews, especially in Hebron

1932–9 Fifth *aliya*

1936–9 Arab Revolt

1937   July: Peel Commission presents first plan for the division of Palestine

1939   17 May: British government issues White Book severely restricting Jewish immigration to and land purchases in Palestine

1944   Jewish parties increase agitation for the founding of a Jewish state, increased resistance to British authorities

1947   29 November: UN General Assembly approves resolution to divide Palestine into a Jewish and an Arab state. Areas designated for Arab state annexed by Jordan, this act recognized only by Great Britain and Pakistan

1947–8   Armed conflict in Palestine in wake of UN resolution

1948   14 May: Israel declares its independence. Hostilities with Arab neighbours begin on same day.
The USA is the first nation to recognize Israel but imposes a *de facto* embargo on deliveries of heavy armament.

1948–9   War of Independence

1949   7 January: ceasefire
24 February: armistice with Egpyt
20 July: final armistice agreement signed with Syria

1948–51   Mass immigration and economic crisis

1952   10 September: reparations agreement signed with Federal Republic of Germany

1956   29 October to 5 November: Sinai Campaign with British and French assistance to reopen the Straits of Tiran (previously blocked by Egypt)

1957   12 March: final Israeli withdrawal from territories occupied during Sinai Campaign after considerable pressure from USA

1960   14 March: Israeli Prime Minister Ben-Gurion and West German Chancellor Adenauer meet in New York

1963   June: Ben-Gurion resigns

1965   May: assumption of diplomatic relations with the Federal Republic of Germany

1966   December: military administration for Israeli Arabs abolished

1967   5 to 10 June: Six Day War with Egypt, Jordan and Syria.
          Following Six Day War: first acts of Palestinian resistance. After
          French President de Gaulle's embargo on arms sales to Israel,
          the USA becomes Israel's chief arms supplier.

1969–70   1 March 1969 to 7 August 1970: War of Attrition with Egypt
          along the Suez Canal

1970   June: West German Chancellor Willi Brandt visits Israel

1973   6 to 26 October: Yom Kippur War with Egypt and Syria. US
          airlift of weapons and ammunition

1974   April: Golda Meir resigns, Y. Rabin becomes prime minister
          May: Richard Nixon first US president to visit Israel

1975   1 September: Sinai Disengagement Agreement with Egypt

1977   17 May: Knesset elections lead to change in governments
          19–21 November: Egyptian President Sadat in Jerusalem

1978   17 September: Camp David Agreement

1979   26 March: signing of Peace Treaty with Egypt

1980   30 July: Israel formally annexes East Jerusalem

1981   Crisis in Lebanon
          7 June: Israeli planes destroy atomic reactor near Baghdad
          14 December: Israel annexes the Golan Heights

1982   6 June: Operation Peace for Galilee mounted against PLO in
          Lebanon
          16–17 September: Israeli officers allow Lebanese Christian
          militia to enter two Palestinian camps near Beirut and a
          massacre ensues

1983   17 May: Israeli–Lebanese accord
          28 August: Prime Minister Begin resigns
          September: Lebanon nullifies accord with Israel

1984   National Unity Cabinet formed during worsening economic
          crisis

1985   Israeli pullback from Lebanon

List of Abbreviations

A	Ahdut
AH	Ahdut Haavoda, social democratic party 1919–29, leftist socialist, agrarian (*kibbutzim*); 'new' AH 1944–68 left Mapai in 1944, joined with HHZ to form Mapam in 1948, which the AH left in 1954
AG	Avisohar Group
AI	Agudat Israel
ALF	Arab Liberation Front
BLG	Basic Law Government
BLR	Blue Red Movement
BP	Beh Porath
CC	(party) central committee
CO	Communist Opposition
CP	Communist Party
CPP	Communist Party of Palestine
CRM	(also CR, and – before and after split – CR1 and CR2) Citizens' Rights Movement, founded in 1973 immediately following Yom Kippur War as anti-establishment party led by Shulamit Aloni
DFP	Democratic Front for Peace and Equality
DM	Democratic Movement
DMC	Democratic Movement for Change, clearly centrist bourgeois party founded in 1977, promising continuity and change, dissolved into various factions in 1978
EC	European Community
FAZ	*Frankfurter Allgemeine Zeitung*
FC	Free Centre, split from Herut in 1967, rightist liberal and extremely nationalistic until 1974, joined DMC in 1977
FF	Farmer's Federation (Hitachdut Haikarim)
FRG	Federal Republic of Germany (West Germany)
Gahal	Bloc formed by Herut and GZ (Liberal Party) in 1965
GDR	German Democratic Republic (East Germany)
GE	Gush Emunim
GI	Greater Israel Movement
GL	Georg Landauer
GZ	General Zionists, right-leaning liberal, formed Liberal Party together with IL 1961–5; joined nationalistic-populistic Herut in forming Gahal bloc after break with IL in 1965
HC	Hebrew Communists
Herut	nationalist, populist party
HHZ	Hashomer Hazair, at first youth-oriented, leftist socialist and Zionist from late 1920s, since 1948 as Mapam

HP	Hapoel Hazair, social reformist party with agrarian orientation, founded in 1905; merged with AH to form Mapai in 1930
HPM	Hapoel Hamisrahi
HPML	Hapoel Hamisrahi Left
IC	Independent Centre
IDF	Israel Defence Forces (Zahal)
IH	Izhar Harari
IIASR	Israel Institute for Applied Social Research
IL	Independent Liberals, 1948–61 as Progressive Party, 1961–5 as Liberal Party (together with the GZ), since 1965 the former Progressive Party as IL
ILP	Israeli Labour Party, fusion of Mapai, Rafi and AH in 1968
IS	Independent Socialists
IZL	Irgun Zvai Leumi
JA	Jewish Agency
JC	Jewish Communist Party
JJ	J. Jitzhaki
JS	Jewish Section
JSP	Jewish State Party
LAO	Law and Administration Ordinance (1948)
Le	Lehi
Likud	Bloc formed by Gahal, SL, GI and FC in 1973
LP	Liberal Party
LU	Left Union
M	Misrahi, 1983 ff. Mazad
Maarah	Bloc formed by Mapai and AH in 1965 (Small Maarah); bloc formed by Mapai, AH and Mapam since 1969 (Big Maarah)
Mapai	'Party of the Workers of Eretz Israel', popular social democratic party founded in 1930, the dominant party until 1977, but never with absolute majority in Knesset and thus always dependent on coalition partners from religious or bourgeois camps
Mapam	'United Workers' Party', leftist socialist, Zionist and agrarian (*kibbutzim*)
MD	Moshe Dayan
MH	Min Hayessod
MK	Member of the Knesset
Mn	Matzpen
MS	Moshe Sneh
NCL	New Communist List (Rakah)
NF	New Force
NFL	National Federation of Labour
NI	New Immigration, centrist to leftist liberal party founded by immigrated German Jews in 1942
NK	Neture Kartha
NLF	National Labour Federation
NRF	National Religious Front
NRP	National Religious Party
NZZ	*Neue Züricher Zeitung*
O	Ometz

OZ	Haolam Haze (Avnery)
PAI	Poale Agudat Israel
PCP	Palestinian Communist Party
PLP	Progressive List for Peace
PMN	Progressive Movement Nazareth
PORI	Public Opinion Research Israel
PP	Progressive Party
PS	Flatto-Sharon
PZ	Poale Zion
PZL	Poale Zion Left, in socialist revolutionary party, partly Zionist, founded in 1922–4
PZM	Poale Zion Marxists, precursor of PZL, founded in 1923
PZSD	Poale Zion Social Democrats
R	Rafi, 'List of Israeli Workers', rightist social democratic splinter group led by Ben-Gurion, broke off from Mapai in 1965
RC	Radical Centre
Rev	Revisionists
RZ	Radical Zionists
S	Shinui
Seph	Sephardim, originally Jews of Spanish ancestry who gradually immigrated to Palestine from the 15th century on, mainly from various regions of the Orient, thus longtime residents of Palestine, in contrast to those Jews who immigrated from Arab-Islamic North African and West Asian nations from 1948 onwards; only the latter are designated here as 'Oriental' or 'Afro-Asian' Jews
SL	State List, group of former Rafi members not prepared to rejoin the ILP in 1968, split into various factions and 'parties', part of the Likud since 1973
SWP	Socialist Workers' Party
SS	Shass
SZ	*Shlomzion* (General Sharon)
T	Tehiya
Ta	Tami
Te	Telem
TF	Tora Front
UKM	United *Kibbutz* Movement
Y	Yahad (Ezer Weizman)
Yem	Yemenites
WL	Workers' Legion
WP	Women's Party
WZO	World Zionist Organization
Z	Zomet
ZBP	Zionist Black Panthers
ZW	Zionist Workers, precursor of Progressive Party/IL
ZY	Zionist Youth

References

(Quoted Publications and Sources)

Abadi, Jacob (1982), *Britain's Withdrawal from the Middle East, 1947–1971, The Economic and Strategic Imperatives* (Princeton, NJ: The Kingston Press).

Abramov, S. Zalman (1976), *Perpetual Dilemma. Jewish Religion in the Jewish State* (Rutherford, NJ: Fairleigh Dickinson University Press and London: Associated University Press).

Ackermann, Walter, *et al.* (eds.) (1982), *Erziehung in Israel*, 2 vols. (Stuttgart: Klett-Cotta).

Africa Contemporary Record. Annual Survey and Documents, 14 vols. to 1985, ed. Colin Legum (New York and London: Holmes & Meier).

Aharoni, Yair (1976), *Structure and Performance in the Israeli Economy* (Hebrew) (Tel-Aviv: Tschrikover).

Allen, David, and Pijpers, Alfred (eds.) (1984), *European Foreign Policy-Making and the Arab–Israeli Conflict* (The Hague, Boston: Nijhoff).

Amir, Shimon (1974), *Israel's Development Cooperation with Africa, Asia and Latin America* (New York: Praeger).

Antonovsky, Aaron, and Arian, Alan (1972), *Hopes and Fears of Israelis. Consensus in a New Society* (Jerusalem: Academic Press).

Antonovsky, Aaron, and Katz, Abraham O. (1979), *From the Golden to the Promised Land* (Darby, Pa.: Norwood Editions and Jerusalem: Academic Press).

Arian, Alan (1971), 'Voting and ideology in Israel', in Lissak and Gutmann, 1971, pp. 257–86.

Arian, Alan (ed.) (1972a), *The Elections in Israel 1969* (Jerusalem: Academic Press).

Arian, Alan (1972b), 'Electoral choice in a dominant party system', in Arian, 1972a, pp. 187–201.

Arian, Asher (ed.) (1975), *The Elections in Israel 1973* (Jerusalem: Academic Press).

Arian, Asher (1979), 'The electorate: Israel 1977', in Penniman, 1979, pp. 59–89.

Arian, Asher (ed.) (1980), *The Elections in Israel 1977* (Jerusalem: Academic Press).

Arian, Asher (1981), 'Elections 1981: competitiveness and polarization', *Jerusalem Quarterly*, no. 21, pp. 3–27.

Arian, Asher (ed.) (1983), *The Elections in Israel 1981* (Tel-Aviv University: Ramot).

Arian, Asher (1985a), *Politics in Israel. The Second Generation* (London: Chatham House).

Arian, Asher (1985b), 'Israeli democracy', in *Journal of International Affairs*, vol. 38, no. 2, pp. 259–76.

Arian, Asher, and Shamir, Michael (1983), 'The primarily political functions of the left–right continuum', in Arian, 1983, pp. 259–79.

Aronoff, Myron J. (1977), *Power and Ritual in the Israeli Labor Party* (Assen-Amsterdam: Van Gorcum).

Aronoff, Myron J. (ed.) (1984a), *Cross-Currents in Israeli Culture and Politics* (New Brunswick, NJ, and London: Transaction Books).

Aronoff, Myron J. (1984b), 'Gush Emunim: The institutionalization of a movement in Israel', in *Political Anthropology*, vol. 3, pp. 63–84.

Aronson, Shlomo (1978), *Conflict and Bargaining in the Middle East. An Israeli Perspective* (Baltimore, Md.: Johns Hopkins University Press).

Avineri, Shlomo (1981), *The Making of Modern Zionism: The Intellectual Origins of the Jewish State* (New York: Basic Books).

Avnat, Alexander, and Leviathan, Uri (1984), 'The *kibbutz* and Israeli society', Haifa University, Kibbutz Studies Institute, unpublished report kindly provided by the authors.

Avruch, Kevin (1981a), *American Immigrants in Israel. Social Identities and Change* (Chicago: University of Chicago Press).

Avruch, Kevin (1981b), 'Becoming traditional: socialization among American immigrants in Israel', *Studies in Comparative International Development*, vol. 16, no. 3–4, pp. 64–83.

Bach, Ami, Weiner, Eynav, Adler, Israel, and Levinsohn, Hannah (1974), *The Positions of the Public on Settlements and Occupied Territories* (Hebrew) (Jerusalem: IIASR and Communications Institute, Hebrew University).

Baker, Henry E. (1976), 'Legal system of Israel', in *Israel Yearbook*.

Baker, Henry E. (1977), 'Legal system of Israel', in *Israel Yearbook*.

Baldwin, E. (1972), *Differentiation and Co-operation in an Israeli Veteran Moshav* (Manchester: Manchester University Press).

Bank of Israel (Jerusalem), annual reports.

Bar-Lev, Mordechai, and Peri, Kedem (1984), Religious observance amongst Jewish university students in Israel' (Hebrew), *Megamot*, vol. 28, no. 2/3 (March), pp. 265–79.

Barnavie, Eli (1982), *Israel au XXe siècle* (Paris: Presses Universitaires de France).

Becker, Helmut, and Leigle, Ludwig (1980), *Israel, Erziehung und Gesellschaft* (Stuttgart: Klett-Cotta).

Behbehani, Hashim S. H. (1981), *China's Foreign Policy in the Arab World 1955–75* (London: Routledge & Kegan Paul).

Ben-Avram, Baruh (1976), *Hewer Hakawutzot, its Social and Ideological Development* (Hebrew) (Tel-Aviv: Am Oved).

Beilin, Yossi (1983), 'Inter-generational friction in three parties in Israel', in *International Journal of Group Tensions*, vol. 13, nos. 1–4, pp. 18–41.

Beling, Eva (1967), *Die gesellschaftliche Eingliederung duetscher Einwanderer in Israel* (Frankfurt am Main: Europäische Verlagsanstalt).

Bendelac, Jacques (1982), *Les Fonds extérieurs d'Israel* (Paris: Economica).

Ben-Eliezer, Yariv (1978), '*Television in Israel*', unpublished PhD dissertation, New York University.

Ben-Meir, Dov (1980), *The Histadrut Lexicon* (Tel-Aviv: Am Oved).

Ben-Meir, Dov (1982), *Histadrut. Die israelische Gewerkshaft* (Bonn and Bad Godesberg: Verlag Neue Gesellschaft).

Ben-Rafael, Eliezer (1982), *The Emergence of Ethnicity: Cultural Groups and Social Conflict in Israel* (Westport, Conn., and London: Greenwood Press).

Bensimon-Donath, Doris (1975), *L'Éducation en Israel* (Paris: Anthropos).

Ben-Sira, Zeev (1983), *The Jewish-Israeli Society: Interethnic Relations* (Hebrew) (Jerusalem: IIASR).

Bentwich, Joseph S. (1965), *Education in Israel* (London: Routledge & Kegan Paul).

Benvenisti, Meron (1984), *The West Bank Data Project. A Survey of Israel's Policies* (Washington, DC: American Enterprise Institute).

Benyamini, Kalman (1981), 'Israeli youth and the image of the Arab', *Jerusalem Quarterly*, no. 20 (Summer), pp. 87–95.

Bernstein, Deborah (1984), 'Conflict and protest in Israeli society: The case of the Black Panthers of Israel', in *Youth and Society*, vol. 16, no. 2, pp. 129–52.

Bilski, Raphaella, et al. (eds) (1980), *Can Planning Replace Politics? The Israeli Experience* (The Hague: Nijhoff).

Bin-Nun, Ariel (1983), *Einführung in das Recht des Staates Israel* (Darmstadt: Wissenschaftliche Buchgesellschaft).

Birrenbach, Kurt (1984), *Meine Sondermissionen. Rückblick auf zwei Jahrzehnte bundesdeutscher Außenpolitik* (Düsseldorf and Vienna: Econ).

Blustein, Jakob (1975), *The Individual and the Bureaucracy* (Hebrew) (Jerusalem: Hebrew University, Academic Press).

Bober, Arie (ed.) (1972), *The Other Israel. The Radical Case against Zionism* (Garden City, NY: Doubleday).

Boim, Leon (1972), 'Financing of the 1969 election', in Arian, 1972a, pp. 132–49.

Boim, Leon (1979), 'The financing of elections', in Arian, pp. 199–225.

Bracha, Baruch (1978), Restriction of personal freedom without due process of law according to the Defence (Emergency) Regulations, 1945', in *Israel Yearbook of Human Rights*, vol. 8 (Tel-Aviv), pp. 296–323.

Braham, R. L. (1966), *Israel: A Modern Education System* (Washington, DC: Government Printing Office).

Brecher, Michael (1972), *The Foreign Policy System of Israel. Setting, Images, Process* (London: Oxford University Press).

Brecher, Michael (1974a), *Decisions in Israel's Foreign Policy* (Oxford: Oxford University Press).

Brecher, Michael (1974b), *Israel, the Korean War and China* (Jerusalem: Academic Press).

Brecher, Michael (1980), *Decisions in Crisis. Israel, 1967 and 1973* (Berkeley, Calif.: University of California Press).

Brichta, Abraham (1972), 'The social, political and cultural background of Knesset members in Israel' (Hebrew), dissertation for the Hebrew University of Jerusalem, published in Arian, 1972a, pp. 109 ff.

Brichta, Abraham (1977), *Democracy and Elections: On Changing the Electoral and Nominations Systems in Israel* (Hebrew) (Tel-Aviv: Am Oved).

Brownstein, Lewis (1977), 'Decision-making in Israeli foreign policy: An unplanned process', in *Political Science Quarterly*, vol. 92, no. 2, pp. 259–79.

Büren, Rainer (1982), *Ein palastinensische Teilstaat? Zur internen, regionalen und internationalen Dimension der Palästinenserfrage* (Baden-Baden: Nomos).

Caiden, Gerald E. (1970), *Israel's Administrative Culture* (Berkeley, Calif.: University of California Press).

Caiden, Gerald E. (1980), *To Right Wrong: The Initial Ombudsman Experience in Israel* (Tel-Aviv: Ashdown Press).

Carta's Historical Atlas of Israel (1977) (Jerusalem: Carta).

Caspi, Dan (1972), 'Patterns of voter fluctuation in Israel' (Hebrew), *State and Government*, no. 3, pp. 81–97; here cited from Lissak and Gutmann, 1977, pp. 268–84.

Caspi, Dan (1976), 'Between legislators and electors. The Knesset members' perceptions of public attitudes' (Hebrew), dissertation for the Hebrew University of Jerusalem.

Caspi, Dan, Diskin, A., and Gutmann, E. (eds.) (1983), *The Roots of Begin's Success. The 1981 Israeli Elections* (London: Croom Helm and New York: St Martin's Press).

Chafets, Zeev (1984), 'Press and government in Israel', in *Israel Yearbook on Human Rights*, vol. 14, pp. 134–47.

Cohen, Adir (1985), *An Ugly Face in the Mirror. National Stereotypes in Hebrew Children's Literature* (Hebrew) (Tel-Aviv: Reshafim).

Cohen, Raanan (ed.) (1984), *The Israeli Arabs* (Hebrew) (Tel-Aviv: Israeli Labour Party).

Cohen, Samy (1974), *De Gaulle, les gaullistes et Israel* (Paris: A. Moreau).

Cohen, S. M. (1983), *Attitudes of American Jews toward Israel and Israelis* (New York: The American Jewish Committee).

Council for Higher Education (1982), *Higher Education in Israel, Statistical Abstract 1980/81* (Jerusalem), August.

Crosbie, Sylvia K. (1974), *A Tacit Alliance. France and Israel. From Suez to the Six Day War* (Princeton, NJ: Princeton University Press).

Daniel, Abraham (1976), *Labor Enterprises in Israel, Vol. 1: The Cooperative Economy, Vol. 2: The Institutional Economy* (Jerusalem: Academic Press).

Darin-Drabkin, & Haim (1963), *The Other Society* (New York: Harcourt, Brace World).

Darin-Drabkin, H. (1967), *Der Kibbutz. Die neue Gesellshaft in Israel* (Stuttgart: Klett).

Davis, Moshe (ed.) (1977), *World Jewry and the State of Israel* (New York: Arno Press).

Davis, Uri (1983), *The Golan Heights under Israeli Occupation 1967–1981* (University of Durham: Centre for Middle Eastern and Islamic Studies).

Davis, W. D. (1982), *The Territorial Dimension of Judaism* (Berkeley, Calif.: University of California Press).

Dent, Brenda (1972), 'Public attitudes toward the use of 'protekzia' in the Israeli administration', in *State and Government* (Hebrew), no. 3, pp. 57–80.

Deutschkron, Inge (1983), *Israel und die Deutschen. Das besondere Verhältnis* (Cologne: Verlag Wissenschaft und Politik, 2nd ed.).

Diner, Dan (1979), *Israel in Palästina* (Königstein: Athenäum).

Diskin, Abraham (1976), 'The competitive multi-party system of Israel (1949–1973)' (Hebrew), dissertation for the Hebrew University of Jerusalem.

Diskin, Abraham (1980a), *Das politische System Israels* (Cologne: Böhlau).

Diskin, Abraham (1980b), 'The 1977 interparty distances: a three-level analysis', in Arian, 1980, pp. 213–29.

Diskin, Abraham (1982a), 'Polarization and volatility in the elections for the Tenth Knesset' (Hebrew), *State, Government and International Relations*, no. 19–20, pp. 44–62; English version in Caspi, Diskin and Gutmann, 1983.

Diskin, Abraham (1982b), 'The 1981 elections: public opinion polls', *Jerusalem Quarterly*, no. 22, pp. 99–104.

Diskin, Abraham, and Wolffsohn, Michael (1977), 'Das Ende des Dominanzpartei-Systems, Israels Wahlen vom 17. Mai 1977', in *Politische Vierteljahresschrift*, vol. 18, no. 4, pp. 771–841.

Diskin, Abraham, and Wolffsohn, Michael (1978), 'Strukturelle Veränderungen in den politischen Parteien Israels', *Jahrbuch des Öffentlichen Rechts der Gegenwart*, new series, vol. 27, pp. 455–99.

Diskin, Abraham, and Wolffsohn, Michael (1979), 'Die organisatorische und ideologische Entwicklung der israelische Parteien', *Orient*, vol. 20, no. 1, pp. 33–52.

Dror, Yehezkel (1971), 'Political Decision-Making Processes in Israel' (Hebrew), in *State and Government*, no. 1, pp. 7–32.

Dror, Yehezkel (1978), *Policy and Administration Improvement in Israel* (Hebrew) (Tel-Aviv: Sifriat Haminhal).

Dror, Yehezkel (1984), 'A guide through the perplexities of Israeli politics after Begin', *The Political Quarterly*, vol. 55, no. 1, pp. 38–47.

Duclos, Louis-Jean (1983), 'La question des frontières orientales d'Israel. Reflexion sur la démultiplication fonctionelle des frontières', *Révue française des sciences politiques*, vol. 33, no. 5, pp. 847–65; also in Études internationales (Quebec), vol. 14, no. 2, pp. 289–301.

Eaton, Joseph W. (1970), *Influencing the Youth Culture. A Study of Youth Organizations in Israel* (London: Sage).

Efrat, Elisha (1984), *Urbanization in Israel* (London: Croom Helm and New York: St Martin's Press).

Eisenmann, Robert H. (1978), *Islamic Law in Palestine and Israel* (Leiden: Brill).

Eisenstadt, S. N. (1964), *Israeli Society* (London: Weidenfeld & Nicolson).

Eisenstadt, S. N. (1973), *Die israelische Gesellschaft* (Stuttgart: Enke).

Eisenstadt, S. N. (1985), *The Transformation of Israeli Society* (Boulder, Colo.: Westview Press).

Elazar, Daniel J. (ed.) (1982), *Governing Peoples and Territories* (Philadelphia, Pa.: Institute for the Study of Human Issues).

Elcott, David M. (1981), 'The political resocialization of German Jews in Palestine, 1933–1939', unpublished PhD dissertation, Columbia University, New York.

Elections (1959), *Results of Elections to the Fourth Knesset and to Local Authorities 1959* (Hebrew) (Jerusalem: Central Bureau of Statistics, 1961).

Elections (1961), *Results of Elections to the Fifth Knesset and to Local Authorities 1961* (Hebrew) (Jerusalem: Central Bureau of Statistics, 1964).

Elections (1965), *Results of Elections to the Sixth Knesset and to Local Authorities 2.11.1965* (Hebrew) (Jerusalem: Central Bureau of Statistics, 1967).

Elections (1969), *Results of Elections to the Seventh Knesset and to Local Authorities 28.10.1969* (Hebrew) (Jerusalem: Central Bureau of Statistics, 1970).

Elections (1973), *Results of Elections to the Eighth Knesset and to Local Authorities 31.12.1973* (Hebrew) (Jerusalem: Central Bureau of Statistics, 1974).

Elections (1977), *Results of Elections to the Ninth Knesset 17.5.1977* (Hebrew) (Jerusalem: Central Bureau of Statistics, 1978).

Elections (1981), Results of Elections to the Tenth Knesset 30.6.1981 (Hebrew) (Jerusalem: Central Bureau of Statistics, 1981).

Elon, Amos (1971), *The Israelis – Founders and Sons* (New York: Bantam).

Elon, Amos (1972), *Die Israelis, Gründer und Söhne* (Vienna and Munich: Molden, Taschenbuchausgabe).

Encyclopaedia Hebraica (1958), Vol. 6, 'Eretz Israel' (Hebrew) (Tel-Aviv: Encyclopaedia Publishing Company).

Encyclopaedia of Social Sciences (1970) (Hebrew), ed. David Knaani, 5 vols. (Merhavia: Sifriat Hapoalim).

Erel, Shlomo (1983), *Neue Wurzeln. 50 Jahre Immigration deutschsprachiger Juden in Israel* (Gerlinger: Bleicher Verlag).

Etzioni-Halevy, Eva, and Shapira, Rina (1977), *Political Culture in Israel. Cleavage and Integration among Israeli Jews* (New York: Praeger).

Falk, Gloria H. (1985), 'Israeli public opinion: Looking toward a Palestinian solution', in *Middle East Journal*, vol. 39, no. 3 (Summer) pp. 247–69.

Falk, Ze'ev W. (1973), 'Religion and state in Israel', *Orient*, vol. 14, no. 4, pp. 423–33.

Fein, Aharon (1984) 'The rate of emigration from Israel', in *Forum on the Jewish People, Zionism and Israel*, no. 53, pp. 53–60.

Fein, Leonhard J. (1976), *Politics in Israel* (Boston, Mass.: Little, Brown).

Feldman, Lily G. (1984), *The Special Relationship between West Germany and Israel* (Boston, Mass.: Allen & Unwin).

Feldman, Shai, and Rechnitz-Kijner, Heda (1984), *Deception, Consensus and War: Israel in Lebanon*, (Tel-Aviv University: Jaffe Center for Strategic Studies).

Fishman, Aryei (1975), 'The religious *Kibbutz*: A study in the Interrelationship of religion and ideology in the context of modernization (Hebrew), PhD dissertation, Hebrew University, Jerusalem.

Fishman, Aryei (1983), 'Judaism and modernization: The case of the religious kibbutzim', *Social Forces*, vol. 62, no. 1 (September 1983), pp. 9–31.

Freedman, Robert O. (ed.) (1982), *Israel in the Begin Era* (New York: Praeger).

Freudenheim, Yehoshua (1973), *Government in Israel, Its Structure and Legal Foundations* (Hebrew), 5th ed. (Jerusalem: Rubin Mass; 1st ed. Munich, 1973).

Friedlander, Dov, and Goldscheider, Calvin (1979), *The Population of Israel* (New York: Columbia University Press).

Friedmann, Menachem (1977), *Society and Religion. The Non-Zionist Orthodox in Eretz Israel, 1918–1936* (Hebrew) (Jerusalem: Yad Yitzhak Ben-Zvi Publications).

Galnoor, Yitzhak (1982), *Communication and Politics. The·Development of Israeli Democracy* (Beverly Hills, Calif., and London: Sage).

Gerber, Haim (1979), 'The population of Syria and Palestine in the nineteenth century', *Asian and African Studies*, vol. 13, no. 1 (March) pp. 58–80.

Gerson, Allan (1978), *Israel, the West Bank and International Law* (London: Frank Cass).

Gertz, A. (ed.) (1947), *Statistical Handbook of Jewish Palestine* (Jerusalem: Jewish Agency).

Giersch, Herbert (ed.) (1980), *The Economic Integration of Israel in the EEC*, (Tübingen: Mohr).

Giladi, Dan (1973), *Jewish Palestine during the Fourth Alija Period 1924–1929. Economic and Social Aspects* (Hebrew) (Tel-Aviv: Am Oved).

Gilbert, Martin (1974), *The Arab–Israeli Conflict. Its History in Maps* (London: Weidenfeld & Nicolson).

Ginor, Fanny (1979), *Socio-Economic Disparities in Israel* (Tel-Aviv: Tel-Aviv University and New Brunswick, NJ: Transaction Books).

Gitelman, Zvi (1982), *Becoming Israelis. Political Resocialization of Soviet and American Immigrants* (New York: Praeger).

Gitelson, Susan A. (1974), *Israel's African Setback in Perspective* (Jerusalem: Hebrew University, Jerusalem Papers on Peace Problems).

Glatt, Joseph (1973), 'The historical development of Histadrut' PhD dissertation, Columbia University, New York.

Globerson, Arye (1970), *The Bureaucratic Elite in the Israeli Civil Service* (Hebrew) (Tel-Aviv: Institute of Management Press).

Golan, Galia (1979), *Yom Kippur and After. The Soviet Union and the Middle East Crisis* (Cambridge: Cambridge University Press).

Goldberg, Giora, and Ben-Zadok, Ephraim (1983), 'Regionalism and territorial cleavage in formation. Jewish settlement in the administered territories' (Hebrew), *State, Government and International Relations*, no. 21, (Spring), pp. 69–94.

Goldberg, Giora (1980), 'Democracy and representation in Israeli political parties', in Arian, 1980, pp. 101–17.

Goldberg, Giora, and Hoffman, Steven A. (1983), 'Nominations in Israel. The Politics of Institutionalization', in Arian, pp. 61–87.

Goldscheider, Calvin, and Friedlander, Dov (1982), 'Religiosity patterns in Israel', in *American Jewish Yearbook 1983* (New York: American Jewish Committee and Philadelphia: Jewish Publication Society of America), pp. 3–39.

Gonen, Amiram (1982), 'The geography of the electoral competition between the Labor alignment and the Likud in Jewish cities of Israel 1965–1981' (Hebrew), *State, Government and International Relations*, no. 19–20, pp. 63–87; in English in Caspi, Diskin and Gutmann, 1983, pp. 63–87.

Goren, Dina (1980), *Secrecy and the Right to Know* (Ramat-Gan: Turtledove).

Gorni, Yosef (1970), 'Changes in the social and political structure of the second *aliyah* (1904–1940)' (Hebrew), in Daniel Carpi (ed.), *Zionism. Studies in the History of the Zionist Movement and the Jews in Palestine*, Vol. 1 (Hebrew into English) (Tel-Aviv: Tel-Aviv University/Hakibbutz Hameuchad), pp. 204–46.

Gorni, Yosef (1973), *Ahdut Haawoda 1919–1930. The Ideological Principles and the Political System* (Hebrew) (Tel-Aviv: Tel-Aviv University/Hakibbutz Hameuchad).

Gottheil, Fred M. (1975), 'Arab immigration into pre-state Israel: 1922–1931', in Michael Curtis *et al.* (eds.), *The Palestinians. People, History, Politics* (New Brunswick, NJ: Transaction Books), pp. 30–41.

Gottlieb, Avi, and Yuchtman-Yaar, Ephraim (1983), 'Materialism, postmaterialism, and public views on socioeconomic policy, the case of Israel', *Comparative Political Studies*, vol. 16, no. 3, pp. 307–35.

Gradus, Yehuda (1983), 'The role of politics in regional inequality', *Annals of the Association of American Geographers*, vol. 73, no. 3, pp. 388–403.

Greenwald, Carol S. (1974), *Recession as a Policy Instrument: Israel 1965–1969* (London: C. Hurst).

Greilsammer, Alain (1978), *Les Communistes israeliens* (Paris: Presses de la Fondation Nationale des Sciences Politiques).

Gutman, Yechiel (1981), *The Attorney-General versus the Government* (Hebrew) (Jerusalem: Edanim).

Gutmann, Emanuel (1958), 'The development of local government in Palestine. Background to the study of local administration in Israel' PhD dissertation, Columbia University, New York.

Gutmann, Emanuel (ed.) (1984), *Israel and the Second Enlargement of the European Community. Political and Economic Aspects* (Jerusalem: Hebrew University, The European Research Center).

Gutmann, Emanuel, and Landau, Jakob M. (1975), 'The political elite and national leadership in Israel', in Lenczowski, 1975, pp. 163–99.

Gutmann, Emanuel, and Levy, Jakob, (eds.) (1976), *Israel's Governmental System. A Collection of Sources* (Hebrew), 3rd ed. (Jerusalem: Kaplan School of Economic and Social Sciences, Hebrew University).

Haberfeld, Jitzhak, and Nadler, Laurence (1979), 'Demographic characteristics of senior civil servants in the Israeli civil service' (Hebrew), *State, Government and International Relations*, no. 13, pp. 114–19.

Hacke, Christian (1985), *Amerikanische Nahost-Politik. Kontinuität und Wandel von Nixon bis Reagan* (Munich and Vienna: Oldenbourg).

Halevy, Nadav, and Klinov-Malul, Ruth (1975), *The Economic Development of Israel* (Hebrew) (Jerusalem: Hebrew University Academon; original American edition, New York: Praeger, 1968).

Harari, Yehiel (1976), *The Arabs in Israel – 1976. Facts and Figures* (Hebrew) (Givat Haviva: Arab and Afro-Asian Sources).

Harkabi, Yehoshafat (1983), *The Bar Kokhba Syndrome* (New York: Rosel Books).

Harel, Aharon (1981), *Analysis of Elections to the Workers' Councils* (Hebrew) (Tel-Aviv: Histadrut, September).

Hareven, Alouph (ed.) (1983), *Every Sixth Israeli. Relations between the Jewish Majority and the Arab Minority in Israel* (Jerusalem: Van Leer Foundation).

Harris, William W. (1980), *Taking Root. Israeli Settlement in the West Bank, the Golan and Gaza-Sinai, 1967–1980* (Chichester: Research Studies Press/Wiley).

Heinsohn, Gunnar (ed.) (1982), *Das Kibbutz-Modell. Bestandsaufnahme einer alternativen Wirtschafts- und Lebensform nach sieben Jahrzehnten* (Frankfurt am Main: Edition Suhrkamp).

Herman, Simon N. (1977), *Jewish Identity. A Social Psychological Perspective* (Beverly Hills, Calif., and London: Sage).

Hérodote (1983), Révue de géographie et de géopolitique: Géopolitiques au proche-orient, no. 29–30, (April–September).

Herzog, Hanna (1984), 'Political ethnicity in Israel' (Hebrew), *Megamot*, vol. 28, no. 2/3 (March), pp. 332–54.

Heth, Michael (1967), *The Legal Framework of Economic Policy in Israel* (New York: Praeger).

Histadrut (1977), *Statistical Yearbook 1968–1977.* (Hebrew) (Tel-Aviv: Allgemeine Histadrut).

Hof, Frederic C. (1985), *Galilee Divided. The Israel–Lebanon Frontier 1916–1984* (Boulder, Colo.: Westview Press).

Hoffman, Jochanon, and Nager, Kamil (1985), 'The readiness for intact social contacts between Jewish and Arab secondary students' (Hebrew), University of Haifa, un-published ms. kindly provided by the authors.

Hoffman, Steven (1980), 'Candidate selection in Israel's parliament. The realities of change', *Middle East Journal*, vol. 34, pp. 285–301.

Hooker, M. B. (ed.) (1983), *Islam in South-East Asia* (Leiden: Brill).

Horowitz, Dan, and Lissak, Moshe (1977), *The Origins of the Israeli Polity. The Political System of the Jewish Community in Palestine under the Mandate* (Hebrew) (Tel-Aviv: Am Oved).

Horowitz, Dan, and Lissak, Moshe (1978), *The Origins of the Israeli Polity. Palestine under the Mandate* (Chicago: University of Chicago Press).

Horowitz, David (1967), *The Economics of Israel* (New York: Pergamon).

Horowitz, David (1972), *The Enigma of Economic Growth: A Case Study of Israel* (New York: Praeger).

Horowitz, David (1973), 'Economic development', in *Israel Pocket Library*, vol. Economy, (Jerusalem: Keter), pp. 1–101.

Ichilov, Orit (1981), 'Citizenship orientations of city and *kibbutz* youth in Israel', *International Journal of Political Education*, vol. 4, pp. 305–17.

Index to International Public Opinion (yearly) (Westport, Conn.: Greenwood Press).

IIASR (1980), *The Public and the Local Elections of November 1978* (Hebrew) (Jerusalem: IIASR).

Immigration (1975), *Immigration to Israel 1948–1972, Part II, Composition by Period of Immigration* (Jerusalem: Central Bureau of Statistics).

Isaac, Rael J. (1976), *Israel Divided. Ideological Politics in the Jewish State* (Baltimore, Md.: Johns Hopkins University Press).

Isaac, Rael J. (1981), *Party and Politics in Israel. Three Visions of a Jewish State* (New York and London: Longman).

Israel Pocket Library (1973 ff.), 15 vols. (Jerusalem: Keter).

Jörgensen, A. (1984), *Israel intern* (Berlin, GDR: Militärverlag).

Kahanman, Ira, and Levinson, Hana (1980), *Public Attitudes towards Minister Hurvitz's New Economic Scheme* (Hebrew) (Jerusalem: IIASR), February.

Kalcheim, Chaim (1979), 'Local income resource and the dependence on central government as viewed by local government spokesmen in Israel' (Hebrew), *State, Government and International Relations*, no. 13 (Winter), pp. 101–10.

Karmon, Yehuda (1983), *Israel. Eine geographische Landeskunde* (Darmstadt: Wissenschafliche Buchgesellschaft).

Katzenstein, Liora (1983), 'From Reparations to Rehabilitation. The Origins of Israeli–German Relations', dissertation, University of Geneva.

Kaufmann, Edy, Shapira, Yoram, and Barromi, Joel (1976), *Israeli–Latin American Relations* (New Brunswick, NJ: Transaction Books).

Kerbe, Nathalie (1975), *L'Ombudsman israélien* (Paris: A. Pedone).

Key, V. O. (1955), 'A theory of critical elections', *Journal of Politics*, vol. 17, pp. 1 ff.

Kieval, Gershon R. (1983), *Party Politics in Israel and the Occupied Territories* (Westport, Conn., and London: Greenwood Press).

Kimmerling, Baruch (1983a), *Zionism and Territory. The Socio Territorial Dimensions of Zionist Politics* (Berkeley, Calif.: University of California Press).

Kimmerling, Baruch (1983b), *Zionism and Economy* (Cambridge, Mass.: Schenkman).

Kiryat Sefer. Bibliographical Quarterly of the Jewish National and University Library (Jerusalem).

Klayman, Maxwell I. (1970), *The Moshav in Israel* (New York: Praeger).

Klein, Claude (1983), *Le Système politique d'Israél* (Paris: Presses Universitaires de France).

Klieman, Aaron S. (1984), *Israeli Arms Sales: Perspectives and Prospects* (Tel-Aviv: Tel-Aviv University).

Klieman, Aaron S. (1985), *Israel's Global Reach. Arms Sales as Diplomacy* (Washington, DC: Pergamon-Brassey's).

Knesset 9 (1975), *Who's Who in the Ninth Knesset?* (Hebrew) (Jerusalem: Knesset).

Knesset 10 (1982), *Who's Who in the Tenth Knesset?* (Hebrew) (Jerusalem: Maariv).

Krauss, Vered (1976), 'The social ranking of professions in Israel', (Hebrew), dissertation for the Hebrew University of Jerusalem.

Krausz, Ernest (ed.) (1980), *Studies of Israeli Society, Migration, Ethnicity and Community* (New Brunswick, NJ, and London: Transaction Books).

Krausz, Ernest (ed.) (1983), *The Sociology of the Kibbutz. Studies of Israeli Society*, Vol. II (New Brunswick, NJ, and London: Transaction Books).

Kressel, G. (1977), *A Guide to the Hebrew Press* (Zug, CH: Interdocumentation Company).

Landau, Jacob M. (1971), *The Arabs in Israel. A Political Study* (Tel-Aviv: Maarahot, and London: Oxford University Press).

Laqueur, Walter Z. (ed.) (1970), *The Israel–Arab Reader* (Harmondsworth: Penguin).

Laqueur, Walter (1972), *A History of Zionism* (London: Weidenfeld & Nicolson).

Laqueur, Walter Z. (1975), *Der Weg zum Staat Israel. Geschichte des Zionismus* (Vienna: Europaverlag).

Latin America and Caribbean Contemporary Record, 2 vols. to 1985, Jack W. Hopkins (ed.) (New York and London: Holmes & Meier).

Lehman-Wilzig, Sam (1981), 'Public protest and systemic stability in Israel, 1960–1979', in Lehman-Wilzig and Susser, 1981, pp. 171–210.

Lehman-Wilzig, Sam N. (1982), 'Public protest against central and local government in Israel, 1950–1979', *Jewish Journal of Sociology*, vol. 24, no. 2, pp. 99–115.

Lehman-Wilzig, Sam, and Goldberg, Giora (1983), 'Religious protest and police reaction in a theo-democracy. 1950–1979', *Journal of Church and State* (Summer), quoted from the authors' copy.

Lehman-Wilzig, Sam, and Susser, Bernhard (eds.) (1981), *Public Life in Israel and the Diaspora* (Ramat-Gan: Bar Ilan University Press).

Lerner, Abba, and Ben-Shahar, Haim (1975), *The Economics of Efficiency and Growth. Lessons from Israel and the West Bank* (Cambridge, Mass.: Ballinger).

Lesch, Ann M. (1983), 'Israeli settlements on the West Bank. Mortgaging the future', *Journal of South Asian and Middle Eastern Studies*, vol. 17, no. 1 (Fall), pp. 3–23.

Leviathan, Uri (1980), 'Attitudes of the Jewish population of Israel towards the *kibbutz* movement and the possibility of living in a *kibbutz*', (Hebrew), *Megamot*, vol. 26, no. 2 (December), pp. 232–6.

Leviathan, Uri (1983): *The Kibbutz and Israeli Society* (Hebrew) (Haifa: University of Haifa Center for Kibbutz Studies).

Levinsohn, Hannah (1979), *The Positions of the Public on Settlements and Autonomy* (Hebrew) (Jerusalem: IIASR and Communications Institute, Hebrew University, 13 August 1979).

Levy, Schlomit, and Gutman, E. L. (1974), *The Will to Stay in Israel* (Hebrew) (Jerusalem: IIASR Communications Institute, Hebrew University).

Levy, Schlomit, and Gutman, E. L. (1978), *Changes in Public Assessments of Government's Handling of Issues, and the Voter's Intentions* (Hebrew) (Jerusalem: Israel Institute of Applied Social Research, Communications Institute, Hebrew University).

Levy, Schlomit, and Gutman, E. L. (1979a), *Changes in the Attitudes of the Voters* (Hebrew) (Jerusalem: Israel Institute of Applied Social Research, Bulletin No. 49).

Levy, Schlomit, and Gutman, E. L. (1979b), *Towards a Prediction of Voting for the Next Knesset* (Hebrew) (Jerusalem: IIASR and Communications Institute, Hebrew University), March.

Levy, Schlomit, and Gutman, E. L. (1981), *The Voters of Tehija* (Hebrew) (Jerusalem: IIASR, May).

Levy, Schlomit, and Gutman, Louis (1971), *Zionism and the Jewish People in the Eyes of the Israeli Public* (Hebrew) (Jerusalem: Israel Institute of Applied Research, Communications Institute, Hebrew University).

Levy, Schlomit, and Gutmann, Louis (1976a), *Values and Attitudes of Israel High School Youth* (Hebrew) (Jerusalem: The Israel Institute of Applied Social Research).

Lichtenstein, J. (1974), '*The Herut movement. Structure and internal processes*', MA thesis, Hebrew University, Jerusalem.

Liebman, Charles S. (1977), *Pressure without Sanctions. The Influence of World Jewry on Israeli Policy* (Rutherford, NJ: Fairleigh Dickinson University Press, and London: Associated University Press).

Liebman, Charles S., and Don-Yehiya, Eliezer (1984a), *Civil Religion in Israel. Traditional Judaism and Political Culture in the Jewish State* (Berkeley, Calif.: University of California Press).

Liebman, Charles S., and Don-Yehiya, Eliezer (1984b), *Religion and Politics in Israel* (Bloomington, Ind.: Indiana University Press).

Likhovski, Eliahu S. (1971), *Israel's Parliament. The Law of the Knesset* (Oxford: Clarendon Press).

Lissak, Moshe (1981), *The Elites of the Jewish Community in Palestine* (Hebrew) (Tel-Aviv: Am Oved).

Lissak, Moshe (1984), 'The ethnic problem and ethnic organizations in the Jewish community in Palestine' (Hebrew), *Megamot* (special issue), vol. 28, no. 2/3 (March), pp. 295–315.

Lissak, Moshe, and Ronel, Nurit (eds.) (1984), 'The Ethnic Problem. Continuity and change' (Hebrew), *Megamot*, vol. 28, no. 2/3 (March).

Local Authorities (1979), *Results of Elections to the Local Authorities 7 November 1978* (Hebrew) (Jerusalem: Ministry of the Interior, Inspector General of Elections).

Lorch, Nathaniel (1982), 'Latin America and Israel', *Jerusalem Quarterly*, no. 22, pp. 70–84.

Louis, Wm Roger (1984), *The British Empire in the Middle East 1945–1951* (Oxford: Clarendon Press).

Luft, Gerda (1977), *Heimkehr ins Umbekannte. Eine Darstellung der Einwanderung von Juden aus Deutschland nach Palästina vom Aufstieg Hitlers zur Macht bis zum Ausbruch des Zweiten Weltkriegs 1933–1939* (Wuppertal: Peter Hamer Verlag).

Lustick, Ian (1980), *Arabs in the Jewish State, Israel's Control of a National Minority* (Austin, Texas, and London: University of Texas Press).

Lustick, Ian (1981), 'Israel and the West Bank after Elon Moreh: The mechanics of de facto annexation', *Middle East Journal*, vol. 35, no. 4, pp. 557–77.

Luttwak, Edward, and Horowitz, Dan (1975), *The Israeli Army* (New York: Harper & Row).

Mahler, Gregory S. (1981), *The Knesset. Parliament in the Israeli Political System* (Rutherford, NJ: Fairleigh Dickinson University Press, and London: Associated University Press).

Mahler, Gregory S. (ed.) (1982), *Readings on the Israeli Political System* (Washington, DC: University Press of America).

Mahler, Gregory S. (1985), *Bibliography of Israeli Politics* (Boulder, Colo.: Westview Press).

Mahler, Gregory S., and Trilling, Richard J. (1975), 'Coalition behavior and cabinet formation, the case of Israel', *Comparative Political Studies*, vol. 8, pp. 200–33.

Malkosh, Noah (1962), *La Histadrouth* (Tel-Aviv: Institut afro-asiatique d'Études Syndicales et Cooperatives).

Mansour, Antoine (1983), 'L'économie israélienne: Le militarisme et l'expansionisme comme solution à la crise', *Peuples méditerranéens*, no. 25 (October–December, pp. 47–62.

Margalit, Elkana (1971), *'Hashomer Hazair' – From Youth Community to Revolutionary Marxism (1913–1936)* (Hebrew) (Tel-Aviv University: Hakibbutz Hameuhad).

Mar'i, Sami Khalil (1978), *Arab Education in Israel* (Syracuse, NY: Syracuse University Press).

Marmorstein, Emilie (1969), *Heaven at Bay* (Oxford: Oxford University Press).

Meari, Mahmoud (1978), *Identity of Arab Academics in Israel* (Jerusalem: IIASR for the Ford Foundation).

Medding, Peter Y. (1972), *Mapai in Israel, Political Organization and Government in a New Society* (London: Cambridge University Press).

Meier-Cronemeyer, Hermann (1969), *Kibbutzim-Geschichte, Geist und Gestalt* (Hannover: Verlag für Literatur und Zeitgeschehen).

Merhav, Peretz (1972), *Die israelische Linke. Zionismus und Arbeiterbewegung in der Geschichte Israels* (Frankfurt am Main: Europäische Verlagsanstalt).

Merhav, Peretz (1980), *The Israeli Left: History, Problems, Documents* (Cranbury, NJ: A. S. Barnes).

Michaely, Michael (1975), *Foreign Trade Regimes and Economic Development, Israel* (New York and London: Columbia University Press).

Middle East Contemporary Survey, ed. Colin Legum *et al.*, vols. 1–7 (1978 ff.) (New York and London: Holmes & Meier), vols. 8 ff. (Boulder, Colo.: Westview Press).

Mielke, Siegfried (ed.) (1983), *Internationales Gewerkschaftshandbuch* (Opladen: Leske & Budrich).

Mintz, Alex (1985), 'Military-industrial linkages in Israel', *Armed Forces and Society*, vol. 12, no. 1, pp. 9–27.

Nachmias, David, and Rosenbloom, David H. (1978), *Bureaucratic Culture. Citizens and Administrators in Israel* (New York: St Martin's Press).

Nadelmann, Ethan A. (1981), 'Israel and Black Africa: A rapprochement?', *Journal of Modern African Studies*, vol. 19, no. 2, pp. 183–219.

Neuberg, Assia (1977), *The State of Israel. An Annotated Bibliography*, 2 vols. (Jerusalem: The Center for Public Libraries in Israel).

Neustadt, Amnon (1983), *Die deutsch-israelischen Bezwihungen im Schatten der EG-Nahostpolitik* (Frankfurt am Main: Haag & Herchem).

Newman, David (ed.) (1985), *The Impact of Gush Emunim Politics and Settlement in the West Bank*, (London: Croom Helm).

Nikitina, Galina S. (1973), *The State of Israel. A Historical Economic and Political Study* (Moscow: Progress Publishers).

Nisan, Mordechai (1978), *Israel and the Territories. A Study in Control, 1967–1977* (Ramat-Gan: Turtledove).

Nyrop, Richard F. (ed.) (1979), *Israel. A Country Study* (Washington, DC: The American University Press).

Oded, Arye (1983), 'Africa, Israel and the Arabs: On the restoration of Israel–African diplomatic relations', *Jerusalem Journal of International Relations*, vol. 6, no. 3, pp. 48–70.

Ophir, Arie (1973), *The Kibbutz in the Labour Movement* (Hebrew) (Tel-Aviv: Am Oved).

Orchan, Eliat, and Samuel, Jitzhak (1981), 'The influence of *kibbutz* attractiveness on the willingness to enter and become a member of a *kibbutz* (Hebrew), *Megamot*, vol. 26, no. 4 (June), pp. 390–404.

Orland, Nachum (1983), *Die Cherut* (Munich: Tuduv).

Osia, Kunirum (1981), *Israel, South Africa and Black Africa* (Washington, DC: University Press of America).

Pack, Howard (1971) *Structural Change and Economic Policy in Israel* (New Haven, Conn.: Yale University Press).

Peled, Elad (1979), 'The hidden agenda of educational policy in Israel: The interrelationship between the political system and the educational system'. PhD dissertation, Columbia University, New York.

Peled, Elad (1984), 'Political power and ideological perceptions – determinants of Israel's educational policy with regard to disadvantaged children' (Hebrew), in Lissak and Ronel, 1984, pp. 355–69.

Peled, Tsiyona, and Bar-Gal, David (1983), *Intervention Activities in Arab–Jewish Relations. Conceptualization. Classification and Evaluation* (Jerusalem: IIASR).

Peled, Yoav, and Shafin, Gershon (1985), 'Thorns in your eyes: The socio-economic basis of the Kach vote', unpublished ms. kindly provided by the authors.

Peled, Ziona (1979), *On Social Distance between Jews and Arabs: Über die gesellschaftliche Distanz zwischen Juden und in Israel* (Hebrew) (Jerusalem: IIASR, Information Sheet No. 50), pp. 8–11.

Peled, Ziona (1980), 'On social distance between Jews and Arabs in Israel', in *Israel Institute of Applied Social Research Report 1978–1979*, ed. Haya Gratch, pp. 19–21.

Penniman, Howard, R. (ed.) (1979), *Israel at the Polls. The Knesset Elections of 1977* (Washington, DC: American Enterprise Institute).

Penniman, Howard R. (ed.) (1984), *Israel at the Polls. The Knesset Elections of 1981* (Washington, DC: American Enterprise Institute).

Peres, Yochanan (1976), *Ethnic Relations in Israel* (Hebrew) (Tel-Aviv: Sifriat Hapoalim).

Peres, Yochanan, and Shemer, Sara (1983), 'The ethnic factor in elections', Caspi, Diskin and Gutmann, 1983, pp. 89–111.

Peretz, Don (1985), *The West Bank. History, Politics, Society and Economy* (Boulder, Colo.: Westview Press).

Peretz, Don, and Smooha, Sammy (1981), 'Israel's Tenth Knesset elections', *Middle East Journal*, vol. 35, no. 4, pp. 506 ff.

Peri, Mordechai (1977), 'The responsiveness of the Israeli national educational policy-making system to demands for change, 1973–1975', PhD dissertation, University of Oregon.

Peri, Yoram (1973), 'Processes of Evolution of a New Civilian Elite of Senior Reserve Officers in Israel' (Hebrew), MA (Sociology), Hebrew University of Jerusalem.

Peri, Yoram (1974), 'The ideological character of the military elite in Israel', *State, Government and International Relations'* no. 6 (Fall), pp. 142–55.

Peri, Yoram (1983), *Between Battles and Ballots, Israeli Military in Politics* (London: Cambridge University Press).

Perlmutter, Amos (1977), *Politics and the Military in Israel. Nation-Building and Role Expansion*, 2nd ed. (London: Frank Cass).

Pijpers, Alfred, and Allen, D. (eds.) (1984), *European Foreign Policy-Making and the Arab–Israeli Conflict* (Den Haag: Nijhoff).

Poll, Salomon, and Krausz, Ernest (eds.) (1975), *On Ethnic and Religious Diversity in Israel* (Ramat-Gan: Bar Ilan University).

Porat-Martin, Hedva (1979), 'Rabbinical and civil courts in Israel: A dual legal system in action' PhD dissertation, University of California.

Preuss, Walter (1965), *The Labour Movement in Israel* (Jerusalem: R. Mass).

Primakov, Y. M. (1979), *Anatomy of the Middle East Conflict* (Moscow: Nauka Publishing House).

Public Complaints Commissioner (1979), *Annual Report*, no. 8 (Hebrew) (Jerusalem).

Quandt, William B. (1977), *Decade of Decisions. American Policy toward the Arab-Israeli Conflict, 1967–1976* (Berkeley, Calif.: University of California Press).

Rabinovich, Itamar, and Reinharz, Jehuda (eds.) (1984), *Israel in the Middle East. Documents and Readings on Society, Politics and Foreign Relations, 1948 to the Present* (Oxford: Oxford University Press).

Rauch, Max (1971), 'Higher education in Israel', PhD dissertation, University of California.

Rayman, Paula (1981), *The Kibbutz Community and Nation Building* (Princeton, NJ: Princeton University Press).

Reich, Bernard (1977), *Quest for Peace. United States–Israel Relations and the Arab–Israeli Conflict* (New Brunswick, NJ: Transaction Books).

Reich, Bernard (1984), *The United States and Israel. The Dynamics of Influence* (New York: Praeger).

Reshef, Yonathan (1983–4), 'Government and Histadrut. An Anatomy of Cooperation and Confrontation' (Hebrew), *State, Government and International Relations*, no. 22 (Winter), pp. 75–90.

Reuveni, Jakob (1974), *The Israeli Civil Service. Its Development in the Years 1948–1973* (Hebrew) (Ramat-Gan: Massada).

Robbins, Marc L. (1981), 'The strategy of innocence: Political resocialization of Oriental Jews in Israel', PhD dissertation, Princeton University.

Robinson, Donna (1970), 'Patrons and saints. A study of the career patterns of higher civil servants in Israel', PhD thesis, Columbia University, New York.

Ro'i, Yaacov (1974), *From Encroachment to Involvement. A Documented Study of Soviet Policy in the Middle East, 1945–1973* (New Brunswick, NJ: Transaction Books).

Ro'i, Yaacov (1980), *Soviet Decision-Making in Practice. The USSR and Israel 1947–1954* (New Brunswick, NJ: Transaction Books).

Rosner, Menachem, *et al.* (eds.) (1978), *The Second Generation. Continuity and Change in the Kibbutz* (Hebrew) (Tel-Aviv: Hakibbutz Haartzi-Hashomer Hatzair-Sifriat Hapoalim).

Rosner, Menachem, and Ovnath, Alexander (1979), 'Seven years later: changes in perceptions and attitudes of *kibbutz*-born adults and their causes', *Journal of Rural Cooperation*, vol. 7, nos. 1–2, pp. 65–85.

Rubenstein, Sondra M. (1985), *The Communist Movement in Palestine and Israel, 1919–1984* (Boulder, Colo.: Westview Press).

Rubinstein, Amnon (1974), *Israeli Constitutional Law*, 2nd rev. ed. (Jerusalem and Tel-Aviv: Schocken).

Rubinstein, Amnon (1980), *Israeli Constitutional Law*, 3rd rev. ed. (Tel-Aviv: Schocken).

Sachar, Howard M. (1977), *A History of Israel. From the Rise of Zionism to Our Time* (Oxford: Blackwell).

Saddy, Fehmy (1983), *Arab–Latin American Relations* (New Brunswick, NJ: Transaction Books).

Safran, Nadav (1978), *Israel, The Embattled Ally* (Cambridge, Mass.: The Belknap Press of Harvard University Press).

Sager, Samual (1985), *The Parliamentary System of Israel* (Syracuse, NY: Syracuse University Press).

Sandler, Shmuel, and Frisch, Hillel (1984), *Israel, the Palestinians, and the West Bank. A Study in Intercommunal Conflict* (Lexington, Mass., and Toronto: Lexington Books).

Sankari, Farouk A. (1979), 'The costs and gains of Israeli pursuit of influence in Africa', *Middle Eastern Studies*, vol. 15, no. 2, pp. 270 ff.

Sassoon, David M. (1968), 'The Israeli legal system', *American Journal of Contemporary Law*, vol. 16 (Baltimore), pp. 405 ff.

Schechtman, Joseph, and Benari, Y. (1970), *History of the Revisionist Movement* (Tel-Aviv: Hadar).

Schiff, Gary S. (1977), *Tradition and Politics. The Religious Parties of Israel* (Detroit, Mich.: Wayne State University Press).

Schiff, Zeev, and Haber, Eitan (1976), *Israel, Army and Defence. A Dictionary* (Hebrew) (Tel-Aviv: Zmora, Bitan, Modan).

Schnall, David J. (1979), *Radical Dissent in Contemporary Israeli Politics. Cracks in the Wall* (New York: Praeger).

Schoneveld, J. (1976), *The Bible in Israeli Education* (Assan and Amsterdam: Van Gorcum).

Seligmann, Rafael (1982), *Israels Sicherheitspolitik* (Munich: Bernard & Graefe).

Seligson, Mitchell A., and Caspi, Dan (1983), 'Arabs in Israel. Political tolerance and ethnic conflict', *Journal of Applied Behavioral Science*, vol. 19, no. 1, pp. 55–66.

Seliktar, Ofira (1980), 'The cost of vigilance in Israel: linking the economic and social cost of defense', *Journal of Peace Research*, vol. 17, no. 4, pp. 339–55.

Semyonov, Moshe, and Krauss, Vered (1983), 'Gender, ethnicity and income inequality. The Israeli experience', *International Journal of Comparative Sociology*, vol. 24, no. 3–4, pp. 258–72.

Shaked, Haim, and Rabinovich, Itamar (eds.) (1980), *The Middle East and the United States. Perceptions and Policies* (New Brunswick, NJ: Transaction Books).

Shamgar, Meir (ed.) (1982), *Military Government in the Territories Administered by Israel 1967–1980* (Jerusalem: Hebrew University).

Shamir, Michal, and Arian, Asher (1982), 'The ethnic vote in Israel's 1981 election', (Hebrew), *State, Government and International Relations*, nos. 19–20, pp. 88–104; in English in Caspi, Diskin and Gutmann, 1983, pp. 88–104.

Shamir, Michal, and Sullivan, John L. (1985), 'Jews and Arabs in Israel. Everybody hates somebody, sometime,' *Journal of Conflict Resolution*, vol. 29, no. 2, pp. 283–305.

Shapira, Rina, Adler, Haim, Lerner, Miri, and Peleg, Rahel (1979), *Blue Collar and White Collar. A Study on the Social World of Youth Movement Graduates in Israel* (Hebrew) (Tel-Aviv: Am Oved).

Shapira, Rina, and Peleg, Rachel (1984), 'From Blue Shirt to White Collar', *Youth and Society*, vol. 16, no. 2, pp. 195–216.

Shapiro, Yonathan (1976), *The Formative Years of the Israeli Labour Party. The Organization of Power 1919–1930* (London: Sage).

Shapiro, Yonathan (1977), *Democracy in Israel* (Hebrew) (Ramat-Gan: Massada).

Sharansky, Ira (1979), *Whither the State? Politics and Public Enterprise in Three Countries* (Chatham, NJ: Chatman House Publications).

Shavit, Yaacov (1978), *Revisionism in Zionism. The Revisionist Movement. The Plan for Colonizatory and Social Ideas 1925–1935* (Hebrew) (Tel-Aviv: Yariv-Hadar).

Shavit, Yossi (1984), 'Tracking and Ethnicity in Israeli Secondary Education', *American Sociological Review*, vol. 49, (April), pp. 210–20.

Sheffer, Gabriel (1984), 'The uncertain future of American Jewry–Israel relations', *Jerusalem Quarterly*, no. 32, pp. 66–80.

Sheffer, Gabriel (ed.) (1986), *Modern Diasporas in International Politics* (London: Croom Helm).

Sherman, Neal (1982), 'From government to opposition: the rural settlement movements of the Israel Labour Party in the wake of the election of 1977', *International Journal of Middle Eastern Studies*, vol. 14, pp. 53–69.

Shichor, Y. (1976), 'The Middle East in China's foreign policy 1949–1974', 2 vols, dissertation, London University.

Shimshoni, Daniel (1982), *Israeli Democracy. The Middle of the Journey* (New York: The Free Press).

Shlaim, Avi, and Tanter, Raymond (1978), 'Decision process. Choice and consequences: Israel's deep penetration bombing in Egypt, 1970', *World Politics*, vol. 30, pp. 483–516.

Shokeid, Moshe (1983), 'Commitment and paradox in sociological research. School integration in Israel', *Ethnic and Racial Studies*, vol. 6, no. 2, pp. 198–212.

Shokeid, Moshe (1984), 'Precepts versus Tradition. Religious Trends among Middle Eastern Jews' (Hebrew), *Megamot*, vol. 28, no. 2/3 (March) pp. 250–64.

Shokeid, Moshe, and Deshen, Shlomo (1977), *The Generation of Transition: Continuity and Change among North African Immigrants in Israel* (Hebrew) (Jerusalem: Ben-Zwi Institute, Hebrew University).

Shokeid, Moshe, and Deshen, Shlomo (1982), *Distant Relations, Ethnicity and Politics among Arabs and North African Jews in Israel* (New York: Praeger).

Sieben, Hermann (1982), *Jugend und Jugendarbeit in Israel. Versuch einer Darstellung* (Bonn: Internationaler Jugendaustauschund Besucherdienst).

Sirkin, Ronald M. (1971), '*Coalition, Conflict and Compromise. The Party Politics of Israel*', PhD thesis, Pennsylvania State University.

Smith, Herbert (1972), 'Analysis of voting', in Arian, 1972, pp. 63–80.

Smooha, Sammy (1978), *Israel, Pluralism and Conflict* (London: Routledge & Kegan Paul).

Smooha, Sammy (1980), *The Orientation and Politicization of the Arab Minority in Israel* (Haifa: The Jewish-Arab Centre, Institute of Middle East Studies).

Smooha, Sammy, and Peretz, Don (1982), 'The Arabs in Israel', *Journal of Conflict Resolution*, vol. 26, no. 3 (September), pp. 451–84.

Society in Israel (1976), *Selected Statistics* (Jerusalem: Central Bureau of Statistics).

Sprinzak, Ehud (1977), 'Extreme politics in Israel', *Jerusalem Quarterly*, no. 5, pp. 33–47.

Sprinzak, Ehud (1981), 'Gush-Emunim. The tip of the iceberg', *Jerusalem Quarterly*, no. 21, pp. 28–47.

State Comptroller (1983), *Yearbook No. 33* (Hebrew) (Jerusalem).

Statistical Abstract of Israel (various years) (Jerusalem: Central Bureau of Statistics).

Stein, Gustav, and Steinbach, Udo (eds.) (1979), *The Contemporary Middle Eastern Scene. Basic Issues and Major Trends* (Opladen: Leske & Budrich).

Steinitz, Ruth (1984), 'Educational policy and the ethnic gap', in Lissak and Ronel, 1984, pp. 370–86.

Stone, Julius (1981), *Israel and Palestine. Assault on the Law of Nations* (Baltimore, Md., and London: Johns Hopkins University Press).

Stone, Russell A., with the collaboration of Louis Gutmann and Shlomit Levy (1982), *Social Change in Israel. Attitudes and Events, 1967–79* (New York: Praeger).

Sullivan, John L., Shamir, M., Walsch, P., and Roberts, N. S. (1985), *Political Tolerance in Context. Support for Unpopular Minorities in Israel, New Zealand, and the United States* (Boulder, Colo.: Westview Press).

Tabory, Ephraim (1982), 'Reform and conservative Judaism in Israel: A social and religious profile', in *American Jewish Yearbook 1983* (New York: American Jewish Committee, and Philadelphia: Jewish Publication Society of America), pp. 41–61.

Talbar, Michael A. (1973), 'Foreign trade', in Israel Pocket Library Volume *Economy* (Jerusalem: Keter), pp. 137–45.

Tatsachen (1975), *Tatsachen über Israel* (Jerusalem: Foreign Office).

Tessler, Mark A. (1977), 'Israel's Arabs and the Palestinian problem', *Middle East Journal*, vol. 31, no. 3, pp. 313–29.

Torgovnik, Efraim (1979), 'A movement for change in a stable system', in Penniman, 1979, pp. 147–171; also in Arian, 1980, pp. 75 ff.

Vital, David (1975), *The Origins of Zionism* (Oxford: Oxford University Press).

Vital, David (1982), *Zionism: The Formative Years* (Oxford: Oxford University Press).

Viteles, Harry (1966–8), *A History of the Cooperative Movement in Israel*, 7 vols. (London: Vallentine, Mitchell).

Wallach, Jehuda L. (1984) '. . . *und mit der anderen hielten sie die Waffe*' (Koblenz: Bernard & Graefe).

Wehling, Gerd-Rudolf (1977), *Die politischen Parteien im Verfassungssystem Israels* (Berlin: Dunker & Humblot).

Weimann, Gabriel (1984), 'Cross-ethnic acquaintance networks. The "small world" experiment in Israel' (Hebrew), in Lissak and Ronel, 1984, pp. 444–54.

Weintraub, Dov, Lissak, Moshe, and Azmon, Yael (1960), *Moshava, Kibbutz and Moshav* (Ithaca, NY: Cornell University Press).

Weisbrod, Lilly (1981), 'Delegitimation and legitimation as a continuous process: A case study of Israel', *Middle East Journal*, vol. 35, no. 4, pp. 527–43.

Weisbrod, Lilly (1984), 'Protest and dissidence in Israel', in Aronoff, 1984a, pp. 51–68.

Weisburd, David, and Vinitzky, Vered (1984), 'Vigilantism as Rational Social Control: The Case of the Gush Emunim Settlers', in Aronoff, 1984a, pp. 69–87.

Wiener, Daniel (ed.) (1984), *Shalom. Israels Friedensbewegung* (Reibek bei Hamburg: Rororo aktuell).

Weiss, Shevah (1979), *The Change of Power. May 1977–November 1978* (Hebrew) (Tel-Aviv: Am Oved).

Weiss, Shevah (1970), *Typology of Local Elected Officials and the Problem of Stability in Israeli Local Politics* (Hebrew) (Jerusalem: Hebrew University, Academic Press).

Weiss, Shevah (1972), *Local Government in Israel* (Hebrew) (Tel-Aviv: Am Oved).

Weiss, Shevah (1973), *Politicians in Israel* (Hebrew) (Tel-Aviv: Achiasaf).

Weiss, Shevah (1977), 'The Ninth Knesset: An initial analysis of its composition and Patterns of Recruitment of Knesset Members', (Hebrew), *State, Government and International Relations*, no. 11, pp. 26–39.

Wilson, Harold (1981), *The Chariot of Israel. Britain, America and the State of Israel* (London: Weidenfeld & Nicolson).

Wolfenson, Avraham (1979), 'Party newspapers in the political process', PhD dissertation, Hebrew University, Jerusalem.

Wolffsohn, Michael (1978), 'Religion and politics in Israel', *Orient*, vol. 19, no. 2, pp. 88–117.

Wolffsohn, Michael (1979a), 'Israel's new economic order', in Stein and Steinbach, 1979, pp. 59–83.

Wolffsohn, Michael (1979b), 'Israel in der Epoche der Mapai/Arbeitspartei (I)', *Neue politische Literatur*, vol. 1, pp. 94–119.

Wolffsohn, Michael (1979c), 'Israel in der Epoche der Mapai/Arbeitspartei (II)', *Neue politische Literatur*, vol. 2, pp. 221–34.

Wolffsohn, Michael (1981), 'Israel's PLO policy, 1977–1981: Towards a dialogue?', *Orient*, vol. 22, no. 3, pp. 413–30.

Wolffsohn, Michael (1982), 'The European Community and the Middle East

1980/81', in Colin Legum *et al.* (eds.), *Middle East Contemporary Survey*, vol. 5, (New York and London: Holmes & Meier) pp. 80–101.

Wolffsohn, Michael (1983a), *Politik in Israel. Entwicklung und Struktur des politischen Systems* (Opladen: Leske & Budrich).

Wolffsohn, Michael (1983b), 'Israel', in Mielke, 1983, pp. 588–96.

Wolffsohn, Michael (1983c), 'Leben im Land der Mörder. Deutschlands Juden im Spannungsfeld zwischen Israel und Diaspora', *Die Zeit*, 27 May 1983, pp. 9–10.

Wolffsohn, Michael (1983d), 'Hochschul- und Studienfinanzierung in Israel', in Michael Zöller (ed.), *Bildung als öffentliches Gut? Hochschul- und Studienfinanzierung im internationalen Vergleich* (Stuttgart: Verlag Bonn aktuell) pp. 189–192.

Wolffsohn, Michael (1984a), 'The European Community and the Middle East 1981/82', in Colin Legum *et al.* (eds), *Middle East Contemporary Survey*, Vol. 6 (New York and London: Holmes & Meier), pp. 55–74.

Wolffsohn, Michael (1984b), *Israel: Politik, Gesellschaft, Wirtschaft* (Opladen: Leske).

Wolffsohn, Michael (1984c), 'Deutsch-israelische Beziehungen im Spiegel der öffentlichen Meinung', *Das Parlament*, 17 November, pp. 19–30.

Wolffsohn, Michael (1985a), *German–Saudi Arabian Arms Deals, 1936–1939, 1981–1985. With an Essay on West Germany's Jews* (Frankfurt am Main: Peter Lang).

Wolffsohn, Michael (1985b), 'The European Community and the Middle East 1983', in Colin Legum *et al.* (eds), *Middle East Contemporary Survey*, vol. VII (New York and London: Holmes & Meier).

Wolffsohn, Michael (1986), *Deutsch-israelische Beziehungen: Umfragen und Interpretationen 1952–1983* (Munich, Bayerische Landeszentrale für politische Bildungsarbeit).

World Opinion Update (monthly) (Westport, Conn.: Greenwood Press).

Yaacobi, Gad (1980), *The Government* (Hebrew) (Tel-Aviv: Am Oved and Zmora, Bitan, Modan; American ed. New York: Praeger).

Yaacobi, Gad (1983), *Kriyat Kivun* (Direction Cries) (Hebrew) (Tel-Aviv: Am Oved).

Yadlin, Asher (1980), *Testimony* (Hebrew) (Jerusalem: Idanim).

Yanai, Nathan (1981), *Party and Leadership in Israel, Maintenance and Change* (Ramat-Gan: Turtledove).

Yegar, Moshe (1981), 'Israel in Asia', *Jerusalem Quarterly*, no. 18, pp. 15–28.

Yishai, Yael (1980) 'Factionalism in the National Religious Party. The quiet revolution', in Arian, 1980, pp. 57–74.

Yishai, Yael (1981), 'Challenge groups in Israeli politics', *Middle East Journal*, vol. 35, no. 4, pp. 544–56.

Yishai, Yael (1984) 'Responsiveness to ethnic demands: The case of Israel', in *Ethnic and Racial Studies*, vol. 7, no. 2, pp. 283–300.

Yogev, Abraham, and Jamsky, Haia (1984), 'Offspring of ethnic intermarriage in Israeli schools. Are they marginal?', in Lissak and Ronal, 1984, pp. 425–43.

Youth Movements (1972), *Youth Movements in Israel* (Hebrew) (Jerusalem: Secretariat of Youth Movements Council).

Yoshitsu, Michael M. (1984), *Caught in the Middle East: Japan's Diplomacy in Transition* (Lexington, Mass.: Lexington Books).

Yuchtman-Yaar, Ephraim, and Semyonov, Moshe (1979), 'Ethnic Inequality in Israeli schools and sports. An expectation-states approach', *American Journal of Sociology*, vol. 85, no. 3, pp. 576–90.

Yuval-Davis, Nira (1977), *Matzpen, The Israeli Socialist Organization* (Hebrew) (Jerusalem: Kaplan School of Economic and Social Sciences, Hebrew University).

Zakai, Dan (1984), *The Economic Development of Judaea. Samaria and the Gaza Strip 1981–1982* (Hebrew) (Jerusalem: Bank of Israel).

Zarzur, Sa'ed (1982), 'Arabische Erziehung', in Ackermann, 1982, pp. 129–89.

Zelniker, Shimshon, and Kahan, Michael (1976), 'Religion and nascent cleavages: the case of Israel's Religious Party', *Comparative Politics*, vol. 9, pp. 21 ff.

Zemah, Mina (1980), *Attitudes of the Jewish Majority towards the Arab Minority* (Hebrew) (Jerusalem: Van Leer Foundation).

Zemach, Mina, and Zin, Ruth (1984), *Opinion of Youths on Democratic Values* (Hebrew) (Jerusalem: Van Leer Foundation).

Zidon, Asher (1971) *The Knesset – Israel's Parliament*, 6 vols. (Hebrew) (Tel-Aviv: Achiasaf; American ed. New York: Herzl Press, 1967).